Voluntary Environmental Programs

STUDIES IN PUBLIC POLICY

Series Editor: Paul J. Rich, Policy Studies Organization

Lexington Books and the Policy Studies Organization's **Studies in Public Policy** series brings together the very best in new and original scholarship, spanning the range of global policy questions. Its multi-disciplinary texts combine penetrating analysis of policy formulation at the macro level with innovative and practical solutions for policy implementation. The books provide the political and social scientist with the latest academic research and the policy maker with effective tools to tackle the most pressing issues faced by government today. Not least, the books are invaluable resources for teaching public policy. For ideas about curriculum use, visit www.ipsonet.org.

Voluntary Environmental Programs

A Policy Perspective

Edited by Peter deLeon and Jorge E. Rivera

LEXINGTON BOOKS
A division of
ROWMAN & LITTLEFIELD PUBLISHERS, INC.
Lanham • Boulder • New York • Toronto • Plymouth, UK

Published by Lexington Books
A division of Rowman & Littlefield Publishers, Inc.
A wholly owned subsidary of The Rowman & Littlefield Publishing Group, Inc.
4501 Forbes Boulevard, Suite 200, Lanham, Maryland 20706
http://www.lexingtonbooks.com

Estover Road, Plymouth PL6 7PY, United Kingdom

British Library Cataloguing in Publication Information Available

Library of Congress Cataloging-in-Publication Data
Voluntary environmental programs : a policy perspective / edited by Peter
deLeon and Jorge E. Rivera.
     p. cm.
  Includes index.
  ISBN 978-0-7391-3322-4 (cloth : alk. paper) — ISBN 978-0-7391-3324-8
(electronic)
  1. Environmental policy—United States. 2. Voluntarism—United States. 3.
Social responsibility of business—United States. I. DeLeon, Peter. II. Rivera,
Jorge E.
  HC110.E5V63 2010
  333.70973—dc22   2009035989

Printed in the United States of America

Contents

v

Acknowledgments

Peter deLeon would like to thank his co-author (and great friend), Dr. Jorge Rivera, for initially introducing him to the concept and practice of Voluntary Environmental Programs. And to our colleagues who contributed articles to this endeavor, having repeatedly responded to our insistent demands and deadlines. Dr. Paul Teske, Dean of the School of Public Affairs (SPA) at the University of Colorado Denver, has been consistently supportive. Lastly, Laurie Manderino, a doctorial candidate at SPA and IGERT Fellow funded by the National Science Foundation, has been an invaluable contributor; her contributions extend far beyond simple co-authorship.

Jorge Rivera recognizes with great appreciation the many individuals and organizations that helped make this edited book possible. At The George Washington University, the grants from the Institutive for Corporate Responsibility, the Center for International Business Research, and the School of Business's Dean Research Scholar Program allowed me the extra time to finish this book. My writing owes its improved clarity to Brian Oetzel's immense patience and attention to detail. Professor Peter deLeon's energy and friendship have been an endless source of inspiration. Lastly, but not least, my parents, Leonor and Jorge, and my wife Jennifer for giving me the love and encouragement that constitutes the sunshine of my life.

Finally, both of us are deeply appreciative of the encouragement of Professor Hank Jenkins-Smith of the University of Oklahoma; Hank deserves special applause for his early recognition and continued comments to our work while serving as Editor of the *Policy Studies Journal;* he was instrumental in encouraging us to consider the possibility of assembling and publishing this volume. Similarly, Dr. Paul Rich, President of the Policy Studies Organization, was pivotal in moving this project to the PSO Publication Series at Rowman/Lexington.

Chapter 1

Voluntary Environment Programs: An Introduction

Peter deLeon, Jorge E. Rivera, and Laurie Manderino

Public policy scholars, for at least a generation now, have deliberated the effectiveness of public-mandated "command and control" regulatory programs, most often in the area of environmental regulatory regimes, as an efficacious means to promote cleaner environment conditions at a reduced cost to the government and, possibly, at a diminished cost to the firm. In a phrase, such voluntary programs would seem to imply a preferred "win-win" strategy (see Potoski and Prakash, 2004). In the United States, such policies go at least as far back as the Clean Air Act of the late 1960s. Typically, they are designed, monitored, evaluated and generally shepherded under the guiding auspices of the Environmental Protection Agency (EPA) and industry associations. Carmin and her colleagues (2003) estimate that government agencies (typically the EPA) and industry have sponsored approximately 150 since the late 1980s, with more than 13,000 participants (Darnall and Carmin, 2005, citing also Mazurek 2002).

Given a series of, at best, mixed evaluations as to the overall effectiveness of command and control regulation (for recent reviews, see Coglianese & Nash, 2006; and Prakash & Potoski, 2006), the concept of a Voluntary Environment Program (VEP) has been increasingly considered as an alternative to extensive governmental rules and regulations mandated under the command and control regimen. In general terms, VEPs reflect self-regulatory agreements reached among and promoted by corporate firms, industrial associations, often non-profit environmental groups and, finally, for legitimacy's sake, the relevant government agencies. The purpose of VEPs is to encourage (as opposed to compel) businesses to enhance their environmental protection performances (see Steelman and Rivera, 2006). Dorothy Daley (2007, p. 165) is on target when she sug-

1

gests the objective of a VEP: "The regulator achieves the desired result with decreased enforcement costs, while the regulated community is provided with more flexibility in meeting societal goals—thus eliminating economic inefficiencies."

The idea underlying the voluntary programs concept was consonant with a widespread changing, deregulatory philosophy of government, and was reflected in a number of policy issue areas, e.g., communications, transportation, and of late and most evident, financial regulation. However, it was in the area of environmental regulation where Voluntary Programs were most noted and discussed, especially under the sponsorship of the EPA (see the Green Lights—later incorporated into Energy Star—and the 33/50 programs; Moon 2008). Still, it is important to recognize that the emergence of VEPs was more than an isolated public policy endeavor. Various industries similarly established their own set of VEPs, often in cooperation with and the assistance of a government agency; for instance, the American Chemical Council created the Responsible Care Program and the National Association of Ski Areas created the Sustainable Slopes Program (see King and Lexon, 2000; Rivera, deLeon, and Koerber, 2006, respectively). Scholars investigating the VEP phenomena have observed that there are a number of reasons for firms or industries to adopt a VEP. They may be seen as one way of reaching out to consumers with a "green" signal (thus abetting their differentiation advantage), or as a means of obtaining new technologies and information (e.g., Green Lights), or as a tactic for deferring or avoiding later, possibly more constraining and invasive government-imposed regulations and accompanying public opprobrium that affects the sacred "bottom line."

Not surprisingly, VEP scholars soon advanced an admittedly limited (but growing) number of VEP-specific evaluations, finding (again not surprisingly) mixed results, suggesting that some VEPs have been more efficacious than others in promoting enhanced corporate environmental performance. These findings were not unexpected. Yet it is important to emphasize that for the most part, the initial empirical studies suggest that VEPs—generally lacking performance-based standards, independent monitoring, and sanctions—tended to attract "dirtier" firms which, after participation in a VEP, did not show improved environmental performance relative to the analogous non-VEP members (Steelman and Rivera, 2006).

With this material as a background, we propose that the VEP phenomenon has largely been studied on a piecemeal basis, relating the specific experience of a company here, a trade association there, with little attention to issues of underlying theories or VEP applications outside the United States (Morgenstern and Pizer, 2007, is an exception to the latter charge). Moreover, of greater concern to us is the scant attention paid to the public policy implication of VEPs. What was sorely lacking was a more systematic investigation of the effects of VEPs writ large, commenting broadly on the effects in a general sense.

For instance, it has long been observed that the environment has been described as a "public good." As articulated by Weimer and Vining (2005, p. 78), a public good is best characterized as both nonexclusionable (one cannot be excluded from its benefits) and nonrivalous (consuming a unit of a particular public good does not preclude another from also consuming it). As such, VEPs fall squarely into the category of initiatives promoting public goods; no one can be excluded from the benefits proffered by a cleaner environment and everybody can partake without fear of compromising others' benefits. The problem, of course, is how to preserve, let alone enforce, a public good when there is no sanction against unlimited engagement. Garrett Hardin (1968) nearly forty years ago presciently cautioned us to this likelihood when he wrote of the "tragedy of the commons," which attracted many less constrained members of the community, or what Olsen (1965) called "outliers" or "free riders" (see Delmas and Keller, 2005). A VEP is a consensual, voluntary policy instrument or agreement between the firm, the government, and ultimately the consumer. In other words, it reflects an understanding whose capacities are mutually and consensually determined, a compact that is typically lacking in enforcement authority or powers (at least in a formal sense), as well as a set of meaningful sanctions to be exercised if the public good is somehow violated or circumvented.

To summarize: VEPs as environmental policy instruments have emerged of late as alternatives to the traditional command and control regulatory policy instruments, in terms of being more conducive and effective policies but also in recognition of a political philosophy that moved decisively towards a reduced—perhaps minimal—role for government intervention or regulation. But VEPs are far from accepted policy interventions, either in their generalized purpose, or more tellingly, in their evaluations, or as agreed-upon theoretic enterprises. With these problems in mind, we approached the existing VEP community of scholars and asked a series of salient questions: Whether a voluntary approach to preserving the environment as a public good is a reliable means for ensuring an adequate level of environmental performance as determined by a polity's public representatives (either appointed or elected)? What factors motivate a firm or industry to voluntarily undertake an environmental protection program, one that well might adversely affect a firm's bottom line? What are the variables or conditions that encourage and maintain a voluntary association? And, ultimately, is the VEP approach to environmental protection a continuingly viable policy instrument, or should it be relegated to the dustbin of yesterday's policy fads? The responses to our solicitations have been especially gratifying, as is evident from the remaining chapters of this volume, which discuss the VEP phenomenon with great insight, sophistication, clarity, and even sympathy.

At this time, let us offer a précis of the book's chapters as a preliminary guidepost, with the firm insistence that the readers will profit immensely by a careful reading of the full chapters from which these synopses were drawn.

*****

Dinah A. Koehler (of the Conference Board's Center for Corporate Citizenship and Sustainability) provides an excellent overview of research on VEPs in her essay "The Effectiveness of Voluntary Environmental Programs—A Policy at a Crossroads?" particularly those targeting pollution-emitting production firms. Her analysis deftly illustrates that a one-size-fits-all approach to VEPS is largely misguided; rather, they should instead be evaluated relative to important contextual elements. One should look not only at VEP participation rates, but also at actual member actions leading to environment impacts beyond a business-as-usual scenario. Koehler examines the limited body of empirical research on VEPs that target pollution abatement via changes in industrial processes, a group that includes the Chemical Industry's Responsible Care Program, the 33/50 Program, and ISO 14001, providing some insight into the performance of members vs. non-members and early vs. late joiners. Most VEPs analyzed have not been associated with significant improvements in environment performance, with the exception of ISO 14001. She poses a pivotal question, "Did the minimal environmental improvement arise because the participants failed the institution, or did the institution fail the participants?" She notes a basic distinction in the posed objectives of a VEP: while VEP participation is often pursued to demonstrate a pro-active environmental stance, decisions to invest in pollution abatement are more driven by economic considerations. Research has shown that VEPs tied to economic gains do, in fact, achieve environmental results. Furthermore, a regulatory threat alone does not necessarily translate into actual improvement in environmental performance by VEP participants; more substantial improvement occurs from the traditional regulatory schemes and enforcement.

"Environmental Public Voluntary Programs Reconsidered" by Thomas Lyon and John Maxwell (from University of Michigan and University of Western Ontario, respectively) looks at the difference in performance of participants and non-participants in public voluntary programs (PVPs). The authors take a critical look at the added value of these programs, many of which serve an information diffusion function while also providing public recognition for firms that assume additional pollution control steps. Previous research on PVPs found little or no effect on participant's behavior but those studies, according to the authors, may have underestimated a more thorough assessment of PVPs. This chapter takes a different approach by modeling the value of VEPs specifically for promoting diffusion of cost-effective pollution abatement techniques. They candidly acknowledge the complexities of such modeling, because of the potential for information produced for PVP participants to also is open to transfer to non-participants, an aspect that has perhaps been overlooked in previous studies. Therefore, the pollution reduction impact of PVPs is not limited to firms participating in the PVPs, but may also extend to the sector as a whole. This potential "spillover" effect argues for new modeling strategies to measure the true overall environmental impact of PVPs.

Madhu Khanna (of the University of Illinois, Urbana-Champaign) and Patricia Koss, Cody Jones, and David Ervin (from Portland State University) collaboratively take the unique approach of looking at both VEPs and Environmental Management Practices (EMPs) in their chapter on "Voluntary Environmental Management: Motivations and Policy Implications." EMPs are practices that firms adopt on their own, such as operational changes and employee training. The researchers expand the VEP focus by examining whether motivations for pursuing VEPs and EMPs differ and if different types of firms are likely to participate. The costs and benefits of undertaking each type of program are not the same; there are important distinctions in both the actions required and the public recognition received. This chapter draws upon the results from a survey of small facilities in six industrial sectors in Oregon, where the researchers found participation rates in VEPs to be relatively low, despite a multitude of programs offered. This essay also shows the influence of existing regulatory approaches on how firms participate in VEPs, since different regulatory structures motivate different types of actions. Public recognition is found to be a more important factor for larger firms, which suggests that the design of current VEPs is better-suited to this sub-group. Large firms are, they find, the group most likely to participate in VEPs. By contrast, firm size was not found to be an important indicator of which firms adopt EMPs. Many more Oregon firms are implementing EMPs than are participating in VEPs, perhaps to avoid certification costs and other costs associated with VEP participation. This makes an argument for more flexible approaches in VEPs. The authors conclude by noting that VEPs are just one potential tool for fostering environmental management and that more research is needed to better understand firms' motivating factors.

"Collective Action through Voluntary Environmental Programs: A Club Theory Approach," by Aseem Prakash and Matthew Potoski (from University of Washington and Iowa State University, respectively) analyzes different aspects of VEP participation, with a theoretic focus on institutional features and analytical dimensions. Program design is modeled as an exogenous determinant of program efficacy, as it influences collective action forces. Further, program design is linked to the stakeholder context in which it occurs, or is likely to occur. This chapter explores how to mitigate potential collective action problems associated with clubs, such as "free-riding" and "shirking," and what design elements lead to success or failure. Institutional design features can also help to establish a credible commitment from participants. Design may address, for instance, information asymmetries, the stringency of standards for club participation, and monitoring and enforcement schemes that strengthen credibility. If one thinks of VEPs as "clubs" that require firms to incur (monetary and institutional) costs not otherwise incurred or mandated, the firms must weigh these costs relative to intangible VEP benefits, such as "branding" through association with the club brand. In reviewing different voluntary club standards, the authors advise that policymakers recognize that different VEP types are suited to different policy contexts and different types of firms. For example, the number of club members impacts the strength and value of the brand and if "crowding" sets in, this can dilute the brand by broadly giving the entire industry a good name. While there is no single blueprint for a voluntary club, one must assess the population characteristics and institutional context when deciding on standards and monitoring and enforcement rules. The challenge is to balance credibility with external stakeholders with being so stringent that potential members are deterred from participating.

Magali Delmas and Ivan Montiel (from University of California at Santa Barbara and University of Texas–Pan American, respectively) look at diffusion of standards and the interaction between voluntary standards adoption and institutional environments in their chapter "The Diffusion of Voluntary International Management Standards: Responsible Care, ISO 9000, and ISO 14001 in the Chemical Industry." Delmas and Montiel inquire: Do VEP standards adopted by industry actually hamper the creation of more stringent standards, or do they pave the way for better standards because of the information diffusion element of VEPs? In an attempt to answer these questions, the authors develop a generalized model to explain the adoption of VEP standards within an industry. Variables to explain international diffusion of standards include support from international NGOs and governments, and trade forces. Specific programs examined include ISO 14001, the Responsible Care Program, and the European Eco-Management and Audit Scheme (EMAS) of the European Union. Their findings show that firms that have previously participated in a voluntary standards program (e.g., ISO 9000) are more likely to later adopt more rigorous standards such as ISO 14001. Another factor positively linked with ISO 14001 adoptions in a country was government endorsement and the role of civil society in raising awareness of environmental issues. There is a cumulative effect of management standards; furthermore, national institutional environments are also important in facilitating the diffusion of international standards. Trade associations can also play an important role in fostering collective action behavior, and industry-specific codes of behavior can co-exist with generalist codes. Therefore, when designing voluntary standards, policymakers should consider existing standards that may be in place through VEPs and analogous attempts to design and implement complementary standards.

Jorge Rivera (from George Washington University), Peter deLeon (from University of Colorado-Denver), and Charles Koerber (from George Washington University) also write about a specific industry in "Is Greener Whiter Yet? The Sustainable Slopes Program After Five Years." They study results of the ski industry-sponsored Sustainable Slopes Program (SSP) over a five-year period, looking at whether VEP participants display superior performance than ski areas that do not join the SSP program, and, if so, in what specific areas of environmental performance. The Sustainable Slopes Program, started in the late 1990s, is a partnership between the industry's ski areas, the EPA, a few non-profit environment groups, and a number of government agencies. Whereas most VEP research looks only at changes in pollution output as a measure of environmental improvement, Rivera and his colleagues look at five dimensions of environmental performance addressed by the SSP. Using data from an environmental scorecard prepared by the Ski Area Citizens' Coalition group, their analysis found no evidence of improved performance in four out of five environmental protection performance areas: 1) overall environmental performance, 2) expansion management, 3) pollution management, and 4) wildlife and habitat management.

The only area showing an improvement was "natural resource conservation," which was, in many ways, the easiest of the five to accomplish. They model various dimensions of ski resorts' environmental performance and show that opportunistic behavior, such as "free-riding," prevails when robust institutional mechanisms are lacking. The authors propose that these standards should include a system of sanctions and rewards, and establish performance standards and independent performance monitoring.

Nicole Darnall and Stephen Sides (from George Mason University) present a meta-analysis of nine VEP studies and 30,000 firms in "Assessing the Performance of Voluntary Environmental Programs: Does Certification Matter?" The analysis uses quantitative methods to perform an overall assessment of the actual environmental outcomes of VEPs. The findings are not encouraging for VEP proponents. Their analysis concludes that environmental performance of non-members actually improves more than the performance of members, particularly in the case of self-monitored VEPs. This research contributes to organizational research on VEP governance in two respects: 1) it provides insights on environmental performance by looking at a large body of literature; and 2) it makes a distinction between programs that are self-monitoring and those with third-party certification, such as ISO 14001, to evaluate the relationship between VEP monitoring regimes and environmental performance. Self-monitoring programs, not surprisingly, were found to offer greater opportunities for free-riding, which demonstrates how design features of VEPs can affect the environmental impact ultimately realized.

"Can Voluntary Environmental Regulation Work in Developing Countries: Lessons from Case Studies" by Allan Blackman (of Resources for the Future) sets out a series of exploratory research questions specific to developing country attempts to utilize VEP practices. In economically developed countries, the hope is that VEPs will encourage over-compliance with mandatory regulations; in developing countries VEPs may be a strategy to remedy rampant non-compliance with existing (often inadequate) regulations. Blackman examines five broad questions: 1) whether VEPs can be successful in light of the weak regulatory background threat that exists in many developing countries; 2) whether the same non-regulatory pressures that prompt firms to react to VEPs in developed countries exist in developing countries; 3) if developing country VEPs are poorly managed, do they actually just impede real progress by delaying mandatory regulations; 4) can VEPs be effective in country settings where industry and government have closely entwined relationships (regulatory capture) that limit effective regulations; and, lastly, 5) can VEPs be effective where small firms dominate in many industrial sectors? In addition, Blackman looks at how limitations on information dissemination in developing countries may affect VEP effectiveness, especially the availability of information on emissions data and pollution control technologies. Three case studies are presented: 1) a series of negotiated agreements with leather tanneries in Mexico; 2) a national voluntary audit program in Mexico; and 3) a public disclosure rating scheme in India targeting four pollution-intensive industries. While only limited observations can be drawn from these three case studies, the insights provide a platform for further research focusing on particular VEP-motivating factors distinguishing between developed and developing countries.

Canadian VEPs are the central focus of the chapter on "Voluntary Environmental Programs: A Canadian Perspective" by Irene Henriques and Perry Sardorsky (both from York University's Schulich School of Business). Canadian programs have emphasized achieving targets and goals through cooperation and negotiations, rather than mandatory emissions limits, thereby providing more flexibility and potentially lower cost of environmental protection (also see Mackendrick, 2005). Of the three types of VEPs addressed (government working directly with a trade association or firm, government offering voluntary program to multiple firms, or industry acting independently of government to establish a voluntary program), the most common form in Canada is unilateral, or industry-initiated VEPs. This form of VEP, most often focused on pollution control, can also be the most difficult form to evaluate because publicly available program data are lacking. This chapter looks at firms' motivations to adopt VEPs and what experience has been to date with the three types of VEPs. Both economic and non-economic motivations are examined, highlighting some firm-specific VEPs and how these programs relate to the firm's primary and secondary stakeholders. Unlike the other chapters, this article also examines government motivations to create VEPs. Institutional, regulatory, and political factors in Canada that may account for the relatively few government-initiated VEPs are discussed. A significant factor was found to be the division of jurisdictional power among provinces and territories with regard to environmental authority. Also, there are few market-based instruments in Canada, a condition exacerbated by a lack of integration between these instruments and VEPs.

*****

This compilation of analytic work on VEPs comes at an especially interesting time, when we can expect to see changes in environmental policy, especially climate change policy, from the new US administration. How these policies will incorporate voluntary vs. market-based vs. command-and control regulations will be a critical element of debate and design. As a number of these chapters note, the regulatory and institutional setting in which different types of VEPs operate have an impact on how they achieve desired environmental impacts. While one can anticipate changes in the regulatory climate surrounding greenhouse gas emissions, whether governing regulations will be at the federal level as opposed to the patchwork of state and local climate change regulations that exist today remains to be seen.

In addition, recent economic events have compelled US lawmakers to reconsider the overall merit of government deregulation, which is viewed by many as the culprit that led us to the current state of upheaval in sectors such as the banking and mortgage industries. The likely result will be a shifting of the political tide to be less hospitable to regulatory approaches such as VEPs that incorporate flexibility and self-monitoring. Any future efforts to expand and refine VEPs will need to keep this state of affairs in mind when initiating policy discussions about the merit and potential application of VEPs for US environmental policy.

Bibliography

Carmin, JoAnn, Nicole Darnall, and Joao Mil-Homens. 2003. "Stakeholder Involvement in the Design of U.S. Voluntary Environmental Programs: Does Sponsorship Matter?" *Policy Studies Journal*. Vol. 31, No. 4: pp. 527–543.

Coglianese, Cary, and Jennifer Nash (eds.). 2006. *Beyond Compliance: Business Decision Making and EPA's Performance Track Programs*. Cambridge, MA: Harvard University, Kennedy School of Government.

Daley, Dorothy M. 2007. "Voluntary Approaches to Environmental Problems: Exploring the Rise of Nontraditional Public Policy." *Policy Studies Journal*. Vol. 35, No. 2: 165–180.

Darnall, Nicole, and JoAnn Carmin. 2005. "Greener and Cleaner? The Signalling Accuracy of the U.S. Voluntary Environmental Program." *Policy Sciences*. Vol. 38, No. 2: 71–90.

Delmas, Magali, and Arturo Keller. 2005. "Free Riding in Voluntary Environmental Programs: The Case of the U.S. EPA WasteWise Program." *Policy Sciences*. Vol. 38, No. 2: 91–106.

Hardin, Garrett. 1968. "The Tragedy of the Commons." *Science*. Vol. 168: 1243–1248.

King, Andrew A., and Michal J. Lenox. 2000. "Industry Self-Regulation Without Sanctions: The Chemical Industry's Responsible Care Program." *Academy of Management Journal*. Vol. 43, No. 4: 698–716.

Mackendrick, Norah A. 2005. "The Role of the State in Environmental Reform: A Case Study of Public Land." *Policy Sciences*. Vol. 38, No. 1: 21–44.

Mazurek, Janaice. 2002. "Government Sponsored Voluntary Programs: An Initial Survey." In T. Dietzz and Paul C. Stern, eds. *New Tools for Environmental Protection: Education, Information, and Voluntary Measures*. Washington DC: National Academy Press.

Moon, Seong-gin 2008. "Corporate Environmental Behavior in Voluntary Programs: Does Timing Matter?" *Social Science Quarterly*. Vol. 89, No. 5: 1102–1120.

Morgenstern, Richard D., and William A Pizer (eds.). 2007. *Reality Check: The Nature and Performance of Voluntary Environmental Programs in the United States, Europe, and Japan*. Washington, DC: Resources for the Future.

Olson, Mancur. 1965. *The Logic of Collective Action*. Cambridge, MA: Harvard University Press.

Potoski, Matthew, and Aseem Prakash. 2004. "The Regulation Dilemma: Cooperation and Conflict in Environmental Governance." *Public Administration Review*. Vol. 64, No. 2 (March/April): 152–163.

Prakash, Assem, and Matthew Potoski. 2006. *The Voluntary Environmentalist*. Cambridge, UK: Cambridge University Press.

Rivera, Jorge, Peter deLeon, and Charles Koerber. 2006. "Is Greener Still Whiter?: The Sustainable Slopes Program after Five Years." *Policy Studies Journal*. Vol. 34, No. 2: 195–224.

Steelman, Toddi A., and Jorge Rivera. 2006. "Voluntary Environmental Programs in the United States: Whose Interests Are Served?" *Organizations & Environment*. Vol. 19, No. 4: 505–526.

Weimer, David L., and Aidan Vining. 2005. *Policy Analysis: Concepts and Practice*. 4th Edition. Upper Saddle River, NJ: Prentice-Hall.

Chapter 2

The Effectiveness of Voluntary Environmental Programs— A Policy at a Crossroads?

Dinah A. Koehler

Voluntary Environmental Programs (VEPs) have been used as a policy tool in the United States since the early 1990s and come in many forms. Early assessments of VEPs targeting changes in production processes showed that industrial participants improved their environmental performance and VEPs were celebrated as a viable alternative to more traditional regulation. Recent analyses using more sophisticated techniques, however, paint a less favorable picture. On the one hand firms appear willing to sign up to VEPs, and in some cases participants may be able to create a shield against future losses in shareholder value. On the other hand, these VEPs targeting production processes appear not to generate significant pollution abatement. The latter finding is particularly disturbing, and this paper discusses various explanations, including institutional failure and participant motivations. Future research needs to focus on understanding the firm motivation to invest in production-related pollution abatement under a VEP. For policy makers, the research offers a warning on the limited impact to date of VEPs targeting production processes. However, the multitude of other VEPs, such as those which target new product development and changing market demands, merit a closer look to determine the overall potential of VEPs to engender positive environmental change.

Introduction

In the United States voluntary environmental programs (VEPs) have become standard in the environmental policy tool kit since the 1990s. This development is at the confluence of several events, including more complex regulations, technical innovation and scientific discoveries, cuts in regulatory budgets (Griffiths, Brouhle et al. 2005), and increased concern with the costs imposed by environmental regulations. In 1981 President Reagan issued Executive Order 12291 (amended with Executive Order 12866) which called for regulatory impact analysis to weigh the potential benefits to society of a regulation with its potential costs. The emphasis on cost raised the profile of environmental economics both within and outside the Environmental Protection Agency (EPA) and in the 1990s helped broaden support for economic instruments, such as emissions trading markets, in lieu of traditional command and control regulation that was increasingly considered less efficient and more costly. In parallel the international business community made a concerted effort to be a proactive participant in debates on environmental protection with the formation of the World Business Council for Sustainable Development (WBCSD) at the 1992 Rio Earth Summit. Business leaders furthermore argued that industry-led environmental change is both viable and necessary (Schmidheiny 1992), if not financially strategic (Schmidheiny and Zorraquin 1996). In 1996 the ISO 14001 Environmental Management System (EMS) standard was issued unleashing a global wave of voluntary certified management systems targeted broadly at improving corporate environmental management.

Today, in 2007 many fundamental questions remain about the effectiveness of VEPs, despite their popularity. It is not clear what types of voluntary programs can yield an incremental improvement in performance compared with a status quo defined by a set of regulations and market conditions, and if so why this should be. Do VEPs achieve environmental and public health results commensurate with the resources invested by firms and government? Most research has focused on the decision to participate in a VEP targeting production process changes and is starting to yield a profile of the type of firm most likely to participate. Far less research has focused on the actual impact on the environment and public health. With the exception of theoretical work (Lyon and Maxwell 2004), very little is known about the interplay between market and regulatory pressures on adoption and action under a VEP. For example, if regulation is anticipated, does firm resistance increase or decrease after joining the associated VEP? Even less is known about the actual effectiveness of various program design elements intended to motivate participation and action. As a result expectations of VEPs may not be properly aligned with the decision-making reality at the firm (or in government) to permit appropriate conclusions on their effectiveness. Should we merely concede that VEPs at best "prepare" firms to address and acknowledge an issue and open the door to green washing?

This paper presents a summary of research to date on VEPs in the United States. Much of the research has been funded through the EPA's Office of Research and Development (ORD) STAR (Science to Achieve Results) program, which since 1997 has helped create a community of scholars with increasingly more sophisticated skills in program (effectiveness) evaluation. After a brief description of VEPs and their standing in the United States the remainder of this paper focuses on research that evaluates US VEPs. I draw from empirical research on non-US VEPs where it complements and ameliorates our understanding of how VEPs in the United States (might) work. It should be emphasized that the empirical research summarized here focuses on VEPs that target pollution abatement via changes in industrial production processes and not changes to product design, as in various eco-labeling schemes. It is important to note at the outset that industrial production process VEPs probably make up a relatively small share of total US or world VEPs given the large number of VEPs targeting areas such as energy efficiency, transportation, food and agriculture, and indoor air quality.

Alberini and Segerson (2002) point out that VEPs can be evaluated from several angles: participation, pollution abatement levels, and the impact on polluting firms and competition. I start with effectiveness determinations based on participation. Two basic mechanisms are thought to motivate participation: (i) positive incentives (e.g. cost-sharing and subsidies) and (ii) the threat of legislation (Segerson and Miceli 1998). Most of the theoretical work has focused on the interplay between the threat of regulation and the firm's desire to avert that threat by entering into a VEP. Alternatively, theorists posit that VEPs can be useful when the threat of regulation is weak (Lyon and Maxwell 2003). The next section presents this theoretical work.

While firms appear willing to participate in a VEP, empirical evidence on increased pollution abatement levels beyond business as usual for industrial production process VEPs is scarce. I find, somewhat surprisingly, that none of the VEPs targeted at production processes initiated by the US government that have been studied show evidence of significant pollution abatement above business as usual, even those programs with specified targets. VEPs managed by the private sector fare no better, with the exception of the ISO 14001 standard, which appears to be mildly successful. In light of what appears to be widespread green washing, I turn to empirical research on corporate compliance behavior to understand how firms respond to regimes with stricter sanctions. I suggest that conclusions on the overall effectiveness of VEPs as a policy tool be postponed until we have additional analysis covering the complete spectrum of VEPs.[1] I conclude with implications for the policy maker and suggestions for further research.

Definition of Voluntary Environmental Programs

The most common taxonomy of voluntary environmental programs (VEPs), alternatively called voluntary environmental agreements (VEAs), is based on which party(s) initiated and designed the programs. The EU Research Network outlined three widely accepted categories: (i) unilateral industry led; (ii) public voluntary VEPs initiated by government where industry is invited to participate; and (iii) negotiated agreements between industry and government.[2] VEPs are in many instances designed to enhance the efficacy and scope of existing regulations. Alternatively, they are used to address issues which do not fall within the current regulatory framework. For example, in the United States a significant number of VEPs address global warming.

Compared with traditional policy tools, such as command-and-control (CAC) regulation, VEPs are thought to encourage proactive industry, reduce transactions costs and accelerate achievement of environmental targets due to less legal action and conflict (Brouhle, Griffiths et al. 2005). VEPs, like taxes and cap-and-trade policies, offer industry greater flexibility and can more readily accommodate specific situations. Participants can benefit from technical asistance, information subsidies and public recognition. Public VEPs often involve a non-binding Memorandum of Understanding (MOU), under which participants commit to environmental goals, but are not subject to a penalty for withdrawal or non-performance. Unilateral industry VEPs, on the other hand, have used the threat of dismissal as a sanction (Mazurek 2002; Griffiths, Brouhle et al. 2005).

The US EPA Commitment to VEPs

According to the 2006 report on EPA partnership programs (PPs) by the EPA's Office of Inspector General there are 54 VEPs currently managed by EPA at the federal level.[3] Climate change is targeted by 18 of these programs. According to their designers, EPA PPs attempt to use a market-based approach to motivate organizations and individuals to engage in environmental protection. These programs do not specifically require external parties to take action by law and EPA retains primary responsibility for program design. Overall individual program budgets are small, with median values at $492,500. Most EPA PPs offer technical assistance and information, PR or the opportunity for partnership with regulatory agencies (both federal and state), while a few offer regulatory flexibility. Some EPA PPs leverage the influence of federal purchasing power and other large, institutional buyers to achieve results. Other EPA PPs in partnership with banks and other financial institutions, help companies and other organizations finance cost-saving pollution prevention measures. Participants range from industry to state and local government and the non-profit sector and are often required to help with recruitment and marketing. While data collection continues to be a challenge, the majority of programs (35) require reporting, and the data is used by the EPA to change programs.

EPA Administrator Steve Johnson has publicly stated support for voluntary environmental management systems (EMS) in 2005. The Position Statement calls for widespread use of EMSs across a range of organizations as a means to achieve improved environmental performance, compliance and pollution prevention. Specifically, the EPA will encourage organizations that use EMSs to demonstrate accountability for performance outcomes through measurable objectives and targets. Additionally, the Agency will encourage organizations to publicly disclose information on the performance of their EMSs. Finally, the EPA will encourage the use of recognized environmental management frameworks, such as the ISO 14001 Standard. Issued in 1996, this ISO standard describes a set of environmental management systems and practices, including the development of environmental objectives and policies, the provision of training and documentation, delegation of responsibilities and internal performance audits (Delmas 2002).[4] Clearly, there is strong support in regulatory and industry circles for VEPs targeting production process changes, though proponents still rely primarily on anecdotal evidence, rather than the increasingly critical empirical research.

Why Do Firms Participate in a VEP?

Theory of Regulatory Threats and Incentives

In the absence of a clear signal from markets the regulator needs to create a situation where firms can gain from VEP participation. The problem is that pollution abatement requires some form of resource investment, and so a firm must perceive a net gain from participation (Alberini and Segerson 2002). The most widely proposed mechanism is the threat of regulation or taxation that prompts industry to either form its own VEP (Lyon and Maxwell 2003) or (if an industry VEP fails)[5] join a public VEP (Segerson and Miceli 1998; Segerson and Miceli 1999; Alberini and Segerson 2002). A firm is more likely to join a VEP if the associated costs are lower compared with the anticipated cost of compliance with (current or expected) government mandates or other schemes, such as eco taxes (Segerson and Miceli 1998). The regulator can increase the appeal of VEP participation by providing sufficient incentives, such as the threat of regulation, financial subsidies, the provision of services, and cost-sharing schemes.

Each of these has implications for the regulator. On the one hand the regulator needs to generate the funds necessary to extend financial subsidies to firms participating in a VEP. On the other hand the threat of regulation needs to be credible enough to induce participation. An important benefit of a credible regulatory threat is that it can reduce the need for government subsidies to induce participation (Khanna 2001). Segerson and Miceli (1998) theorize that a VEP can be reached even when the regulatory threat is weak, however, the level of abatement achieved will be lower than what could be achieved with mandatory standards. Such a minimal amount of voluntary abatement is in the firm's economic self-interest, as long as it serves to preempt regulation (Khanna 2001). In circumstances where there is low political will to impose mandatory controls and it is not costly (both politically and financially) to provide subsidies, a regulator is more likely to design a VEP with subsidies to attract participants (Lyon and Maxwell 2003). If, on the other hand, the probability of regulation is high enough the first best pollution abatement outcome (possible under mandatory standards) can occur with a VEP (Segerson and Miceli 1999). In this circumstance a complementary, and perhaps necessary, policy is for the regulator to implicitly promise not to regulate if a VEP can adequately achieve the desired environmental goals. These models suggest that the level of abatement depends on the probability of regulation and a cost/benefit analysis for both regulator and regulated.

Alternatively, when the regulation(s) is already in place the regulator is conceivably in a stronger position and can extend exemptions to VEP participants. This approach, however, requires potentially expensive monitoring systems (Alberini and Segerson 2002) and an appropriate regulatory setting. Regulatory relief has been a popular approach in Europe, but faces legal challenge in the United States, because Congress has not extended this authority to the EPA. Thus, the EPA relies upon legally non-binding agreements that do not require congressional approval and cannot rely on tough sanctions to punish defecting firms (Delmas and Terlaak 2001; Delmas and Terlaak 2002; Mazurek 2002).[6] Without this bargaining position the EPA is constrained to offering a more limited set of incentives such as technical assistance, analytical tools, product differentiation, brand enhancement, and public recognition.

An important concern with VEPs is the potential for participating and non-participating firms to "free-ride" and gain the benefits from a VEP without investing resources in pollution abatement. For example, when a VEP is created to address an industry-wide regulatory threat and only some firms actively participate, the entire industry is thought to benefit from preemption of regulation, because regulation related costs are avoided (Dawson and Segerson 2003). A subset of firms will therefore still opt to participate in a VEP despite the free-rider problem. However, it is the non-participants who gain more.

Business Strategy

As an alternative to the above regulator-industry model of VEPs, researchers theorize that market forces can shape firm environmental behavior. For example, firms may be more inclined to participate in a VEP if they perceive a shift in demand and supply toward more green products. Market pressures can arise not only from consumers and suppliers, but also customers, competitors, trade associations, community groups and investors (Henriques and Sardosky 1996). Participating in VEPs is one manner in which a firm can demonstrate its environmental consciousness to these various audiences. At another level VEPs help firms to signal reduced production costs via improved environmental management and reduced financial risk through better management of environmental risks and liabilities (Reinhardt 1999b).

Yet another avenue of research is informed by neo-institutional sociologists who claim that compliance can be achieved through informal mechanisms, including shaming and public exposure (Braithwaite 1989) and the emergence of new values and norms that guide and alter members' preferences for collective action (Hoffman 1997). In the absence of a clear regulatory threat corporate managers might still perceive a net gain from participation associated with personal satisfaction from being an environmental steward (Alberini and Segerson 2002). The desire for social legitimacy therefore also influences management choices and practices (Meyer and Rowan 1977). An analogous debate has been between those who suggest that industry self-regulation will work only if explicit sanctions are included to prevent free-riding (Grief 1997) and those who argue that sanctions are not necessary. In lieu of sanctions researchers have theorized that the institutional structure of industry self-regulation[7] may control behavior through informal means of coercion, the transfer of norms and the diffusion of best practices (Nash and Ehrenfeld 1997; King and Lenox 2000).

Evidence

The majority of research on US VEPs that target production processes has focused on the decision to participate and has explored most of the above mentioned factors. Most papers use a discrete choice model to evaluate the decision to participate (or not) and evaluate the relative impact of various factors using regression analysis. Factors, such as regulatory pressure, environmental performance, market pressures, competitive pressures and financial performance that have empirically been shown to influence the decision to participate are listed in Table 2.1. The table also lists the VEPs where these factors have been found to influence participation and associated paper(s), the majority of which have been published.

What is striking from a perusal of Table 2.1 is the consistency of influential factors across analyses of several VEPs, including those initiated by the EPA and DOE (e.g. 33/50, Green Lights, WasteWi$e, and Climate Challenge) and those managed by industry (e.g. ISO 14001 EMS, Responsible Care, Responsible Distribution Processes, Sustainable Slopes, Sustainable Forestry Initiative and Encouraging Environmental Excellence). It should be noted that this perceived consistency is also a function of data availability to evaluate environmental performance and collective learning in the research community of which factors appear to influence participation and need to be included in an analysis. Thus, for example, a significant number of analyses have used the Toxic Release Inventory (TRI) database, because it is a longitudinal database (starting in 1987) of toxic chemicals released from a broad swath of manufacturing facilities. As a result 33/50, an EPA initiated VEP to reduce toxic chemical emissions, has been analyzed by six different author teams (Arora and Cason 1995; Arora and Cason 1996; Khanna and Damon 1999; Videras and Alberini 2000; Sam and Innes 2005; Gamper-Rabindran 2006) and the TRI is the most common measure of environmental performance.

If we consider which factors appear statistically significant despite differences across studies in sample, sampling period, and econometric analysis, the research to date shows that a combination of market and non-market forces influences the decision to participate in a VEP, as has been posited in theoretical work. The evidence, based upon the number of studies finding the same statistically significant results, indicates that VEP participants tend to be large, more polluting firms which face more regulatory pressure or future environmental liability, that are image and brand conscious in highly competitive industries, are more innovative global market players and have engaged in one or more voluntary environmental management activities, such as Green Lights or ISO 14001.

More specifically, high levels of pollution (usually measured with TRI data) induce participation in multiple EPA partnership programs (33/50, Green Lights, WasteWi$e) and industry VEPs (Responsible Care, Sustainable Forestry Initiative, ISO 14001). Similarly, higher levels of CO_2 emissions per unit output are a motivator for participation in the Climate Challenge program (Karamanos 1999). From the perspective of EPA as a designer of VEPs, the goal of attracting more highly polluting firms (or industries) appears successful. It bears mentioning that EPA has strategically targeted high polluters, as in the 33/50 program where the first wave of invitations went out to the highest 600 polluting firms who in total generated 66% of 33/50 chemicals in 1988 (Khanna 2007).

What is somewhat surprising is that high level polluters, who bear a greater cost of pollution abatement, are more likely to participate in an industry initiated VEP, such as ISO 14001 or Responsible Care (King and Lenox 2000; Khanna and Anton 2002). This implies that participants join not to signal higher levels of performance already achieved, but rather it would appear that the decision to participate is motivated by the desire to improve performance, at a minimum create the appearance that such improvements are taking place or in the making, or preempt future regulation that is likely to be more costly to heavy polluters. From a game theoretic standpoint, a firm may be motivated by the desire to build leverage with the regulator and thereby influence future regulatory actions and legislation. The private sector tends to view VEPs as a manner to promote regulatory goodwill and generate positive public opinion (Mazurek 2002). Scholars have also theorized that these dirty firms have the most to gain from institutionalized improvement strategies and from reducing the adverse risks of increased regulator and activist scrutiny if they continue to operate too close to or fluctuate around regulated pollution thresholds (Russo and Fouts 1997; Lyon and Maxwell 2002). In fact, research has shown that facilities with water pollution discharges build up a regulatory buffer by discharging far below permitted levels due to the high variability in discharge levels (Gunningham, Kagan et al. 2003; Bandyopadhyay and Horowitz 2006). A similar risk management logic may underlie the decision to participate in a VEP.

Table 2.1 Factors Influencing Participation in VEPs

Influential Factors		VEP	Reference
Environmental Performance/ Regulatory Pressure	High toxic chemical emissions	33/50, Green Lights, WasteWi$e, Responsible Care, Responsible Distribution Processes, Sustainable Forestry Initiative, Encouraging Environmental Excellence, ISO 14K	Arora & Cason, 1995, 1996; Videras & Alberini, 2000; King & Lenox, 2000; Khanna & Damon, 1999; Potoski & Prakash, 2005; Gamper-Rabindran, 2006; Lenox, 2006; Lenox & Nash, 2003; King et al, 2005; Toffel, 2006
	High Hazardous Air Pollutant (HAPs) emissions	33/50, EMS	Khanna & Damon, 1999; Khanna & Anton, 2002; Gamper-Rabindran, 2006
	Low toxic chemical emissions	ISO 14K	Toffel, 2006
	Poor air quality (NAAQS criteria pollutants)	Climate Challenge, 1605(b)	Karamanos, 1999; Lyon & Kim, 2006
	High inspections	ISO 14K, 33/50	Potoski & Prakash, 2005; Gamper-Rabindran, 2006
	More Superfund sites	33/50, WasteWi$e, EMS	Khanna & Damon, 1999; Videras & Alberini, 2000; Khanna & Anton, 2002
	High pollution abatement costs (proxy for regulation)	EMS, Climate Challenge	Khanna & Anton, 2002; Delmas & Montes-Sancho, 2007
	Carbon emissions per unit output	Climate Challenge, 1605(b)	Karamanos, 2000; Lyon & Kim, 2006
	High environmental group membership	Climate Challenge	Karamanos, 1999; Welch et al, 2000
	Perceived regulatory pressures	EMS, 33/50, ISO 14K, Sustainable Slopes	Henriques & Sadorsky, 1996; Dasgupta, Hettige & Wheeler, 2000; Khanna & Damon, 1999; Potoski & Prakash, 2005; Rivera et al, 2006; King et al, 2005; Coglianese & Nash, 2006
Market Pressure/PR	Perceived pressures from share-holders, lobby groups, neighborhood & community groups, trade associations, educated employees and management	33/50, EMS, ISO 14K	Henriques & Sadorsky, 1996; Khanna & Damon, 1999; Dasgupta, Hettige & Wheeler, 2000; Potoski & Prakash, 2005; Gamper-Rabindran, 2006; Coglianese & Nash, 2006
	Final goods producers; consumer pressures	33/50, Green Lights, WasteWi$e, EMS	Khanna & Damon, 1999; Henriques & Sadorsky, 1996; Arora & Cason, 1995, 1996
	More visible, concern with public image	33/50, Responsible Care	Celdran et al, 1996; King & Lenox, 2000; Coglianese & Nash, 2006
	Higher advertising expenditures per unit sales	33/50, Green Lights, WasteWi$e	Arora & Cason, 1996; Videras & Alberini, 2000

Continued on next page

(Table 2.1—continued)

Influential Factors		VEP	Reference
	Publish environmental report	WasteWi$e, Green Lights	Videras & Alberini, 2000
	Industry association membership	33/50, Climate Challenge	Khanna & Damon, 1999; Delmas & Montes-Sancho, 2007
Competition/ Competitive-ness	Participation in Green Lights	33/50	Arora & Cason, 1996
	Less concentrated industries subject to more competition	33/50	Arora & Cason, 1995
	Older equipment	33/50, EMS	Khanna & Damon, 1999; Khanna & Anton, 2002; Videras & Alberini, 2000
	More innovative, high R&D expenditure	EMS, 33/50, Green Lights, WasteWi$e, ISO 14K	Khanna & Anton, 2002; Arora & Cason, 1996; DeCanio & Watkins, 1998; Videras & Alberini, 2000; King & Lenox, 2001a; Khanna & Anton, 2002
	More foreign presence & subject to greater global competition	EMS	
	Foreign-owned	Responsible Care, Responsible Distribution Processes, Sustainable Forestry Initiative, Encouraging Environment Excellence, ISO 14K	Lenox & Nash, 2003; King & Lenox, 2001a
	Greater Distance to buyers, foreign buyers, ongoing relationships with buyers	ISO 14K	King et al., 2005
	Certification to ISO 9000	ISO 14K	King & Lenox, 2001b
	Existing EMS	ISO 14K	King et al., 2005
	Large firms (by sales, output or employees or property)	33/50, Green Lights, Responsible Care, Responsible Distribution Processes, Sustainable Forestry Initiative, Encouraging Environmental Excellence, ISO 14001, Climate Challenge, WasteWi$e, Sustainable Slopes	Arora & Cason, 1995, 1996; Khanna & Damon, 1999; DeCanio & Watkins, 1998; Karamanos, 2000; Videras & Alberini, 2000; King & Lenox, 2000, 2001a; Dasgupta et al. 2000; Karamanos, 1998; Welch et al, 2000; Lenox 2006; Lenox & Nash, 2003; Jorge et al. 2006; Coglianese & Nash, 2006
Financial Performance	High ratio of capital asset to sales & more dependent on capital markets	EMS	Khanna & Anton, 2002
	High earnings per share, growth in earnings per share	Green Lights	Decanio & Watkins, 1998

The finding that VEP participants tend to come from industries that are final goods producers and are more visible and concerned with maintaining a strong brand or public image indicates that perceived pressures from various external stakeholders are strong motivators (Henriques and Sardosky 1996). These perceived pressures may also indicate either an increase in green demand or concern with higher visibility (i.e. marketing) (Alberini and Segerson 2002). Similarly, it appears that participants generally are subject to greater (global) competition or tend to be foreign owned and use VEP participation (e.g. ISO 14001 certification) to signal environmental excellence to distant trading partners.

However, a murkier picture emerges on the question of whether participating firms operate in more competitive industries and are more innovative with greater R&D. While in some studies these factors appear to positively influence VEP participation (Arora and Cason 1995; 1996; Decanio and Watkins 1998; Videras and Alberini 2000; King and Lenox 2001a; Khanna and Anton 2002), other studies, often by the same authors, find no such effect or find a negative impact on participation (Arora and Cason 1996; Khanna and Damon 1999; Videras and Alberini 2000; Khanna and Anton 2002). It is also not clear from this research whether more profitable firms tend to participate (Arora and Cason 1995; Decanio and Watkins 1998; Khanna and Damon 1999; Videras and Alberini 2000). It would appear that firms with older equipment and subject to greater investor scrutiny are more likely to participate (Khanna and Damon 1999; Khanna and Anton 2002). These attributes are not necessarily mutually exclusive and overall paint a picture of participating firms that attempt to use VEP participation to differentiate themselves in highly competitive consumer products markets where profit margins are tight and investor perception is tied closely to maintaining a good brand image and reputation. In addition, enterprises that are global market players subject to greater supply chain pressures are more likely to participate.

How Effective Are VEPs?

As noted earlier, VEPs can be evaluated from several angles, including pollution abatement levels, and the impact on polluting firms and competition. In this section I focus on research of VEP effectiveness in inducing participants to abate production-related pollution beyond what could be expected in a business as usual scenario and the potential to gain competitive advantage from participation. Multiple scholars have noted that VEPs lack monitoring and reporting requirements, which could yield data that can be used as a comparative baseline in effectiveness analyses (Alberini and Segerson 2002; Lyon and Maxwell 2002).[8] The lack of baseline data in part explains the fact that most VEP research to date has focused on the participation question.

Table 2.2 provides a summary of various VEPs, both public VEPs launched by the EPA and industry-led VEPs, that have been evaluated from the environmental performance perspective; some of which have also analyzed participation. The table shows a program's inception date, any precipitating event that influenced program launch, and a brief program description. Changes in corporate behavior are summarized along with the study time frame and study sample, and the unit of analysis (facility, firm, industry) for each research paper. It becomes quickly evident that several programs were studied by different research teams, which puts us in a stronger position to draw general conclusions on program effectiveness, program design and methodological issues that might impact the research findings.

I start with the 33/50 program, initiated in 1991 in response to a Science Advisory Board (1990) report on risks of exposure to toxic chemicals and improved transparency based upon data coming from the EPA's Toxic Release Inventory (TRI) starting in 1989 (based on 1987 emissions results) (Khanna 2007). This program was designed to reduce releases and transfers of 17 high volume chemicals listed in the TRI by 33% in 1992 and 50% in 1995 relative to 1988 baseline levels. Firms were specifically invited by the EPA to join and engage in pollution prevention of these chemicals across various media according to their own reduction goals and time tables. 1,294 firms participated over the lifetime of the program. According to two studies (Khanna and Damon 1999; Sam and Innes 2005), the 33/50 program was successful in reducing emissions of the 17 program chemicals, whereas two others show a limited or mixed impact of the program (Vidovic and Khanna 2005; Gamper-Rabindran 2006). One obvious difference between these studies is that the former two analyses are at the level of the firm, whereas the latter two focus on changes at the facility and industry level. It is less likely that the facility vs. firm difference will have an impact, since all researchers assumed that changes in emissions levels at *all facilities* owned by a participating firm were associated with program participation. This assumption should yield industry samples composed of similar facilities. The difficulty in creating a finer distinction between true and estimated participating facilities is due to the fact that the EPA kept a record of participating 33/50 *firms*, while the TRI data used to evaluate the program is gathered at the *facility* level. Alternatively, the length of study period can impact findings, however this is a less plausible explanation since three out of the four studies capture the entire program period.

A more plausible explanation of the differences in 33/50 program effectiveness evaluations is the confounding impact of regulation and strategic reporting in analyses using TRI data. The toxic chemicals listed in the TRI are often targeted by multiple regulations, and if these emissions reducing influences are not accounted for in an analysis, results will likely yield false positives. Researchers have found evidence of strategic behavior by facilities that have to report to the TRI (Bennear 2008) and potentially very significant impacts on reported emissions levels due to changes in regulation, such as the Clean Air Act Maximum Available Control Technology (MACT) standards and other regulations (Bui 2005; Koehler and Spengler 2007). In general omitting key confounding variables in this type of analysis means that the program under study will appear to be more effective than merited. Based on their 33/50 analysis, Vidovic and Khanna (2005) conclude that the decline in observed emissions from 1991–95 was likely the result of an independent trend rather than a direct consequence of 33/50.

Gamper-Rabindran (2006) specifically excludes 33/50 chemicals that are ozone depleting substance (ODS), which are regulated under the Clean Air Act (in accordance with the 1989 Montreal Protocol), and finds that 33/50 participants shifted emissions to media which were not included in the program (i.e. off-site recycling). In addition, while fabricated metal and paper industry emissions decreased, chemical and primary metals industry emissions increased! This is a direct contrast with Khanna and Damon's earlier analysis of 33/50 emissions reductions by chemical industry program participants, yet they did not exclude the two ODS substances. These two chemicals alone accounted for the greatest percentage reductions between 1990 and 1996 of all 17 chemicals in the 33/50 program (Khanna 2007). This important omission in earlier analyses of 33/50 leads me to conclude that there is stronger evidence that the program was not effective in reducing toxic chemical emissions beyond the levels to be expected under business as usual.

Four studies analyze various federal initiatives to reduce greenhouse gas emissions (GHG) (Welch, Mazur et al. 2000; Lyon and Kim 2006; Delmas and Montes-Sancho 2007; Morgenstern, Pizer et al. 2007). These studies consistently find that the programs, sponsored by the EPA and Department of Energy, had no or a transient impact on GHG emissions reductions beyond business as usual. These findings are somewhat nuanced by differences in behavior by early vs. late participants. It should be noted that many of these VEPs have been terminated several years ago and are not widely considered among the more successful VEPs by practitioners.

Finally, research into the effectiveness of the EPA's Performance Track program finds that, because the program does not adequately recognize and reward the best environmental performers and does not motivate many firms to become high performers, change in environmental performance will be minimal. At best the program can offer a view inside the firms or facility regarding management decision-making with respect to environmental performance (Coglianese and Nash 2006).

Various industry-led VEPs have been studied, including Responsible Care, ISO 14001 Environmental Management Systems (EMS), and Sustainable Slopes. The majority of research has been on the first two VEPs, and raises interesting questions on the effectiveness of VEP design elements, such as the role of sanctions and third party auditing. The Responsible Care (RC) program was created in 1989 to achieve two goals: (i) to improve the environmental and safety performance of members of the Chemical Manufacturers Association (CMA),

Table 2.2 Analysis of VEP Effectiveness

Program (Start Date; Precipitating Event)	Associated Regulation	Program Description	Changes in Corporate Behavior	Industry (Unit of Analysis)	Study Time Frame	Reference
33/50 (1991; 1990 Science Advisory Board report on risks of exposure to toxic chemicals)	1986 CRTK Act, 1990 Pollution Prevention Act; 1990 Clean Air Act Amendments (MACT standards)	Reduce releases and transfers of 17 chemicals by 33% in 1992 and 50% in 1995 relative to 1988 baseline levels	Reduction in toxic chemical emissions - 28% of reduction attributable to 33/50.	Chemical (firm)	1988-93	Khanna & Damon, 1999
			Releases lowered from 1992 until end of program in 1995. Reduced inspections under Clean Air Act.	Multiple (firm)	1989-1995	Sam & Innes, 2005
			Decline in observed emissions likely the result of an independent trend, and not a direct consequence of the Program.	Multiple (facility)	1991-95	Vidovic & Khanna, 2005
			Exclude ODS, find participants shift emissions to non-program medium (off-site recycling). Chemical and primary metal industry emissions increased, fabricated metal and paper industry emissions decreased.	Paper, Fabricated metal, chemical & primary metal, electronic, transport (facilities, industries)	1990-96	Gamper-Rabindran, 2006
Climate Challenge (1995; 1992 UN Convention on Climate Change)	N/A	Agreement to voluntarily reduce, avoid, or sequester greenhouse gases by the year 2000; participating firms may benefit by getting credits for emissions reduction in future tradable permit system	Larger, dirtier and more fossil fuel intensive entities under higher direct regulatory pressure set higher reduction targets. However, level of emissions reductions is not affected by decision to participate. Firms predicted to pledge higher reduction levels found to exhibit lower actual reductions of CO_2, SO_2, NOx.	Utilities (firm)	1995-97	Welch et al. 2000
			No overall impact on CO_2 emissions. Early adopters abate, while later adopters do not, indicating free riding. Late adopters undertake less abatement than non-participants.	Utilities (firm)	1995-2000	Delmas & Montes-Sancho, 2007

Continued on next page

(Table 2.2—Continued)

Program (Start Date; Precipitating Event)	Associated Regulation	Program Description	Changes in Corporate Behavior	Industry (Unit of Analysis)	Study Time Frame	Reference
Climate Wise (1993; 1992 UN Convention on Climate Change)	N/A	Agreement to voluntarily reduce, avoid, or sequester greenhouse gases by 2000; participating firms may benefit by getting future credits for emissions reduction in possible tradable permit system	Shift from fossil fuels to electricity use, indicating possible 3% reduction in emissions, transient effect for 1 year.	Multiple (facility)	1992-2001	Morgenstern & Pizer, 2007
1605(b) (1992)	Energy Policy Act 1992	Voluntary registry for GHG reductions at program level. Later revised guidelines: participants must report entity-wide reductions	No significant effect on carbon intensity	Utilities (firm)	1996-2003	Lyon & Kim, 2006
Performance Track (2000)	N/A	Voluntary general environmental management	Program does not adequately recognize and reward the best environmental performers and does not motivate many firms to become high performers change in environmental performance will be minimal. At best illuminates the firms or facility regarding environmental management	Multiple Firms		Coglianese & Nash, 2006
Responsible Care (1989; 1984 Bhopal accident)	1986 CRTK Act	Improve industry reputation, accept to ten Responsible Care guiding principles and adopt any combination management practices to improve plant safety, community awareness, pollution prevention and emergency response	Members reduce toxic chemical emissions slower than non-members	Chemical (firm)	1987-96	King & Lenox, 2000
			Dirtier firms join RC, possibly due to lack of direct sanction, such as expulsion	Chemical (firm)	1996	Lenox & Nash, 2003

Continued on next page

(Table 2.2—Continued)

Program (Start Date; Precipitating Event)	Associated Regulation	Program Description	Changes in Corporate Behavior	Industry (Unit of Analysis)	Study Time Frame	Reference
			A negative event at a chemical firm caused increased negative effects on stock returns of the entire industry, especially to firms in same industry subsector. The negative spillover was decreased after creation of Responsible Care. Being an RC member did not result in reduced spillover from accidents at other firms. If an accident occurred at a RC member, the spillover to other firms is reduced. RC is protective of outsiders.	Chemical (firm)	1980-2000	Barnett & King, 2006
			After inception of RC, the financial performance of RC participants improved, however, non members experienced financial performance higher than RC members. While RC did not reduce RATE of emissions reductions, the existence of RC created value. Absolute emissions may have gone down, but not at a faster rate. 70% of chemical firms chose not to participate in RC.	Chemical (firm)	1987-96	Lenox, 2006

Continued on next page

(Table 2.2—Continued)

Program (Start Date; Precipitating Event)	Associated Regulation	Program Description	Changes in Corporate Behavior	Industry (Unit of Analysis)	Study Time Frame	Reference
ISO 14001 EMS (1996)	N/A	A standard for environmental management systems and practices, including the development of environmental objectives and policies, the provision of training and documentation, delegation of responsibilities and internal performance audits	Virtually no difference exists in the performance of facilities with certified systems compared to those without certified systems. Certified facilities have more enforcement actions and pay high fines. Improvements in environmental performance did not accelerate from past performance after EMS implementation and certified to the ISO 14001 standard; some facilities had worse performance.	Automobile assembly (facility)	1993-2001	Matthews et al., 2005
			Certification to ISO 9001 influences ISO 14001 certification; lower emitters adopt ISO 9000. Plants with lower inventory levels have lower toxic chemical emissions	Multiple (facility)	1991-96	King & Lenox, 2001b
			Existence of EMS improves environmental performance; certification does not improve performance. Certification provides evidence of existing EMS, but does not signal improved performance	Multiple (facility)	1994-2002	King et al. 2005
			Certification to ISO 14001 decreases toxic chemical emissions relative to non-participants	Multiple (facility)	1995-6, 2000-01	Potoski & Prakash, 2005a
			Facilities who certify are out of compliance less	Multiple (facility)	1995-6, 2000-01	Potoski & Prakash, 2005b
			Certified facilities reduced TRI emissions, and emissions intensity; early adopters reduce emissions more than late adopters	Multiple (facility)	1991-2003	Toffel, 2006

Continued on next page

(Table 2.2—Continued)

Program (Start Date; Precipitating Event)	Associated Regulation	Program Description	Changes in Corporate Behavior	Industry (Unit of Analysis)	Study Time Frame	Reference
			Facilities with both EMS mandates and EMS were more likely to report improvements but differences were modest. There were no significant improvements for air or water pollution.	Motor Vehicle Parts and Accessories, Chemicals, Plastic Products, Coating, Engraving, and Allied Services (facilities)	2003	Andrews et al., 2006
Sustainable Slopes (2000, 1998 arson attack on Vail ski lodge)	N/A	Commit to good environmental stewardship; provide a framework for resorts to implement best practices, assess environmental performance, and set goals for future improvement	Larger properties, facing more regulatory pressure tend to participate. No significant reduction in pollution Less dirty firms join, possibly due to active use of expulsion as sanction for non-compliance	Ski resorts	2001-2005	Rivera et al., 2006
Sustainable Forestry Initiative (1994)	N/A	Set of principles to improve environmental health and safety practices at facilities		Pulp & Paper (firm)	1996	Lenox & Nash, 2003

and (ii) to improve the public perception of the industry. Participants were encouraged to adopt the RC principles and to annually submit a self-assessment to the CMA. Failure to demonstrate progress on implementation did not lead to expulsion, though it could provoke greater peer-to-peer scrutiny. However, members were not held to a particular level of performance. All CMA members were required to adopt RC as a condition of membership (King and Lenox 2000). In all 70% of chemical firms chose not to join the program, many of them smaller chemical manufacturers (Lenox 2006).

In the first significant empirical analysis of Responsible Care, researchers King and Lenox (2000) find that RC membership did not translate into improvement in the rate of environmental performance. In fact, they find that members improved their performance more slowly than non members. Thus, while toxic chemical emissions for the entire chemical industry decreased, emission from RC members did not decrease any faster. They conclude that explicit sanctions may be needed by informed outsiders to avoid this type of opportunistic behavior, or green washing if you will.[9]

In a related analysis, Lenox and Nash (2003) hypothesize that industry associations that incorporate sanctions in the form of expulsion for noncompliance with an industry code will attract less polluting firms. Of the four programs studied only two employed the threat of expulsion, the Sustainable Forestry Initiative and the Responsible Distribution Process program (see Table 2.2 for summary). They find mixed support for their hypothesis. Specifically, participants in Responsible Care (without threat of expulsion) were more polluting on average than other chemical firms, while participants in the Sustainable Forestry Initiative were less polluting on average than other pulp and paper firms. Since 1996, when this study was conducted Responsible Care and the Responsible Distribution Process programs have introduced third party verification of implemented of program aspects and program elements aligned with the ISO 14001 EMS standard.

There is a considerable amount of research on ISO 14001, including research on participation and effectiveness. As noted above, the research finds that adopters are large more R&D intensive facilities that have previously adopted similar quality management schemes (such as ISO 9001 quality management standards). Certified facilities are also under pressure from foreign firms to demonstrate environmental management. Finally, more polluting facilities (measured in absolute TRI emissions) tend to join (King and Lenox 2001c; King, Lenox et al. 2005). According to these researchers, certifying facilities are thus not signaling higher levels of environmental performance. However, when pollution is measured not in *absolute* levels of emissions, but emissions *intensity* (air emissions per production volume), *cleaner* facilities were more likely to adopt ISO 14001 (Toffel 2006). Since larger facilities tend to join VEPs, they will also emit at higher levels, which can explain the King and Lenox result, and does not necessarily contradict the Toffel result. It may simply be that the larger facilities in Toffel's sample are less emissions-intensive.

In contrast, Khanna and Anton (2002) find that when TRI emissions are disaggregated into on-site emissions (released into the air, water and soil) and off-site transfers (which are managed) per unit sales (based on Compustat data), firms with *larger on-site releases* per unit sales and firms with *lower off-site transfers* per unit sales adopt a more sophisticated EMS.[10] Air emissions, as utilized by Toffel, fall within the on-site category of the TRI database, and thus his finding that cleaner facilities certify contradicts the Khanna and Anton paper.[11] The point in this discussion is that choice of environmental performance measure affects results, and it is wise to reserve judgment on whether cleaner or dirtier facilities pursue a sophisticated EMS and certify to ISO 14001.

Research on whether certification to ISO 14001 leads to improved environmental performance also yields a complex picture. We would expect that certification to ISO 14001 verifies the existence of an environmental management system (EMS) and various related management practices that should in turn lead to changes in environmental performance.[12] Researchers do find that it is the *underlying* EMS which leads to future improvements and not certification itself (King, Lenox et al. 2005), yet this result is sensitive to econometric model specification. Another study (Toffel 2006), which does not specifically control for the existence of an EMS, finds that *certification to ISO 14001 itself* is associated with improvements, measured in absolute pounds of toxic chemical emissions and emissions intensity per production volume. Similarly, an analysis that does not take account of the existence of an EMS finds that certification reduces both time out of compliance with clean air regulations and TRI emissions, compared with non certifying facilities, at least for the short 1995–96 and 2000–2001 time frames (Potoski and Prakash 2005a).

Based on a 2003 survey of 3,189 manufacturing facilities, Andrews et al (2006) did a simple comparative analysis between those who had a certifiable EMS to those without. They find that facilities with an EMS were characterized by modest environmental improvements, such as decreases in energy use, increased use of recycled inputs and recycling of waste, decreases in hazardous and non-hazardous waste generation, and decreased incidence of severe leaks or spills (i.e. "low-hanging fruit").[13] They find no significant improvements for air and water pollution and material inputs, which might require more costly capital investments. Similarly, an empirical analysis based upon survey results and publicly available databases finds that at automobile assembly facilities there was virtually no difference between the environmental performance of facilities with and without ISO certified EMSs (Matthews 2001). Furthermore, despite the focus on regulatory compliance, certified auto assembly facilities had more enforcement actions and paid high fines. Finally, at auto assembly facilities with an ISO certified EMS improvements in environmental performance did not accelerate from past performance. In some cases, facility performance was actually worse.

Despite these mixed results, the research on EMS does suggest the possibility of institutional learning (and level of comfort with VEPS) and the development of corporate norms of environmental management through participation in various VEPs, as proposed by neo-institutional sociologists (see discussion earlier). The propensity to participate in multiple programs, indicated in Table 2.1, may represent an institutional commitment to VEPs. In support of this conjecture, researchers have found that facilities that adopt the ISO 9000 total quality management (TQM) standard are more likely to adopt ISO 14001 (King, Lenox et al. 2005). TQM practices, such as lean production, are found to be associated with reduced toxic chemicals waste generation (King and Lenox 2001d). Firms who adopt total quality environmental management (TQEM) adopt more sophisticated pollution prevention activities (Anton, Deltas et al. 2004). In fact a "consensus" EMS has developed across certifying facilities that is aligned with the ISO 14001 standard and focuses on regulatory issues (Matthews 2001). A further testament to institutional learning is that firms with past experience with pollution prevention engage in more pollution prevention activities going forward (Khanna, Deltas et al. 2005).

Institutional and organizational aspects of a firm can also impact the corporate response to environmental initiatives, including VEPs. In a recent analysis of the Performance Track program, researchers find that internal organizational dynamics rather than environmental performance distinguish participants from non-participants (Coglianese and Nash 2006). For example, institutional pressures from different stakeholders are channeled to different organizational functions, which influence how they are received by facility managers and ultimately the firm's response (Delmas and Toffel 2004; Delmas and Toffel 2004a). Thus firm legal departments are more involved in addressing non-market (e.g. regulatory agencies, local community, media, environmental NGOs) pressures, while market pressures (e.g. consumers, suppliers, competitors, socially responsible investors, trade associations) are handled by corporate marketing departments. When the pressure is coming from market constituents, firms are more likely to adopt ISO 14001. Pressure from non-market constituents, however, is found to compel firms to adopt government-initiated voluntary programs and less so ISO 14001. Based on this and other analyses, researchers suggest that market pressures, rather than non-market pressures, applied through the regulator, are generally more effective at initiating beyond compliance behavior (i.e. participation in VEPs) (Khanna and Anton 2002; Delmas and Toffel 2004). Significantly, these market pressures do not appear to motivate higher levels of pollution abatement (beyond regulated levels) according to the majority of VEP research summarized here.

The role of free-riders in VEPs has been explored by some researchers. Comparing early and late joiners to the Climate Challenge Program, Delmas and Montes-Sancho (2007) find that early joiners reduced emissions more than later joiners, who in fact reduced emissions more slowly than non-participants. As a result of free-riding by later joiners, the program in the aggregate appears not to have had an impact on CO_2 emissions reductions. Similarly, in Denmark early joiners in the agreements on industrial energy efficiency achieved more profitable gains than late joiners, indicating the possibility of a first mover advantage (Morgenstern and Pizer 2007).[14] Analysis of ISO 14001 finds that early adopters, who tend to be more pollution intensive, reduce their TRI emissions more than late adopters (Toffel 2006). This type of effect appears to be at play with various VEPs and should be incorporated in future analyses.

Other research supports the theoretical conclusions of Dawson and Seger-son (2003), who propose that an entire industry can benefit economically from a VEP, *though free-riders benefit more*. Research on Responsible Care (RC) finds that while the rate of emissions reductions did not increase after RC creation, RC members benefited from improved financial performance, measured in To-bin's Q (market value over value of tangible assets) (Lenox 2006). However, non-participating chemical firms benefit even more in terms of improved To-bin's Q after inception of RC. Lenox concludes that, even though RC yields no environmental improvements and suffers from free-riders, the institution contin-ues to exist because participants and non-participants reap some degree of finan-cial reward. Similarly, the shareholder value of chemical industry firms did not decrease as significantly after an accident at a chemical firm once RC existed, indicating a protective effect of the VEP. Conversely, negative financial spillov-er increased for the chemical industry after the deadly chemical accident in Bhopal, India (Barnett and King 2006a; Barnett and King 2006b). However, RC is more protective of non-members. Thus, when an accident occurred at non-member firms, RC members were not protected from a negative financial im-pact. Non-members, however, did not suffer as significant a negative financial impact when the accident occurred at an RC member firm.

Discussion

From the summary in Table 2.2 it appears that most VEPs targeting production process changes that have been studied are not associated with significant im-provements in environmental performance. Several federal VEPs that have been analyzed seem to be unsuccessful or lead to short lived efforts, with minor nuances due to early vs. late adopters. Of the industry-led VEPs studied only ISO 14001 seems to be associated with some environmental improvements, which tend to be focused at end-of-pipe measures rather than pollution preven-tion or innovation. The authors of several chapters in Morgenstern and Pizer (2007) found that the various international climate change VEPs demonstrate a 5% improvement in energy efficiency during the study period, which while not trivial does suggest that VEPs might inherently have some limitations. Similarly, case studies of voluntary approaches to climate change in the UK, Switzerland and Denmark found that these VEPs did achieve goals and could improve the efficacy of CO_2 tax policies, but that the goals were not often very demanding (Baranzini and Thalmann 2004). However, it cannot be emphasized enough that there are many VEPs, particularly more recent ones or those targeting greener product design which might conceivably be more effective. The results pre-sented here are indeed troubling from the perspective of environmental protec-tion and present a fundamental question: did the minimal environmental im-provement arise because the participants fail the institution or did the institution fail participants?

Let's start with the institution: Various researchers have suggested that tigh-ter requirements might improve the performance of VEPs, such as sanctions, rewards, public disclosure or independent monitoring and verification (Rivera, Leon et al. 2006). Environmental targets are set by participating firms in several VEPs. However, the analysis of 33/50, Climate Wise and Climate Challenge indicate that this requirement did not motivate significantly higher pollution abatement above the business as usual scenario, possibly because participating firms set very low performance targets. Lenox and Nash (2003) find only limited support for their hypothesis that sanctions in the form of expulsion for non-compliance with a voluntary industry code will attract less polluting firms. VEPs with stronger requirements, such as monitoring and public disclosure used in Performance Track or 33/50, are thought to perform better than weak form programs, such as ISO 14001, which does not employ public disclosure but requires monitoring (Potoski and Prakash 2005). However, the research summarized here does not support this conjecture.

Attempts to strengthen VEP requirements have had limited success. VEP designers rightly fear that introducing a more stringent process for participant target setting will scare them away and/or not motivate significant environmental improvements. In fact, though EPA raised the level of rewards for Performance Track participants to compensate for higher entry requirements, the net result was reduced participation rates indicating an important trade-off between level of effort required and willingness to participate (Coglianese and Nash 2006). Considering five VEPs targeted at energy-efficiency in the United States, Germany, the United Kingdom, Denmark and Japan with varying levels of sanction (ranging from taxes, further regulation to industry coercion), Morgenstern and Pizer (2007) conclude that increased stringency does not seem to improve environmental performance. For example, the United Kingdom and Danish climate change VEPs were designed as an exemption to a significant tax, but this heavy handed approach nevertheless did not yield significantly better VEP performance.

In contrast, sanctions (e.g. inspections, penalties and fines) do work in regulated areas to various degrees. Enforcement activity increases compliance and pollution abatement for pulp and paper facilities and at publicly owned treatments works (POTWs) (Dietrich 2004; Gray and Shadbegian 2005). Penalties appear to improve environmental performance and compliance behavior (Foulon, Lanoie et al. 2002), but for some industries (e.g. pulp and paper plants) the impact lasts only one year (Shimshack and Ward 2005). Other researchers find that penalties are generally more effective at smaller plants with lower financial resources (Thornton, Gunningham et al. 2005). Not surprisingly, higher costs of compliance and more complex regulations combined with decreased inspection and detection rates are found to increase the likelihood of violations (Stafford 2006). Finally, the mere *threat of legal sanctions* implied by promulgation or enforcement of laws and regulations is much more salient than the imminent threat of legal punishment (Thornton, Gunningham et al. 2005). In other words, while the ultimate punishment, penalties, appears to spur compliance behavior, particularly at small facilities, the threat of regulation and associated uncertainty may be a more significant driver of compliance behavior.

The impact of regulation and regulatory uncertainty has been considered in the empirical research on VEPs. Various researchers (Davies, N. Darnall et al. 1996; Videras and Alberini 2000; Alberini and Segerson 2002) have suggested that VEPs with a direct link to an *existing* regulatory framework, such as Waste Wi$e or 33/50, are more successful because there is a clearer connection to cost savings arising from pollution reduction. For 33/50, however, I conclude that it was in fact direct regulation (under the Montreal Protocol) rather than a "linked" VEP that engendered the significant portion of toxic chemical reductions. Others suggest that various proxy variables for potential *future* regulatory pressures, such as environmental group membership are motivators for voluntary pollution abatement (Karamanos 1999; Maxwell, Lyon et al. 2000; Welch, Mazur et al. 2000), though the evidence is not definitive. My own experience as an industry participant in crafting a packaging waste management VEP in Hungary supports the notion that VEPs preempt regulation or at least weaken and postpone it (Koehler 2002).

However, it is noteworthy that the regulatory threat as a motivation to participate does not appear to translate into actual improvements in environmental performance by VEP participants. In contrast, in the traditional compliance regimes regulatory uncertainty appears to motivate pollution abatement, which may lend support to theories that the perceived seriousness of regulatory threats and subsequent enforcement activities guide the decision to invest in pollution abatement. As noted by numerous scholars, VEPs are popular when the threat of regulation is low. Thus, the weak institutional framework for VEPs, both in terms of program design and regulatory threats, partially can explain the lack of effectiveness.

Now consider whether it is the participants who have failed the VEP as an institution. Some of the compliance research provides hints that firms tend to sort themselves into good or bad environmental stewards, and will do so more likely due to industry fixed effects (e.g. technology), market pressures and peer pressure than regulatory pressure. Research finds that a relatively small number of plants are responsible for most violations of environmental regulations (Horowitz 2002), and a positive correlation in the probability of violation across facilities owned by the same firm (Stafford 2006). Pulp and paper plants that are old, large, host a more pollution intensive pulp mill, and violate water pollution or OSHA regulations tend to violate air regulations (Gray and Shadbegian 2005). At the other end of the spectrum, firms that are already committed to compliance for normative and reputational reasons view themselves as responsible corporate citizens who need not fear the social and economic costs that can be triggered by serious violations (Thornton, Gunningham et al. 2005). In fact, day-to-day environmental management practices appear to have a greater influence on variation in levels of environmental performance (in the pulp and paper industry) than differences in regulatory stringency (Gunningham, Kagan et al. 2003), indicating that firm internal decisions are critical, and may also explain VEP participation decisions within a neo-institutional framework.

There appear to be some parallels between those firms who do not comply and those who participate in VEPs: large and polluting, see Table 2.1. It would be useful to know if these are the same firms, or if industry membership makes a difference. For example, large polluting intermediate goods firms may be less inclined to comply than large polluting final goods firms, lending support to theories that consumer and customer demand plays a role in VEP participation; though this continues to be debated (Alberini and Segerson 2002; Gunningham, Kagan et al. 2003; Salzmann, Steger et al. 2006). Alternatively, large polluting firms in final goods industries may be less compliant, but nevertheless partici- pate in a VEP to gain regulator goodwill and greenwash.[15] Perhaps it is the large polluting *final goods* firms that join a VEP earlier and actively engage in pollu- tion prevention, while large polluting *intermediate goods* industries join later and do not engage in pollution prevention, effectively negating the efforts of early joiners with their free-riding behavior. There are multiple possibilities that would need to be examined by more comparative industry analysis. It would also be very interesting to tease out whether more or less compliant firms join VEPs as this could help illuminate why VEPs are not as effective as hoped and which type of sanctioning methods might work better, given the research on compliance behaviour referenced above.

Finally, it may be factors other than the institutional design and regulatory framework of a VEP or the *a priori* proactive environmental attitude of certain types of firms that influence participant commitments under VEPs. Researchers suggest that beyond-compliance behavior cannot be explained purely in terms of threats and moral obligations, but rather can be better explained as an interplay of societal pressures and economic constraints (Gunningham, Kagan et al. 2004). Ramus and Montiel (2005) find evidence that coercive, normative and mimetic institutional pressures determine whether firms make a public commit- ment or not to environmental actions, whereas economic incentives determine whether they actually implement their commitment.

In other words, the problem may be that while firms are willing to demon- strate a proactive environmental policy by participating in VEPs it may not be economically advantageous to subsequently invest in pollution abatement. We know from research that US facilities tend to face significant marginal abate- ment costs (McClelland and Horowitz 1999; Rezek and Campbell 2007), which would imply that unless forced to do so, most facilities are unlikely to invest in pollution abatement technology. It is striking that of the VEPs studied (e.g. ISO 14001 and climate change programs) the changes that have been made appear minimal, hardly distinguishable from business as usual, and probably low- hanging fruit. The ineffectiveness of Performance Track and other VEPs may be because the incentives that can be legally offered by the EPA to participating firms do not appear to offer sufficient economic reward to compensate for po- tentially significant investments in production processes required to achieve (costly) improved environmental performance. The final goods firms may have joined these VEPs in expectation of raising their market appeal, but low levels of environmental performance may indicate that these pressures are insufficient or market players are informationally challenged and cannot "punish" lackluster performance. On the other hand, research on the voluntary Costa Rican Certifi- cation for Sustainable Tourism shows that those participants who achieve superior (presumably more costly) performance are able to command price premiums for hotel rooms (Rivera 2002) and that proximity to the country's eco-parks, which attract eco-tourists and more government scrutiny, predicts participation (Rivera 2004).

Theoretical work and empirical research indicate that the national political context can be an important influence on the decision to participate in a VEP (Lyon and Maxwell 2004; Potoski and Prakash 2004) and undertake pollution abatement. For example, implementation of the European Union's Eco-Audit and Mangament Scheme (EMAS) is quite variable based upon domestic factors, including standard promotion and dissemination, stakeholder demands and the extent of regulatory relief offered by national governments (Glachant, Schucht et al. 2002; Kollman and Prakash 2002). Public disclosure of environmental performance appears to have a marked effect on pollution levels in Indonesia and Canada (Foulon, Lanoie et al. 2002; Garcia, Sterner et al. 2006). In the latter case researchers find that appearing on a list of out of compliance firms is more effective at reducing water pollution than traditional sanctions, such as fines.[16] Kollman and Prakash (2001) suggest that in an adversarial economy (or what Lyon and Maxwell (2004) call a "pluralist" political setting), industry willingness to engage in a VEP is influenced by whether individuals and citizen groups or NGOs can use litigation as a means to enforce good environmental behavior. In the United States the reluctance of firms to adopt ISO 14001 arises in part from concerns that evidence gathered by a third-party auditor can be used in a court of law. Similarly, members of the US forestry product industry preferred to certify to the domestic private Sustainable Forest Initiative rather than join the more rigorous NGO-sponsored international Forest Stewardship Council to preserve an element of control in an adversarial context (Sasser, Prakash et al. 2006).

In the United States the design of VEPs is constrained by regulatory requirements. As noted earlier, the EPA is constrained in its ability to offer regulatory relief without congressional authorization and therefore may not be able to offer enough economic incentive to spur pollution abatement. Furthermore, antitrust laws limit the types of sanctions participating firms can levy against members who fail to comply with the codes of an industry (self-regulatory) VEP. VEP participants cannot coerce other firms to participate or impose internal sanctions that would impact production costs for competitors (Lenox and Nash 2003; Lenox 2006). Another concern in the United States is the potentially adverse impact on VEPs of third party legal complaint, such as actions initiated by environmental groups (Kollman and Prakash 2001; Delmas and Terlaak 2002; Potoski and Prakash 2004).

In combination, these findings can leave the policy maker in a quandary. To what degree is regulator involvement sufficient or necessary for the success of a VEP in the United States? How do institutional inertia, a pluralistic political setting and a history of adversity impede VEP adoption and performance? If the regulator increases sanctions in an existing VEP within the limited playroom given by Congress, this may launch widespread defection or have no effect at all on environmental performance. If the regulator increases the threat of *future* regulation it is not clear whether this will increase industry effort, though this has been suggested in theory and anecdotally. In the United States at best regulatory threats appear to induce greater levels of VEP participation, though it is notable that early adopters appear to engage in more pollution abatement for reasons that remain to be explored. For participants the lack of significant improvement may in fact be due to the lack of economic incentive or to very conservative target-setting and a wait-and-see attitude. For outside observers, including the EPA, consumers and/or third party auditors, the information asymmetry may be so great as to make it difficult if not impossible to determine whether VEP participants are setting ambitious targets and performing beyond business as usual. This phenomenon has been noted in several climate change VEPs included in the Morgenstern and Pizer (2007) volume. It is not helpful in this regard, that many EPA VEPs (i.e. Partnership Programs) have not established baselines which would readily lend themselves to effectiveness analysis.

Conclusions and Future Research

As the EPA considers the effectiveness of EPA sponsored VEPs and whether this type of policy can be depended on to achieve environmental results, particularly in priority areas, the research offers several warnings. Based on what we know today, VEPs in the United States that target pollution arising from production processes can attract participants, but do not incrementally yield significant environmental improvement. It may be that on the margin a VEP can spur higher rates of improvement in production processes in areas where pollutants are already regulated elsewhere, such as the 33/50 program, or regulation is anticipated, e.g. climate change. However, we have yet to research this question.[17] In lieu of blind faith in VEPs as an option for changing production processes, policy makers need to understand that these VEPs are used by industry as a public relations tool, intended to appease critics in government and consumer circles alike. For significant change in production-related emissions different policies, including regulation, will be necessary. Indeed, Khanna and Anton (2002) find that first-order practices, such as environmental staffing, audits and internal policies are attributable to legal and regulatory factors, whereas second-order practices (e.g. total quality management) are driven by market factors.

The research does suggest that expectations of VEPs are not properly aligned with the decision-making reality at the firm (or in government) to permit appropriate conclusions on the effectiveness of VEPs. It would appear that theories of regulatory threats, market pressures and neo-institutional factors can explain the decision to participate, yet require more work to explain why participants do not improve environmental performance. The strongest reason I believe, is that it is economically unfavorable to invest in pollution abatement under a voluntary regime in the current socio-political situation in the United States, which is not thoroughly explored in the theoretical and empirical work. In other words, the rewards, whether they be offered by the government or expectations of consumer demand, are not sufficient to compensate for what are likely to be the expensive investments in production processes that could achieve notable change.

According to some researchers, regardless of the lack of significant environmental improvement by participants, participation in a VEP may in itself be a public good (Morgenstern and Pizer 2007). The more participants, the greater the potential benefit. In fact, the existence of a VEP improves the image of both regulator and regulated by signaling the willingness by both sides to engage in a more flexible process of environmental protection. However, a blind pursuit of high participation numbers such as EPA's strategy of first inviting a high profile group of organizations to participate in a VEP, is an open invitation for late adopters to free-ride and thereby jeopardizes the overall effectiveness of the program (Delmas and Montes-Sancho 2007); or as noted by Morgenstern and Pizer (2007) lead to short-lived efforts.

It is notable that of the VEPs studied using empirical methods researchers tend to focus on industrial production processes. A central reason is that the available environmental performance data come from the EPA, which, through a variety of regulations focused primarily on production processes, has required primarily large facilities to collect a vast array of production-related environmental data. Therefore, the main theoretical thrust of environmental economists to explain the motivation to join a VEP has been to explore the risk of regulation of production processes, and not of products. In other words, both theoretical and empirical work on VEPs is colored by the prevailing method of environmental protection in the United States: control of industrial production processes. In this setting a VEP may be doomed for a variety of reasons, including the adversarial relationship between regulator and regulated, costly abatement, high levels of regulatory interference that make it particularly difficult to empirically isolate an incremental impact associated with a VEP, and environmental databases (from the EPA) that essentially track compliance and do not always lend themselves to beyond compliance analysis without very careful sleuthing to evaluate various confounding variables.

As an institution VEPs should not merely be discarded. Rather, the role of EPA should be more carefully explored in terms of the market failure that is being targeted and the key drivers creating the failure. It is entirely conceivable that the EPA can play an effective and unique role in resolving the failure, not only through the provision of technical information at a below market cost.[18] It is in areas where there are clear economic incentives to innovate and invest in pollution reduction that VEPs can help accelerate improvements beyond what can be expected of mandatory emissions levels alone. I would argue that by focusing on products and leveraging market developments the EPA is in a better position to align economic and environmental performance in its VEP programs rather than by focusing on production-related pollution abatement alone, which will still fundamentally be considered a cost in markets. The fact that final goods producers tend to participate in VEPs is clear indication that this is based upon a rationale more closely aligned with market conditions than simply compliance requirements. Consequently, EPA can help create clear market signals and rewards for environmentally friendly product design, such as Energy Star.

A growing body of research indicates that VEPs which are clearly tied to economic gains can achieve environmental results. These VEPs tend to focus on energy efficient lighting (Horowitz 2001; 2004),[19] energy efficient electronics (Webber, Brown et al. 2000), energy efficient motors,[20] green building,[21] land conservation easements,[22] wildlife conservation income tax check-off,[23] transportation demand management,[24] and eco-labeling (Teisl, Roe et al. 2002). This body of research merits careful attention in the debate on VEP effectiveness.

The research on ISO 14001 certification in the US tentatively reveals small improvements in environmental performance, which may be due to scheduled third party auditing and the desire to attract new business across the supply chain. By encouraging the frequency and quality of third party auditing, as with ISO 14001, the EPA can leverage a private sector "enforcement" mechanism that appears to be yielding positive environmental results. Government monitoring and government sponsored transparency in (quasi) voluntary schemes, such as Indonesia's PROPER (Garcia, Sterner et al. 2006) and Costa Rica's Certification for Sustainable Tourism (Rivera 2002; 2004) appear to stimulate higher levels of environmental effort.

The literature on VEPs summarized here shows some interesting behavior that would benefit from a closer look in future research. Particularly intriguing, I find, is the potential role of networks, geographic clusters, peer pressure, trade associations, and a precipitating event that creates a de-facto group more willing to engage in a VEP. The research on Responsible Care begins to illuminate the beneficial impact of a VEP (sponsored by a trade association), at least for the financial well-being of participants (King and Lenox 2000). EPA experts on VEPs have noted that trade associations can play a positive role by increasing the pressure to participate and assisting with information exchange, and should therefore be leveraged by policy makers. Indeed multiple papers find that industry association membership is crucial in the formation of and recruitment into VEPs (King and Lenox 2000; Potoski and Prakash 2004; Rivera 2004; Sasser, Prakash et al. 2006).

We would also benefit from more neo-institutional research to understand the role of networking and geographic clusters in environmental protection, both compliance and beyond compliance measures. For example, researchers have found that more inspections at a plant, nearby plants, and other plants in the same state are associated with greater compliance (Gray and Shadbegian 2007). Penalty actions against other mills in the same state for water discharge violations result in reduced discharge levels for all facilities, both those that are already compliant and those which are noncompliant (Shimshack and Ward 2006). Research on the US hazardous waste management industry finds that local competition increases compliance (Stafford 2007). With most compliance enforcement happening at the regional and state level, this appears to be creating clusters of high performers dependent on the extent of enforcement action and local peer pressure. VEPs that are state-run may be more effective than those developed and administered at the federal level for the very reason that continuous local networking and peer pressure appear to play an important role in pollution abatement. It would therefore be very interesting to understand whether firms fear sanctions from the regulator more than sanctions from other firms. If it is the former, then regulatory threats and VEP sanctions need to be heightened. If it is the latter, then the policy maker should leverage this peer-to-peer oversight mechanism.

Finally, we need more research to understand when a voluntary agreement is most effective or appropriate. This issue has not been addressed properly by the empirical research to date, and few of the theoretical models presented and tested are designed to provide an answer. This is, however, the predominant concern for the EPA, which must determine the environmental effectiveness of various policies, including mandatory and voluntary approaches, which has been explained in theory (Stranlund 1995; Lyon and Maxwell 2003). One possibility would be cost effectiveness analysis of the relative advantage of VEPs compared with traditional regulation, which remains to be explored (Alberini and Segerson 2002). We might expect economies of scale to appear as more firms join a VEP and a reduction in firm compliance costs, because government programs, such as those that provide information on pollution prevention opportunities, can partially substitute for private effort. The benefits can be even greater when the government program provides "nonrival" (i.e. non-replicate/duplicate) efforts to firms. In fact, researchers (perhaps optimistically) theorize that the benefit of government services associated with a VEP can eventually outweigh mandatory programs as more firms are targeted to participate (Wu and Babcock 1999). Thus, a social welfare analysis of VEPs needs to consider the industry costs incurred by participation and the costs avoided by not having to comply with mandatory requirements in addition to the net costs to the regulator (Stranlund 1995).

For the EPA to effectively use VEPs there has to be greater understanding of the strategic linkage between public policy and industry behavior, both compliance and beyond compliance. There may be contradictory tendencies and complementary assets that need to be understood and leveraged. Research has yet to provide more insights into the mechanism by which VEPs might work and the interplay between various motivating and demotivating factors for participants. For example, did VEP creation forestall regulation or inflate frustration at the lack of action at the federal level? Empirical analysis is not necessarily suited to this type of research and more promising avenues of research lie in fields such as experimental economics and psychology. Finally, the distinction among different types of VEPs by researchers, policymakers, and the public is critical to understanding the mechanisms of corporate response. Failure to make these distinctions will result in unforeseen consequences and invalid expectations (Welch, Mazur et al. 2000).

Acknowledgments

The author wishes to thank Stephan Sylvan for his insights into VEP typology and effectiveness. I have relied on Jon Silberman and Stephan's extensive list of lists to guide the literature included here. Two anonymous reviewers provided helpful comments. The author is solely responsible for the content of this article. This work does not represent either EPA policy or the perspective of EPA officials.

Bibliography

Alberini, A. and K. Segerson (2002). "Assessing Voluntary Programs to Improve Environmental Quality." *Environmental and Resource Economics* 22(1/2): 157–84.

Andrews, R. N. L., A. M. Hutson, et al. (2006). Environmental Management under Pressure: How Do Mandates Affect Performance? *Leveraging the Private Sector: Management Strategies for Environmental Performance*. N. J. Coglianese C. Washington, DC, Resources for the Future Press.

Anton, W. R. Q., G. Deltas, et al. (2004). "Incentives for Environmental Self-Regulation and Implications for Environmental Performance." *Journal of Environmental Economics and Management* 48(1): 632–54.

Arora, S. and T. N. Cason (1995). "An Experiment in Voluntary Environmental Regulation: Participation in EPA's 33/50 Program." *Journal of Environmental Economics and Management* 28: 271-286.

———. (1996). "Why do Firms Volunteer to Exceed Environmental Regulation? Understanding Participation in EPA's 33/50 Program." *Land Economics* 72(4): 413–432.

Bandyopadhyay, S. and J. Horowitz (2006). "Do Plants Overcomply with Water Pollution Regulations? The Role of Discharge Variability." *Topics in Economic Analysis & Policy* 6(1): Article 4.

Baranzini, A. and P. Thalmann, Eds. (2004). *Voluntary Approaches to Climate Policy*. Cheltenham, Edward Elgar.

Barnett, M. and A. King (2006a). Privatizing in Reputations: An Institutional Explanation of Industry Self-Regulation, University of South Florida.

———. (2006b). "Good Fences Make Good Neighbors: An institutional Explanation of Industry Self-Regulation." *under review.*

Bennear, L. S. (2008). Strategic Response to Regulatory Thresholds: Evidence from the Massachusetts Toxic Use Reduction Act. *Nicholas School of the Environment,* Duke University.

Blackman, A. and J. Boyd (2002). "Tailored Regulation: Will Voluntary Site-Specific Environmental Performance Standards Improve Welfare?" *Southern Economic Journal* 69(2): 309–326.

Braithwaite, J. (1989). *Crime, Shame, and Reintegration*. Cambridge, Cambridge University Press.

Brouhle, K., C. Griffiths, et al. (2005). The Use of Voluntary Approaches for Environmental Policymaking in the U.S. *The Handbook of Environmental Voluntary Agreements*. E. Croci, Kluwer Academic Publisher.

Bui, L. (2005). Public Disclosure of Private Information as a Tool for Regulating Environmental Emissions: Firm-Level Responses by Petroleum Refineries to the Toxics Release Inventory, Brandeis University.

Celdran, A., H. Clark, J. Hecht, E. Kanamaru, P. Orantes, and M. Santaello Garguno. 1996. "The Participation Decision in a Voluntary Pollution Prevention Program: The USEPA 33/50 Program as a Case Study." In Developing the Next Generation of the USEPA's 33/50 Program: A Pollution Prevention Research Project [Report], Duke University Nicholas School of the Environment, Durham, NC.

Coglianese, C. and J. Nash (2006). Beyond Compliance—Business Decision Making and US EPA's Performance Track Program, Harvard University, JFK School of Government.

Dasgupta, S., H. Hettige, and D. Wheeler. 2000. What improves environmental compliance? Evidence from Mexican Industry. *Journal of Environmental Economics and Management* 39:39–66.

Davies, T., N. Darnall, et al. (1996). Industry Incentives for Environmental Improvement: Evaluation of U.S. Federal Initiatives. Washington, DC, Global Environmental Management Initiative, Resources for the Future.

Dawson, N. L. and K. Segerson (2003). Voluntary Agreements with Industries: Particiation Incentives with Industry-Wide Targets. Dept of Economics Working Paper Series, University of Connecticut.

Decanio, S. J. and W. E. Watkins (1998). "Investment in Energy Efficiency: Do the Characteristics of Firms Matter?" *Review of Economics and Statistics* 80(1): 95–107.

Delmas, M. and M. J. Montes-Sancho (2007). Voluntary Agreements to Improve Environmental Quality: Are Late Joiners the Free Riders? Working paper, Donald Bren School of Environmental Science and Management. Santa Barbara, CA, University of California.

Delmas, M. and M. Toffel (2004). Institutional Pressures and Environmental Management Practices. *New Perspective in Research on Corporate Sustainability: Stakeholders, Environment and Society.* S. Sharma and M. Starik. Northampton, MA, Edward Elgar Publishing.

———. (2004a). "Stakeholders and Environmental Management Practices: An Institutional Framework." *Business Strategy and the Environment* 13(209–222).

Delmas, M. A. (2002). "The Diffusion of Environmental Management Standards in Europe and the United States: An Institutional Perspective." *Policy Sciences* 35: 91–119.

Delmas, M. A. and A. K. Terlaak (2001). "A Framework for Analyzing Environmental Voluntary Agreements." *California Management Review* 43(3).

———. (2002). "Regulatory Commitment to Negotiated Agreements: Evidence from the United States, Germany, The Netherlands, and France." *Journal of Comparative Policy Analysis: research and practice,* 4: 5–29.

Dietrich, E. (2004). "Regulatory Factors Shaping Environmental Performance at Publicly-Owned Treatment Plants." *Journal of Environmental Economics and Management* 48: 655–681.

Foulon, J., P. Lanoie, et al. (2002). "Incentives for Pollution Control: Regulation or Information?" *Journal of Environmental Economics and Management* 44: 169–87.

Gamper-Rabindran, S. (2006). "Did the EPA's Voluntary Industrial Toxics Program Reduce Emissions? A GIS Analysis of Distributional Impacts and By-Media Analysis of Substitution." *Journal of Environmental Economics and Management* 52: 391–410.

Garcia, J., T. Sterner, et al. (2006). Public Disclosure of Industrial Pollution: The PROPER Approach for Indonesia? *Department of Economics.* Gothenburg, Sweden, University of Gothenburg.

Glachant, M., S. Schucht, et al. (2002). "Companies' Participation in EMAS: The Influence of the Public Regulator." *Business Strategy and the Environment* 11(4): 254–266.

Gray, W. and R. Shadbegian (2007). "The Environmental Performance of Polluting Plants: A Spatial Analysis." *Journal of Regional Science* February: 63–84.

———. (2005). "When and Why do Plants Comply? Paper Mills in the 1980s." *Law and Policy* April: 238–261.

Grief, A. (1997). Microtheory and Recent Development in the Study of Economic Institutions through Economic History. *Advances in Economic Theory and Econometrics.* D. Kreps and K. Wallis. Cambridge, UK, Cambridge University Press.

Gunningham, N., R. Kagan, et al. (2004). *Social License and Environmental Protection: Why Businesses Go Green,* ABA.

———. (2003). *Shades of Green, Business, Regulation and Environment.* Stanford, Stanford University Press.

Hamilton, J. T. (2005). *Regulation through Revelation, the Origin, Politics, and Impacts of the Toxics Release Inventory Program.* New York, Cambridge University Press.

Henriques, I. and P. Sardosky (1996). "The Determinants of an Environmentally Responsive Firm: An Empirical Approach." *Journal of Environmental Economics and Management* 30(3): 381–395.

Hoffman, A. J. (1997). *From Heresy to Dogma: An Institutional History of Corporate Environmentalism.* San Francisco, CA, The New Lexington Press.

Horowitz, J. (2002). Over-compliance in Point Source Water Pollution. *STAR Grant Final Report,* US EPA:
http://cfpub.epa.gov/ncer_abstracts/index.cfm/fuseaction/display.abstractDetail/abstract/213/report/F.

Horowitz, M. J. (2001). "Economic Indicators of Market Transformation: Energy Efficient Lighting and EPA's Green Lights." *Energy Journal* 22: 95–122.

———. (2004). "Electricity Intensity in the Commercial Sector: Market and Public Program Effects." *Energy Journal* 25: 139–144.

ISO (2005). The ISO Survey of Certifications. Geneva, Switzerland, International Standards Organization: http://www.iso.org/iso/en/iso9000-14000/pdf/survey2005.pdf (accessed 2/2007.

Karamanos, P. (1999). Voluntary Environmental Agreements for the Reduction of Greenhous Gas Emissions: Incentives and Characteristics of Electric Utility Participants in the Climate Challenge Program. *School of Public and Environmental Affairs.* Bloomington, IN, Indiana University.

Khanna, M. (2001). "Non-Mandatory Approaches to Environmental Protection." *Journal of Economic Surveys* 15(3): 291–324.

———. (2007). The U.S. 33/50 Voluntary Program: Its Design and Effectiveness. *Reality Check: The Nature and Performance of Voluntary Environmental Programs in the United States, Europe, and Japan.* R. Morgenstern and W. Pizer. Washington, DC, Resources for the Future.

Khanna, M. and W. R. Q. Anton (2002). "Corporate Environmental Management: Regulatory and Market-Based Incentives." *Land Economics* 78(4): 539–558.

Khanna, M. and L. A. Damon (1999). "EPA's Voluntary 33/50 Program: Impact on Toxic Releases and Economic Performance of Firms." *J. Environ. Econom. Management* 37: 1–25.

Khanna, M., G. Deltas, et al. (2005). Adoption of Pollution Prevention Techniques: The Role of Management Systems, Demand-Side Factors and Complementary Assets. *Dept of Economics.* Urbana, University of Illinois.

King, A. and M. Lenox (2000). "Industry Self-Regulation without Sanctions: The Chemical Industry's Responsible Care Program." *The Academy of Management Journal* 43(4): 698–716.

———. (2001a). "Does It Really Pay to Be Green? Accounting for Strategy Selection in the Relationship between Environmental and Financial Performance." *Journal of Industrial Ecology* 4(4 Fall): 105–116.

———. (2001b). "Who adopts management standards early? An examination of ISO 14001 Certifications." Academy of Management Proceedings, pp. A1–A6.

————. (2001c). "Who Adopts Management Standards Early? An Examination of ISO 14001 Certifications." *Academy of Management Proceedings:* A1–A6.

————. (2001d). "Lean and Green: An Empirical Examination of the Relationship between Lean Production and Environmental Performance." *Production and Operations Management* 10(3): 244–256.

King, A. A., M. J. Lenox, et al. (2005). "The Strategic Use of Decentralized Institutions: Exploring Certification with the ISO 14001 Management Standard." *Academy of Management Journal* 48(6): 1091–1106.

Koehler, D. A. (2002). Navigating Toward a Hungarian Packaging Waste Management Solution. *Voluntary Environmental Agreements: Process, Practice and Future Use.* P. t. Brink, Greenleaf Publishing, UK.

Koehler, D. A. and J. D. Spengler (2007). "The Toxic Release Inventory: Fact or Fiction? A Case Study of the Primary Aluminum Industry." forthcoming *Journal of Environmental Management.*

Kollman, K. and A. Prakash (2001). "Green by Choice? Cross-National Variations in Firms' Responses to EMS-based Environmental Regimes." *World Politics* 53: 399–430.

Kollman, K. and A. Prakash (2002). "EMS-Based Environmental Regimes as Club Goods: Examining Variations in Firm-level Adoption of ISO 14001 and EMAS in U.K., U.S. and Germany." *Policy Sciences* 35(1): 43–67.

Lenox, M. (2006). The Role of Private Decentralized Institutions in Sustaining Industry Self-Regulation. *Fuqua School of Business.* Durham, Duke University.

Lenox, M. and J. Nash (2003). "Industry Self-Regulation and Adverse Selection: A Comparison across Four Trade Association Programs." *Business Strategy and the Environment* 12: 343–356.

Lyon, T. and J. Maxwell (2002). Voluntary Approaches to Environmental Regulation: A Survey. *Economic Institutions and Environmental Policy.* M. Frazini and A. Nicita. Aldershot and Hampshire, U.K, Ashgate Publishing.

————. (2003). "Self-Regulation, Taxation and Public Voluntary Environmental Agreements." *Journal of Public Economics* 87(7): 1453–1486.

Lyon, T. P. and E.-H. Kim (2006). Greenhouse Gas Reductions or Greenwash? The DOE's 1605(b) Program. Stephen M. Ross School of Business. Ann Arbor, University of Michigan.

Lyon, T. P. and J. W. Maxwell (2004). *Corporate Environmentalism and Public Policy.* Cambridge, Cambridge University Press.

————. (2006). Greenwash: Corporate Environmental Disclosure under Threat of Audit. School of Business. Ann Arbor, University of Michigan.

Matthews, D. (2001). Assessment and Design of Industrial Environmental Management Systems, Carnegie Mellon University.

Matthews, D. H., L. Lave, and C. Hendrickson. 2005. "Environmental Management Systems: Informing Organizational Decisions." Final report, National Center for Environmental Research, Washington, DC.

Maxwell, J. W., T. P. Lyon, et al. (2000). "Self-Regulation and Social Welfare: The Political Economy of Corporate Environmentalism." *Journal of Law and Economics* XLIII(October): 583–617.

Mazurek, J. (2002). Government-Sponsored Voluntary Programs for Firms: An Initial Survey. *New Tools for Environmental Protection: Education, Information and Voluntary Measures.* T. Dietz and P. C. Stern. Washington, NAS.

McClelland, J. and J. Horowitz (1999). "The Costs of Water Pollution Regulation in the Pulp and Paper Industy." *Land Economics* 75: 220–232.

Meyer, J. and B. Rowan (1977). "Institutional Organizations: Formal Structure as Myth and Ceremony." *American Journal of Sociology* 80: 340–363.

Morgenstern, R. and S. Al-jurf (1999). "Does the Provision of Free Technical Information Really Influence Firm Behavior." *Technological Forecasting and Social
Change* 61: 13–24.

Morgenstern, R. D. and W. A. Pizer (2007). *Reality Check, the Nature and Performance
of Voluntary Environmental Programs in the United States, Europe, and Japan.*
Washington, DC, Resources for the Future.

Morgenstern, R. D., W. A. Pizer, et al. (2007). Evaluating Voluntary U.S. Climate Pro-
grams: The Case of Climate Wise. *Reality Check: The Nature and Performance of
Voluntary Environmental Programs in the United States, Europe, and Japan.* R. D.
Morgenstern and W. A. Pizer. Washington, DC, Resources for the Future.

Nash, J. and J. Ehrenfeld (1997). "Codes of Environmental Management Practice: Assessing Their Potential as a Tool for Change." *Annual Review of Energy and the Environment* Vol. 22 (November): 487–535.

Potoski, M. and A. Prakash (2004). "The Regulation Dilemma: Cooperation and Conflict
in Environmental Governance." *Public Administration Review* 64(2): 152-163.

———. (2005). "Covenants with Weak Swords: ISO 14001 and Facilities' Env Performance." *Journal of Policy Analysis and Management* 24(4): 745–769.

Potoski, M. and A. Prakash (2005a). "Green Clubs and Voluntary Governance: ISO
14001 and Firms' Regulatory Compliance." *American Journal of Political Science*
49(2): 235–248.

Ramus, C. A. and I. Montiel (2005). "When Are Corporate Environmental Policies a
Form of Greenwashing?" *Business and Society* 44: 377–415.

Reinhardt, F. (1999b). "Market Failure and the Environmental Policies of Firms." *Journal of Industrial Ecology* 3(1): 9–21.

Rezek, J. P. and R. Campbell (2007). "Cost Estimates for Multiple Pollutants: A Maximum Entropy Approach." *Energy Economics* 29: 503–519.

Rivera, J. (2002). "Assessing a Voluntary Environmental Initiative in the Developing
World: The Costa Rican Certification for Sustainable Tourism." *Policy Sciences* 35:
333–360.

———. (2004). "Institutional Pressures and Voluntary Environmentanl Behavior in Developing Countries: Evidence from the Costa Rican Hotel Industry." *Society and
Natural Resources* 17: 779–797.

Rivera, J., P. d. Leon, et al. (2006). "Is Greener Whiter Yet? The Sustainable Slopes Program after Five Years." *The Policy Studies Journal* 34(2): 195–221.

Russo, M. V. and P. A. Fouts (1997). "A Resource-Based Perspective on Corporate Environmental Performance and Profitability." *Academy of Management Journal* 40(3):
534–559.

SAB (1990). Reducing Risk: Setting Priorities and Strategies for Environmental Protection. Washington, DC, EPA Science Advisory Board.

Salzmann, O., U. Steger, et al. (2006). Inside the Mind of Stakeholders—Are They Driving Corporate Sustainability? *Forum for Corporate Sustainability Management.*
Lausanne, Switzerland, IMD.

Sam, A. G. and R. Innes (2005). Voluntary Pollution Reductions and the Enforcement of
Environmental Law: an Empirical Study of the 33/50 Program. *Department of Agricultural and Resource Economics.* Tucson, University of Arizona, College of Agriculture and Life Sciences.

Sasser, E., A. Prakash, et al. (2006). "Direct Targeting as an NGO Political Strategy:
Examining Private Authority Regimes in the Forestry Sector." *Business and Politics*
8(3): 1–32.

Schmidheiny, S. (1992). *Changing Course: A Global Business Perspective on Development and the Environment.* Boston, MIT Press.

Schmidheiny, S. and F. Zorraquin (1996). *Financing Change, The Financial Community, Eco-Efficiency and Sustainable Development.* Cambridge, MIT Press.

Segerson, K. and T. J. Miceli (1998). "Voluntary Environmental Agreements: Good or Bad News for Environmental Protection?" *Journal of Environmental Economics and Management* 36(2): 109–130.

———. (1999). Voluntary Approaches to Environmental Protection: The Role of Legislative Threats. *Voluntary Approaches in Environmental Policy.* C. Carraro and F. Leveque, Kluwer Academic Publishing.

Shimshack, J. P. and M. B. Ward (2005). "Regulator Reputation, Enforcement, and Environmental Compliance." *Journal of Environmental Economics and Management* 50: 519–540.

———. (2006). Enforcement and Overcompliance, Tufts University Working Paper.

Stafford, S. (2007). "Can Consumers Enforce Environmental Regulations? The Role of the Market in Hazardous Waste Compliance." *Business and Economics* 31(1): 83–107.

Stafford, S. L. (2006). "Rational or Confused Polluters? Evidence from Hazardous Waste Compliance." *Contributions to Economic Analysis & Policy* 5(1): Art. 21.

Stranlund, J. K. (1995). "Public Mechanisms to Support Compliance to an Environmental Norm." *Journal of Environmental Economics and Management* 28(2): 205–222.

Teisl, M. F., B. Roe, et al. (2002). "Can Eco-Labels Tune a Market? Evidence from Dolphin-Safe Labeling." *Journal of Environmental Economics and Management* 43(3): 339-359.

Thornton, D., N. A. Gunningham, et al. (2005). "General Deterrence and Corporate Environmental Behavior." *Law and Policy* 25(2): 262–288.

Toffel, M. W. (2006). Resolving Information Assymetries in Markets: The Role of Certified Management Programs. *Harvard Business School.* Cambridge.

Videras, J. and A. Alberini (2000). "The Appeal of Voluntary Environmental Programs: Which Firms Participate and Why?" *Contemporary Economic Policy* 18: 449–461.

Vidovic, M. and N. Khanna (2005). Can Voluntary Pollution Prevention Programs Fulfill Their Promises? Further Evidence from the EPA's 33/50 Program, presented at 2006 Third World Congress of Environmental and Resource Economists.

Webber, C. A., R. E. Brown, et al. (2000). "Savings Estimates for the ENERGY STAR Voluntary Labeling Program." *Energy Policy* 28(15): 1137–1150.

Welch, E., A. Mazur, et al. (2000). "Voluntary Behavior by Electric Utilities: Levels of Adoption and Contribution of the Climate Challenge Program to the Reduction of Carbon Dioxide." *Journal of Policy Analysis and Management* 19(3): 407–425.

Wu, J. and B. A. Babcock (1999). "The Relative Efficiency of Voluntary vs. Mandatory Environmental Regulations." *Journal of Environmental Economics and Management* 38(4): 158–175.

Ziegler, A. and K. Rennings (2004). Determinants of Environmental Innovations in Germany: Do Organizational Measures Matter? A Discrete Choice Analysis at the Firm Level. *Centre for European Economic Research.* Mannhaim, Germany.

Notes

1. VEPs can have various targets: 1) Production process VEPs (e.g. 33/50, Responsible Care, EMS, Performance Track, ClimateWise); 2) Commercial building VEPs (e.g. Green Lights, Energy Star Buildings, LEED Green Building Certification, Voluntary workplace smoking bans); 3) Product VEPs (e.g. Energy Star product labeling, dolphin safe label, organic food labeling, sustainable seafood labeling, Forest Stewardship Coun-

cil label, GreenSeal, Energy Star Homes, Sustainable Slopes); 4) Citizen action VEPs (e.g. anti-littering programs, adopt-a-highway programs, forest fire prevention programs (e.g. Smokey the Bear), SunWise and other sun protection programs, Radon Protection Program, anti-idling); 5) Transportation VEPs (e.g. SmartWay Transport program, diesel retrofit program/National Clean Diesel Campaign, Best Workplaces for Commuters, other commuter-benefit Transportation Demand Management programs (telework), bike to work campaigns); 6) Government action VEPs (e.g. Environmentally preferable purchasing, Federal Electronics Challenge, Landfill Methane Program); 7) Negotiated environmental performance agreements (e.g. National Vehicle Mercury Switch Recovery Program).

2. See "Voluntary Approaches," Environmental Policy Research Brief #1, European Union Research Network on Market-based Instruments for Sustainable Development, undated.

3. There are multiple programs at the state and local level.

4. As of 2005, 111,162 facilities have certified to the standard around the world ISO (2005). The ISO Survey of Certifications. Geneva, Switzerland, International Standards Organization: http://www.iso.org/iso/en/iso9000-14000/pdf/survey2005.pdf (accessed 2/2007.

5. Lyon, T. and J. Maxwell (2003). "Self-regulation, taxation and public voluntary environmental agreements." *Journal of Public Economics* 87(7): 1453–1486.

6. The problems encountered with EPA's Project XL arose both from this legal constraint and from disagreements within EPA on the extent of feasible regulatory relief to offer. See Blackman, A. and J. Boyd (2002). "Tailored Regulation: Will Voluntary Site-Specific Environmental Performance Standards Improve Welfare?" *Southern Economic Journal* 69(2): 309–326.

7. Industry self-regulation has been defined as trade-association sponsored industry standards. King, A. and M. Lenox (2000). "Industry Self-Regulation without Sanctions: The Chemical Industry's Responsible Care Program." *The Academy of Management Journal* 43(4): 698–716.

8. The EPA is increasingly introducing reporting requirements in its Partnership Programs, but many still lack a baseline against which the program can be evaluated. The majority of PPs (87%) report the existence of a baseline measure though the quality of the reported data remains uncertain.

9. Due in part to the results of this study, the American Chemistry Council (ACC) today requires third party verification of Responsible Care compliance as a condition of membership. The ACC will also begin ranking its members based on their environmental performance and will publish the results. By December 2007, member firms will be required to have facilities externally certified to a new Responsible Care management system which is based upon the ISO 14001 EMS standard. Lenox, M. and J. Nash (2003). "Industry Self-Regulation and Adverse Selection: A comparison across four trade association programs." *Business Strategy and the Environment* 12: 343–356.

10. Sophistication, or "comprehensiveness", of EMS is defined by the number of environmental management practices adopted by a firm based upon an Investor Research Responsibility Center (IRRC) survey.

11. There are multiple interpretations of these differences. One possibility is that EMS certified facilities have shifted toxic emissions from on-site (emissions) to off-site management of toxic chemicals, usually via land treatment. Thus the aggregate toxicity of their production has not changed. It turns out that off-site transfers reported to the TRI have increased over time, while on-site releases have decreased over time at an even greater rate. Air emissions have decreased the most from 1988–2004.

12. ISO 14001 certificated facilities are not required to report their environmental performance. Therefore certification does not directly inform on the environmental performance of a firm.

13. Recent research indicates that EMS's are not associated with environmental innovation. In particular, a cross-sectional analysis found only a minimal positive association between ISO 14001 certification and environmental innovation, while no such relationship was found between environmental innovation and certification to the EU's EMAS. See Ziegler, A. and K. Rennings (2004). Determinants of Environmental Innovations in Germany: Do Organizational Measures Matter? A Discrete Choice Analysis at the Firm Level. *Centre for European Economic Research.* Mannhaim, Germany.

14. However, because the entry barriers to VEP participation and membership requirements tend to be low, early joiners appear unable to prevent "lazy" late joiners from jeopardizing their efforts to improve environmental performance. Not surprisingly participants in the Swiss climate policy are pushing for CO_2 taxes to punish free riders. Baranzini, A. and P. Thalmann, Eds. (2004). *Voluntary Approaches to Climate Policy.* Cheltenham, Edward Elgar.

15. The interested reader should consider a recent theoretical paper on greenwashing, which explores the variable impacts of EMS certification and disclosure policies on greenwashing behavior. Lyon, T. P. and J. W. Maxwell (2006). Greenwash: Corporate Environmental Disclosure under Threat of Audit. *School of Business.* Ann Arbor, University of Michigan.

16. Research in the US has not yet provided robust evidence of the effectiveness of public disclosure via the TRI, due in part to the regulatory confounding impacts noted earlier in this paper. Early research by Hamilton argues that TRI is effective, while EPA funded research is ongoing. *See* Hamilton, J. T. (2005). *Regulation through Revelation, the origin, politics, and impacts of the toxics release inventory program.* New York, Cambridge University Press.

17. To assess this one would have to redo the Gamper-Rabindran analysis and not exclude the two ODS substances, but rather include them and assess whether the rate of ODS pollution abatement increased for 33/50 participating firms after the launch of the program relative to non-participants.

18. Research on the provision of technical information by electric utilities was found to positively influence the adoption of high efficiency lighting technology in commercial office buildings. Morgenstern, R. and S. Al-jurf (1999). "Does the provision of free technical information really influence firm behavior." *Technological Forecasting and Social Change* 61: 13–24.

19. "Energy Savings Estimates of Light Emitting Diodes in Niche Lighting Applications," Building Technologies Program Office of Energy Efficiency and Renewable Energy U.S. Department of Energy, November 2003.

(http://www.netl.doe.gov/ssl/PDFs/Niche%20Final%20Report.pdf)

20. Oak Ridge National Laboratory by XENERGY, Inc. "Evaluation of U.S. Department of Energy Motor Challenge program." 2000.

www1.eere.energy.gov/industry/bestpractices/pdfs/mceval1_2.pdf

August, 1995, U.S. Department of Energy's Motor Challenge Program: A National Strategy for Energy Efficient Industrial Motor-Driven Systems by *Paul E. Scheihing U.S. Department of Energy, Industrial Technologies Program Washington, DC, USA*

http://www1.eere.energy.gov/industry/bestpractices/motor_challenge_national_strat egy.html

21. "SmartMarket Report Green Building, Design & Construction Intelligence, 2006 Green Building Issue," McGraw Hill Construction in conjunction with the U.S. Green Building Council, 2006.

22. "Private Land Trusts: A Free-Market Forest Conservation Tool," Washington Policy Center Policy Brief, October 2002 (http://www.washingtonpolicy.org/Environment/PBMontagueForestLandTrusts.html).

23. The Federation of Tax Administrators. http://www.taxadmin.org/FTA/rate/ co_chart03.html; Montana Wildlife Division. "Projects Supported by Nongame Checkoff Funds".   January   2005,   http://fwp.mt.gov/FwpPaperApps/wildthings/projects.pdf; Colorado Herpetological Society. http://coloherp.org/cb-news/Vol-28/cbn-0102/ Tax-Checkoff.html; Kentucky Nature Preserves Commission. http://www.naturepreserves.ky. gov/helping/taxcheckoff.htm.

24. The Congestion Mitigation and Air Quality Improvement Program: Assessing 10 Years of Experience—Special Report 264 (2002) published by the Transportation Research Board of the National Academy of Sciences. See: http://www8.national acade-mies.org/onpinews/newsitem.aspx?RecordID=10350; "Do Employee Commuter Benefits Reduce Vehicle Emissions and Fuel Consumption? Results of the Fall 2004 Survey of Best Workplaces for Commuters" published in Proceedings from the TRB 2006 Annual Meeting (www.bwc.gov/pdf/evaluation-survey-findings-2005.pdf).

Chapter 3

Environmental Public Voluntary Programs Reconsidered

Thomas P. Lyon and John W. Maxwell

Introduction

For years environmental regulators have relied upon various forms of taxes, subsidies and command and control regulations to remedy environmental problems. Recently, however, new tools—including environmental public voluntary programs, or PVPs —have been added to the regulator's tool box. Public voluntary programs typically invite firms to set and achieve environmental goals, and offer modest subsidies to encourage firms to participate. These subsidies consist of various combinations of favorable publicity, technical assistance and opportunities for positive interactions with regulators. PVPs have been developed to address a variety of issues, including agriculture, air quality, energy efficiency and climate change, labeling, pollution prevention, waste management, and water. Among these, the areas with the most PVP activity are pollution prevention and climate change.

Perhaps the best known US PVP was the 33/50 Program operated by the Environmental Protection Agency (EPA) between 1991 and 1995.[1] This program identified seventeen high-priority toxic chemicals, and invited thousands of industrial companies to join the program and reduce their emissions of these chemicals 33% by 1992 and 50% by 1995. According to the EPA's Final Report on the Program, the most important feature of the program was that the agency "encouraged participants to set their own reduction goals, oriented to their own time frames, and most did so. Of the 1,294 companies participating, 1,066 set measurable goals for reducing their releases and transfers of the 17 targeted chemicals against the 1988 baseline."[2] The EPA was very pleased with the apparent success of the program, claiming that "The 33/50 Program achieved its goal in 1994, one year ahead of schedule, primarily through program participants' efforts."[3]

President Clinton's Climate Change Action Plan (CCAP), released in October 1993, spawned many public voluntary programs including Green Lights, Climate Wise, Motor Challenge and Energy Star Buildings, among many others. As in the case of 33/50, participants in these PVPs were provided with case studies detailing the cost savings of other program participants, and were offered technical information aimed at aiding the development of a program action plan. The programs also offered access to question hotlines, seminars at which firms could exchange information about cost savings, free software, and access to databases of equipment suppliers and financing programs.

Despite government enthusiasm for PVPs, econometric analysis of PVPs suggests that they are largely ineffective.[4] However, our analysis of PVPs and their design suggests that identifying the effects of PVPs is inherently difficult. An important aspect of most PVPs is an attempt to diffuse information about pollution abatement throughout industry, but this information may be received by non-participants as well as participants. If so, there will be little or no difference in performance between firms that join an information-oriented PVP and those that do not. It is possible that a difference would be observed in the early phases of a program, when the government is trying to attract participants who already have information to share. Once the program moves to the dissemination stage, however, there is likely to be no measurable difference between participants and non-participants. This is a point that has not been recognized in the empirical literature on PVPs, and that demands a reinterpretation of the findings in this literature.

To put PVPs in perspective alongside other policy instruments, we present a framework in which conventional regulation and PVPs can be considered in a unified political/economic approach, thereby allowing a sharper comparison of their relative merits. We show that in the absence of significant political opposition, a mandatory regulatory policy can produce greater environmental improvement than a PVP. However, if there is strong political opposition to mandatory measures, then PVPs may be preferable.

The modest subsidies implicit in PVPs can be provided in a variety of ways, with potentially important implications for the effectiveness of such programs. Hence, we analyze the structure of PVPs in detail, arguing that PVPs can enhance the diffusion of cost-effective techniques for pollution abatement, so long as the information involved is not competitively sensitive. We conclude that PVPs have a role to play in environmental policy, but that it is much more restricted than is sometimes portrayed by advocates of voluntary approaches.

The paper is organized as follows. The following section provides an overview of the voluntary programs sponsored by the US EPA, and their key features. The section on the Empirical Evidence on the Performance of PVPs reviews recent empirical findings on the performance of PVPs. The section on the Political Economic Context of PVPs provides a political-economic framework for understanding PVPs, which raises serious questions about the proper interpretation of the results obtained in the empirical literature to date. The section on the Implications for Empirical Research discusses the implications of our framework for future empirical work on PVPs, as well as its implications for the use and design of future PVPs.

An Overview of EPA PVPs

In this section we review all the PVPs listed on the EPA's "Partnership Programs" webpage on September 1, 2007.[5] Based on a careful reading of the materials on the website, we identify the key environmental issues to which PVPs have been applied, and analyze the key elements of the various PVPs.

The EPA identifies twelve categories in which they have PVPs, which are listed below with the number of programs in each category in parentheses:

- Agriculture (3)
- Air Quality (15)
- Energy Efficiency and Global Climate Change (26)
- Pollution Prevention (13)
- Product Labeling (1)
- Regulatory Innovation (1)
- Sector Programs (1)
- Technology (1)
- Transportation (13)
- Waste Management (6)
- Water (12)
- EPA's Regional Partnership Programs (None Listed)

Summing over all twelve categories yields a total of 92 programs. However, because many programs are listed in more than one category, the total number of independent PVPs is actually only 60. The three categories that encompass the vast bulk of PVPs are Energy Efficiency and Global Climate Change (many of which are also listed as Air Quality or Transportation programs), Pollution Prevention, and Water. Together, these three categories account for over 80% of the EPA's partnership programs.

The EPA Partnership Programs vary greatly in their form and substance. Many are basically websites with links to various documents and other websites.[6] Others are essentially programs run by industry trade associations with the encouragement of EPA, such as the Green Suppliers Network, Partnership for Safe Water,[7] and Sustainable Slopes.[8] Still others, such as the Carpet America Recovery Effort (CARE) and Hospitals for a Healthy Environment (HHE) are the result of specific agreements between industry and government, with multi-year goals and monitoring of industry progress toward reaching them.[9]

In order to get a better understanding of the structure of the EPA's partnership programs, we conducted a thorough review of the partnership website, with an eye to identifying the key program elements for each partnership program. The results are presented in Table 3.1, which reveals certain common features found in many of these programs and characterizes each partnership program according to which features it includes.

The Table shows that the two most common elements of PVPs are: 1) Disseminating information about abatement techniques more broadly throughout firms in particular industries and 2) Providing public recognition to those companies that go beyond compliance with existing regulations. In addition, there are several other techniques that are sometimes used in PVPs. Some PVPs provide regulatory benefits in the form of reduced priority for inspection (Performance Track) or improved access to EPA officials (Climate Leaders).[10] Other programs provide third-party certification of the environmental effectiveness of certain technologies (Environmental Technology Verification Program), or a reliable compendium of information about the environmental attributes of competing products (Green Vehicle Guide).[11]

Overall, it seems appropriate to characterize PVPs as primarily informational in nature.[12] As Table 3.1 shows, there are several different types of information-oriented PVPs. First, five involve government-sponsored research aimed at creating new knowledge, which can then be diffused throughout an industry. Second, twenty-eight programs codify the knowledge of certain leading firms through case studies, and make that information available to other firms in the industry. Third, twenty-four programs include peer-to-peer sharing of information, in addition to transmitting information through the regulator as intermediary. Each of these types of programs has certain special characteristics, which we now discuss.

Government-sponsored research is relatively unusual among PVPs. Design for the Environment and Green Chemistry are among the more prominent programs that utilize this approach. Even Design for the Environment sponsored little original research. Its focus was instead on pulling together the existing body of knowledge on the environmental impacts of alternative technologies in particular industries, an approach we discuss in more depth below. Government-sponsored original research seems to be used primarily in industries where there are no or few large firms that can generate the knowledge themselves. For example, one of the first projects under the Design for the Environment program was aimed at the dry cleaning industry, whose firms are too small to undertake projects aimed at generating new knowledge (or even staying abreast of the existing knowledge base) on the environmental impacts of alternative dry cleaning technologies.

Table 3.1 EPA Voluntary Partnership Program Characteristics

Primary Category	Program	Software	Cases	Lists	Tech Info	Tech. Asst.	P2P Exchange	Govt. R&D	Certification	Public Recognition	Regulatory Benefits	Coordination
					(Information Provision)							
1 Water	Adopt Your Watershed											
2 EEGCC	ASTAR											
3 EEGCC	Best Workplaces for Commuters											
4 WM	Carpet America Recovery Effort											
5 Water	Clean Marinas		•		•					•		
6 Air Quality	Clean School Bus USA				•							
7 Water	Clean Water Act Recognition Programs		•		•					•		
8 EEGCC	Climate Leaders		•		•					•		
9 EEGCC	Coal Combustion Products Partnership		•		•							
10 EEGCC	Coalbed Methane Outreach Program		•		•							
11 EEGCC	Combined Heat and Power Partnership	•			•	•				•		
12 Water	Decentral. Wastewater Treatment Syst. Program	•	•		•							
13 PP	Design for the Environment	•			•	•						
14 Air Quality	Diesel Retrofit Program				•			•	•			
15 EEGCC	ENERGY STAR		•	•	•				•	•		
16 Technology	Environmental Technology Verification Program				•				•	•		
17 PP	Environmentally Preferable Purchasing	•		•	•							
18 Water	EPA's Volunteer Monitoring Program			•	•							
19 PP	Federal Electronics Challenge											
20 Water	Five Star Restoration Program	•	•		•					•		
21 EEGCC	Great Amer. Woodstove Changeout Campaign		•		•							
22 PP	Green Chemistry		•		•			•		•		
23 PP	Green Engineering				•							
24 EEGCC	Green Power Partnership		•	•	•					•		
25 EEGCC	Green Vehicle Guide			•	•							
26 EEGCC	GreenScapes	•	•		•							
27 EEGCC	HFC-23 Emission Reduction Program											
28 PP	High Production Volume Challenge				•		•					
29 WM	Hospitals for a Healthy Environment	•	•		•		•					
30 EEGCC	Improving Air Quality through Land Use Activities	•			•							
31 Air Quality	Indoor Air Quality Tools for Schools	•			•							
32 Air Quality	Indoor Environments				•							
33 EEGCC	It All Adds Up to Cleaner Air	•			•							
34 EEGCC	Labs 21	•			•							
35 EEGCC	Landfill Methane Outreach Program (LMOP)	•			•		•					
36 PP	Lawns and the Environment				•							
37 EEGCC	Methane to Markets Partnership				•		•					
38 EEGCC	Mobile Air Cond. Climate Protection Partnership				•		•					
39 PP	National Environmental Performance Track				•		•			•		•
40 Water	National Fish Contamination Program				•							
41 Water	National Nonpoint Source Management Program		•		•							
42 EEGCC	National Partnership for Environmental Priorities		•		•							
43 EEGCC	Natural Gas STAR Program		•		•		•					
44 Water	Partnership for Safe Water		•		•							
45 AG	Pesticide Environmental Stewardship Program				•							
46 WM	Plug-in to eCycling		•		•							
47 AG	Reduced Risk for Conventional Pesticides†		•		•							
48 Sector	Sector Strategies Program		•		•							
49 EEGCC	SF6 Partnership for Electric Power		•		•		•			•		
50 EEGCC	SF6 Partnership for Magnesium Industry		•		•		•			•		
51 EEGCC	SmartWay Transport Partnership	•	•		•							
52 PP	Sustainable Futures Initiative				•							
53 Water	Sustainable Slopes				•							
54 PP	The Green Suppliers Network		•		•					•		
55 EEGCC	The SunWise School Program				•					•		
56 EEGCC	Voluntary Aluminum Industrial Partnership		•		•		•			•		
57 EEGCC	Voluntary Children's Chem. Eval. Program		•		•							
58 EEGCC	Waste Wise		•		•					•		
59 Water	Water Sense		•		•					•		
	Number of Programs with Feature	13	28	15	32	7	24	5	6	25	3	4

EEGCC = Energy Efficiency and Global Climate Change
PP = Pollution Prevention
WM = Waste Management
AG = Agriculture
Sector = Sector Program

Table 3.1 –Continued
Glossary of Terms

Software	Computer programs made available by EPA, dealing with how to measure or control emissions and/or costs.
Cases	Case studies of successful abatement efforts by participants in the program.
Lists	Compilations of suppliers of technical assistance or products.
Tech. Info	Written documents explaining the scientific or technical aspects of pollution generation, or of technologies for abatement.
Tech Assist	Live interaction with human experts who can provide customized technical advice.
P2P Exchange	Opportunities for peer-to-peer exchange between program participants of information about effective abatement strategies. Typically done through conferences, but sometimes also through online dialogues.
Govt. R&D	Government funded research on abatement technologies, the results of which are disseminated through the program.
Certification	Government-backed assurance that certain technologies or practices achieve their abatement claims.
Public Recognition	Plaques and awards that can be displayed prominently within participating organizations, and assistance with external media public relations.
Regulatory Benefits	Opportunities for interaction with EPA officials or promises of reduced inspection priority.
Coordination	Encourages all participants to adopt similar policies.
Funding	Financial grants or incentives for selected applicants.
Info. Disclosure	Participants expected to disclose data on their environmental performance.
Goal Setting	Participants expected to set goals for environmental improvement.

Programs that codify the existing knowledge of leading firms are perhaps the most common tool used within the family of EPA partnership programs. For example, many PVPs provide case studies of successful projects undertaken by participating firms. Some types of knowledge, of course, are difficult for the EPA to generate directly, such as learning-by-doing, that is, knowledge that accrues during the process of conducting business. Government-sponsored research is a poor means for attempting to create this knowledge. Even if the knowledge could be generated directly through government sponsorship, at least in principle, it is often more efficient for the regulator to collect data on the experience firms have already accumulated rather than to try and generate new knowledge on its own, assuming firms can be persuaded to share their existing stock of information.

Peer-to-peer information sharing is an aspect of PVPs that is distinct from the transmission in written form of codified knowledge and case studies. Ongoing interactions with give and take are particularly useful when firms are engaged in long-term processes of continuous improvement in the environmental arena. One-time achievements can be documented and posted on the web, but web postings will always lag behind the ongoing creation of new knowledge. Face-to-face interactions are also helpful when one cannot simply replicate one firm's experience in another firm's operational setting. In such cases, the opportunity for immediate feedback helps firms to determine just how applicable other firms' experience is for their own idiosyncratic problems. This may have particular value when the technological processes involved are complex, and are difficult for EPA officials to convey accurately without having actual industry experience.

The second key design feature of many PVPs is the provision of public recognition for the firm. This may be quite attractive to firms, since the EPA is likely to be viewed as a more credible source of information about the firm's good works than is self-promotion by the firm itself. The EPA's recognition programs can also help to boost employee morale within the firm, by highlighting the efforts of individuals who have played important roles in environmental improvement. For firms that use their environmental performance as a way to attract quality employees, this benefit can have substantial value.

We will refer back to this discussion of the structure of PVPs in the following section below, where we discuss its implications for empirical evaluation of PVPs, and later, where we discuss in more detail how regulators can design PVPs to function most effectively as information diffusion programs.

Empirical Evidence on the Performance of PVPs

In this section we review the still small body of hard quantitative evidence on how well PVPs perform. While there are many qualitative case studies of individual programs,[13] and quite a few papers that study which firms are likely to join PVPs,[14] our interest here is on whether these programs have any measurable impact on the behavior of firms that join. We begin by discussing the most widely studied PVP, the EPA's 33/50 Program, then turn to climate change PVPs, and finally discuss other programs, including WasteWise, the Sustainable Slopes program for ski areas and the EPA's Performance Track Program. Overall, the empirical results suggest that participation in these PVPs had little or no impact on firms' environmental performance.

Toxic Chemical Emissions: The 33/50 Program

The EPA's 33/50 program was initiated in 1988, and is considered the grandfather of all voluntary programs. Its primary goal was to convince companies to set goals for reducing toxic chemical emissions by 50% by the year 1995, from a 1988 baseline. The program emerged shortly after the deadly chemical release from Union Carbide's plant in Bhopal, India, which killed over 3,000 people. Chemical industry leaders became seriously concerned about the industry's "license to operate," especially after survey results found that the chemical industry's reputation among the public was in the same league with the tobacco and the nuclear industries, both of which had been saddled with intrusive and burdensome regulations. Indeed, the Chemical Manufacturer's Association was concerned enough to create the Responsible Care program to improve the public's trust of the industry.[15]

It was in this context that William Reilly, EPA Administrator and former head of the World Wildlife Fund, called a small group of chemical industry leaders into his office and told them he expected substantial reductions in toxic emissions, which could be accomplished voluntarily or through regulations. The industry representatives preferred a voluntary approach, but there was clearly a regulatory threat looming behind the program.[16]

According to the EPA the program consisted of four major elements: "outreach to companies to encourage commitments; public recognition of companies for their commitments, pollution prevention efforts, and achievements; technical assistance to help companies overcome barriers and achieve commitments through pollution prevention practices; and evaluation of the effectiveness of both industry and government efforts in a voluntary, cooperative program."[17]

Outreach was accomplished by sending solicitation letters to companies directly, inviting them to participate. In addition, EPA convened "a series of about a dozen meetings with top executives from different industrial manufacturing sectors: chemicals; transportation related; machinery and electrical equipment; iron, steel, and primary metals; pulp and paper; petroleum refining; pharmaceuticals; wood and metal furniture; rubber and related products; and metal finishings and coatings. Trade associations, such as the Chemical Manufacturers Association, were instrumental in helping arrange these sessions."[18]

Public recognition was to be created in "program publications, press releases, and in speeches and other routine federal and state communications. Companies submitting reduction commitments receive a formal certificate of participation from EPA."[19]

With regard to technical assistance, there were five components: 1) A series of workshops across the country with industry to exchange information on pollution prevention theory and practices; 2) the Pollution Prevention Information Exchange System, a free computer bulletin board containing technical and policy information on pollution prevention; 3) bibliographic reports on pollution prevention and recycling techniques; 4) a pollution prevention resource guide, which identifies key pollution prevention documents, industry specific guidance manuals, fact sheets, and videos; and 5) a list of successful and innovative pollution prevention practices companies have implemented as part of the 33/50 Program.[20]

Because the program builds upon the readily-accessible information reported through the EPA's Toxic Release Inventory (TRI), it is the most widely studied of voluntary programs. However, researchers are divided on the impacts of the program. All four papers that we discuss below employ a two-stage methodology of the sort pioneered by Heckman (1979), in which the first stage predicts the probability a given firm participates in the program, and the second stage estimates performance controlling for the likelihood of participation. This method avoids the selection bias that occurs if one simply includes program participation as a variable without controlling for the antecedents that explain participation.

Khanna and Damon (1998) were the first to study whether 33/50 participation made a difference in the level of chemical reductions undertaken by firms over the period 1991-1993, and concluded that 33/50 Program participants reduced emissions significantly more than did other firms in the chemical industry during this period. This paper has been widely cited as evidence that PVPs work. Sam and Innes (2007) also analyze the 33/50 Program, using a larger set of explanatory variables and a longer time horizon, and also conclude program participation reduced emissions, but only had a significant impact on emissions in 1991 and 1992. In later years they find no evidence that program participants reduced emissions any more than did non-participants.

Vidovic and Khanna (2007), in contrast, find no impact at all from 33/50 Program participation. They include a variable measuring emission reductions during the two years prior to the inception of the 33/50 Program, and find that once this variable is included, the predicted probability of participation has no impact on emissions at the firm level. They thus conclude that most of the reported impact of the program came from "free riding" by early joiners who had already accomplished significant reductions without the benefit of the program. This is consistent with raw data reported in US EPA (1999, p. 2), which shows that industry had already achieved a 32.1% reduction in emissions by 1991, when EPA began inviting companies to participate.

Finally, Gamper-Rabindran (2006) revisits the 33/50 Program's effectiveness, accounting for some measurement problems inherent in the program.[21] He finds that participants in the fabricated metals and paper industries cut emissions relative to non-participants, while in the chemical and primary metals industries participants actually did less emissions reduction than non-participants.[22] Furthermore, even in the industries where participation seemed to be beneficial, the vast bulk of the apparent emission reductions were really transfers off-site rather than true pollution prevention. Gamper-Rabindran thus concludes that the program has been ineffective in achieving its goals.

Climate Change

Most of the US climate change PVPs aim to increase investments in energy efficiency. They emphasize the private benefits to firms and individuals of adopting energy efficient equipment, and attempt to solve the "market failures" that limit the spread of these technologies. The climate change VAs were begun under the first Bush Administration after President Bush promised to be the "environmental president." Most of them, however, were promulgated as part of the Clinton Administration's efforts to achieve reductions in greenhouse gases after the "Earth Summit" in Rio de Janeiro in June 1992.

In contrast to the 33/50 Program's origins, there does not appear to have been a substantial regulatory "threat" driving the adoption of climate-oriented PVPs. Indeed, the first Bush Administration opposed strong actions to combat global warming, and was publicly derided by US environmental groups and by most other nations of the world for its refusal at the "Earth Summit" to agree to a timetable with specific targets for reducing emissions of greenhouse gases.

After President Clinton was elected in November of 1992, one of his early actions was to announce support for stronger measures to prevent climate change. In the early months of 1993, his administration floated a variety of proposals to tax energy, including a carbon tax and a broader-based "BTU tax" based on the energy content of fuels as measured in British Thermal Units. The political backlash was fast and furious, and within a few months the Administration had abandoned the BTU tax initiative. When the Administration presented its Climate Change Action Plan (CCAP) later in the year, the focus was shifted away from mandatory regulations to subsidies (including $200 million per year to stimulate the adoption of more energy-efficient technologies) and voluntary programs. The environmental community was not impressed. Alden Meyer, director of the program on climate change and energy at the Union of Concerned Scientists, argued that the plan placed too much emphasis on voluntary measures, "with no prospect of hammers or sticks to bring us into compliance if those don't work."[23]

Released in October 1993, the President's Climate Change Action Plan (CCAP) spawned many public voluntary programs including Green Lights, Climate Wise, Motor Challenge and Energy Star Buildings among many others. Unfortunately, there is little work that attempts to measure the impact of these programs on emissions, although there is a large literature describing the programs, and a few papers that assess empirically the factors driving firms to participate and the benefits claimed by participants.[24] However, the Climate Challenge program for electric utilities, sponsored by the Department of Energy (DOE), has been studied by Welch, Mazur and Bretschneider (2000) and Delmas and Montes-Sancho (2007).

The Climate Challenge program invited utilities to set their own targets for carbon dioxide emissions reductions, develop their own approaches to achieving reductions, and self-report on their progress. Stated benefits of participation included the possibility of preempting binding legislation, public relations advantages, cost savings, and the possibility of obtaining early reduction credits in the event that mandatory climate change legislation is passed.[25] Welch et al. (2000) find that participation in the Climate Challenge program most likely had no impact on greenhouse gas emissions, although some of their results suggest it may have actually had a detrimental impact. They point out that there was no real regulatory threat during the time period they studied (1995 to 1997), and that this may explain why the program had little effect on participant behavior.

It is also important to note that on average, the 50 large utilities in their sample cut CO_2 emissions by 6.3 million tons per firm over the sample period. The average reduction pledged by program participants was 3 million tons, which is less than half the average actual reductions achieved by all firms. Thus, it is not the case that participants took no action; it is just that non-participants reduced emissions just as fast as participants. As a result, it is possible that DOE is correct when it claims that "A significant effect of the Climate Challenge program is the shift in thinking of electric utility management and strategic planners to include the mitigation of greenhouse gas emissions into their corporate culture and philosophy," and that "Climate Challenge has served as a catalyst for utility support of many of the voluntary CCAP actions."[26]

Delmas and Montes-Sancho (2007) also studied the Climate Challenge program, but they distinguished between the behavior of early joiners and late joiners. Like Welch et al. (2000), they found no overall difference in emissions reductions between program participants and non-participants. However, early joiners actually did reduce emissions significantly more than non-participants; the problem was that this beneficial effect was cancelled out by the behavior of the late joiners. The authors argue that late joiners were free-riding on the substantive efforts of the early joiners, and were participating in a purely symbolic way to obtain benefits with relevant stakeholders. This suggests their participation can be viewed as a form of greenwash designed to deflect attention from their actual environmental performance.[27] Delmas and Montes-Sancho (2007) find that the two groups differed in important ways: early joiners were larger and subject to greater political pressure than late joiners, had higher regulatory expenses, and were better connected to the industry trade association.

Morgenstern and Pizer (2007, chapter 7) study the EPA's Climate Wise program, a PVP initiated in 1993 and targeted at the non-utility industrial sector, with an emphasis on encouraging energy efficiency, renewable energy and pollution prevention techniques. In 2000, Climate Wise was renamed and placed under EPA's Energy Star umbrella. The main requirements for a participant were that they develop a baseline estimate of its greenhouse gas (GHG) emissions, pledge future reductions, and make periodic progress reports. Like most PVPs, the program offered public recognition and technical assistance to participants. At its peak, the program had over 600 members with thousands of facilities nationwide. Morgenstern and Pizer's basic conclusion is that the program had only a transient effect on fuel use and emissions, with the best estimate being a 3% reduction during the program's initial phase. They note that there is also some evidence that participants actually increased their electricity use in achieving these apparent reductions, so the program's overall impact on the environment is unclear. Interestingly, they speculate that "it may be fair to say that the effect of Climate Wise was to accelerate energy-saving behavior that eventually arose among program participants and nonparticipants alike."[28]

Other Programs

There have also been empirical assessments of the EPA's WasteWise program, EPA's Performance Track program, and the Sustainable Slopes Program, a voluntary environmental initiative established by the U.S. National Ski Areas Association in partnership with federal and state government agencies.

Delmas and Keller (2005) studied the EPA's WasteWise program, created in 1994 to promote waste reduction in businesses and other organizations. WasteWise encourages participants to design their own waste reduction and recycling programs, and to use emerging technologies in the manufacturing and design process of materials. It offers technical information, free technical assistance, and opportunities for peer-to-peer networking. Although the authors did not have information about actual waste reduction outcomes, they were able to assess whether participants followed through on their commitments to report their results to the EPA. Based on surveys of participating firms, Delmas and Keller (2005) found that firms joining the WasteWise program in 1999 were significantly less likely to report on their environmental performance (as required by the program) than were firms that joined in earlier years.

Coglianese and Nash (2007) study the EPA's Performance Track Program. This program cut across various industry sectors, and offered additional regulatory flexibility and reduced inspection frequency to firms that had demonstrated a track record of environmental compliance. Although the authors' analysis does not present a formal quantitative analysis of the performance impacts of participation, they conclude that "it appears that many businesses simply do not perceive the rewards offered by government to be very significant at all. . . . The conclusion from this analysis is that the level of participation in programs like Performance Track will likely remain quite modest."[29]

Rivera and de Leon (2004) study the Sustainable Slopes Program, which was created in response to growing criticism by environmentalists of the western ski industry's expansion plans, which emphasized concerns about landscape destruction, deforestation, water and air pollution, and damage to wildlife habitats. The program, created by the National Ski Areas Association (NSAA) in 2000 with the EPA as a partner, aims to promote "beyond compliance" principles that cover 21 general areas of environmental management. Participant ski areas are expected to implement annual self-assessment of their environmental performance; it does not include specific environmental performance standards or third party oversight for participants. In its first year of operation, 160 ski areas enrolled in the program, a number that increased to 170 in 2001, and has since remained constant at 173 ski areas. The self-assessment survey of environmental performance distributed by the program was completed by 79 ski areas in 2003, about 11% less than in 2001 and 2002.

Rivera and de Leon measure the performance of the program using ratings created by the Ski Area Citizens Coalition, an alliance of American environmental organizations. They find that "participant ski areas appear to be correlated with lower third-party environmental performance ratings."[30] They attribute the poor performance of the program to loosely specified performance criteria and lax reporting requirements.[31]

Overall Empirical Conclusions

The papers we have reviewed here indicate that PVPs have had little or no impact on the behavior of participants. Even the 33/50 Program, for which initial studies found significant impacts, seems under further study to have had little effect overall. Climate Wise appeared to create a small and transient beneficial effect on greenhouse gas emissions, Climate Challenge had no measurable effect overall, and Sustainable Slopes arguably had a negative impact. These findings are broadly consistent with the case study literature, as represented in Morgenstern and Pizer (2007). Some case studies suggest a cautiously optimistic conclusion that PVPs may offer modest benefits. However, as Morgenstern and Pizer (2007, p. 184) conclude: "[N]one of the case study authors found truly convincing evidence of dramatic environmental improvements. Therefore, we find it hard to argue for voluntary programs where there is a clear desire for major changes in behavior."

The Political Economic Context of PVPs

The extensive and continued use of PVPs by the EPA stands in marked contrast to the empirical literature that suggests the programs are ineffective. In this section we discuss whether extant empirical results on the effectiveness of PVPs have been interpreted correctly. First, we argue that once one considers the political environment within which PVPs arise, the objectives of regulators, and the structure of most PVPs, the expectation that PVPs will result in large changes in corporate behavior is misplaced. Second, we argue that the information-oriented design of most PVPs means that the econometric techniques commonly used in the literature may not actually identify the effects of these programs.

Motives for Voluntary Reductions

As the discussion in an earlier section illustrates, PVPs arise in a setting in which society believes that businesses are engaging in activities that produce significant environmental harm. What constitutes significant harm is more often than not a political issue as much as it is a scientific issue. Consequently, participants and non-participants alike may face a variety of pressures to reduce the environmental harm they are deemed to cause. These pressures might manifest themselves in the market place, via legislative or regulatory threats, or through threats from non-governmental organizations (NGOs). Econometric studies need to be careful to control for these factors if they are to obtain unbiased and efficient estimates.

Market-based motivations for voluntary pollution reductions can take several forms. Porter and van der Linde (1995) suggested a so-called "win-win" motive for voluntary pollution reductions: firms may clean up their production processes voluntarily because cleaner production processes are cheaper than dirtier ones. While many economists doubt that this hypothesis can explain widespread pollution abatement, Palmer, Oates and Portney (1995), in rebuttal to Porter and van der Linde, do find support for the notion that clean production may lower firm costs once the costs of current and possible future regulations are taken into account.

Green consumerism is a commonly suggested driver of voluntary pollution reduction efforts.[32] If consumers are willing to pay a premium for environmentally friendly goods, any firm that can verifiably reduce its pollution in a cost-effective manner should engage in such efforts voluntarily. Employees have also been suggested as an important driver for voluntary corporate pollution reduction efforts. Most employees want to feel good about the company where they spend so much of their lives. One way companies try to attract and retain the best employees is by making environmental commitments that are aligned with those employees' environmental values.[33]

Some studies suggest that even if pollution efforts result in a net cost to the corporate bottom line, green investors may exist in sufficient numbers to prevent the market from disciplining voluntary pollution reduction efforts. Graff Zivin and Small (2005) show that if investors prefer to make their social donations through bundled corporate activities rather than through direct charitable contribution, then companies may find it profit-maximizing to engage in actions such as voluntary pollution abatement to attract investors. Baron (2006) shows that even when activities such as voluntary pollution abatement may lower the value of the firm, its shares trade at a premium, reflecting the utility green investors obtain from holding them.

There is a large theoretical and empirical literature that suggests that voluntary emissions reduction efforts may be motivated by the desire to preempt legislative and/or regulatory threats. Maxwell, Lyon and Hackett (2000) show that industry self-regulation of pollution emissions can be effective in preempting legislative threats for two reasons. First, self-regulation lowers consumers' desires for additional emissions reductions and, second, it serves as commitment mechanism for industry to fight harder against legislative efforts aimed at extracting further emissions reductions. In a related vein, Segerson and Miceli (1998) show that if a regulator anticipates legislation that may be forthcoming and costly to enforce, it may negotiate a voluntary agreement with industry aimed at preempting the legislation.

A legislative threat is the manifestation of a desire by the broader public to regulate the emissions activities of firms. However, in some cases industry may hold sway over the political process, effectively blockading any legislative threats. In this situation, NGOs that wish to change corporate environmental behavior must turn to what David Baron (2001, 2005, 2006, 2007) has termed "private politics," in which NGOs directly pressure firms and/or industries to undertake actions to improve their corporate social performance (via boycotts, negative information campaigns etc.)

We have dwelt upon the various motives for corporate greening for two reasons. First, as mentioned above, econometric studies of PVPs need to be careful to control for these various drivers of behavior, which may affect incentives to join a PVP. Second, and more subtly, these drivers affect the incentives for firms to make use of information about pollution reduction opportunities, whether that information comes through participation in a PVP or through other, more indirect, channels.[34]

Remark 1: Firms' incentives to join PVPs, and their incentives to use the information provided by PVPs, will depend upon the strength of market drivers for corporate greening, including opportunities for cost reductions; the presence of green consumers, employees and investors; and threats of regulation or negative campaigns by NGOs.

Mandatory vs. Voluntary Programs

The previous subsection illustrates that when a regulator offers a PVP firms may be subject to a myriad of pressures aimed at pushing them to undertake emissions reductions efforts. The 33/50 program is a case in point. At the time the program was introduced, firms were already required by law to report their toxic chemical emissions to the Toxic Releases Inventory (TRI). Because information in the TRI is public, firms (especially the largest emitters) would have already been subject to public pressures to reduce their emissions of the TRI chemicals.[35] The fact that firms were required to report emissions of specific chemicals, and the fact that the 33/50 program identified a specific subset of the TRI chemicals, is a strong indication of a regulatory threat. Additionally, the fact that the share prices of the largest emitters experienced abnormal negative returns on the date that emissions information was released suggests that market forces, including green investors, employees, and possibly even green consumers, likely played a role in motivating firms to engage in emissions reduction.[36]

Although firms face growing pressures to engage in pollution abatement, Bagnoli and Watts (2003) show that market forces are unlikely to be strong enough to induce firms to undertake socially optimal levels of abatement. Assuming there is a need for government intervention, what motivates a government agency to offer a PVP as opposed to using another policy instrument? The best-known theoretical model of PVPs is that of Lyon and Maxwell (2003), which argues that PVPs are chosen based on the regulator's expectations about the political and market responses of industry to mandatory as opposed to voluntary policy alternatives.

Lyon and Maxwell (2003) follow Carraro and Siniscalco (1996) in modeling the public voluntary agreement as a subsidy payable to any plant that adopts the environmental technology.[37] They compare it to a mandatory policy that takes the form of an environmental tax, although their main points would apply to an environmental standard or a cap-and-trade program as well. They assume that the benefits of the PVP can only be collected by plants that participate in the PVP program. In addition, they assume plants that adopted the environmental technology before the PVP was established cannot be excluded from receiving the benefits of participating in the PVP.[38] As we discuss below, regulators may seek firms that have already undertaken abatement actions to be "early joiners" and often seek to reward such firms with positive publicity.

Using this basic setup, Lyon and Maxwell (2003) show that the welfare gains from taxation, relative to government inaction, come in three parts. First, there are social gains from forcing inefficient plants to exit the industry, since the profits these plants generate are less than the environmental damage they cause. Second is the social value of the tax revenues raised from the emissions tax, which can offset the need to raise public funds through other means. Third are the social gains from adoptions of the environmental technology by efficient plants.

When regulators do not face political opposition from industry, the optimal pollution tax generates greater social benefits than does the optimal public voluntary program. There are two key reasons for this. First, a fundamental limitation of the PVP is that it cannot subsidize plants to exit the industry; plants must stay in business in order to collect any benefits from the PVP program. Second, in a world with costly public funds, a tax that generates public revenues is preferable to a subsidy that drains public coffers. Both effects make a tax preferable to a PVP when political pressures are irrelevant.

Remark 2: An environmental tax is inherently a more effective instrument than a PVP.

Remark 2 serves as a caution to researchers seeking to investigate the effectiveness of PVPs. As PVPs will provide firms with weaker incentives than traditional regulatory tools, one should not expect PVPs to induce dramatic changes in firm behavior.

If PVPs are necessarily a weaker tool than regulation, resulting in perhaps small differences between participants and non-participants, why should regulators include PVPs in their regulatory toolkit? The answer is that PVPs may be useful in achieving regulatory goals either as a complement to existing or forthcoming regulations, or as an alternative when the traditional legislative and regulatory processes have been blockaded. As we noted earlier, many PVPs are structured to enhance information flows about pollution prevention technologies and processes. This is a step that can be taken even when there is no political will to impose mandatory regulations, and can at least help eliminate pollution whose origin is in inefficient production processes. In the following section we discuss how the structure of a PVP may assist both participants and non-participants to achieve pollution reduction goals, and we discuss the implications of this structure for empirical studies of PVP effectiveness.

The Structure of PVPs

As we mentioned above, PVPs can be viewed as modest subsidies designed to induce participating firms to adopt cleaner production processes. We now turn to investigating the nature of these subsidies in more detail. The subsidies offered by PVPs do not take the form of direct cash payments, but are instead implicit subsidies created through offering public recognition, regulatory benefits, or information and technical assistance. The first two of these are basically private benefits whose magnitude is unlikely to induce large investments in pollution reduction. The public recognition that government agencies give firms for pollution reduction efforts is likely to have only a small impact on the corporate bottom line. Similarly, regulators are constrained in the level of favorable treatment they can offer to firms with positive environmental profiles. The third form of subsidy is essentially a public good, as we have noted previously, so joining the PVP may not be necessary to collect this subsidy.[39] Why then do firms join PVPs and how do they assist firms in achieving environmental goals?

Firms constantly seek investments that achieve positive returns. The benefit from environmental investments may take the form of a reduction in energy usage, increased employee morale and productivity, or enhanced consumer, community and regulatory relations. These benefits may vary across firms for several reasons. For example, if there are economies of scale in building em-ployee morale, then larger firms may benefit more from an increase in morale than smaller firms. Similarly, firms that deal with regulatory authorities on a regular basis may benefit more from improved regulatory relations than firms that interact infrequently with these authorities. For these reasons, large firms may find it worthwhile to invest in acquiring information about opportunities for environmental improvement, while smaller firms may be unable to afford this type of investment. A PVP can then be structured so as to enhance information collection from firms that have already undertaken environmental investments, and then to speed the diffusion of information about pollution-abating technolo-gies and practices to firms that would otherwise lack incentives to gather that information.

Since government subsidies are small, firms will be unwilling to provide in-formation concerning investments that give them a competitive advantage. However, many environmental investments may lower a firm's fixed costs ra-ther than variable costs, and are therefore unlikely to result in a dramatic advan-tage in the firm's competitive position. In these cases small incentives, such as public recognition and enhanced regulatory relations, may be enough to induce knowledgeable firms to join a PVP that ultimately diffuses their information to other firms. These incentives will be enhanced if the PVP serves to assist indus-try in preempting costly regulations.

Once the government agency has obtained the relevant information, and de-cided upon the mechanism it wishes to use to diffuse it, the government must decide with whom should the information be shared. Should it restrict informa-tion access to participants in PVPs, or should it to attempt to diffuse the infor-mation as broadly as possible? For an agency charged with protecting the natural environment, it is clearly desirable to share information as widely as possible, thereby having the greatest possible beneficial impact on the environment. Once firms join the PVP, the EPA would still have incentives to make information available more broadly. The only reason for the agency to withhold information from non-participants would be to "prove" that PVPs work.

Remark 3: Once a government agency has acquired pollution abatement in-formation, environmental benefits are greatest if it is made available to all firms who might benefit from it, regardless of whether they participate in a PVP or not.

This remark has strong implications for empirical analysis of PVPs. It means that there may be no good reason to expect a difference in performance between firms that join a PVP and those that do not. It is possible that a difference would be observed in the early phases of a program, when the government is trying to attract participants who already have information to share. Once the program moves to the dissemination stage, however, there is likely to be no measurable difference between participants and non-participants. This is a point that generally has not been recognized in the empirical literature on PVPs,[40] and suggests that a reinterpretation of the findings in this literature may be necessary. Existing papers have focused on whether participants in PVPs achieve higher environmental performance than non-participants. While these papers have provided useful insights, they do not answer the broader question of whether PVPs have had beneficial effects in the aggregate. Since this latter question is the important one from a policy perspective, we would argue that existing empirical analyses are misspecified for the purpose of policy evaluation.

Remark 4: Given that the information offered by a PVP will gradually diffuse beyond PVP members, performance differences between participants and non-participants should diminish over time.

It is worth noting that government agencies are unlikely to be the only source of information diffusion. Many environmental investments involve the adoption of new technologies. The suppliers of those technologies have strong economic incentives to promote their innovations to PVP participants and non-participants alike. Consequently, even if a regulator does not proactively diffuse information beyond the PVP membership base, it is still reasonable to expect that PVP non-participants will become aware of profitable environmental investments and practices over time.

Even if firms do not need to join a PVP to acquire information, some of them will still have incentives to join. The most obvious motivation for joining is to obtain public recognition provided by the program, but some programs also offer the potential for improved relations with regulators. Larger firms and those facing greater external pressure from NGOs are more likely to find that these benefits outweigh the administrative costs of participating, as we mentioned above. Of course, there are also costs to participation. In addition to the administrative costs of filling out the required paperwork, joining a PVP can impose the risk of being targeted by activists for "greenwashing."[41] The expected cost of that risk may exceed the subsidy associated with joining, and thus some firms that make environmental improvements might choose not to join the PVP.

Implications for Empirical Research

In this section we elaborate on the implications of the previous section, Political Economic Context of PVPs, for empirical research attempting to identify the effects of PVPs. As discussed earlier, our analysis sees PVPs unaccompanied by a regulatory threat as a form of modest subsidy aimed at assisting companies engage in pollution reduction. As a result, expectations should be low regarding what is possible through PVPs. In addition, it is difficult to disentangle the effect of a PVP from other motivating factors such as state and federal regulatory threats or market forces (from green consumers, employees or investors). This suggests that useful studies will need to have large numbers of data points, so as to generate small standard errors and facilitate inference.

The framework presented in the previous section implies that recent empirical analyses finding that PVPs have no impacts are mis-specified. If information on pollution abatement techniques diffuses to non-participants as well as participants, then the empirical studies evaluating PVPs have pursued empirical strategies that cannot possibly identify the true impact of these programs. If a PVP is effective in disseminating information about pollution prevention throughout the manufacturing sector, then all firms would be reducing their emissions at roughly the same rate—which appears to be the case. There would be no evidence that PVP participants performed better than non-participants, even if the program actually achieved meaningful goals.

This perspective suggests that different econometric strategies are required to measure the true impact of public voluntary programs. It is not enough simply to apply a Heckman-style two-stage estimation in which the first stage estimates the probability of a firm participating in the PVP and the second estimates the effectiveness of the PVP, conditional on the probability of participation.[42] As mentioned above, this approach will not capture the effects of PVPs if information diffuses to non-participants.

We believe that progress in the empirical analysis of PVPs will be facilitated if researchers emphasize that PVPs are information-oriented programs designed to diffuse abatement technologies and practices. In this view, many firms are not operating on the production possibilities frontier, and environmental process improvements can be studied as a form of technology diffusion that may be enhanced by PVPs.

As economists, we are naturally reluctant to believe there are $20 bills lying on the ground, but as business school professors we speak with enough corporate managers to realize that there is considerable waste within industry. Indeed, Leibenstein's (1966) notion of X-inefficiency refers to exactly this failure to squeeze out all waste from the production process.[43] We do not find it hard to believe that there really are "win/win" opportunities for companies to cut emissions and costs at the same time, by reducing waste. Porter and van der Linde

(1995) provide numerous examples of firms that increased their resource use efficiency, reducing pollution and costs at the same time.

There is a small empirical literature demonstrating that providing managers with information on their environmental performance can produce meaningful improvements. Blackman, Afsah and Ratunanda (2004) study the PROPER program in Indonesia, a mandatory rating system for large water polluters, which assigns to each plant a color indicating its performance (from worst to best the ratings are black, red, blue, green and gold). They find that plants rated black or red improved significantly after the ratings, and that the most important reason was simply that managers previously lacked information about their low performance, although concerns about ISO-14001 certification and shareholder value were also important. Blackman, Lyon, Narain and Powers (2007) study India's similar Green Rating Program, and also find that pulp and paper plants receiving the lowest rating improved significantly afterwards.

The studies of PROPER and the Green Rating Program support the notion that information diffusion programs can help firms to move up onto the production possibility frontier. In neither case did high-performing plants improve due to the programs, but low performers were able to rapidly improve their environmental performance.

Once we recognize that firms may be operating below the production possibility frontier, it becomes important to come up with a way to control for the true state of efficiency (and, implicitly, of information) possessed by program non-participants. One approach is the use of Data Envelopment Analysis (DEA), a tool pioneered by Charnes, Cooper and Rhodes (1978) that is used to estimate how far individual firms are from the production possibilities frontier. The resulting distance measure gives an indication of the internal inefficiency of each firm, which can be taken as a proxy for a lack of information on pollution control opportunities. Delmas and Montes-Sancho (2007) use DEA to compute the productive efficiency of firms, and then use this measure as an independent variable to help explain participation in the Climate Challenge program. They find that productive efficiency has important explanatory power. Highly efficient firms were more likely to join the program early, which is consistent with our argument that government wants to attract these firms so as to codify their knowledge and share it with other, less efficient, firms. Interestingly, they also found that even late joiners tended to be more efficient than non-participants, but they also tended to spend less on environmental efforts than did non-participants. This last finding suggests that including a measure of environmental efficiency (as well as pure productive efficiency) might also be worthwhile as a way to estimate the state of the firm's environmental knowledge.

Our argument suggests that measures of a firm's productive and environmental efficiency should also be included in the second stage of empirical assessments, where researchers estimate the effects of program participation on environmental performance. We expect that less efficient firms will exhibit greater performance improvement, as all firms in the industry gradually converge to the production frontier. Of course, this is likely to be true of program non-participants as well as participants, although non-participants may exhibit improvement with a greater lag than participants. If this lag is found in the empirical data, it would support our hypothesis that information diffuses beyond the boundaries of PVP participation.

It may be possible to make use of information on the network structure of particular industries to identify the effects of a PVP. If information is transmitted across the links of industrial networks, as argued by Kranton and Minehart (2001), then firms that join a PVP are more likely to diffuse information to firms with whom they share a link. The notion that social networks may play an important role in diffusion processes is supported by the computer simulations of Abrahamson and Rosenkopf (1997). Empirical research could potentially use information on links between firms to trace out the process of information diffusion. Membership in trade associations is one simple way to get at inter-firm linkages, but more nuanced network data would be more helpful in assessing the role of PVPs.

Another approach to identifying the effects of a PVP would be to select a program oriented towards a specific industry, and then create a control group consisting of firms from an industry with similar production processes that are not part of the PVP. It would be especially helpful if the industries were different enough that they could not easily share knowledge on environmental efficiency improvement.

Another identification strategy would be to exploit geographical information, such as policy differences across states or countries. With this strategy, a key issue will be to control for the extent of information spillovers across political boundaries. It should also be possible to learn from the literature on technology diffusion, which has begun to estimate spillover effects explicitly.[44] By including a range of independent variables from the diffusion literature that have not traditionally been part of empirical analyses of PVPs, we may be able to identify the effects of PVPs much more precisely.[45] In particular, it may be worthwhile to control for the geographic proximity of firms, as Audretsch and Feldman (1996) have shown that innovations are more likely to diffuse between firms that are located closer together.

An alternative approach would involve exploiting patterns in the dynamics of PVP participation to test hypotheses regarding PVP performance. In particular, we might expect joiners to perform better than non-joiners early on, as found by Delmas and Montes-Sancho (2007) and Sam and Innes (2007). However, it is not yet clear exactly why these results are observed. It may be that, as Delmas and Montes-Sancho suggest, late joiners are simply free-riding on the reputation of the PVP. Alternatively, it is possible that the designers of a PVP attempt to first attract those firms that already have knowledge about pollution reduction, and then to draw in firms that can benefit from this information. Empirical results may depend in part upon the strength of regulatory threats at a given time.

It may be some time before the next generation of empirical studies on PVPs establishes with confidence the overall effectiveness of these programs in improving the environmental performance of industry. In the meantime, our analysis—for better or worse—gives the managers of PVPs at the DOE and EPA a bit more ammunition with which to defend their programs in the face of the growing empirical assault on their effectiveness.

Implications for the Use and Design of PVPs

The goal of a government agency in offering a PVP is to assist as many firms as possible in enhancing their environmental records, not to ensure that participants outperform non-participants. Given that PVPs involve the use of costly public funds, it is important to structure PVPs to enhance their efficiency and to use PVPs only when they improve social welfare. In this section we draw on the findings of the existing theoretical literature on PVPs to offer suggestions regarding their use and design.

Concerning the use of PVPs, Lyon and Maxwell (2003) have shown the optimal use of a PVP involves consideration of strategic corporate behavior in the lobbying process over a tax or regulation. In this context, they derive the following result.

Remark 5: Offering a PVP may increase industry political resistance to a tax, thereby reducing the effectiveness of the tax and its likelihood of passage.

The intuition behind Remark 5 is simple: if the industry knows a PVP will be offered after a tax fails, it has more incentive to oppose the tax so it can collect the subsidy that is offered under the PVP. Whether the possibility of a PVP is likely to have negative incentive effects depends upon political circumstances. If society has reached the point where there is a reasonable likelihood of passing strong environmental legislation, then it would be best if the regulator could commit *not* to offer a PVP. This would help to maintain the political pressure for strong regulation. In contrast, when the chances of strong legislation are minimal, offering a PVP is unlikely to prevent passage of a strong bill but can offer at least some environmental improvement. In such a situation, a PVP may be a worthwhile policy.

A well-designed PVP can enhance the diffusion of information about pollution-abating technologies and practices to firms that would otherwise lack incentives to gather that information. A regulator attempting to enhance the diffusion of information about pollution control opportunities is faced with two decisions. First, it must decide how to acquire information about the value of alternative pollution abatement technologies, and second, it must decide how to distribute this information to firms. With regard to the first decision, the regulator has two options: it could undertake research and development itself or it could attempt to obtain information from firms that are already informed. In some cases, such as those in which firm-level experience with the environmental investment is necessary for learning, only the latter option will be open to the regulator.

Obtaining information from firms that are already informed is the most desirable option for the regulator to follow as long as the information being passed to the uninformed firms does not threaten the competitive position of the informed firms and hence undermine their incentives to participate. The EPA's Green Lights program provides such an example. The installation of an energy-efficient lighting system tends to lower a firm's overhead and should consequently have little impact on the firm's competitive position. Furthermore, lighting is used in all types of industries, so much of the sharing will be with firms in other industries. In this case, informed firms need to be offered only minor inducements to provide information to the regulator. Typical benefits provided by PVPs include access to EPA officials, highly visible publicity, or a widely-recognized logo that can be used on the firm's products—which may be enough to convince informed firms to participate when information is not competitively sensitive.

Remark 6: A cost-effective PVP should offer informed firms inducements that cover their costs of sharing information. It then subsidizes the cost of providing that information to uninformed firms.

Remark 6 is consistent with the work of Darnall (2003), who reports results from a small-scale survey that asked companies to identify their rationales for participation in the EPA's Environmental Management System Pilot Program, and the benefits actually obtained. Among the findings was a striking difference between privately held and publicly traded firms. For example, privately held firms were more likely to report learning valuable new information from participation than were publicly traded companies. In our framework, these firms are uninformed firms that did not invest in gathering information on their own.

To improve the effectiveness of PVPs, it may be useful to target the benefits of public recognition more narrowly towards those firms that join during the information collection phase of the program, and that are sharing valuable information with government. Firms that join the program during the dissemination phase are more properly viewed as consumers of information, and should not need (and arguably do not deserve) public recognition for finally implementing cost-effective pollution reduction processes. More careful targeting of public recognition might help to eliminate concerns about free-riding behavior from late joiners of PVPs.

For competitively valuable information, firms will be reluctant to share the information with rivals. Any benefits government regulators can provide are unlikely to outweigh damage to a firm's market position. Hence, PVPs are unlikely to be effective unless the information involved is not competitively sensitive.

Remark 7: PVPs should focus on information that is less competitively sensitive so as to enhance information provision by participating firms.

Once the regulator learns the value of a given abatement technology, it must then decide whether and how to transmit the information to uninformed firms. There are a variety of ways for sharing information, which subsidize information acquisition to different extents and in different ways. For example, in many cases the regulator places case studies on its website, which provide at least partial information to firms at a cost to the government that is virtually zero. In other cases, such as the Climate Leaders program and the Green Power Partnership, the regulator offers direct technical assistance to participating firms. In still other cases, such as the Natural Gas Star program, the regulator facilitates meetings at which firms can share information among themselves. Such meetings may allow for fuller information transmission, but it is costly for firms to travel to meetings and allocate employee time to attending them. They may be necessary, however, if the information to be shared takes the form of tacit knowledge, which is hard to codify in verbal form.[46] Thus, there is a range of options for the regulator regarding the extent to which it subsidizes the information acquisition of uninformed firms.

Remark 8: Regulators have a variety of options for enhancing information diffusion. Written documentation of case studies and other technical information may suffice for relatively simple information. Personalized technical assistance may be required for more complex information that must be tailored to a firm's unique circumstances. Peer-to-peer knowledge exchange is helpful when firms' experiences are heterogeneous and idiosyncratic.

In summary, there are several implications to conceiving of PVPs as information diffusion programs. Regulators using information programs effectively focus on industries where there is likely to be a lack of knowledge about opportunities for cost-effective pollution abatement. Even so, the regulator's expectations are kept modest, since information alone is not likely to be enough to induce large, costly changes in corporate behavior. Regulators are careful not to deploy PVPs when their presence may undermine the demand for more effective policies. Regulators seek out the least-cost means of acquiring useful information, which may often be from well-informed firms. There is no need to try and draw all firms in an industry into a PVP. Membership in the PVP can be limited to leading firms with knowledge to share, unless peer-to-peer interaction is needed for successful information transfer. Regulators diffuse the relevant information to a broad array of firms in the industry, regardless of whether they participate in the PVP. Finally, regulators use sophisticated econometric tools for evaluating the success of programs, understanding that simple empirical tools may be unlikely to identify much program impact.

Conclusions

There appears to be a growing consensus that PVPs are at best of modest impact and at worst a form of greenwash that diverts public attention from important environmental problems. However, our analysis suggests that these conclusions are premature. Given that these programs are typically created out of political weakness, there is no reason to expect them to have large impacts. However, recent empirical findings that PVPs have no impacts seem to us to be misspecified. If we are correct that information on pollution abatement techniques diffuses to non-participants as well as participants, then the empirical studies evaluating PVPs have arguably pursued empirical strategies that cannot possibly identify the true impact of these programs. If a PVP is effective in disseminating information about pollution prevention throughout the manufacturing sector, then all firms would be reducing their emissions at roughly the same rate—which appears to be the case. There would be no evidence that PVP participants performed better than non-participants, even if the program was achieving meaningful goals.

Our analysis suggests that new econometric strategies are required to measure the true impact of public voluntary programs. The problem is that it is very difficult to control for the true state of information possessed by program non-participants. We have suggested a number of potential approaches to identifying the effects of PVPs empirically, and are hopeful that our analysis will spark a new generation of papers that produce more refined estimates of the impact of these programs. In the meantime, our analysis gives the managers of PVPs at the DOE and EPA a bit more ammunition with which to defend their programs in the face of the growing empirical assault on the effectiveness of these programs.

Bibliography

Abrahamson, E., and L. Rosenkopf. 1997. "Social Network Effects on the Extent of Innovation Diffusion: A Computer Simulation." *Organization Science* 8 (3): 289–309.

Arora, Seema, and Tim Cason. 1996. "An Experiment in Voluntary Environmental Regulation: Participation in EPA's 33/50 Program." *Journal of Environmental Economics and Management* 28: 271–86.

Arora, Seema, and Subhashis Gangopadhyay. 1995. "Toward a Theoretical Model of Emissions Control." *Journal of Economic Behavior and Organization* 28: 289–309.

Audretsch, David B., and Maryann P. Feldman. 1996. "R&D Spillovers and the Geography of Innovation and Production." *American Economic Review* 86: 630–40.

Aydogan, Neslihan, and Thomas P. Lyon. 2004. "Spatial Proximity and Complementarities in the Trading of Tacit Knowledge." *International Journal of Industrial Organization* 22: 1115–35.

Bagnoli, Mark, and Susan G. Watts. 2003. "Selling to Socially Responsible Consumers: Competition and the Private Provision of Public Goods." *Journal of Economics and Management Strategy* 12 (3): 419–45.

Baron, David P. 2001. "Private Politics, Corporate Social Responsibility, and Integrated Strategy." *Journal of Economics and Management Strategy* 10: 7–45.

———. 2005. "Competing for the Public through the News Media." *Journal of Economics and Management Strategy* 14: 339–76.

———. 2006. "The Positive Theory of Moral Management, Social Pressure, and Corporate Social Performance." Working Paper, Stanford University.

———. 2007. "Corporate Social Responsibility and Social Entrepreneurship." *Journal of Economics and Management Strategy* 16: 683–718.

Baron, David P., and Daniel Diermeier. 2007. "Strategic Activism and Nonmarket Strategy." *Journal of Economics and Management Strategy* 16: 599–634.

Blackman, Allen, Shakeb Afsah, and Damayanti Ratunanda. 2004. "How Do Public Disclosure Pollution Control Programs Work? Evidence from Indonesia." *Human Ecology Review* 11: 235–46.

Blackman, Allen, Thomas P. Lyon, Urvashi Narain, and Nicholas Powers. 2007 "Does Public Disclosure Reduce Pollution? Evidence from India's Pulp and Paper Industry." Working Paper, University of Michigan.

Brekke, Kjell Arne, and Karine Nyborg. 2004. "Moral Hazard and Moral Motivation: Corporate Social Responsibility as Labor Market Screening." Working Paper, Ragnar Frish Center, University of Oslo.

Carraro, Carlo, and Domenico Siniscalco. 1996. "Voluntary Agreements in Environmental Policy: A Theoretical Appraisal." In *Economic Policy for the Environment and Natural Resources,* ed. Anastasios Xepapadeas. Cheltenham: Edward Elgar.

Charnes, A., W. Cooper, and E. Rhodes. 1978. "Measuring the Efficiency of Decision-making Units." *European Journal of Operational Research* 2: 429–44.

Coglianese, Cary, and Jennifer Nash, eds. 2007. *Beyond Compliance: Business Decision Making and the U.S. EPA's Performance Track Program.* Washington, DC: Resources for the Future Press.

Darnall, Nicole. 2003. "Motivations for Participating in a Voluntary Environmental Initiative: The Multi-state Working Group and EPA's EMS Pilot Program." In *Research in Corporate Sustainability,* ed. Sanjay Sharma and Mark Starik. Boston: Edward Elgar Publishing, 123–54.

DeCanio, Stephen J. 1998. "The Efficiency Paradox: Bureaucratic and Organizational Barriers to Profitable Energy-saving Investments." *Energy Policy* 26: 441–54.

DeCanio, Steven J., and William E. Watkins. 1998. "Investment in Energy Efficiency: Do the Characteristics ĥ Firms Matter?" *Review of Economics and Statistics* 80: 95–107.

Delmas, Magali, and Arturo Keller. 2005. "Free Riding in Voluntary Environmental Programs: The Case of the U.S. EPA WasteWise Program." *Policy Sciences* 38: 91–106.

Delmas, Magali A., and Maria J. Montes-Sancho. 2007. "Voluntary Agreements to Improve Environmental Quality: Are Late Joiners the Free Riders?" University of California, Santa Barbara, ISBER Paper 07.

Delmas, Magali, and Ann Terlaak. 2001. "A Framework for Analyzing Environmental Voluntary Agreements." *California Management Review* 43 (3): 44–63.

European Environment Agency. 1997. *Environmental Agreements: Environmental Effectiveness,* Vols.1 and 2. Copenhagen: European Environment Agency.

Feddersen, Timothy J., and Thomas W. Gilligan. 2001. "Saints and Markets: Activists and the Supply of Credence Goods." *Journal of Economics and Management Strategy* 10 (1): 149–71.

Fichman, Robert G. 1992. "Information Technology Diffusion: A Review of Empirical Research." *Proceedings of the Thirteenth International Conference on Information Systems,* Dallas, Texas, pp. 195–206.

Gamper-Rabindran, Shanti. 2006. "Did the EPA's Voluntary Industrial Toxics Program Reduce Emissions? A GIS Analysis of Distributional Impacts and By-media Analysis of Substitution." *Journal of Environmental Economics and Management* 52: 391–410.

Graff Zivin, Joshua, and Arthur Small. 2005. A Modigliani-Miller Theory of Altruistic Corporate Social Responsibility." *Topics in Economic Analysis and Policy* 5 (1): 1–19.

Haddad, Brent M., Richard Howarth, and Bruce Paton. 2004. "Energy Efficiency and Greenhouse Gas Emissions: Correcting Market Failures Using Voluntary Participation Programs." In *Voluntary Agreements in Climate Policies,* ed. Andrea Baranzini and Philippe Thalmann. Cheltenham, UK: Edward Elgar, 189–206.

Heckman, James J. 1979. "Sample Selection Bias as a Specification Error." *Econometrica* 47: 153–61.

Heyes, Anthony G., and John W. Maxwell. 2004. "Private vs. Public Regulation: Political Economy of the International Environment." *Journal of Environmental Economics and Management* 48 (2): 978–96.

Irwin, Douglas A., and Peter J. Klenow. 1994. "Learning-by-doing Spillovers in the Semiconductor Industry." *The Journal of Political Economy* 102: 1200–27.

Karamanos, Panagiotis. 1999. "Voluntary Environmental Agreements for the Reduction of Greenhouse Gas Emissions: Incentives and Characteristics of Electric Utility Participants in the Climate Challenge Program." Working Paper, School of Public and Environmental Affairs, Indiana University.

Karshenas, Massoud, and Paul Stoneman. 1993. "Rank, Stock, Order and Epidemic Effects in the Diffusion of New Process Technologies: An Empirical Model." *RAND Journal of Economics* 24: 503–28.

Khanna, Madhu, and Lisa A. Damon. 1999. "EPA's Voluntary 33/50 Program: Impact on Toxic Releases and Economic Performance of Firms." *Journal of Environmental Economics and Management* 37: 1–25.

King, Andrew A., and Michael J. Lenox. 2000. "Industry Self-regulation without Sanctions: The Chemical Industry's Responsible Care Program." *Academy of Management Journal* 43 (4): 698–716.

Kranton, Rachel, and Deborah Minehart. 2001. "A Theory of Buyer-seller Networks." *American Economic Review* 91: 485–508.

Liebenstein, Harvey. 1966. "Allocative Efficiency vs. X-Efficiency." *American Economic Review*, 56: 392-415.

Lyon, Thomas P., and John W. Maxwell. 2003. "Self-regulation, Taxation, and Public Voluntary Environmental Agreements." *Journal of Public Economics* 87: 1453–86.

———. 2004. *Corporate Environmentalism and Public Policy.* Cambridge: Cambridge University Press.

———. 2007. "Greenwash: Corporate Environmental Disclosure under Threat of Audit." Working Paper, University of Michigan.

Maxwell, John W., and Christopher S. Decker. 2006. "Voluntary Environmental Investment and Regulatory Responsiveness." *Environmental and Resource Economics* 33: 425–39.

Maxwell, John W., Thomas P. Lyon, and Steven C. Hackett. 2000. "Self-regulation and Social Welfare: The Political Economy of Corporate Environmentalism." *Journal of Law and Economics,* XLIII (October): 583–618.

Morgenstern, Richard D., and William A. Pizer, eds. 2007. *Reality Check: The Nature and Performance of Voluntary Environmental Programs in the United States, Europe and Japan.* Washington, DC: RFF Press.

Organization for Economic Cooperation and Development. 2003. *Voluntary Approaches to Environmental Policy: Effectiveness, Efficiency and Usage in Policy Mixes.* Paris: OECD.

Palmer, Karen, Wallace E. Oates, and Paul R. Portney. 1995. "Tightening Environmental Standards: The Benefit-cost or the No-cost Paradigm?" *The Journal of Economic Perspectives* 9 (4): 119–32.

Porter, Michael, and Claas van der Linde. 1995. "Toward a New Conception of the Environment-Competitiveness Relationship." *The Journal of Economic Perspectives* 9 (4): 97–118.

Rivera, Jorge, and Peter deLeon. 2004. "Is Greener Whiter? Voluntary Environmental Performance of Western Ski Areas." *Policy Studies Journal* 32: 417–37.

Rivera, Jorge, Peter deLeon, and Charles Koeber. 2006. "Is Greener Whiter Yet? The Sustainable Slopes Program after Five Years." *Policy Studies Journal* 32 (3): 417–37.

Sam, Abdoul, and Robert Innes. 2007. "Voluntary Pollution Reductions and the Enforcement of Environmental Law: An Empirical Study of the 33/50 Program." Working Paper, University of Arizona.

Segerson, Kathleen, and Thomas Miceli. 1998. "Voluntary Environmental Agreements: Good or Bad News for Environmental Protection?" *Journal of Environmental Economics and Management* 36: 109–30.

Stevens, William K. 1993. "U.S. Prepares to Unveil Blueprint for Reducing Heat-trapping Gases." *New York Times* (October 12): C4.

U.S. Environmental Protection Agency (EPA). 1992. *33/50 Program: Second Progress Report,* EPA-TS-792A. Washington, DC: U. Environmental Protection Agency.

———. 1999. *33/50 Program: The Final Record,* EPA-745-R-99-004. Washington, DC: U.S. Environmental Protection Agency.

Videras, Julio, and Anna Alberini. 2000. "The Appeal of Voluntary Environmental Programs: Which Firms Participate and Why?" *Contemporary Economic Policy* 18: 449–60.

Vidovic, Martina, and Neha Khanna. 2007. "Can Voluntary Pollution Prevention Programs Fulfill Their Promises? Further Evidence from the EPA's 33/50 Program." *Journal of Environmental Economics and Management* 53: 180–95.

Welch, Eric W., Allan Mazur, and Stuart Bretschneider. 2000. "Voluntary Behavior by Electric Utilities: Levels of Adoption and Contribution of the Climate Challenge Program to the Reduction of Carbon Dioxide." *Journal of Policy Analysis and Management* 19: 407–25.

Notes

1. Toxic reductions were measured against a 1988 baseline, but according to US EPA (1999) companies were not invited to participate until the spring of 1991, hence we consider that as the beginning of the program.

2. US EPA (1999), p. 4.

3. US EPA (1999), p. 1.

4. We review several prominent empirical papers on PVPs in section 3.

5. Clearly this misses some important programs from the past, such as the 33/50 Program and Project XL. Nevertheless, our approach has the virtue of providing a complete snapshot at a given point in time. For a more comprehensive review of PVPs, see Lyon and Maxwell (2004), chapter 6.

6. Many of the water-related programs appear to be of this type, e.g. Adopt Your Watershed, Clean Marinas, EPA's Volunteer Monitoring Program, Decentralized Wastewater Treatment Systems Program, Improving Air Quality through Land Use Activities, and National Nonpoint Source Management Program.

7. For example, the site for the Partnership for Safe Water is maintained by the American Water Works Association. A visit to the site on September 3, 2007, turned up a web page with the information: "Unable to Find Content." The Partnership does not appear to be defunct, however. Searching the AWWA website did produce webpages on the Partnership, including photos of a US EPA representative handing out plaques to award recipients at a June 27, 2007, meeting of water utility managers. According to the website, the Partnership was created after a 1994 EPA study found that 12% of Americans were served by water utilities that were in violation of public health standards. "Immediate concern for safety, and the overall realization that appropriate legislation might take years to implement, lead to the innovative cooperative effort called the Partnership for Safe Water. The Partnership brings regulators and drinking water suppliers together in synergistic   advancement   rather   than   an   adversarial   negotiation." http://www.awwa.org/Resources/utilitymanage.cfm?ItemNumber=3790&navItemNumber=29263 Thirteen years later, appropriate legislation has still not appeared, according to the 2007 report of the Partnership: "The *Partnership* program seeks improved water quality, not by meeting more stringent regulations, but by using flexible technical tools that allow each plant to customize performance improvements at their own pace with limited capital spending." http://www.awwa.org/files/Resources/PSWInfoCenter/AR08AnnualReport2007.pdf

8. The EPA website merely provides a link to a site maintained by the National Ski Areas Association at http://www.nsaa.org/nsaa/environment/sustainable_slopes/

9. The HHE program echoes the EPA's earlier 33/50 program in calling for "a thirty-three percent (33%) reduction in total waste volume in all hospitals by 2005 and an overall goal of achieving a fifty percent (50%) reduction by 2010." See http://www.h2e-online.org/docs/h2emou101501.pdf

10. Maxwell and Decker (2006) present a model of programs like Performance Track that reward good corporate behavior with a reduced likelihood of inspection.

11. A few PVPs involve helping industry to solve coordination problems that can inhibit the adoption of environmentally friendly practices. The EPA's Water Alliances for Voluntary Efficiency has helped hotels to coordinate on encourage hotel guests to re-use towels instead of washing them each day. Similarly, EPA's EnergyStar program helped

the VCR industry coordinate on the use of inexpensive circuitry that reduces power consumption during periods when the VCR is not in use.

12. This is consistent with Delmas and Terlaak's (2001) argument that PVPs are likely to be most effective in promoting the diffusion of best practices throughout an industry.

13. See European Environment Agency (1997) or OECD (2003). For links to numerous other case studies, see http://www.euractiv.com/en/environment/environmental-voluntary-agreements/article-117478

14. See, for example, Arora and Cason (1996), DeCanio and Watkins (1998), Karamanos (1999) or Videras and Alberini (2000).

15. See King and Lenox (2000) for a more complete discussion of the Responsible Care program.

16. Personal communication from David Buzzelli, Retired Vice President and Director, Dow Chemical, March 14, 2003.

17. US EPA (1992), p. 3.

18. US EPA (1992), p. 4.

19. Ibid.

20. Ibid, p. 5.

21. First, he excludes two ozone depleting substances (ODS)—carbon tetrachloride and methylchloroform (or 1.1.1-trichloroethane)—that were included in the 17 chemicals on the 33/50 Program's list, but whose reduction can better be attributed to mandatory phase-outs under the Clean Air Act. Their reduction accounted for one-fifth of the aggregate reduction of 33/50 chemicals from all Toxic Release Inventory (TRI) plants. He also excludes chemicals whose changes in reporting requirements led to paper reductions in emissions. Changes in the reporting requirement of ammonium sulfate in 1994 accounted for 27 percent of the total reduction in toxic releases reported for 1988-91, while the delisting of non-aerosol sulphuric and hydrochloric acid in 1994 and 1995 led to similar paper reductions.

22. Gamper-Rabindram's results for the chemical industry parallel King and Lenox's (2000) study of the chemical industry's self-regulatory Responsible Care program. King and Lenox find that participants in the program did not reduce emissions more rapidly than non-participants. If anything, they may have reduced less rapidly than non-participants.

23. William K. Stevens, "U.S. Prepares to Unveil Blueprint for Reducing Heat-Trapping Gases," *New York Times*, October 12, 1993, page C4.

24. DeCanio (1998) finds that firms participating in the Green Lights program reported rapid payback on their investments, and questions why more firms did not join the program.

25.   Climate   Challenge   Executive   Summary, http://www.climatevision.gov/climate_challenge/execsumm/execsumm.htm

26. Ibid.

27. For an economic model of greenwash, see Lyon and Maxwell (2007).

28. Morgenstern and Pizer (2007), p. 134.

29. Coglianese and Nash (2007), p. 112.

30. Rivera and deLeon (2004), p. 417.

31. Rivera, deLeon and Koeber (2006) conduct a longitudinal analysis of the first five years of the Sustainable Slopes Program, and find little difference between the five-year time horizon and the earlier one year snapshot.

32. Arora and Gangopadhyay (1995) were the first to formally model green consumerism as a motivation for firm abatement efforts that exceeded levels required by law. The notion that consumers are willing to pay a premium for environmentally friendly products has been adopted in many contexts, see, e.g, Feddersen and Gilligan (2001), Heyes and Maxwell (2004) and Baron and Diermeier (2007).

33. Brekke and Nyborg (2004), model a job market that includes environmentally concerned workers. Companies desire to attract these individuals, since it is assumed they are less likely to engage in shirking on the job. One way they can screen for these employees is by adopting socially responsible practices. The authors find that if abatement is inexpensive, the gains from labor market screening outweigh the costs of the abatement needed to accomplish it.

34. The effects of these drivers may depend upon the details of a particular PVP. For PVPs where peer-to-peer information exchange is critical, strong opportunities for cost reduction may make firms more likely to join a PVP. But for PVPs where information can readily be codified through case studies or technical documents, firms facing strong pressure from green consumers or NGOs will be more likely to join.

35. In addition, as we explained earlier, many large emitters of toxins were under general social and political pressures due to events such as the Bhopal disaster.

36. See Lyon and Maxwell (2004, Chapter 1) for a discussion of studies linking corporate environmental and firm financial performance.

37. They do not assume that voluntary actions are cheaper than actions mandated by law, as doing so would bias the outcome toward simplistic conclusions about the superiority of voluntary measures. They also assume away the possibility of "win-win" solutions in which the adoption of environmentally-friendly technology lowers cost.

38. For example, in the area of climate change, leading firms that have already begun reducing carbon dioxide emissions hope to acquire "early reduction credits" that they can trade in for emissions credits if and when a mandatory system is put in place. In the case of PVPs based on the provision of technical information, as discussed in Haddad, Howarth and Paton (2004), matters may be somewhat different, since information on environmentally-friendly technology is redundant for firms that have already adopted the technology. Firms that have already adopted then have no incentive to join the program, which would tend to hold down the cost of running the PVP.

39. Indeed, Irwin and Klenow (1994) find that even for firms in a highly competitive industry like the dynamic random-access memory (DRAM) chip industry, knowledge spillovers across firms were extensive. This is likely to be much more true of government programs designed to push information out to industry.

40. Notable exceptions are Delmas and Keller (2005) and Delmas and Montes-Sancho (2007).

41. Lyon and Maxwell (2007) present a formal model in which NGOs target firms they suspect of greenwashing.

42. This is the standard approach in the literature, and builds on the pathbreaking work of Heckman (1979).

43. For example, he cites evidence from International Labor Organization (ILO) "productivity missions" in which labor productivity was frequently increased by 25% or more, even in technically advanced countries such as Israel.

44. See, for example, Audretsch and Feldman (1996) and Karshenas and Stoneman (1993).

45. Fichman (1992) suggests a typology of diffusion situations and the variables appropriate for each.

46. See Aydogan and Lyon (2004) for a model of information sharing in an industry where tacit knowledge is important.

Chapter 4

Voluntary Environmental Management: Motivations and Policy Implications

Madhu Khanna, Cody Jones, David Ervin, and Patricia Koss

Firms are increasingly undertaking initiatives to proactively improve their environmental performance and go beyond simply complying with regulatory standards. Some firms are adopting an internally-structured mix of environmental management practices (EMPs) that reflect a commitment to integrating environmental considerations into operational decisions. These EMPs include the establishment of internal standards, goals and policies for environmental performance improvements, use of environmental cost accounting methods, and training and compensating employees to improve environmental performance. Firms have flexibility in the mix of practices they adopt, and can tailor the mix to suit the needs of their organization. Firms also have a choice of participating in one or more voluntary environmental management programs (VEPs)—such as ENERGY STAR, Climate Savers, and ISO 14001—established by regulatory agencies, trade associations or third parties. While some programs such as ENERGY STAR and green building programs require firms to adopt specific equipment or certain types of materials, others, such as ISO 14001, require firms to adopt management practices that meet standards specified by the program.

This chapter classifies voluntary environmental initiatives by firms into two categories, participation in VEPs and adoption of EMPs. It investigates the factors motivating firms to undertake each type of initiative and explores any differences in the types of firms likely to participate in VEPs and those likely to adopt EMPs. Although there is likely to be some overlap among the firms that participate in VEPs and those that adopt EMPs, there could also be differences because the costs and benefits of undertaking the two types of initiatives are not the same. Participation in VEPs may allow firms to obtain credible recognition for their environmental actions since many of these programs allow participating firms to display logos on their products or recognize firms through newsletters, websites and awards. This recognition may help differentiate firms from competitors and appeal to consumers with green preferences or suppliers who view VEP participation as an element of sound risk management. These good faith efforts may also enable firms to preempt future regulations or mitigate the stringency of existing regulations. However, participation in VEPs can be costly, since modification of equipment or certification to meet program standards is typically required.

On the other hand, adoption of internal EMPs without formal certification enables firms to avoid certification costs and remain flexible regarding the intensity of EMP implementation, although it may not provide the same level of public recognition. Moreover, EMPs typically must be tailored to meet a firm's needs, thereby requiring greater managerial innovativeness. By contrast, with at least some VEPs, firms can simply adopt off-the-shelf processes, practices, and labeled equipment.

Furthermore, firms may differ not only in whether they join a VEP or adopt an EMP, but also in the extent to which they engage in each type of activity. Since each VEP is typically focused on one environmental issue, facilities that seek to improve environmental performance across multiple indicators may be willing to participate in several VEPs. Firms may also adopt multiple EMPs because an individual practice by itself may achieve little. Synergistic relations between various practices may necessitate joint adoption to achieve meaningful and effective change in organizational behavior.

To explain differences in the number of voluntary activities being adopted by facilities while taking into account the discrete, non-negative, and count nature of the data, we estimate Poisson regression models for each of the two alternative measures of voluntary environmental activity—the count of VEPs in which a firm participates and the count of EMPs adopted. We examine the importance of a variety of external and internal factors in influencing the extent to which a firm engages in each type of voluntary activity. The external factors considered here proxy for pressures a facility might face from regulators, consumers, investors, and competing firms while the internal factors include technical capabilities of the facility and availability of internal resources.

We undertake this analysis using data gathered from a survey conducted in 2005 of facilities located in Oregon operating in six sectors. Unlike previous studies of corporate environmental management, the respondents consist primarily of small facilities (the majority having fewer than 24 employees) under private ownership. We focus this analysis on facilities located in Oregon where public and private initiatives to foster improved business environmental management have proliferated since the 1990s.[1] Our survey identified well over 100 VEPs available in Oregon, compared to over 200 VEPs available nationally (Carmin et al., 2003). Facilities in our sample reported participating in a variety of VEPs, ranging from local recycling programs such as the Clackamas County Recycling Partnership to international certification programs (ISO 14001), with the largest proportions of participants participating in energy efficiency and green building programs.

The existing literature indicates several motivations for firms to participate in specific VEPs or to adopt one or more EMPs (see surveys in Khanna, 2001; Khanna and Brouhle, 2007). In general, this literature shows that large, visible firms subject to regulatory pressures are more likely to participate in voluntary programs sponsored by regulators and industry associations. Such firms are also more likely to adopt a more comprehensive environmental management system and obtain ISO 14001 certification. Additionally, innovative firms that are more R&D intensive are more likely to adopt a more comprehensive environmental management system; however, evidence of their willingness to participate in voluntary programs is less clear. The findings of these studies have tended to be specific to the VEP or one or more EMPs examined.[2] Therefore, comparing the extent to which firms that participate in VEPs have similar/different characteristics than firms that adopt EMPs requires comparisons across studies based on different samples of firms. Moreover, these studies have typically analyzed participation in federal voluntary programs and have focused on large and publicly traded firms for which secondary information is available. Firms in our study participated in regional and industry-specific VEPs. We seek to explain the behavior of all except very small business facilities (with fewer than 10 employees) using primary survey information. By analyzing motivations for broad types of voluntary behavior, we seek to provide more general insights on the determinants of program participation and its implications for effective program design and public policy.

The analysis in this chapter has several policy implications. It shows the influence of existing regulatory approaches on fostering firms' voluntary environmental activities and the types of activities the regulations are more likely to motivate. By distinguishing between different types of regulatory pressures, the analysis sheds light on how the various pressures induce different types of voluntary behavior. The results obtained here also highlight the importance of providing technical assistance to facilities that may not have the capacity to unilaterally undertake innovative environmental activities. Lastly, by identifying the types of facilities less likely to be self-motivated to undertake voluntary activities, this analysis has implications for the design and targeting of policy initiatives that seek to encourage voluntary environmental behavior across the full spectrum of firms.

The rest of this chapter is organized as follows. The following section presents the conceptual framework underlying our empirical analysis. This discussion is followed by a description of the empirical model, which is in turn followed by a description of the data. Finally, results are presented, followed by a discussion of the policy implications and conclusions.

A Rationale for Voluntary Environmental Initiatives

The conventional view in environmental economics has considered the firm as being a competitive price taker in the output and input markets and maximizing profits while reacting passively to regulatory constraints. Environmental actions in this framework impose costs and divert productive resources; consequently such firms could be expected to undertake environmental protection only to the extent that they were coerced to do so by regulatory constraints or by citizen actions, such as private lawsuits or boycotts (Cropper and Oates, 1992). Firms in this setting would have no incentive to go beyond compliance with the regulatory constraints they face.

More recent literature, however, suggests that even economically rational firms may see it as being in their self interest to voluntarily undertake actions to improve their environmental performance beyond compliance. This is because such actions could enable them to influence markets for their products, obtain higher prices for their products, lower the costs of labor, capital and environmental regulations, and gain access to government assistance and payments (Khanna, 2001; Carpentier and Ervin, 2002). This literature suggests that the potential to preempt the threat of mandatory regulations, shape future regulations, gain competitive advantage and market share (by appealing to consumers and suppliers and lowering costs and improving internal efficiency), build a corporate reputation with communities and environmental interest groups and lower the costs of capital by reducing risks of liabilities for lenders and stockholders can provide economic incentives for firms to voluntarily invest in environmental activities. Our empirical analysis examines whether decisions about whether to participate in VEPs and/or adopt EMPs, and the extent of participation/adoption, can be explained by differences in firms' anticipated benefits and costs from these actions. Following is a discussion of some of the factors that may motivate firms to adopt EMPs and/or to participate in VEPs, and the explanatory variables we use as proxies for these factors. These motivations could stem from a desire to mitigate pressures or exploit market advantages for improved environmental performance created by various external stakeholders such as regulators, consumers, and investors. The extent to which a firm may respond, however, is likely to be tempered by its technical and resource capacities, which influence its ability to bear the costs of voluntary initiatives.

Firms may participate in VEPs and/or adopt EMPs to mitigate regulatory pressures because the resulting improvement in environmental performance reduces the cost of complying with existing environmental regulations. Firms may also undertake these voluntary activities to signal to regulators that they are making good faith efforts to improve their environmental performance, thereby mitigating the stringency with which existing regulations are enforced, or preempting future regulations. Firms that face higher costs of compliance with existing regulations and the threat of stringent enforcement may have greater incentives to participate in VEPs or adopt EMPs. These voluntary actions may deflect enforcement activity away from such firms, serve to preempt or lessen stringent regulations in the future, and possibly lower the costs of anticipated compliance by mitigating potential environmental problems before they become serious issues.

There is fairly consistent evidence across various program-specific empirical studies that facilities that are subject to more extensive regulation are more likely to participate in voluntary programs and implement EMPs (Khanna, 2001; Khanna and Brouhle, 2007). Regulatory pressures have been proxied by the stringency of enforcement of existing regulations (e.g. frequency of inspections, number of penalties) and the threat of liabilities for Superfund sites. Firms subject to more frequent inspections in the past, greater government oversight, and other pressures for environmental improvement were more likely to participate in the 33/50 program, Sustainable Slopes, and ISO 14001 and adopt more EMPs (Khanna and Anton, 2002; Rivera and de Leon, 2004; Potoski and Prakash, 2005a, b; Sam and Innes, 2005; Rivera et al., 2006).

We use two alternative proxies for regulatory pressure based on information obtained from the facilities about whether they were subject to environmental regulations for up to six different environmental impacts. The specific impacts queried about in the survey were customized for the different sectors. A dummy variable equal to one if a facility was regulated for a particular impact and zero otherwise was constructed. The first proxy, REGSUM, is a sum of these dummies (with a range between zero and six). In a second model, we replaced this with the individual dummies for four impacts common to the entire sample: water pollution (WATER), solid waste (WASTE), hazardous/toxic waste (HAZ), and hazardous air emissions (HAZAIR) to examine if the incentives for voluntary effort varied across type of regulatory pressure (Table 4.1).

In addition to undertaking voluntary environmental initiatives in response to regulatory pressures, firms might also face market-based incentives to proactively improve environmental performance from competing facilities, consumers, suppliers, and investors. Pressures originating from the market are being facilitated by an increasing availability of information about corporate environmental practices and performance released by government agencies, environmental interest groups, and the media. This information enables consumers, investors and suppliers to signal their environmental preferences to corporations through their purchasing or selling decisions in product, input and capital markets (Reinhardt, 2000; Esty and Winston, 2006).

In the presence of environmentally conscious investors and consumers, firms may seek to differentiate their products and thereby increase product prices over competitive levels, and/or access "green" markets to expand sales. This presumes that consumer interest in green product or process attributes translates into an effective willingness to pay for those attributes. Patagonia's green reputation may be a good example of this effect (Reinhardt, 2000). Rivera (2002) finds that hotels that participated in the Costa Rican Certification for Sustainable Tourism program and showed certified superior environmental performance were able to obtain price premiums and higher sales volume. Firms may also be able to earn higher stock market returns by pursuing a strategy of responsible environmental management (Khanna et al., 1998). To the extent that the adoption of EMPs or participation in VEPs serves as a signal of efforts to improve environmental performance, firms that are final good producers and publicly traded, and thereby more visible and vulnerable to consumer and investor reactions, have greater incentives to adopt EMPs and participate in VEPs.

Table 4.1 Descriptive Statistics of the Independent Variables

Variable	Mean Values*	Description 1 = Yes, 0 = No (Except as noted)
Independent Variables		
EMPLOYEES	0.71 (1.5)	Number of employees at the facility in 100's, range 0.1 to 18.67
REGSUM	2.91 (1.67)	Number of environmental impacts on which the facility is subject to regulations, range 0 to 6
PUB	0.09 (0.29)	Facility or parent firm is publicly traded on a stock exchange
MC	0.12 (0.33)	Facility or parent firm is a multinational corporation
RD	0.15 (0.36)	Facility has onsite research and development (R&D) capacity
RETAIL	0.47 (0.50)	Facility sells directly into retail markets
COMP	0.49 (0.50)	Facility reported having six or more close competitors
ISSUE	0.55 (0.50)	The environment is a significant issue for the facility
CONSTR	0.20 (0.40)	Facility operates primarily in the construction sector, NAICS 236
FOOD	0.17 (0.38)	Facility operates primarily in the food sector, NAICS 311
WOOD	0.19 (0.39)	Facility operates primarily in the wood sector, NAICS 321
ELEC	0.09 (0.29)	Facility operates primarily in the electronics sector, NAICS 334
TRANSP	0.16 (0.37)	Facility operates primarily in the transport sector, NAICS 484
ACCOM	0.18 (0.39)	Facility operates primarily in the accommodation sector, NAICS 721
WASTE	0.73 (0.44)	Facility is subject to solid waste regulations
HAZ	0.72 (0.45)	Facility is subject to hazardous or toxic waste regulations
WATER	0.68 (0.47)	Facility is subject to water pollution regulations (e.g., wastewater or stormwater management)
HAZAIR	0.59 (0.49)	Facility is subject to hazardous air emissions or fugitive dust (construction) regulations

Note(s): * Standard deviations are in parentheses. Mean values estimated for N=425.

Studies have found that firms more exposed to consumer pressure or those producing final goods, and those in industries with larger advertising expenditures were more likely to participate in the 33/50 Program (Arora and Cason, 1996; Khanna and Damon, 1999), in WasteWise and in Green Lights (Videras and Alberini, 2000). A recent analysis of participation in the EPA's National Environmental Performance Track concluded that firms that value external recognition were more likely to participate (Coglianese and Nash, 2006). Henriques and Sadorsky (1996) find that pressure from shareholders was significant in motivating the adoption of an environmental plan.

Firms might also be influenced to participate in VEPs and adopt EMPs to differentiate themselves from their rivals or to "raise rivals' costs" (Sam and Innes, 2005). Firms in concentrated industries may have a stronger motivation to participate in such initiatives and help set tighter environmental standards for the industry that would be disadvantageous for rival firms (Innes and Bial, 2002). They might also have greater potential to coordinate voluntary activities to preempt future regulations on the industry and find it easier to appropriate returns from R&D investment in environmental management, thus encouraging voluntary effort. However, it is also possible that a lower degree of competition may breed bureaucratic inertia and discourage innovative activity and reduce the incentives to differentiate the facility's products based on their environmental attributes. Khanna and Anton (2002) and Arora and Cason (1995) find that firms operating in less concentrated industries are more likely to adopt a more comprehensive environmental management system and to participate in the 33/50 Program, respectively.

In this study, we proxy market pressures from final consumers by RETAIL, a dummy variable equal to one if a facility sold goods and services directly to customers in the retail market and zero otherwise. We proxy pressure from shareholders by PUB, a dummy variable equal to one if the facility belonged to a publicly traded firm and zero otherwise. We measure pressure from competitors by COMP, equal to one if a facility reported having six or more competing firms and zero otherwise. We choose six as the threshold to define COMP=1 because six was the median number of competitors identified by reporting facilities. We also include a dummy variable MC equal to one if a facility belonged to a multinational corporation and zero otherwise (Table 4.1).

We also seek to examine if facilities that considered environmental issues to be a significant concern were more likely to adopt more EMPs and participate in more VEPs to address these issues. Another study found that a farm manager's perception of the degree of soil erosion problem significantly increased the number of management practices and extent of erosion control effort applied (Ervin and Ervin, 1982). We queried facility managers about whether they considered environmental issues to be a significant concern for their facility. We use this to construct a dummy variable ISSUE equal to one if they answered yes and zero otherwise. The inclusion of this explanatory variable could potentially pose two problems. First, it could be correlated with the explanatory variables (for example, if facilities with certain characteristics, such as a high REGSUM, were more likely to consider environmental issues to be important), making it difficult to identify the separate effects of these variables. Second, a facility's perception that ISSUE=1 could be influenced by its adoption of EMPs and participation in VEPs, making ISSUE an endogenous variable.[3] We find, however, that neither of these were the case. The correlation of ISSUE with any of the explanatory variables included here ranged between -0.01 and 0.2. We also test the null hypothesis that ISSUE is exogenous using the Hausman Test (Greene, 1997). We find that we fail to reject the null hypothesis in all models presented below.

The technical and resource capacity of a facility to undertake proactive environmental management is expected to be important in explaining voluntary effort by facilities, although their effect may vary across different types of initiatives. Some voluntary initiatives, particularly the adoption of EMPs, are not easily imitable and require firm-specific internal expertise in the form of human capital, R&D capability, and other resources. Surveys suggest that firms that are more innovative in general are more likely to adopt innovative management practices (Florida, 1996; Florida and Davidson, 2001). Both Arora and Cason (1995) and Khanna and Damon (1999) do not find strong evidence that innovative firms or firms in more innovative industries are more likely to participate in the 33/50 program. However, Khanna and Anton (2002) find that innovative firms were statistically significantly more likely to adopt more EMPs. Such firms are already engaged in improving production systems and products and are likely to be more forward looking, resourceful and capable of undertaking organizational change and absorbing associated costs. We proxy innovative capacity by a dummy variable RD, equal to one if a facility has an R&D department and zero otherwise. We expect RD to have a more significant influence on adoption of EMPs than on participation in VEPs, since the latter often require the adoption of specific equipment or methods and possibly impose low learning and search costs.

Additionally, we examine the impact of facility size on incentives to participate in VEPs and adopt EMPs. Larger facilities may have greater capacity to bear the fixed costs of participating in VEPs and adopting EMPs, seeking certification, and providing environmental training to personnel. Such facilities may also have greater external pressures from regulators, competitors, and the public, since they are more visible and more vulnerable to the negative impacts of a tarnished image. Larger facilities may also be more exposed to liabilities because they have "deeper pockets." On the other hand, larger facilities may also have higher costs of coordinating and training employees, as well as of tracking and collecting information needed to improve environmental management in the facility. Empirical evidence appears to support the former hypothesis: larger firms, measured either by total sales or number of employees, are more likely to participate in a voluntary program (Arora and Cason, 1995, 1996; DeCanio and Watkins, 1998; Videras and Alberini, 2000), join Responsible Care (King and Lenox, 2000) and adopt ISO 14001 practices (Dasgupta, Hettige, and Wheeler, 2000). We measure size of the facility by the number of EMPLOYEES. In addition to the variables described above, we include sector dummies (FOOD, WOOD, ELEC, TRANSP, and ACCOM with CONSTR as the base) to control for industry-specific factors that could also influence the voluntary behavior of facilities.

Empirical Model

We use two different measures of the extent to which a firm undertakes voluntary activities: the first is the count of VEPs in which a facility participates (VEPSUM) and the second is the count of EMPs adopted by a facility (EMPSUM) (as in previous studies by Dasgupta, Hettige, and Wheeler, 2000; Khanna and Anton, 2002; Anton, Deltas, and Khanna, 2004). A count of practices (programs) adopted equally weights all practices (programs) and does not allow us to distinguish between the effects of alternative combinations of practices (programs) having the same count. However, given the large number of practices (programs) being considered here including them individually would make our empirical model less tractable, and summing them up using weights other than 1 for each would be subjective.[4]

The discrete non-negative nature of the two dependent variables, VEPSUM and EMPSUM, generates non-linearities that make the usual linear regression models inappropriate, because some of the basic assumptions such as the normality and homoscedasticity of the residuals or the linear adjustment of the data are no longer fulfilled. The use of linear regression methods with a discrete non-negative dependent variable would result in inefficient, inconsistent and biased estimates (Cameron and Trivedi 1998). We therefore estimate a count data econometric model which explains the variation in the number of occurrences of the dependent variable by the variation in covariates. In this case the variations in VEPSUM and EMPSUM, respectively, are explained by the variation in covariates described above.

We estimate a Poisson regression model in which the scalar dependent variable is the observed number of occurrences of adoption by the nth firm, $w_n=0,1,2...J$ where J is the maximum number of VEPs or EMPs available. The Poisson model stipulates that each w_n is drawn from a Poisson distribution with parameter λ_n which is linearly related to a vector of regressors, v_n, such that $\lambda_n = \beta'v_n$ and the

$$Probability(w_n) = \frac{e^{-\lambda_n}\lambda_n^{w_n}}{w_n!}, \quad w_n = 0,1,2....J \qquad [1]$$

Table 4.2 Descriptive Statistics of the Dependent Variables

Variable	Mean Values*	Description 1 = Yes, 0 = No (Except as noted)
Dependent Variables		
EMPSUM	2.09 (2.43)	Count of EMPs in place at the facility, range 0 to 10
Practices Included in EMPSUM		
TRAIN	0.41 (0.49)	Environmental training for employees
STDS	0.37 (0.48)	Internal environmental standards
POLICY	0.25 (0.43)	Documented environmental policy
GOALS	0.25 (0.43)	Well-defined environmental goals
AUDITS	0.23 (0.42)	Environmental audits at regular intervals
GPUR	0.17 (0.38)	Green purchasing policy
COST	0.17 (0.37)	Environmental cost accounting
SUPSTD	0.14 (0.35)	Environmental standards for suppliers
PUBINFO	0.10 (0.30)	Periodic public publishing of environmental information
EMPCOM	0.02 (0.15)	Employee compensation for contributions to environmental performance
VEPSUM	0.39 (0.79)	Count of VEPs the facility participates in, range 0 to 6
Voluntary Programs included in VEPSUM		
ESTAR	0.07 (0.25)	Facility participated in ENERGY STAR
OTHENGY	0.04 (0.19)	Facility participated in another energy program
LEED	0.04 (0.19)	Facility participated in LEED
EARTH	0.03 (0.17)	Facility participated in the Earth Advantage green building program
OTHGB	0.01 (0.12)	Facility participated in another green building program

Continued on next page

Table 4.2—Continued

Variable	Mean Values*	Description 1 = Yes, 0 = No (Except as noted)
RECYCLE	0.03 (0.16)	Facility participated in a recycling program
ISO	0.05 (0.21)	Facility had obtained ISO 14001 certification
CLIMATE	0.01 (0.11)	Facility participated in a greenhouse gas emission program
GENERAL	0.02 (0.14)	Facility participated in a program designed to reduce multiple impacts, e.g., Oregon Natural Step Network
INDUST	0.02 (0.13)	Facility participated in an industry specific program, such as Design for the Environment (DfE)
OTHER	0.05 (0.20)	Facility participated in another type of program such as water conservation, stormwater management, etc.

Note(s): * Standard deviations are in parentheses. Mean values estimated for $N=425$.

with $\lambda_n = E(w_n) = Var(w_n) > 0$. In our sample, $J=6$ for VEPSUM and 10 for EMPSUM. The marginal effect of the Poisson model measures the change in the conditional mean λ_n if the *mth* regressor changes by one unit, and is given by $\hat{\beta}_m \hat{\lambda}_n$.

To allow for the possibility that the count data in our sample are overdispersed relative to a Poisson distribution we undertake two types of corrections. First, we obtain standard errors from the Huber-White robust covariance matrix constructed from the regression residuals which yields asymptotically consistent covariance matrix estimates without making distributional assumptions. It provides consistent estimates of the covariance matrix for parameter estimates even when the fitted parametric model fails to hold. We report both the classical standard errors and the robust standard errors.

Second, we estimate a zero-inflated Poisson (ZIP) model to account for overdispersion when the incidence of zero counts is greater than expected for a Poisson distribution. The ZIP regression assumes the population consists of two classes, one where observations always have zero counts, and the other where observations have zero or positive counts. The likelihood of belonging to either class is estimated using logit, while the counts in the second class are estimated using Poisson (Greene, 1997). In this case w_n has a ZIP distribution if with probability p the only possible observation is 0, and with probability $1 - p$ a Poisson (w_n) random variable is observed; thus:

$$Probability\ (w_n = 0) = p_n + (1 - p_n)e^{-\lambda_n}$$

$$Probability\ (w_n \geq 0) = (1 - p_n)e^{-\lambda_n} \lambda_n^{w_n} / w_n!$$ [2]

$$for\ w_n = 0, 1, 2, \dots J$$

For a ZIP distribution $E(w_n) = (1-p_n)\lambda_n$ and $Var(w_n) = E(w_n) + [p_n/(1-p_n)]\ E(w_n)^2$. This model is therefore less restrictive than a Poisson, which assumes that the conditional variance of the distribution is equal to its conditional mean (Mullahy, 1986).[5]We use the Vuong statistic to test for the validity of the ZIP vs. Poisson model. This test statistic has a standard normal distribution, with large positive values (greater than 1.96) favoring the ZIP model, and large negative values (less than -1.96) favoring the Poisson model.

Description of the Data

Survey Design and Implementation

This study assesses environmental management at for-profit facilities in Oregon.[6] The sample comprised all facilities employing at least 10 employees, operating in one of the following sectors:[7] Construction of Buildings (Construction; NAICS3 236) Food Manufacturing (Food; NAICS 311), Wood Product Manufacturing (Wood; NAICS 321), Computer and Electronic Product Manufacturing (Electronics; NAICS 334), Truck Transportation (Transport; NAICS 484), Accommodation (Accommodation; NAICS 721). This led to a sample of 1,964 facilities. These sectors are among those that employ the greatest numbers of individuals, that operate the greatest numbers of facilities, and that generate the most substantial corporate tax revenues in Oregon (ORS, 2005; DOR, 2004; USCB, 2003). The survey was developed and administered using a Tailored Design Method protocol (Dillman, 2000) and responses were obtained for the 2004 calendar year. A total of 689 responses were obtained, representing a response rate of 35 percent.

Self-selection bias is a concern in surveys of corporate environmental behavior because facilities with stronger environmental programs may be more inclined to respond than those with poor observations. We tested for potential self-selection bias in several ways. First, we compared the proportions of responding facilities and nonresponding facilities that had received notices of noncompliance and notices of violation (summed together for a total enforcement score) from the Oregon Department of Environmental Quality (DEQ) in 2004. A larger proportion of respondents had received a notice than nonrespondents (2.8 percent compared to two percent), but this difference was not statistically significant at the 95 percent confidence level.

Second, we conducted a follow-up telephone survey on nonrespondents to further query the reasons for the lack of response. The survey included questions about the facility's environmental record and why the facility had not responded. The most frequently cited reason for not responding to the mail survey was that the survey was too long and required too much time. These findings give us confidence that our results are not affected by non-response bias.

We conducted additional assessments by comparing the facility size and geographic location of the sample of 1,964 facilities identified to receive the survey and the completed sample of 689 respondents. We found no statistically significant differences in average or median employment levels, or proportions of facilities located in each county between these groups. Additionally, the DEQ operates three geographic regulatory regions. We found no bias based on comparisons of proportions of facilities located in these regions in the set of respondents. For more detailed information on bias assessments, refer to Jones (2005; 2008).

Data on number of employees at each facility and the primary industrial sector were obtained from the Oregon Employment Department (OED) data. All other data used in this analysis and described below were obtained from the survey. Only those facilities with non-missing data for explanatory and dependent variables used in this study are included. This resulted in a sample of 425 facilities ranging in size from 10 to 1,867 employees and operating in all six selected sectors.

Description of Voluntary Environmental Initiatives

The dependent variable, EMPSUM is constructed as the count of practices, described in Table 4.1, that were implemented by the facility. Of the 425 facilities in our sample, over 60 percent of facilities had implemented at least one practice. Among these facilities, 26 percent reported implementing one or two EMPs, nearly 28 percent reported implementing between three and six EMPs, and just over 7 percent reported implementing seven or more EMPs; on average, these facilities had implemented over three EMPs. The entire sample had implemented two EMPs on average. The most widespread practice, employee training had been implemented at 41 percent of facilities, followed by internal environmental standards, implemented at 37 percent of facilities. Only 2 percent reported having implemented employee compensation for contributions to environmental performance.

Respondents to the survey identified over 30 different VEPs in which they participated, e.g. ECOTEL Certification, ENERGY STAR, LEED (Leadership in Energy and Environmental Design) Certification, and the Smartway Transport Partnership. Less than one-quarter of the sample, 22 percent, reported participating in VEPs, with less than 7 percent of the sample participating in two or more programs. Among participants, 70 percent reported participating in a single voluntary program while one facility reported participating in six programs, the maximum observed. Previous estimates have indicated similar participation rates, ranging from 14 percent to 50 percent of eligible facilities (Khanna and Damon, 1999; Videras and Alberini, 2000). Among the respondents, nearly 11 percent of firms participated in an energy efficiency program, 9 percent participated in a green building program, and 5 percent had ISO certification. Remaining program participants participated primarily in solid waste reduction and climate change mitigation programs.

The VEPs and categories of programs that respondents reported participating in are described below. Details are provided for the most popular individual programs in this study, while general descriptions are offered for the categories and the other programs. These programs and categories are listed in Table 4.2.

ENERGY STAR®

This well-known program, jointly sponsored by the U.S. EPA and the U.S. Department of Energy (U.S. DOE), started as a voluntary labeling program to identify energy efficient products. The first products to be labeled were computers and monitors; the program has expanded to include labeling for appliances, lighting, home improvement products, and commercial and residential buildings. This is an impact-specific program, emphasizing energy conservation, which also results in greenhouse gas reductions if energy conserved would have been obtained from fossil fuels. Today, the program works with more than 12,000 partner organizations to deliver technical information and tools to organizations and consumers to assist them in choosing energy-efficient solutions and best management practices. Partners include manufacturers, retailers, educational and governmental organizations, and a wide variety of other types of facilities. In this study, 6 percent of respondents reported participating, which indicates that the facility purchases, installs, or manufactures ENERGY STAR rated products. Facilities that join ENERGY STAR as partners earn the right to display the labels on their products or facilities, which indicates that they pledge to buy ENERGY STAR labeled products and upgrade equipment as feasible. In addition to the public recognition of using the label, the benefits would be the reductions in energy use, greenhouse gas emissions, and reduced costs associated with these reductions (EPA, 2008b).

The other energy programs in which facilities reported participating varied in characteristics. Some facilities participated in green power purchasing programs through their local utilities, primarily wind power, while other facilities had obtained an Oregon Business Energy Tax Credit, which offsets the cost of energy efficiency and renewable energy projects.

In this study, participation in green building programs was second only to participation in ENERGY STAR. The most popular programs were LEED and Earth Advantage, but participants also reported constructing projects to the U.S. DOE High Performance Building standards and other similar standards.

LEED® (Leadership in Energy and Environmental Design)

This green building rating system is a national, consensus-based voluntary rating system for developing high-performance buildings. LEED can be applied to all building types, manufacturing and non-manufacturing alike. Structures are rated in five areas: sustainable site development, water conservation, energy efficiency, materials and resources selection, and indoor environmental quality and may earn bronze, silver, gold, or platinum status depending on the level of energy and environmental performance. The green building industry is experiencing phenomenal growth, with membership in LEED's sponsor organization, the U.S. Green Building Council, tripling since the program's inception in 2000, and projections that 10 percent of all new construction starts will be "green" by 2010 (USGBC,

2008a). Program benefits include public recognition, savings in energy and water use; reduced greenhouse gas emissions, reported increased productivity due to greater worker comfort; and possible regulatory relief associated with reduced habitat mitigation requirements when sites are selected sustainably. Benefits are somewhat divided: recognition often is given to developers, while performance benefits accrue to building occupants and operators. Costs, however, are incurred during construction or retrofit, and can range from just a few thousand dollars to tens of thousands of dollars for registration and the various design and construction reviews required for certification, depending on facility size (USGBC, 2008b). In this study, three percent of facilities reported participating in LEED.

Earth Advantage®
Two percent of respondents reported participating in Earth Advantage, a residential green building program which originated as a utility-sponsored conservation initiative, and which is now an independent not-for-profit devoted to assisting developers in constructing and remodeling homes for sustainability. The program also offers home certification, including a plan review, site inspection, and performance testing. The program originated in Oregon, but now has licensees in California and Massachusetts (Earth Advantage, 2008).

Recycling Programs
Minimum levels of solid waste recycling are mandated in most Oregon counties, and collection bins and pickup service are provided through the local waste collection provider to facilitate recycling. Less than 3 percent of respondents reported participating in a formal recycling program, and almost all of these facilities participated in what they termed to be the "local recycling program." Costs and other program characteristics vary by locale, but the benefits are typically reduced disposal costs of remaining solid wastes, and avoided enforcement costs for non-compliance. The various awards programs which offer public recognition for exceptional recycling efforts are sponsored by not-for-profit business groups and other organizations, and local government agencies are eligible to receive awards themselves (AOR, 2008; Clackamas, 2008).

WasteWise
Only two facilities in our sample reported participating in WasteWise, the national waste reduction initiative sponsored by the U.S. EPA. There is no charge for membership in WasteWise, and the program allows members to design their own waste reduction programs to suit their circumstances. Members are provided with press and promotional materials and are eligible for awards. Members have access to information, tools, and networking opportunities, and they track and report performance to WasteWise administrators. Participation as a percentage of eligible facilities is low even nationwide, with only 1,900 members, possibly due to the prevalence of local recycling programs (EPA, 2008c).

ISO 14001 Certification
The International Organization for Standardization (ISO) has produced over 17,000 international standards covering a variety of industries and practices. ISO 14001 specifies the requirements for an environmental management system that ensure the organization developing the system has methods for adhering to legal and other requirements, as well as managing environmental aspects and impacts of the organization's activities (ISO, 2008). Any facility that establishes and implements an EMS may pursue certification, and some business customers are requiring vendors to maintain a certified EMS. Multinational corporations also may choose to certify if they operate in markets where ISO 14001 certification is required or common practice.

Climate Programs
Climate change mitigation programs are becoming increasingly popular as impending carbon taxes become more likely. In this study, five respondents reported participating in Climate Savers, sponsored by the World Wildlife Federation, and three facilities reported participating in programs designed to reduce emissions from diesel equipment. These programs focus on increased efficiency as a way to reduce emissions. The diesel retrofit programs emphasize increasing engine efficiency and adjusting idling time, while Climate Savers emphasizes improving energy efficiency in computers and other equipment, and reducing electricity use overall through behavior modifications and other measures, in order to reduce associated emissions generated by electricity production (EPA, 2008d; WWF, 2008).

General Programs
General programs are those that assist facilities in reducing environmental impacts across a range of media (air, land, water, solid waste, and more), through a variety of practices. The two most popular general programs in this study are described below.

The Oregon Natural Step is a framework based on principles of natural science that enables corporations to integrate environmental considerations into strategic decisions and daily operations. The program emphasizes reductions in the concentrations of toxins, prevention of overextraction and overharvesting of resources, and preserving the ability of humans to meet their needs. Annual membership fees range from $100 to nearly $3,000 based on membership level and facility revenue. Members are allowed flexibility in meeting the program conditions, and benefits include discounted events, access to networks, coaching, and other assistance and information exchange. Less than 1 percent of facilities in this study reported participating. The program had more than 300 members as of 2008 (ORTNS, 2008).

The National Environmental Performance Track, sponsored by the U.S. EPA, is a voluntary partnership program that recognizes and rewards private and public facilities that exhibit beyond-compliance performance. This is a general or multiple-impact reduction program, where members work to improve performance in a variety of areas. The program is designed to complement existing programs with new tools and strategies that protect humans and the environment, and that offer cost reductions while inducing technological innovation. As of August 2008, the program had attracted 506 members in 17 industrial sectors. The majority of members, 74 percent, are involved in some sort of production, but the remaining members were non-manufacturers, suggesting that the Performance Track can appeal to a broad spectrum of firms. Primary benefits of participation include recognition, networking, regulatory relief (reduce inspections and self-reporting), and mentoring and other technical guidance. Requirements include implementation and third-party assessment of an environmental management system, public outreach, sustained compliance, and continuous improvement. Requirements are modified for small firms, defined as any facility with fewer than 50 employees (EPA, 2008a). In this study, three respondents, two manufacturers and one large hotel, reported participating in the Performance Track.

Remaining program participation was classified as participating in an industry-specific initiative, or in another type of program that was not easily classified into one of the other categories. Industry-specific initiatives included such programs as ECOTEL certification and the U.S. EPA's suite of Design for the Environment (DfE) programs, which are targeted to specific industrial sectors. Other programs included voluntary streambank restoration and habitat rehabilitation undertaken by facilities in conjunction with local authorities and not-for-profit groups which typically focused efforts on a specific watershed or region.

Descriptive Statistics about Facility Characteristics

Unlike other studies of voluntary environmental management, facilities in our study are primarily privately owned and do not belong to multinational corporations. Only 9 percent of facilities are publicly owned and 12 percent belong to multinational corporations. These facilities are also small in size, averaging 71 employees, and only 15 percent have an R&D department. Despite the small size and private status of many of these facilities, over one-half (55 percent) of the respondents stated that environmental issues are a significant concern. In response to a subsequent question asking respondents to identify specific issues, water issues were mentioned most often, including water conservation, wastewater treatment, and stormwater management. The next most commonly mentioned issue was solid waste, including hazardous waste. Other issues frequently mentioned were energy conservation, compliance with permits and regulations, and environmental stewardship.

Results

Table 4.3 presents the results of three alternative specifications of the Poisson and ZIP models explaining the motivations for adopting EMPs. Model 1 examines the effects of facility size (EMPLOYEES), public trading status (PUB), multinational status (MC), R&D capacity (RD), retail status (RETAIL), market competitors (COMP), the significance of the environment (ISSUE), and regulatory intensity (REGSUM) on the number of environmental practices implemented (EMPSUM). Model 2 includes industry sector dummies and examines the effect of belonging to various sectors compared to the Construction sector. Model 3 replaces REGSUM with the four common environmental impacts (WASTE, HAZ, WATER, HAZAIR)[8]. The log-likelihood value suggests that Model 3 is the preferred specification. Moreover, the over-inflate constant and the Vuong statistic are statistically significant, indicating the appropriateness of the ZIP model as compared to the standard Poisson model for all three specifications. We present both the classical standard errors of the Poisson and the robust standard errors, but rely on the latter to interpret our findings.

We find that EMPLOYEES and PUB have a positive and statistically significant effect on EMPSUM in the Poisson models but not in the ZIP models. Instead the three ZIP models provide robust evidence that RD, ISSUE and regulatory pressures, particularly those from WASTE and HAZ, have a positive and statistically significant impact on EMPSUM. Regulations on WATER have a positive but weaker impact on EMPSUM. These impacts remain significant even after the inclusion of industry sector dummies in Model 2. Moreover, we find that facilities belonging to WOOD were statistically significantly more likely to have a higher EMPSUM as compared to CONSTR. We do not find any evidence for the effects of RETAIL and COMP on EMP implementation.

Table 4.4 presents the results for the determinants of participation in VEPs using the same three model specifications as described above. Again, the log-likelihood value suggests that Model 3 is the preferred specification. Here we find that neither the over-inflate constant nor the Vuong statistic is statistically significant, providing evidence in favor of the Poisson model.

We find consistent evidence across these models (with the exception of ZIP Model 1) that facilities with larger EMPLOYEES are statistically significantly more likely to participate in VEPs. Based on robust standard errors with the Poisson Model 3, we also find evidence that facilities belonging to a multinational corporation are more likely to participate in VEPs, while firms with more competitors are less likely to participate in VEPs. Some factors that influence adoption of EMPs and also participation in VEPs are regulatory pressures (particularly solid waste regulations) and ISSUE.

Table 4.3 Factors Motivating Adoption of Environmental Management Practices

Independent Variables	Model 1		Model 2		Model 3	
	Poisson	ZIP	Poisson	ZIP	Poisson	ZIP
Constant	0.45	0.24	-0.69	-0.06	-0.80	-0.17
	$(0.11)^a$	$(0.14)^c$	$(0.14)^a$	(0.18)	$(0.15)^a$	(0.19)
	$(0.16)^a$	(0.21)	$(0.21)^a$	(0.24)	$(0.20)^a$	(0.24)
Inflate Constant		-0.81		-0.85		-0.90
(ZIP Models)		$(0.14)^a$		$(0.14)^a$		$(0.15)^a$
		$(0.15)^a$		$(0.16)^a$		$(0.16)^a$
EMPLOYEES	0.04	0.02	0.04	0.02	0.05	0.03
	$(0.01)^a$	(0.02)	$(0.02)^a$	(0.02)	$(0.02)^a$	(0.02)
	$(0.02)^b$	(0.02)	(0.02)	(0.02)	$(0.02)^b$	(0.02)
PUB	0.33	0.20	0.27	0.15	0.22	0.10
	$(0.11)^a$	$(0.12)^c$	$(0.11)^b$	(0.12)	$(0.12)^c$	(0.12)
	$(0.16)^b$	(0.13)	$(0.15)^c$	(0.13)	(0.15)	(0.13)
MC	0.23	0.19	0.18	0.17	0.21	0.21
	$(0.11)^b$	$(0.11)^c$	(0.11)	(0.11)	$(0.11)^c$	$(0.11)^c$
	(0.16)	(0.13)	(0.16)	(0.14)	(0.17)	(0.14)
RD	0.23	0.28	0.31	-0.31	0.29	0.29
	$(0.09)^a$	$(0.09)^a$	$(0.10)^a$	$(0.11)^a$	$(0.10)^a$	$(0.09)^a$
	$(0.13)^c$	$(0.11)^b$	$(0.14)^b$	$(0.13)^b$	$(0.14)^b$	$(0.12)^b$
RETAIL	0.05	-0.07	0.11	-0.04	0.13	0.02
	(0.07)	(0.08)	(0.08)	(0.09)	$(0.08)^c$	(0.09)
	(0.10)	(0.09)	(0.11)	(0.11)	(0.11)	(0.12)
COMP	-0.08	-0.03	-0.10	-0.03	-0.11	-0.04
	(0.07)	(0.08)	(0.07)	(0.08)	(0.07)	(0.08)
	(0.10)	(0.09)	(0.11)	(0.10)	(0.11)	(0.10)
ISSUE	0.69	0.38	0.66	0.38	0.67	0.39
	$(0.08)^a$	$(0.09)^a$	$(0.08)^a$	$(0.09)^a$	$(0.08)^a$	$(0.10)^a$
	$(0.13)^a$	$(0.14)^a$	$(0.13)^a$	$(0.13)^a$	$(0.13)^a$	$(0.13)^a$
REGSUM	0.18	0.16	0.19	0.17		
	$(0.03)^a$	$(0.03)^a$	$(0.03)^a$	$(0.03)^a$		
	$(0.04)^a$	$(0.04)^a$	$(0.04)^a$	$(0.04)^a$		
FOOD			0.09	0.17	0.01	0.07
			(0.14)	(0.15)	(0.14)	(0.15)
			(0.20)	(0.19)	(0.19)	(0.19)
WOOD			0.45	0.38	0.40	0.31
			$(0.12)^a$	$(0.13)^a$	$(0.12)^a$	$(0.13)^b$
			$(0.17)^a$	$(0.16)^b$	$(0.17)^b$	$(0.16)^c$
ELEC			0.25	0.27	0.17	0.20
			(0.16)	(0.17)	(0.16)	(0.17)
			(0.27)	(0.24)	(0.26)	(0.23)

Continued on next page

Table 4.3—Continued

Independent	Model 1		Model 2		Model 3	
Variables	Poisson	ZIP	Poisson	ZIP	Poisson	ZIP
TRANSP			0.32	0.30	0.22	0.20
			$(0.12)^a$	$(0.14)^b$	$(0.12)^c$	(0.14)
			$(0.18)^c$	$(0.17)^c$	(0.18)	(0.17)
ACCOM			0.19	0.32	0.12	0.22
			(0.12)	$(0.14)^b$	(0.13)	(0.14)
			(0.19)	$(0.19)^c$	(0.20)	(0.19)
WASTE					0.43	0.35
					$(0.14)^a$	$(0.15)^b$
					$(0.21)^b$	$(0.18)^b$
HAZ					0.42	0.32
					$(0.12)^a$	$(0.14)^b$
					$(0.19)^b$	$(0.18)^c$
WATER					0.25	0.26
					$(0.12)^b$	$(0.13)^b$
					(0.18)	(0.17)
HAZAIR					-0.16	-0.09
					$(0.09)^c$	(0.10)
					(0.13)	(0.11)
Log Likelihood	-859.04	-786.01	-849.61	-781.13	-838.97	-776.64
Vuong Statistic		4.51		4.31		4.11
(significance)		(0.00)		(0.00)		(0.00)

Note(s): Standard Errors (upper) and robust standard errors (lower) are in parentheses.
N=425 for all regressions.[a]Statistically significant at the 1% level.
[b]Statistically significant at the 5% level.[c]Statistically significant at the 10% level.

The significance of the magnitude of estimated parameters on the expected number of EMPs implemented and VEPs in which the facility participates is evaluated by estimating the marginal effects of each of the explanatory variables on EMPSUM and VEPSUM. Marginal effects are estimated as a one standard deviation change in the continuous variable (EMPLOYEES), for a one-unit change in the number of regulations (REGSUM), and for a change from 0 to 1 for the dummy variables. Marginal effects from the ZIP Model 3 for EMPSUM and from the Poisson Model 3 for VEPSUM (both with robust standard errors) are presented in Table 4.5 and Table 4.6 shows the Impact of Environmental Concerns on Voluntary Environmental Action.

We find that larger facilities were significantly more likely to participate in VEPs; an increase in one standard deviation in EMPLOYEES (150 employees) increases the expected number of programs by 0.03. However, EMPLOYEES has a statistically insignificant impact on adoption of EMPs. The perception of the environment as a significant issue (ISSUE) increases the expected value of EMPSUM by 0.68. It also has a statistically significant impact on VEPSUM and increases the expected number of VEPs by 0.11. Solid waste related regulations create statistically significant incentives to adopt EMPs (0.56) and participate in

VEPs (0.20). R&D capacity increases EMPSUM significantly, by 0.57, but does not have a statistically significant influence on VEPs. Participation in VEPs is affected by multinational status (it increases the expected value of VEPSUM by 0.13) and negatively by a larger number of competitor firms (the expected value of VEPSUM decreases by 0.12 if the number of competitors is greater than six).

Since ISSUE has a statistically significant impact on both EMPSUM and VEPSUM, we explore differential behavior by facilities that considered environmental issues to be a significant concern as compared to other facilities. We examine if they responded differently to various motivating factors as compared to facilities that did not consider environmental issues to be significant by splitting the sample into those with ISSUE=1 and those with ISSUE=0 and estimating the specification in Model 3 for each group of facilities. The results presented in Table 4.5 are from the models that provide the best fit to the data: the ZIP Model 3 for EMPSUM and the Poisson Model 3 for VEPSUM. We find that facilities in the two groups did respond very differently to the motivations proxied by the various explanatory variables included in Model 3.

We find that regulatory pressures related to WATER affect EMP adoption whether ISSUE is equal to one or zero. However, larger facilities are likely to implement more EMPs only if ISSUE=1 although they are likely to participate in more VEPs whether ISSUE is equal to one or zero. This suggests that the benefits due to improved public image following participation in VEPs outweigh the costs of participation, even for facilities where environmental issues are not a significant concern. The benefits from adoption of more EMPs are more likely to be internal (through waste reduction, gains in process efficiency and reduced costs of environmental compliance) and large enough to induce adoption only by facilities where environmental issues are of significant concern. We also find that facilities with R&D departments are more likely to implement EMPs only if ISSUE=1 but not otherwise. This suggests that even if facilities have the technical and resource capacity to make changes to their management system they do so only if the expected returns (or anticipated environmental problems in the absence of any action) are large enough. Presence of R&D departments has no effect on number of VEPs in which a facility participates whether ISSUE=1 or 0. We find that facilities with ISSUE=1 and subject to WASTE are more likely to participate in VEPs and less likely to adopt EMPs as compared to facilities with Issue=0. On the other hand, for facilities with ISSUE=1, HAZ or WATER are likely to motivate adoption of EMPs but not have a statistically significant impact on participation in VEPs.

Table 4.4 Determinants of Voluntary Environmental Program Participation

Independent Variables	Model 1		Model 2		Model 3	
	Poisson	ZIP	Poisson	ZIP	Poisson	ZIP
Constant	-1.85	-1.02	-1.03	-0.46	-1.26	-0.70
	$(0.26)^a$	(0.33)	$(0.29)^a$	(0.35)	$(0.32)^a$	$(0.38)^c$
	(0.31)	$(0.42)^b$	$(0.34)^a$	(0.41)	$(0.36)^a$	$(0.41)^c$
Inflate Constant (ZIP Models)		0.13		-0.27		-0.31
		(0.26)		(0.33)		(0.33)
		(0.34)		(0.46)		(0.43)
EMPLOYEES	0.08	0.04	0.11	0.08	0.10	0.08
	$(0.03)^b$	(0.04)	$(0.04)^a$	$(0.04)^b$	$(0.04)^a$	$(0.04)^b$
	$(0.03)^b$	(0.03)	$(0.04)^a$	$(0.04)^c$	$(0.04)^b$	$(0.04)^c$
PUB	0.12	0.27	0.34	0.43	0.30	0.36
	(0.29)	(0.34)	(0.31)	(0.34)	(0.31)	(0.35)
	(0.27)	(0.26)	(0.28)	$(0.25)^c$	(0.29)	(0.28)
MC	0.39	0.05	0.38	0.06	0.45	0.15
	(0.26)	(0.31)	(0.27)	(0.31)	(0.28)	(0.32)
	(0.25)	(0.28)	(0.23)	(0.29)	$(0.23)^c$	(0.25)
RD	-0.09	-0.09	0.18	0.31	0.21	0.36
	(0.24)	(0.27)	(0.28)	(0.33)	(0.28)	(0.34)
	(0.27)	(0.25)	(0.29)	(0.32)	(0.30)	(0.34)
RETAIL	-0.16	-0.13	-0.12	-0.09	-0.13	-0.11
	(0.18)	(0.21)	(0.18)	(0.21)	(0.19)	(0.21)
	(0.23)	(0.25)	(0.24)	(0.24)	(0.24)	(0.25)
COMP	-0.38	-0.41	-0.50	-0.47	-0.51	-0.48
	$(0.18)^b$	$(0.21)*$	$(0.18)^a$	$(0.21)^b$	$(0.18)^a$	$(0.21)^b$
	$(0.22)*$	$(0.24)*$	$(0.22)^b$	$(0.23)^b$	$(0.21)^b$	$(0.22)^b$
ISSUE	0.38	0.36	0.46	0.36	0.47	0.35
	$(0.19)^b$	$(0.21)^c$	$(0.19)^b$	$(0.22)^c$	$(0.19)^b$	(0.22)
	(0.24)	(0.25)	$(0.24)^b$	(0.24)	$(0.24)^b$	(0.25)
REGSUM	0.20	0.20	0.14	0.15		
	$(0.06)^a$	$(0.07)^a$	$(0.06)^b$	$(0.07)^b$		
	$(0.07)^a$	$(0.07)^a$	$(0.06)^b$	$(0.06)^a$		
FOOD			-1.56	-1.51	-1.57	-1.56
			$(0.35)^a$	$(0.40)^a$	$(0.36)^a$	$(0.41)^a$
			$(0.40)^a$	$(0.43)^a$	$(0.40)^a$	$(0.43)^a$
WOOD			-0.89	-0.90	-0.90	-0.92
			$(0.25)^a$	$(0.28)^a$	$(0.26)^a$	$(0.29)^a$
			$(0.29)^a$	$(0.28)^a$	$(0.29)^a$	$(0.28)^a$
ELEC			-1.19	-1.13	-1.15	-1.15
			$(0.37)^a$	$(0.42)^a$	$(0.37)^a$	$(0.42)^a$
			$(0.43)^a$	$(0.42)^a$	$(0.42)^a$	$(0.41)^a$
TRANSP			-1.56	-1.46	-1.59	-1.51
			$(0.35)^a$	$(0.39)^a$	$(0.36)^a$	$(0.39)^a$
			$(0.43)^a$	$(0.45)^a$	$(0.44)^a$	$(0.45)^a$

Continued on next page

Table 4.4—Continued

Independent Variables	Model 1		Model 2		Model 3	
	Poisson	ZIP	Poisson	ZIP	Poisson	ZIP
ACCOM			-0.56	-0.44	-0.59	-0.52
			$(0.24)^b$	(0.35)	$(0.25)^b$	$(0.29)^c$
			(0.35)	(0.43)	(0.34)*	(0.37)
WASTE					0.97	1.03
					$(0.35)^a$	$(0.38)^a$
					$(0.42)^b$	$(0.40)^b$
HAZ					-0.16	-0.09
					(0.28)	(0.32)
					(0.39)	(0.39)
WATER					0.04	0.01
					(0.26)	(0.29)
					(0.30)	(0.28)
HAZAIR					-0.02	-0.07
					(0.22)	(0.26)
					(0.29)	(0.29)
Log Likelihood	-323.39	-310.87	-303.87	-297.02	-300.26	-293.41
Vuong Statistic		1.65		1.24		1.29
(significance)		(0.05)		(0.11)		(0.10)

Note(s): Standard Errors (upper) and robust standard errors (lower) are in parentheses.
N=425 for all regressions. [a]Statistically significant at the 1% level.
[b]Statistically significant at the 5% level. [c]Statistically significant at the 10% level.

It is interesting to note that the impact of HAZ or WATER on EMP adoption is not statistically significant on average, but is significant for facilities with ISSUE=1. This could be because facilities may be best able to address hazardous toxic release problems and water pollution problems through changes in management practices, while solid waste reduction could be achieved at relatively low cost by participating in local recycling programs that were easily accessible. VEPs to address hazardous emission reduction or water pollution reduction are targeted towards specific impacts, and may not be as widely applicable as solid waste reduction programs.

We also find that the presence of fewer competitors and a multinational status lead to participation in more VEPs only for facilities with ISSUE=1. This suggests that the potential for differentiation and gaining a competitive advantage through publicly visible voluntary environmental activities is important in motivating participation in VEPs, particularly among facilities that are otherwise vulnerable to reputational losses due to their environmental impacts.

Table 4.5 Marginal Effects of Determinants of the Independent Variables

Independent Variables	EMPSUM ZIP	VEPSUM Poisson
EMPLOYEES	0.04	0.03
	(0.03)	(0.01)[b]
PUB	0.18	0.08
	(0.24)	(0.09)
MC	0.39	0.13
	(0.29)	(0.08)[c]
RD	0.57	0.06
	(0.26)[b]	(0.08)
RETAIL	0.03	-0.03
	(0.20)	(0.06)
COMP	-0.07	-0.12
	(0.17)	(0.05)[a]
ISSUE	0.68	0.11
	(0.21)[a]	(0.05)[b]
FOOD	0.12	-0.25
	(0.34)	(0.05)[a]
WOOD	0.60	-0.17
	(0.34)[c]	(0.05)[a]
ELEC	0.38	-0.18
	(0.48)	(0.05)[a]
TRANSP	0.37	-0.25
	(0.35)	(0.05)[a]
ACCOM	0.40	-0.12
	(0.39)	(0.06)[b]
WASTE	0.56	0.20
	(0.27)[b]	(0.07)[a]
HAZ	0.52	-0.39
	(0.28)[c]	(0.10)
WATER	0.44	0.01
	(0.27)	(0.07)
HAZAIR	-0.16	-0.00
	(0.20)	(0.07)

Note(s): Marginal effects are presented for Models 3 from Tables 4.2 and 4.3. Robust standard errors are in parentheses. The average predicted value of EMPSUM is 1.72. The average predicted value of VEPSUM is 0.25. [a]Statistically significant at the 1% level. [b]Statistically significant at the 5% level. [c]Statistically significant at the 10% level.

Table 4.6 Impact of Environmental Concerns on Voluntary Environmental Action

Independent Variables	EMPSUM (ZIP Model 3)		VEPSUM (Poisson Model 3)	
	Issue=0	Issue=1	Issue=0	Issue=1
Constant	-0.89	0.58	-2.07	-0.67
	$(0.37)^b$	$(0.19)^a$	$(0.54)^a$	(0.42)
	$(0.41)^b$	$(0.25)^b$	$(0.62)^a$	(0.47)
EMPLOYEES	0.18	0.05	0.99	0.11
	(0.15)	$(0.02)^a$	$(0.31)^a$	$(0.04)^a$
	(0.13)	$(0.02)^a$	$(0.40)^b$	$(0.05)^a$
PUB	-0.21	0.08	0.80	0.05
	(0.32)	(0.14)	(0.68)	(0.39)
	(0.37)	(0.14)	(0.60)	(0.38)
MC	0.39	0.18	-0.19	0.58
	(0.26)	(0.13)	(0.68)	$(0.32)^c$
	(0.34)	(0.16)	(0.66)	$(0.27)^b$
RD	0.24	0.29	-0.27	0.27
	(0.22)	$(0.13)^b$	(0.51)	(0.35)
	(0.23)	$(0.14)^b$	(0.54)	(0.41)
RETAIL	0.06	0.05	0.35	-0.24
	(0.18)	(0.10)	(0.36)	(0.23)
	(0.21)	(0.13)	(0.40)	(0.30)
COMP	-0.00	-0.08	-0.28	-0.57
	(0.16)	(0.09)	(0.32)	$(0.23)^b$
	(0.18)	(0.11)	(0.35)	$(0.25)^b$
FOOD	0.35	-0.17	-0.89	-2.11
	(0.33)	(0.17)	$(0.50)^c$	$(0.54)^a$
	(0.30)	(0.20)	(0.60)	$(0.53)^a$
WOOD	0.82	0.06	-0.77	-1.06
	$(0.27)^a$	(0.15)	(0.47)	$(0.34)^a$
	$(0.26)^a$	(0.17)	(0.68)	$(0.32)^a$
ELEC	1.27	-0.35	-0.70	-1.38
	$(0.31)^a$	$(0.21)^c$	(0.64)	$(0.45)^a$
	$(0.34)^a$	(0.24)	(0.66)	$(0.54)^b$
TRANSP	0.39	0.11	-1.28	-1.72
	(0.32)	(0.15)	$(0.64)^b$	$(0.43)^a$
	(0.33)	(0.19)	$(0.64)^b$	$(0.58)^a$
ACCOM	0.59	0.02	-1.32	-0.39
	$(0.29)^b$	(0.16)	$(0.57)^b$	(0.30)
	$(0.33)^c$	(0.21)	$(0.57)^b$	(0.41)

Continued on next page

Table 4.6—Continued

Independent Variables	EMPSUM (ZIP Model 3)		VEPSUM (Poisson Model 3)	
	Issue=0	Issue=1	Issue=0	Issue=1
WASTE	0.88	-0.01	0.70	1.08
	(0.28)[a]	(0.18)	(0.51)	(0.45)[b]
	(0.28)[a]	(0.18)	(0.55)	(0.48)[b]
HAZ	-0.13	0.37	-0.31	0.06
	(0.27)	(0.16)[b]	(0.51)	(0.36)
	(0.30)	(0.21)*	(0.54)	(0.45)
WATER	0.48	0.35	-0.15	-0.01
	(0.21)[b]	(0.16)[b]	(0.46)	(0.33)
	(0.24)[b]	(0.19)[c]	(0.46)	(0.36)
HAZAIR	0.02	-0.08	0.79	-0.38
	(0.19)	(0.11)	(0.39)[b]	(0.28)
	(0.19)	(0.13)	(0.38)[b]	(0.32)
Log Likelihood	-253.38	-486.60	-102.57	-181.61
Vuong Statistic (significance)	3.43 (0.00)	2.81 (0.00)	0.88 (0.19)	0.73 (0.23)

Note(s): N=192 for Issue=0 and 233 for Issue =1.
Standard Errors (upper) and robust standard errors (lower) are in parentheses
[a]Statistically significant at the 1% level. [b]Statistically significant at the 5% level.
[c]Statistically significant at the 10% level.

Conclusions and Policy Implications

Previous studies of business environmental management have focused predominantly on participants in major governmental environmental programs and on large firms. While these studies have yielded valuable insights about the factors influencing program participation and environmental management efforts in major firms, environmental management at small and medium sized facilities and the full spectrum of environmental practices generally have not been examined. This study provides one of the first in-depth analyses of a representative cross-section of facilities operating in manufacturing and non-manufacturing sectors.

Major Findings

In general, the results of this analysis support previous empirical findings by Henriques and Sadorsky (1996), Dasgupta, Hettige, and Wheeler (2000) and Khanna and Anton (2002) that regulatory pressures are associated with firms' decisions to implement EMPs and participate in VEPs. In our study, both voluntary program participation and the implementation of EMPs increase as firms become subject to more extensive regulations across different media. However we find that the various regulatory pressures examined here differ in the type of voluntary behavior they promote and the type of firms that are more likely to be motivated. We find that solid waste regulations are more likely to induce both VEP participation and EMP adoption, water and hazardous or toxic waste regulations induce only EMP adoption, and hazardous air regulations are not found to influence either behavior.

Although VEPs are becoming a popular tool to encourage business environmental management, our survey indicates that overall participation remains low, as others have found (Khanna and Damon, 1999). The evidence that larger facilities are more likely to participate in VEPs is particularly strong, suggesting that the design of programs currently offered is better suited for larger facilities and/or that the overt public recognition is more valuable to large firms. It could also be that larger facilities are better able to bear the costs of participation in VEPs. Conversely, we find that facility size does not influence EMP adoption.

Interestingly, facilities with R&D capacity, especially those that considered environmental concerns important were more likely to adopt EMPs, but not more likely to participate in VEPs. This implies that firms can be independently motivated to pursue environmentally friendly activities without the payoff of the public recognition offered by formal programs if they have appropriate internal resource capacity.

On average, multinational corporations were found to be more likely to participate in VEPs, possibly to benefit from standardization in management practices, to differentiate themselves from competitors, and to gain positive reputation effects. The latter are more likely achieved through participation in VEPs rather than EMPs alone, which may explain why we find that multinationals are more likely to participate in VEPs than adopt EMPs.

Among respondents identifying the environment as an important issue, participation in voluntary programs was found to be more likely if the firm had fewer competitors. But these firms were not more likely to adopt EMPs. This suggests that perhaps voluntary program participation is used by firms operating in imperfectly competitive markets to signal product or production process differentiation, and attract increased market share from consumers with a preference for environmentally responsible products or production methods.

Our findings do not offer support for the hypothesis that retail firms are more likely to invest in environmental improvements, presumably due to customer pressures. Similarly, our findings do not allow us to conclude that publicly traded firms are more inclined to engage in voluntary environmental management to attract green investors.

Policy Implications

The study's overarching conclusions inform the design of policies to foster voluntary environmental program participation and environmental management practice use. First, we find that Oregon business facilities have access to a wide variety of VEPs yet participation remains low overall. Only 20 percent of respondents in this survey reported participating despite the extensive selection of programs available. This suggests that the existing portfolio of VEPs may have significant effects on certain types of firms, segments of industries or specific pollutants but likely will not cause a major improvement in environmental quality in general. The precise reasons for low participation and coverage overall cannot be determined from this dataset. However, we find that large and/or multinational facilities are more likely to participate, perhaps because the benefits of public recognition outweigh the fixed costs. Smaller facilities may not perceive sizable public recognition benefits from VEPs. Therefore policies that lower the labor and capital costs or provide technical or financial assistance for smaller domestic facilities could foster broader participation.

Second, we find that Oregon business facilities are generally using multiple environmental management practices, most of which are not part of formal VEPs. For the facilities responding to the survey, over 60 percent had implemented at least one EMP and just over 7 percent reported implementing seven or more EMPs; on average, these facilities had implemented over three EMPs. As just noted, less than one-quarter of the sample reported participating in VEPs, with less than 7 percent of the sample participating in two or more programs. This suggests that most facilities are choosing to practice environmental management on their own without VEP assistance. This finding likely reflects the desire by facilities to tailor their practices to their individual situations to maximize their cost-effectiveness. It reinforces the need for policies to permit flexible approaches to advance EMP use across a heterogeneous set of facilities.

Third, our analysis shows that regulatory intensity generally induces both participation in formal VEPs and the adoption of EMPs. Importantly, the Oregon data cover a broader array of facilities than previous studies, which suggests that the effect of regulatory pressure extends down from large to smaller facilities. The policy implication of this finding is that regulations are complements to voluntary business environmental management initiatives, not substitutes. However, different types of regulations, e.g., water and solid waste, vary in their effects on VEPs and EMPs. This suggests that a simple ratcheting up of regulatory standards will not be uniformly effective across environmental media and industrial sectors. Theory and our empirical findings suggest that tailored or targeted approaches will be more effective depending upon the industry in question and the objective.

Fourth, the perception that environmental issues are a significant concern for the facility exerts a significant and positive effect on business environmental management. We found facilities that recognized environmental issues as significant concern for their facility responded very differently to potential motivations for voluntary participation. This finding suggests that educational programs to accurately inform managers about the roles their facilities play in determining environmental conditions and the effect of managing environmental issues on their long-term economic viability could increase voluntary participation.

Finally, our survey showed the rich diversity of facilities in operation and our analysis suggests the need for a portfolio of policy approaches. The predominance of small facilities without adequate resources, particularly R&D capacity, to design and implement their own environmental management programs may be the largest policy challenge to accelerating participation in voluntary initiatives. Increased availability of technical expertise and information sharing among firms may be needed to stimulate the design of environmental management systems tailored to suit the needs of individual firms.

In closing, our study finds that facilities are engaged in a rich diversity of voluntary environmental initiatives. It affirms the significant role of credible regulations as a complement to voluntary environmental programs to encourage firms to participate in such initiatives. Market and other forces may either not be strong enough or simply lead some firms to make symbolic efforts at environmental management. This study also shows that some facilities, particularly small, R&D intensive facilities, are clearly engaging in environmental management outside of formal programs, suggesting that formal government voluntary programs are just one potential tool for fostering environmental management. Future research should focus on better understanding of the motivations for and constraints to informal voluntary environmental actions by business. It should also focus not just on program participation and adoption of practices, but the efficacy or performance of those practices. Our data did not permit an assessment of the effects of the patchwork of voluntary program participation and environmental management practices on ambient environmental conditions. Designing innovative policy approaches to stimulate cost-effective voluntary environmental management hinges on understanding the behavior of facilities of all sizes and ownership structure and their proclivity for formal and/or informal environmental actions that lead to environmental improvement.

Bibliography

Anderson, S., Daniel, J., and Johnson, M. "Why firms seek ISO certification: Regulatory compliance or competitive advantage?" *Production and Management* 8, no. 1 (January 1999): 28–43.

Anton, W., Deltas, G., and Khanna, M. "Environmental management systems: Do they improve environmental performance?" *Journal of Environmental Economics and Management* 48, no. 1 (July 2004): 632–654.

Arora, S., and Cason, T. "Why do firms volunteer to exceed environmental regulations: Understanding participation in EPA's 33/50 Program." *Land Economics* 72, no. 4 (November 1996): 413–432.

———— "An experiment in voluntary environmental regulation: Participation in EPA's 33/50 program." *Journal of Environmental Economics & Management* 28, no. 3 (May 1995): 271–287.

Association of Oregon Recyclers (AOR). "2008 recycler awards." Available at http://www.aorr.org/2008_recycler_awards.htm. Accessed August 25, 2008.

Cameron, A. C., and Trivedi. P. K. *Regression analysis of count data.* Econometric Society Monograph No.30. Cambridge: Cambridge University Press, 1998.

Carmin, JoAnn, Darnall, N., and Mil-Homens, J. "Stakeholder involvement in the design of U.S. voluntary environmental programs: Does sponsorship matter?" *Policy Studies Journal* 31, no. 4 (December 2003): 527–543.

Carpentier, C. L., and Ervin, D. E. "Business approaches to agri-environmental management: Incentives, constraints and policy issues." Paris: Organization for Economic Cooperation and Development (OECD), 2002.

Clackamas County. "Waste Prevention—Commercial: The BRAG Program." Available at http://www.clackamas.us/transportation/recycling/preventioncom.htm. Accessed August 25, 2008.

Clark, L. A., and Watson, D. (1995). "Constructing validity: Basic issues in objective scale development." *Psychological Assessment* 7, no. 3 (September 1995): 309–319.

Coglianese, C., and Nash, J. (Eds). *Beyond compliance: Business decision making and the US EPA's Performance Track Program.* Harvard University: Regulatory Policy Program, Massaavar-Rhamani Center for Business and Government, John F. Kennedy School of Government, 2006.

Cordano M., and Frieze, I.H. "Pollution reduction preferences of US environmental managers: Applying Ajzen's theory of planned behavior." *Academy of Management Journal* 43, no. 1 (February 2000): 627–641.

Cropper, M. L., and Oates, W. E. "Environmental economics: A survey." *Journal of Economic Literature* 30, no. 2 (June 1992): 675–740.

Darnall, N., and Edwards, D. J. "Predicting the cost of environmental management system adoption: The role of capabilities, resources and ownership structure." *Strategic Management Journal* 27, no. 4 (April 2006): 301–320.

Dasgupta, S., Hettige, H., and Wheeler, D. "What improves environmental compliance? Evidence from Mexican industry." *Journal of Environmental Economics and Management* 39, no. 1 (January 2000): 39–66.

DeCanio, S. J., and Watkins, W. E. "Investment in energy efficiency: Do the characteristics of firms matter?" *Review of Economics & Statistics* 80, no. 1 (February 1998): 95–107.

Delmas, Magali A., and Toffel, M.W. "Institutional pressures and environmental strategies." Manuscript, University of California, Santa Barbara, CA, 2005.

———. "Institutional pressure and environmental management practices: An empirical analysis." Presented at the U.S. EPA conference on Corporate Environmental Behavior and the Effectiveness of Government Interventions, April 26–27, 2004. Washington D.C: EPA National Center for Environmental Economics and National Center for Environmental Research.

Dillman, Don A. *Mail and Internet surveys: The Tailored Design Method, Second Edition.* New York: John Wiley & Sons, 2000.

Dowell, G., Hart, S., and Yeung, B. "Do corporate global environmental standards create or destroy market value?" *Management Science* 46, no. 8 (August 2000): 1059–1074.

Earth Advantage. "Earth Advantage Homes." Available at http://www.earthadvantage.com/default.asp. Accessed August 25, 2008.

Ervin, Christine A., and David E. Ervin. "Factors affecting the use of soil conservation practices: Hypotheses, evidence, and policy implications." *Land Economics* 58, no. 3 (August 1982): 277–292.

Esty, D. C., and A. S. Winston. *Green to Gold: How smart companies use environmental strategy to innovate, create value, and build competitive advantage.* New Haven, CT: Yale University Press, 2006.

Florida, R. "Lean and green: The move to environmentally conscious manufacturing." *California Management Review* 39, no. 1 (September 1996): 80–105.

Florida, R., and Davison, D. (2001). "Why do firms adopt advanced environmental practices (and do they make a difference)?" Pp. 82–104 in *Regulating from the Inside: Can Environmental Management Systems Achieve Policy Goals?,* edited by Cary Coglianese and Jennifer Nash. Washington DC: Resources for the Future, 2001.

Greene, W. H., *Econometric analysis, third edition.* Upper Saddle River, NJ: Prentice Hall, 1997.

Harrington, D. R., Khanna, M., and Deltas, G. "Striving to be green: The adoption of total quality environmental management." *Applied Economics*, forthcoming.

Henriques, I., and Sadorsky, P. "The determinants of an environmentally responsive firm: An empirical approach." *Journal of Environmental Economics and Management* 30, no. 3 (May 1996): 381–395.

Innes, R., and Bial, J. J. "Inducing innovation in the environmental technology of oligopolistic firms." *Journal of Industrial Economics* 50, no. 3 (September 2002): 265–287.

International Organization for Standardization (ISO). "ISO 14004:2004 Environmental management systems—General guidelines on principles, systems and support techniques." Available at http://www.iso.org/iso/iso_catalogue/catalogue_tc/catalogue_detail.htm?csnumber=31807. Accessed August 25, 2008.

Johnson, R. J., and Scicchitano, M. J. "Uncertainty, risk, trust, and information: Public perceptions of environmental issues and willingness to take action." *Policy Studies Journal* 28, no. 3 (September 2000): 633–647.

Jones, Cody. What's regulation go to do with it? Examining the Impact of Regulatory Intensity on Facility Environmental Management and Performance. Doctoral dissertation, Portland State University, 2008

Jones, Cody. "An overview of environmental impacts, applicable regulations, and available voluntary initiatives for six industry sectors." Working paper. Portland, OR: Portland State University, 2005.

Khanna, M. "Non-mandatory approaches to environmental regulation: A survey." *Journal of Economic Surveys* 15, no. 3 (July 2001): 291–324.

Khanna, M., and Anton, W. R. Q. "Corporate environmental management: Regulatory and market-based pressures." *Land Economics* 78, no. 4 (November 2002): 539–558.

Khanna M., and Brouhle, K. "Effectiveness of Voluntary Environmental Initiatives." Manuscript, Department of Agricultural and Consumer Economics, University of Illinois, Urbana-Champaign, 2007.

Khanna, M,. and Damon, L. "EPA's voluntary 33/50 program: Impact on toxic releases and economic performance of firms." *Journal of Environmental Economics and Management* 37, no. 1 (January 1999): 11–25.

Khanna, M., Quimio, W., and Bojilova, D. "Toxic release information: A policy tool for environmental protection." *Journal of Environmental Economics and Management* 36, no. 3 (November 1998): 243–266.

King A. A., and Lenox, M. J. "Industry self–regulation without sanctions: The chemical industry's Responsible Care Program. *Academy of Management Journal* 43, no. 4 (August 2000): 698–716.

Mullahy, J. "Specification and testing of some modified count data models." *Journal of Econometrics* 33, no. 3 (December 1986): 341–365.

Nakamura, M., Takahashi, R., and Vertinsky, I. "Why Japanese firms choose to certify: A study of managerial responses to environmental issues." *Journal of Environmental Economics and Management* 42, no. 1 (July 2001): 23–52.

Oregon Natural Step Network. "Membership." Available at http://www.ortns.org/members.htm. Accessed August 23, 2008.

Potoski, M., and Prakash, A. (2005a) "GreencClubs and voluntary governance: ISO 14001 and firms' regulatory compliance." *American Journal of Political Science*; 49, no. 2 (April 2005): 235–248.

———. (2005b). "Covenants with weak swords: ISO 14001 and facilities' environmental performance." *Journal of Policy Analysis & Management* 24, no. 4 (Autumn 2005): 745–769.

Reinhardt, F. L. *Down to earth: Applying principles to environmental management.* Boston: Harvard Business School Press, 2000.

Rivera, J., and de Leon, P. "Is greener whiter? The Sustainable Slopes Program and the voluntary environmental performance of western ski areas." *Policy Studies Journal* 32, no. 3 (September 2004): 417–437.

Rivera, J., de Leon, P., and Koerber, C. "Is greener whiter yet? The Sustainable Slopes Program after five years." *Policy Studies Journal* 34, no. 2 (April 2006): 195–224.

Sam, A. G., and Innes, R. "Voluntary pollution reductions and the enforcement of environmental law: An empirical study of the 33/50 Program". Manuscript, Department of Agricultural and Resource Economics, University of Arizona, Tucson, 2005.

State of Oregon. *Oregon Revised Statutes(ORS), 2005 Edition, Statute 657.665(3).* Available at http://www.leg.state.or.us/ors/657.html. Accessed August 24, 2007.

State of Oregon. Department of Environmental Quality. *Permit Handbook.* Available at: http://www.deq.state.or.us/pubs/permithandbook/toc.htm. Accessed July 23, 2006.

State of Oregon. Department of Revenue (DOR). Oregon corporate excise and income tax: Characteristics of corporate taxpayers, 2004 edition, covering fiscal year 2004 corporate tax receipts and tax year 2002 corporate tax returns, report 150-102-405, revised December 2004. Available at: http://www.oregon.gov/DOR/STATS/docs/102-405-FY04/102-405-FY04.pdf. Accessed August 24, 2007.

U.S. Census Bureau (USCB). "Statistics of U.S. business." Available at http://www.census.gov/csd/susb/. Accessed December 29, 2006.

U.S. Environmental Protection Agency (EPA) (2008a). "The National Environmental Performance Track." Available at: http://www.epa.gov/performancetrack/. Accessed August 23, 2008.

———. (2008b). "ENERGY STAR." Available at: http://www.energystar.gov/. Accessed August 23, 2008.

———. (2008c). "WasteWise: Preserving resources, preventing waste." Available at: http://www.epa.gov/wastewise/. Accessed August 25, 2008.

———. (2008d). "SmartWay: The smart way to save fuel, money, and the environment." Available at: http://www.epa.gov/smartway/. Accessed August 25, 2008.

————. "Toxics release inventory." Available at: http://www.epa.gov/tri. Accessed July 23, 2006.

U.S. Green Building Council (USGBC) (2008a). "Green Building Facts: Green Building by the Numbers." Available at http://www.usgbc.org/ShowFile.aspx?DocumentID=3340. Accessed August 23, 2008.

U.S. Green Building Council (USGBC) (2008b). "Green Building Facts: Green Building by the Numbers." Available at http://www.usgbc.org/DisplayPage.aspx?CMSPageID=65. Accessed August 23, 2008.

Videras, J., and Alberini, A. "The appeal of voluntary environmental programs: Which firms participate and why?" *Contemporary Economic Policy* 18, no. 4 (October 2000): 449–461.

Welch, E.W., Mazur, A., and Bretschneider, S. "Voluntary behavior by electric utilities: Levels of adoption and contribution of the Climate Challenge Program to the reduction of carbon dioxide." *Journal of Policy Analysis and Management* 19, no. 3 (x 1999), 407–425.

World Wildlife Federation (WWF). "Climate Savers - Mobilizing companies to cut carbon dioxide." Available at http://www.worldwildlife.org/climate/item3799.html. Accessed August 25, 2008.

Notes

1. The Oregon Legislature created a Green Permits Program (http://www.deq.state.or.us/programs/greenpermits) in 1999 to achieve environmental results that are significantly better than those required by law. In January 2007, business and government leaders endorsed sustainable business as a core element of the state's economic development strategy (http://www.oregonbusinessplan.org/). The City of Portland, Oregon, has a "green buildings" program to promote cost-effective solutions that lessen environmental impacts of commercial buildings (http://www.green-rated.org/). Private sector (for-profit and not-for-profit) examples include the emergence of business sustainability consulting firms (e.g., http://www.brightworks.net/), the Forest Stewardship Council's certification program (http://fscus.org/), the Food Alliance certification system (http://www.thefoodalliance.org), and the Oregon Natural Step Network (http://www.ortns.org/).

2. A large number of empirical studies have sought to explain the motivations for firms to participate in government sponsored voluntary programs, such as the 33/50 Program, WasteWise, Green Lights, and Climate Challenge (see surveys in Khanna, 2001; Khanna and Brouhle, 2007). Others have examined motivations for seeking ISO certification (Anderson et al., 1999; Potoski and Prakash, 2005a, b) and for participation in industry association programs such as Responsible Care (King and Lenox, 2000) and Sustainable Slopes (Rivera and de Leon, 2004; Rivera et al., 2006). A few studies have investigated the incentives for adopting one or more EMPs, such as an environmental plan (Henriques and Sadorsky, 1996), Total Quality Environmental Management (Harrington, Khanna, and Deltas, forthcoming) and a comprehensive environmental management system (Khanna and Anton, 2002; Anton et al., 2004; Dasgupta et al., 2000).

3. Casual examination of the data suggests that the likelihood of these problems is small. For instance, the same proportion of facilities in the accommodation sector as in the wood sector responded with ISSUE=1, even though the latter is much more regulated than the former. Fewer facilities in the construction sector responded with ISSUE=1 than with ISSUE=0 even though a large proportion of them participated in green building programs.

4. We do, however, check correlations among the individual EMP adoption decisions and find a positive correlation. This indicates that firms considered these practices to be complementary rather than substitutes. Thus the adoption of a larger number of practices does reflect greater voluntary environmental effort.

5. The Negative Binomial is also less restrictive than the Poisson distribution in that it allows for over-dispersion. However, we were unable to estimate a negative binomial model due to the estimate of the variance matrix of the estimates being singular. The variance of the random variable in a ZIP model has the same form as that in a Negative Binomial model.

6. Facilities were selected as the appropriate business unit to survey because studies suggest that environmental management can vary substantially across the different facilities in a company, environmental permits are typically issued at the facility level (or issued for specific equipment installed in a particular facility), and emission data are typically reported at the facility level (DEQ 2006; EPA 2006; Delmas and Toffel, 2004).

7. Facility names, location, number of employees and primary industry classification were obtained from the OED, which is authorized by Oregon Revised Statutes (ORS) 657.665(3) to release information to state agencies for the purposes of socioeconomic

analysis. No individual persons are identified and information is provided subject to strict confidentiality rules (Graham Slater, OED, personal communication, 2005). The North American Industry Classification System (NAICS) replaces the earlier Standard Industry Classification (SIC) system. NAICS codes contain up to six digits; however, sectors were defined at the 3-digit level in this study.

8. We also estimated these models while excluding ISSUE as an explanatory variable. It did not affect the signs and significances of the other coefficients, with the exception of making EMPLOYEES have a statistically significant impact on EMPSUM. This is possibly due to the positive correlation (although only 0.2) between ISSUE and EMPLOYEES. Results without ISSUE are not reported for brevity.

Chapter 5

Collective Action Through Voluntary Environmental Programs: A Club Theory Approach

Aseem Prakash and Matthew Potoski

It is now well recognized that voluntary environmental programs are important policy instruments for environmental governance, with programs sprouting up across continents and policy domains. Program by program, scholars have studied conditions under which firms join the programs and the factors that influence their efficacy. We now have a sense that while some programs are "greenwashes" that do little to encourage firms to improve their environmental performance, others require participants to take progressive environmental action they would not have taken in the absence of the program, leading them to improve their superior environmental performance.

Examples of both types abound. Ski resorts participating in the Sustainable Slopes Program were not greener than non-participants (Rivera and deLeon, 2004, Rivera, deLeon, and Koerber, 2006). Chemical firms participating in the Responsible Care program did not reduce the emission of toxic chemicals any faster than non-participants (King and Lenox, 2000). Participants in the US Department of Energy's Climate Wise program did not reduce their CO_2 emissions any more than non-participants (Welch, Mazur, and Bretschneider, 2000). On the successful side of the ledger, firms that joined the Environmental Protection Agency's (EPA) 35/50 voluntary program reduced their emissions of toxic pollutants more than the non-participants (Khanna and Damon, 1999). Our own work suggests that ISO 14001 improved participating firms' environmental performance (Potoski and Prakash, 2005) and compliance with government regulations (Potoski and Prakash, 2004).

The upshot is that while there are several useful studies about the effectiveness of individual programs, scholars have yet to systematically tie these studies and their findings together.[1] Indeed, scholars have begun to recognize this issue and have responded in two ways. First, sensing the absence of theory, some have developed inductive approaches to study voluntary programs, an "area studies approach"[2] that can go only so far because the theories are tailored and ultimately limited to individual programs (Cashore et al., 2004). The second response has been comparative analyses of voluntary clubs (Lenox and Nash, 2003; Darnall and Carmin, 2005). While such cross-program studies can shed light on why some programs are successful and others are not, advancing research and practice requires an encompassing theoretical and analytic framework that identifies voluntary clubs' important features and ties them to program efficacy, thereby leading to better understanding of what types of voluntary clubs work, where, and why. Such a theoretical framework should facilitate comparisons not only among voluntary programs but also with other policy instruments.

This is where we seek to make a contribution to the study of voluntary environmental programs and the broader environmental governance literature. Drawing on the economic theory of clubs, we outline a deductive framework for the study of voluntary programs, focusing on specific institutional features and analytic dimensions. We highlight the diversity in program design, the variable that policymakers and program sponsors can influence, and relate design to specific collective action issues that influence program efficacy.

After modeling program design as an exogenous determinant of program efficacy, we highlight how the design itself might be endogenous to the institutional and stakeholder context in which the program is established and functions.[3] By doing so, our framework clarifies the determinants of program efficacy and identifies empirically verifiable hypotheses. Finally, our perspective can help voluntary program scholars place their work within the expansive and established governance literature and therefore contribute to broader the dialogue on institutions and governance.

Our essay is structured in the following way. In the first part, expanding on our previous work (Prakash and Potoski, 2006a), we outline a generalizable framework for the study of voluntary clubs, based on an economic club model. We conceptualize voluntary environmental programs as clubs that require firms to incur costs not required by law that lead to the production of positive environmental externalities. In return, voluntary clubs provide branding benefits[4] such as shared reputation and goodwill to participating firms that emanate from their association with the voluntary club brand.[5] In the second part of the paper, we discuss important issues for the study of voluntary environmental programs and illustrate how our club approach can help policymakers design superior voluntary programs.

Collective Action, Program Design, and the Club Framework

Rational actors are generally unwilling to pay private costs to produce positive social externalities. An externality implies that actors do not fully internalize the costs and benefits of their actions. Consequently, goods with negative externalities are over-produced and goods with positive externalities are under-produced. Pollution is a classic negative externality (but see Coase, 1960), and from the other side of the coin, decreasing pollution is a positive externality. A firm might reduce pollution by improving production processes or by adopting new technologies or management systems. In many cases, these are expensive actions for which firms would want some offsetting payoff. The policy challenge for environmental governance is to design institutions that create incentives for actors to incur the costs of pollution reduction, or in other words, to induce polluting actors to internalize their negative externalities.

Ever since Pigou (1960), government regulations have been viewed as the primary mechanism for compelling firms to internalize costs they would otherwise externalize. Regulations change firms' cost calculus by mandating that firms cut pollution, and some regulations stipulate the means for doing so. The case for governmental regulations solving externalities rests on three assumptions. First, public regulations are democratic and fair because governments respond to public concerns (not private interests). Second, governments have the capacities to correctly estimate the cost of externalities and then design regulations to compel firms to internalize them. Third, the state has the capacity to enforce regulations and firms tend to adhere to the law.[6]

These assumptions are all too often problematic (Fiorino, 1999; Coglianese and Nash, 2001), particularly in the context of developing countries. Many countries are not fully functioning democracies,[7] and even in established democracies, governments might be unduly influenced, if not captured by, interest groups. In most developing countries, governments have little power to enforce regulations, or even maintain internal order and protect property rights.[8]

An effective voluntary environmental program can be a corrective for government failure. In Mexico, which ranked well in the bottom half of the failed state indexes, Dasgupta et al. (2000) report that adopting environmental management practices along the lines prescribed by ISO 14001 significantly improved Mexican facilities' self-reported compliance with public law. Haufler (forthcoming) shows how the international diamond industry has developed a voluntary club (Kimberly Process) to curb the flow of "blood diamonds" mined illegally in failed African states and used to fund the internal wars.

The upshot of this discussion is that governance mechanisms should be carefully scrutinized for their strengths *and* deficiencies: one should not compare "imperfect" voluntary clubs with a "perfect" governmental regulation or viceversa. If we accept that all institutions can fail, the scholarly and policy challenge is to identify the conditions and institutions that lead to success and failure.

Voluntary clubs are an important policy instrument in this regard because they can induce participating firms to produce positive environmental externalities not only in response to legal mandates but to exceed them. They implicitly respond to the externality problems resulting from governments' failure to adequately supply or enforce regulations. But how do these programs induce firms to pay the costs of solving externality problems? Below we explain how voluntary clubs mitigate collective action problems inherent in the voluntary provision of such externalities.

Buchanan Clubs and Voluntary Clubs

Clubs are institutions that supply impure public goods. The club literature is well established in public finance and dates back to at least the 1950s (Pigou, 1960; Tiebout, 1956; and Wiseman, 1957). James Buchanan (1965) is generally credited with introducing the theoretical concept of clubs. In the Buchanan theory, clubs are institutions for producing and allocating goods that are neither fully private (rivalrous and excludable), nor fully public (non-rivalrous, nonexcludable). Unlike pure public goods where the benefits one recipient receives are made available to all, club goods provide excludable benefits that are given only to those who join (and pay for) the club and withheld from all others. Club goods are non-rivalrous in that what one individual consumes is still available for others to consume as well. A good example of a club in this traditional sense is a movie theatre: the excludable benefit club members receive is the opportunity to watch a movie on a big screen with excellent acoustics. Purchased tickets offset the cost of the movie and facilities. If you do not purchase the ticket, you are excluded from watching the movie (excludable benefit) and several patrons can watch a movie at a time (non-rival benefit). Club membership can be allocated efficiently because if there are persistent, long lines for tickets, the theater owner can hike ticket prices while entrepreneurs can construct new theatres.

Unlike traditional "Buchanan" clubs, whose central purpose is the production of club goods, the central purpose of voluntary clubs is to produce positive social externalities. Voluntary clubs provide club goods to firms that produce positive externalities beyond what government regulations require. Unlike in traditional economic clubs, membership costs in voluntary clubs are not direct payments to sponsors. Rather, they are the monetary and non-monetary costs of adopting and adhering to the club's membership requirements.

From the perspective of (potential) members, voluntary clubs can generate three kinds of benefits:

- *Social externalities* that constitute the policy payoff of voluntary clubs.
- *Private* benefits that accrue to a single member firm only.[9]
- *Club goods* that accrue to club members only and are central motivation for members to join the club.

The production of positive social externalities is the important welfare gain to society and the central justification for voluntary clubs. The positive social externalities voluntary club members produce can have the attributes of private goods (a voluntary club obligating participating firms to pay higher wages to indigenous coffee growers), public goods (a voluntary club obligating participating firms to lower air pollution), common property resources (protecting a fishery) or even club goods (a voluntary club obligating participating forestry firm not to cut trees which are revered by an aboriginal group).

The private benefits of voluntary club membership accrue only to individual club members, not to other club members, and certainly not to nonmembers. For example, a voluntary club designed to protect the environment might require firms to uncover waste in their production process, and thereby increasing profits as Porter and Van der Linde (1995) suggest in the context of governmental regulations. Such private benefits, however, have limited analytical utility for evaluating voluntary clubs because an instrumental actor (such as a profit-oriented firm) is likely to take these actions unilaterally, without joining the club, in order to enjoy the private benefits such actions produce. If the private gain from unilaterally taking such action were sufficient to induce the firm to produce enough positive social externalities, then voluntary clubs would not be necessary.[10]

The central, analytically salient benefit that the members receive for producing the voluntary club's positive externalities is the affiliation with the club's positive brand reputation, a non-rival but excludable benefit as we discuss below. In its broadest sense, voluntary club membership signals to firms' stakeholders about members' environmental programs, policies, and performance, which can be quite valuable to stakeholders because so much of firms' activities are unobservable (though different stakeholders may have different information about firms' environmental activities). In other words, because outside stakeholders—such as consumers, regulators, investors, and suppliers—are unable to monitor firms' environmental programs and verify firms' claims, voluntary club membership can solve information asymmetries between firms and their stakeholders. Affiliation with a voluntary club and its reputation thus help build firms' reputations which in turn shapes their relations and interactions with stakeholders (Carpenter, 2001).

While the voluntary club brand reduces information costs for stakeholders to differentiate environmentally progressive firms from laggards, stakeholders vary in their abilities to interpret such brand signals, their preferences for the social externalities the firms produce as club members, and their capacities to translate these preferences into rewards or sanctions for firms. Thus, while we focus on voluntary club design as the driver of branding benefits, we recognize that other factors shape the value of a program's brand benefit, such as the stakeholder and institutional context, firm characteristics, and sponsors' attributes.[11]

Mitigating Collective Action Dilemmas Through Institutional Design

All institutions can fail: governments and market failures have been well documented, and voluntary environmental clubs have been shown to fail as well. From a policy perspective, the objective is to understand the conditions under which voluntary clubs fail and how their institutional design, as the key independent variable in their efficacy, can mitigate their failure.[12] The roots of voluntary club failure are collective action problems associated with free-riding and shirking. Firms may want to enjoy a reputation for environmental responsibility without having to actually pay the costs of being environmentally responsible. Firms hope that the goodwill created by environmentally responsible firms will spill over to them because the stakeholders, who can not always identify which firms are doing the good deeds, will spread their rewards broadly. Effective voluntary clubs seek to solve such free riding because they make excludable the benefits from producing positive externalities: stakeholders can target their rewards only to firms that have joined the club. Thus, the club's brand curbs free riding; the more credible is the brand, the more attractive it is for firms to join the club and produce the positive externalities it requires.[13]

Another type of free riding pertains to shirking: firms can join a voluntary club and claim to produce positive social externalities but fail to live up to their promises. The club therefore needs to establish mechanisms to compel participants to adhere to program obligations. Widespread shirking undermines the production of environmental externalities and thereby dilutes its credibility. Willful shirking occurs because: (1) the goals of participants and voluntary club sponsors diverge, and (2) participants are able to exploit information asymmetries (regarding their adherence to club standards) between themselves and sponsors and stakeholders.[14] Information asymmetries prevent stakeholders from differentiating program shirkers from non-shirkers.

Voluntary clubs can mitigate shirking by establishing monitoring and sanctioning mechanisms. A voluntary club with a reputation for effectively policing and sanctioning its participants is likely to have a stronger standing among its stakeholders and therefore have a stronger brand reputation among its firms' stakeholders.

The Olsonian Dilemma, Brand Benefits
and Club Standards

With public regulations as the baseline, club standards specify what beyond-compliance actions are required for firms to join the voluntary club and remain members in good standing. Some standards specify performance requirements (sometimes called outcome standards) while other standards may be more process oriented, such as requirements that members adopt a management system, or that members regularly consult with community groups. Finally, club standards may limit membership to those that have already established high standards of environmental performance. In effect, club standards are signals to members' stakeholders regarding what the voluntary club wants members to accomplish, particularly their production of environmental externalities. The standards' stringency serves as a proxy signal for the level of externalities members generate (per capita) and therefore affects the branding benefits members can expect to receive from stakeholders.

While voluntary clubs establish regulations outside the scope of mandatory government law, it is through reference to the requirements of mandatory government regulations that we can observe the "voluntary" component of voluntary clubs and assess the levels of externalities the programs produce. The voluntary nature of these programs stems from firms' behavior that produces "positive" social outcomes—positive social externalities—beyond what public law requires. This means of course that the same action that is voluntary in a jurisdiction with less stringent public law could be mandatory in a jurisdiction with stringent public law.

Public law also is the analytic referent for measuring the policy contribution of a program to social welfare: how much more positive social externality does a voluntary club compel its members to produce than they would produce in the absence of the program? The marginal contribution to public welfare from a voluntary club is the value added from its participants' activities that are beyond the applicable legal requirements. Again, this means that a voluntary club may contribute to public welfare in a jurisdiction with less stringent public law but may offer little or no contribution in a jurisdiction with stringent public law.

To simplify our discussion, we identify two types of club standards. Lenient club standards require little social externality production from members beyond what government regulations require. These are low-cost voluntary clubs for the members but create marginal levels of social externalities, and therefore the value of their brand among stakeholders is relatively low. Of course, even lenient club standards must mandate that members produce some positive social externality, or else the voluntary club would be a mere empty gesture (as some voluntary clubs indeed are).

Stringent club standards require members to produce high levels of positive social externalities, well beyond what government regulations require. For potential participants, these can be high cost clubs. The advantage of stringent standards is that the club's brand would be more credible and serve as a low cost tool for signaling voluntary club members' commitment to the club's social objective. Stakeholders would easily and confidently distinguish leaders (members) from laggards (non-members) among firms. Armed with this information, stakeholders could reward and punish firms accordingly.[15]

Shirking Dilemma:
Monitoring and Enforcement Rules

Shirking is the second source of institutional failure for voluntary clubs. Shirking implies that some participants formally join the club but do not implement and practice the club standards. In doing so, shirkers seek to free-ride on the efforts of other members who build the voluntary club's reputation. While non-members are excluded from enjoying the benefits of club membership, shirkers enjoy club benefits unless they are discovered and expelled from the voluntary club. As word spreads about large scale shirking, the club's reputation is likely to diminish and the brand reputation undermined.

Willful shirking is facilitated by information asymmetries between voluntary club participants and club sponsors and/or between participants and club stakeholders.[16] By information asymmetries we mean that voluntary club sponsors and stakeholders cannot observe the levels to which an individual participant is adhering to club standards because such activities are inherently difficult to observe or are observable only at significant cost. The net effect is that information asymmetries impose costs on sponsors and stakeholders seeking to differentiate program shirkers from non-shirkers.

Shirking violates appropriate behavior norms (March and Olson, 1989), which suggests that shirking can be curbed by sociological pressures (normative, mimetic, and coercive) from other participating firms or even stakeholders. It would be important to understand the general conditions under which such sociological pressures would persuade instrumental firms not to shirk.[17] As scholars interested in studying the consequences of institutional design on collective action, we are more interested in studying how institutional design can address the issue of shirking.

Instead of relying on sociological pressures alone, a voluntary club might seek to mitigate shirking through its institutional design. Monitoring and enforcement mechanisms can compel members to adhere to club standards, particularly if they contain three central components: third-party monitoring, public disclosure of audit information, and sanctioning by program sponsors.[18] It should be noted, however, that some voluntary environmental clubs have none of these components—the Sustainable Slopes Program (Rivera and deLeon, 2004) is an example. Based on the design features, we expect such clubs to exhibit high levels of shirking and therefore generate very small amounts of positive externalities, if any. Indeed, Rivera and deLeon (2002) report that club Sustainable Slopes participants were no greener than non-participants. Our framework suggests that policymaker and stakeholders should be skeptical of clubs without any monitoring and enforcement rules.

Voluntary programs begin to have some credibility regarding their capacity to curb shirking if they exhibit at least one of the three features. Third-party monitoring means that firms are required by the program sponsor to have their policies audited by accredited, external auditors. Thus, the program might stipulate that a periodic approval granted by a third-party auditor is necessary to retain program membership. In some cases, program sponsors may require public disclosure of audit information (as in the European Union's Eco-Management and Audit Scheme). The idea is that by such disclosure, the stakeholders can reward and punish as they deem fit. Finally, the sponsoring organization may itself act upon the audit information and sanction the shirkers.

With a nod towards Hobbes (1651) for his astute observation in Chapter 17 of the *Leviathan* that "covenants without swords are but words, and of no strength to secure a man at all," we characterize a club's monitoring and enforcement programs as "swords." Strong sword clubs have all three components —audits, disclosure and sanctioning mechanisms—and are most likely to curb shirking because they provide for a monitoring mechanism, mitigate information asymmetries between participants and club sponsors/stakeholders and create mechanism for sponsors to sanction shirkers. In extreme cases, sponsors may expel participants from the program, an undesirable outcome for firms if they value the benefits of voluntary club membership. While strong sword clubs should experience less shirking, they can impose more costs on members. Thus, in thinking about program design, policy makers need to examine the marginal addition to overall branding benefits by strengthening club's swords.

Medium sword clubs require third-party audits and public disclosure of the audit findings. Although they do not provide for sanctioning by the sponsoring organization, they are likely to curb shirking because, with public disclosure of audit information, external stakeholders can punish the shirkers for failing to live up to their commitments as program members. The EPA's 33/50 program and the European Union's Eco-Management and Audit Scheme (EMAS) are examples of medium sword clubs. In both these voluntary clubs, firms are subjected to third-party audits and the information on their environmental performance is available to the public. Because it is not clear whether stakeholders have the willingness and resources to sanction shirkers, we place them in the medium sword category.

Weak swords clubs require only third-party audits. ISO 14001 is an example of a "weak sword" club. The International Organization for Standardization, the sponsoring organization, is not known to aggressively sanction the shirkers.

Importantly, the absence of public disclosure of audit information weakens stakeholders' ability to sanction shirking. However, these are also low cost voluntary clubs and therefore within the financial means of a larger number of firms, as witnessed by the more than 110,000 facilities across 138 countries had joined the ISO 14001 club as of December 2005.

Based on the above discussion, we identify six voluntary club types (Table 5.1). Important arenas for future research include: how does the institutional-stakeholder environment along with firm characteristics (the relative salience of leaders versus laggards in the population) influence the emergence of various voluntary club types; what is the aggregate impact of a voluntary club in terms of the production of positive environmental externalities, defined as the product of externalities produced by each firm and the total number of club participants. In some instance, policymakers might favor lenient standard clubs to attract a large roster as opposed to stringent standard clubs with limited membership. In other instances, lenient standard clubs might be labeled as greenwashes and attract few members simply because they cannot generate significant branding benefits. Thus, instead of one-type-fits-all, policymakers should recognize that different voluntary club types are likely to best fit different policy contexts for different types of firms. While stringent standard clubs with strong swords might seem the best from an externality generation perspective, these are high cost clubs that most firms might not find worth their while. On the other hand, weak sword clubs with lenient standards might generate low levels of externalities per capita, but by attracting a large roster of firms, might lead to the generation of high levels of externalities in the aggregate.

Table 5.1 Analytic Typology of Voluntary Clubs

Club Standards	Enforcement and Monitoring Rules		
	Weak Sword	Medium Sword	Strong Sword
Lenient Standards	Social Externalities: low Shirking: high Branding benefits: marginal Cost: low	Social Externalities: low-moderate Shirking: moderate Branding benefits: low-moderate Cost: low-moderate	Social Externalities: moderate Shirking: low Branding benefits: low-moderate Cost: low-moderate
Stringent Standards	Social Externalities: low Shirking: high Branding benefits: marginal Cost: moderate-high	Social Externalities: moderate Shirking: moderate Branding benefits: moderate Cost: moderate	Social Externalities: high Shirking: low Branding benefits: high Cost: high

Theoretical and Analytic Complexities in Studying Voluntary Clubs

Scholars confront a complex web of causal connections among the features of a voluntary club: the club's institutional design, the sponsor's standing, the type of firms that join the club, and their environmental performance. In statistical terms, this means many of the relationships are likely to be endogenous: firms choose to join a voluntary club (and produce the environmental externalities it requires) in response to the costs of externality production and the returns from affiliating with the voluntary club brand. The reputational benefit of brand affiliation, in turn, is influenced by the sponsors' reputation, the club's institutional design, the practices of other club members, and their stakeholders' effective demand for the externalities. Voluntary club sponsors are likely to design rules and standards in anticipation of likely members. Causal complexities demand stronger research designs that exploit variability across firms, clubs, sponsors and institutional contexts, particularly as club rules and membership rosters change over time. While quasi-experimental designs have been popular among the empirically-oriented scholars seeking to study program efficacy (Khanna and Damon, 1999; King and Lenox, 2001; Rivera and deLeon, 2004; Prakash and Potoski, 2006a), one might design creative experimental techniques to sort out endogeneity issues—a promising approach demonstrated in the common-pool resource literature (Ostrom et al., 1994).

In confronting this complexity, rigorous theoretical analysis should guide empirical inquiry by clearly articulating causal contingencies. Harbaugh et al. (2006), for example, show that uncertainty over what certification means leads consumers to infer that the club's standards are weak, and consequently the taint of association leads cleaner firms to avoid voluntary clubs that dirtier firms have joined. Further empirical and theoretical advances are required to identify not just whether voluntary clubs work, but under why and under what conditions. Our aim in the remainder of this essay is to identify several frontiers of this inquiry: club size and crowding, voluntary club governance, building voluntary club brands, and the reputational commons.

Voluntary Club Size and Crowding

The size of a voluntary club's membership roster affects the strength and value of its brand. More members create opportunities to capture economies of scale in building the club's reputation (McGuire, 1972), a dynamic akin to network effects (Bessen and Saloner, 1988). Network effects are the changes in the benefit that an actor derives from a good when the number of other actors consuming the same good changes. Positive network effects create increasing returns to scale: with every additional unit, the marginal cost of production decreases. Language groups can be thought of as voluntary clubs amenable to network effects: the more people speak a given language, the higher are the benefits from learning it. Having more members helps advertise a voluntary club broadly among stakeholders as one member's socially desirable activities generates positive reputational and goodwill externalities for other members, so that the value a member derives increases as others join.

The benefits of voluntary club membership are non-rival because the positive branding benefits one member enjoys can be simultaneously enjoyed by other members. However, at some point, crowding may set in—a question that has so far not been systematically examined in the voluntary program literature.[19] While a voluntary club with universal membership would do little to identify which firms were producing desirable social goods, industry-sponsored clubs might desire universal membership of the firms operating in their industry, as is the case with National Ski Areas Association's Sustainable Slopes Program, the American Chemistry Council's Responsible Care program, and the American Forestry and Paper Association's Sustainable Forestry Initiative. Thus, similar to the traditional club literature on optimal club size (Cornes and Sandler, 1996), there are significant opportunities to examine this issue in the context of voluntary clubs.

Firms within an industry benefit asymmetrically from affiliating with a voluntary club brand. Large or more profitable firms might benefit more from the club because they are more vulnerable to the negative reputational externalities generated by others in the industry. Firms in a "privileged group" (Olson, 1965) that disproportionately benefit from a shared reputation (or are disproportionately hurt by its degradation) are likely to take the lead in establishing an industry club. Indeed, this is the story of Responsible Care in the chemical industry (Prakash, 2000) and the Sustainable Forestry Initiative in the forestry industry (Cashore et al., 2004).[20] The optimal club size from firms' perspective might vary across firms, even for firms within the same industry.

Voluntary Club Governance and Credible Commitments

Firms constantly look to improve their standing with stakeholders. One might wonder as to what is the point of joining a voluntary club if firms can act on their own to boost their standing with stakeholders. Indeed, it is not hard to think of companies with well-earned reputations for environmental leadership. Club membership offers several advantages over unilateral action for enhancing firms' environmental reputations among stakeholders. Unilateral commitments to desirable environmental action may be less credible because they are less institutionalized. When individual firms make their own rules, they can easily change them as well. Of course, a firm may devise some measure to credibly commit to a rule system and not opportunistically change them—as the "credible commitment" literature suggests (North and Weingast, 1989).

As institutionalized systems, voluntary clubs enjoy a degree of legitimacy that a firm alone may find difficult to acquire. By joining voluntary clubs whose rules they cannot change in the short-run, firms signal their willingness to incur private costs to create positive environmental externalities. However, to capitalize on this legitimacy, clubs themselves must solve two credible commitment problems, one towards firms' stakeholders and a second towards its own members. Failure to solve these problems can undermine the club's standing among firms and stakeholders.

The credible commitment problem towards firms' stakeholders is that after gaining a reputation for strong environmental standards program sponsors may then surreptitiously dilute the standards—capitalizing on reputations' sticky nature (Weigelt and Camerer, 1988; Schultz, Mouritsen, and Gabrielsen, 2001). Anticipating this possibility, stakeholders may withhold the benefits from members until they are confident that sponsors are committed to maintaining the stringency of club standards. Voluntary clubs established by industry associations may be especially vulnerable to such credible commitment problems.

The credible commitment problem towards potential participants is that the voluntary club may tighten its standards after firms have joined, opportunistically exploiting the fact that exiting the program might be costly for firms. Club membership might require investments in infrastructure, technology or competency assets that are specific to the program and are difficult to apply to alternative uses (Williamson, 1985). Firms may be reluctant to join a club that requires asset specific investments that would leave them vulnerable to opportunistic exploitation by sponsors. Retribution costs may also impede firms' ability to leave a program, as stakeholders are likely to punish firms for exiting the club. Because the exit option is costly, voluntary clubs, particularly those sponsored by NGOs, need to signal to potential members that they will not opportunistically tighten the program standards.

We can identify three institutional features voluntary clubs can adopt to counter credible commitment problems. First, voluntary clubs grant external stakeholders—including participating firms and NGOs—political authority in any future changes of its rules, such as the procedures such as the notice and comment provisions of the United States under the Administrative Procedures Act.[21] Voluntary clubs can therefore stipulate "rules for making rules" or "collective choice rules" as Ostrom (1990) terms them, in ways that assure stakeholders that club requirements will not be diluted or changed surreptitiously. The industry-sponsored Sustainable Forestry Initiative is an interesting example of a voluntary club which has designed collective choice rules to mitigate its credible commitment problem. The club sponsors have sought to tie their own hands by creating an External Review Board comprising of "18 independent experts representing conservation, environmental, professional, academic, and public organizations. . . . The volunteer Panel provides external oversight with their independent review of the current SFI program while seeking steady improvements in sustainable forestry practices.[22]

The second credible commitment mechanism is stipulating super-majority voting rules for changing club standards. Consider the case of the International Organization for Standardization which requires that new standards it develops as well as changes in existing standards need to be approved by two-thirds of the members that have participated in the standards development process, and by three-fourths of all voting members of the club.[23] Thus, super-majority voting rules mean the standards cannot be changed easily. In any case, the process of standard development is reasonably transparent and outside observers, even when not represented on technical committees, have a fair amount of information about the deliberations.

A third institutional feature for addressing the credible commitment problem is to submit the voluntary club to an external certification standard how the program is managed. Indeed, we can see the beginnings of an interesting example of a supra voluntary club for certifying quality of other voluntary clubs. The International Social and Environmental Accreditation and Labeling (ISEAL) Alliance is an international NGO made up of international standards setting organizations.[24] ISEAL's Code of Good Practice for Social and Environmental Standard Setting, launched in 2004, is a set of program standards to guide the development, implementation and oversight of voluntary social and environmental clubs. The Code's standards specify processes for developing a program's standards, such as extensive stakeholder participation, and procedures for handling disputes. The Code's monitoring and enforcement mechanisms are being refined: there is currently a peer review procedure in place and ISEAL is in the process of developing tools and processes to assess compliance. The goal is to help sponsors develop their clubs by providing best practices benchmarks, and provide governments, NGOs, citizens and other stakeholders a way to evaluate the quality of different voluntary clubs.

Reputational Commons or Reputations Held in Common

Voluntary clubs are sometimes tailored for firms in a single industry, such as the chemical industry's Responsible Care program or the forestry industry's Sustainable Forestry Initiative, and at other times for firms across industries, such as ISO 14001 and the Performance Track. Industry clubs raise important theoretical issues about the nature of the branding benefits. It is clear that an industry can acquire a reputation of its own. The tobacco industry, for example, has a reputation for misleading advertising, stifling research about the health consequences of smoking, and so on, even if individual tobacco companies engage in such skullduggery to varying degrees and perhaps some not at all. Yet, an industry's reputation reflects on its individual firms in that people make inferences about a firm based on the reputation of the industry in which it operates.[25] It is therefore fair to say that firms operating in a given industry share a common reputation, or to put it differently, the industry reputation is held in common by firms. Below we conduct a theoretical analysis of industry reputations, and the nature of the policy problem underlying them.

Some scholars characterize industry reputations and industry clubs as "reputational commons" and relate their production and appropriation to the broader literature on common-pool resources (Barnett and King, 2002). We believe a more appropriate characterization would be to say industry reputations are "held in common" by members of the industry. As we show below, a *reputation held in common* by firms operating together in an industry (or as part of the same cross-industry voluntary program) is not equivalent to a *reputational commons*, in a common-pool resource sense (Ostrom, 1990; Dolsak and Ostrom, 2003). The distinction between the two is not about semantics because the collective action dilemmas—and the institutional means to solving them—are quite different for each.

The reputational commons concept can indeed be confusing, so we begin with some conceptual clarifications. The phrase "commons" has a specific connotation in political economy and public policy. Where a club good is non-rival and excludable, a common-pool resource (often simply called a "common") is rival and non-excludable.

To illustrate the difference between a good held in common and a common-pool resource, it is useful to return to Garrett Hardin's (1968) pasture, a celebrated example of a common-pool resource. For Hardin the tragedy of the commons arises because one herdsman cannot exclude others from increasing the flock size, dictated by the non-excludability dimension in the Ostrom (1990) framework. Because the pasture can support only up to a certain number of sheep (rivalry dimension), adding additional sheep decreases the availability of the good for other herdsmen, leaving each herdsman with the incentives to increase the size of their own herd because s/he expects others to do so in short order. The herdsman wants to be the first-mover—the first to put more sheep on the common—lest s/he loses out on gains from the commons. The herdsman realizes that by adding a sheep to his heard s/he enjoys the benefit of raising an extra sheep but bears only a small portion of the incremental cost associated with degrading the pasture. Thus, it is rational for the herdsman to add sheep to his herd without limit. As all herdsmen seek to appropriate the resource before others do, the commons are degraded. Note that the rivalry dimension is accentuated by the non-excludability dimension because the first-mover advantage associated with over-consumption compels participants to move quickly.

Hardin's pastures are open access resources: anybody can appropriate them and to any extent they want. To avert the commons tragedy, the access to the resource needs to limited only to a given group of herdsmen. That is, rules are required to create excludability. Addressing the rivalry dimension also reduces the commons tragedy. If rules limit herd size, then every herdsman will be prohibited from increasing the herd size indefinitely and will also have the assurance that others face the same constraint. With diminished possibility of facing a "sucker's payoff," the herdsman is less likely to over consume the pasture. In sum, the solution to the commons problem is to establish property rights that limit the size of the group allowed to appropriate the commons (excludability) *and* the amount each group member is allowed to appropriate (rivalry).

Applying the herding analogy to industry reputations suggests focusing on whether a given industry's reputation is rivalorous (as in common-pool resources) or not rivalrous (as in club goods). We suggest that an industry's (or voluntary club's) reputation is a non-rivalrous good held in common by firms of the industry (or club). A firm "consumes" a positive (or negative) industry reputation by enjoying goodwill (or suffering ill will) from stakeholders that see the industry—and consequently the firm—in a positive (or negative) light. While a firm has "consumed" the reputation in this way, this reputation is still available for other firms to "consume": they too can receive goodwill (ill will) from stakeholders as a consequence of the industry's reputation. If the reputation were rivalrous, once the first firm had "consumed" the reputation, it would no longer be available for the second firm to consume, and firms would consequently race to lower their own environmental standards to exploit the limited and dwindling stock of industry reputation— a dynamic similar to Hardin's herdsmen racing to add sheep to their heard before the pasture is completely overgrazed by sheep of other herdsmen. Since the industry reputation is non-rivalrous, it is not a common-pool resource.

Actions of one firm in an industry have positive or negative consequences for the other industry firms, which is what we mean when we say that the industry reputation is "held in common" by firms. Environmental mishaps by one firm impose negative reputational externalities on other firms in the industry, thereby diminishing the industry's reputation. Firms in an industry realize they all sink or swim together: one firm cannot externalize the costs of the diminished industry reputation on to others. While Hardin's herdsman bears only 1/nth of the incremental cost of his commons consumption, firms all bear the full brunt of the declining industry reputation simply because all firms get tarred by the same negative brush.

The upshot of this discussion is that industry reputations are a shared, non-rivalrous resource. Actions that enhance an industry's reputation, such as by creating an industry-level club, create non-rivalrous benefits for all and actions that diminish an industry's reputations impose non-rivalrous costs for all. The implication for institutional design is that clubs rules should focus on the excludability dimension so that the reputational gains of taking beyond-compliance environmental actions are appropriated only by members of the club. Because free-rider incentives are strong—firms in an industry cannot be excluded from enjoying the benefits of a positive industry reputation—industry clubs need to ensure that all firms in the industry join the club. This explains why industry associations such as the American Chemistry Council and the American Forest and Paper Association *require* their members to join their own voluntary clubs.

In contrast, solving the commons problems requires not only an exclusion mechanism, but also a partitioning mechanism for solving the rivalry problem. A partitioning mechanism would enable the division of the reputation among industry members. In the herdsman example, an exclusion mechanism would limit the number of herdsman allowed to use the pasture while a partitioning mechanism would limit the number of sheep any herdsman can place into the common pasture. The partitioning mechanism would counter herdsmen's incentives to move first and quickly consume the commons before other herdsmen did the same. We do not think any industry-level club has mechanisms to partition its shared reputation among its members, most likely because the industry reputation is a non-rivalrous good that is quite difficult to partition.

Conclusion

Several policy implications follow from our club perspective and our typology. Voluntary clubs offer no magic bullet to respond to environmental challenges. Policymakers need to assess the situations under which such programs can usefully supplement public regulation. Further, there is no single blueprint for a voluntary club. One needs to carefully assess the population characteristics as well as the institutional context in which the club functions to decide about appropriate stringency of club standards as well as monitoring and enforcement rules.

Designing voluntary clubs requires balancing competing imperatives. On the one hand, to enhance the club's credibility with external stakeholders, sponsors may prefer stringent standards. On the other hand, such standards may lead to low membership—and smaller network effects and scale economies in building the voluntary club brand—as few firms are able to meet demanding membership requirements. Further, with a roster of firms with established superior environmental credentials, club membership might not with increase environmental externalities simply because the firms already are at the top of the performance continuum. From a policy perspective, while such clubs might serve as a useful signaling tool and help stakeholders to differentiate the leaders from the laggards, the overall welfare gains associated with pollution reduction may be marginal. Thus, voluntary club sponsors might instead pitch club standards at a level appropriate for potential participants and acceptable to key stakeholders. Higher levels of heterogeneity in the pool of potential participants and among stakeholders are therefore likely to be associated with higher variations in standards adopted by voluntary clubs operating in the same policy context.

This book on Voluntary Environmental Programs is being published at an opportune time. While much has been written about voluntary clubs, it is time now to take stock of this research and carefully identify concepts that would transform this multi-disciplinary research into a theoretically grounded and coherent research program. We hope our paper makes a contribution towards this end.

Our key contribution is to provide a deductive framework for analyzing voluntary environmental programs and tying together the findings generated by the strong first-generation studies. Our framework should help future scholars by identifying voluntary environmental programs' i mportant institutional design features and the collective action problems programs must solve to be effective. Future research can draw on this paper as a unifying framework to study how the interplay among varying sponsors' attributes, stakeholder and institutional contexts, and firm characteristics influence programs' efficacy. The second generation research, we hope, will consider not only specific programs but systematically compare various programs, and hopefully compare voluntary clubs with other policy instruments.

Bibliography

Akerlof, G. A. The Market for 'Lemons': Quality Uncertainty and the Market Mechanism. *Quarterly Journal of Economics* 84(3), 488–500, 1970.

Alberini, A. and Segerson, K. Assessing Voluntary Programs to Improve Environmental Quality. *Environmental and Resource Economics,* 22 (1/2), 157–84, 2008.

Arora, S. and Cason, T. N. Why do Firms Volunteer to Exceed Environmental Regulations? Understanding Participation in EPA's 33/50 program. *Land Economics* 72(4), 413–432, 1996.

Ayres, I. and J. Braithwaite. *Responsive Regulation.* Oxford: Oxford University Press, 1992.

Barnett, M. L. and King, A. A. Good Fences Make Good Neighbors: An Institutional Explanation of Industry Self-Regulation. *Paper presented at the Academy of Management Best Paper Proceedings,* Atlanta, GA, 2002.

Bessen S. M. and Saloner, G. *Compatibility Standards and the Market for Telecommunication Services.* Santa Monica, CA: Rand, 1988.

Buchanan, J. M. An Economic Theory of Clubs. *Economica* 32: 1–14. 1965.

Carpenter, D. P. *The Forging of Bureaucratic Autonomy.* Princeton: Princeton University Press, 2001.

Cashore, B., Auld, G. and Newsom, D. *Governing Through Markets.* New Haven: Yale University Press, 2004.

Coase, R. H. The Problem of Social Cost. *Journal of Law and Economics* 3, 1–44, 1960.

———. *Nobel Prize Lecture.* http://www.nobel.se/economics/laureates/1991/coase-lecture.html; 1991. Retrieved on 08/15/2007.

Coglianese, C. and Nash, J. (Eds.). Regulating from the Inside. Washington, DC: Resources for the Future, 2001.

Cornes, R. and Sandler, T. *The Theory of Externalities, Public Goods, and Club Goods. 2nd edition.* Cambridge, UK: Cambridge University Press, 1996.

Darnall, N. and Carmin, J. Greener and Cleaner? *Policy Sciences* 38(2-3), 71–90, 2005.

Dasgupta, S., H. Hettige, and D. Wheeler. 2000. What improves environmental compliance? Evidence from Mexican Industry. *Journal of Environmental Economics and Management* 39:39–66.

Delmas, M. and Keller, A. Strategic Free Riding in Voluntary Programs: The Case of the US EPA Wastewise Program. *Policy Sciences* 38, 91–106, 2005.

Delmas, M. and Montes-Sancho, M. 2007. Voluntary Agreements to improve Environmental Quality. ISBER Working Paper; http://repositories.cdlib.org/cgi/viewcontent.cgi?article=1006&context=isber; accessed 08/23/2008, 2007.

Dolsak, N. and Ostrom, E. (Eds.) *The Commons in the New Millennium*. Cambridge, MA: The MIT Press, 2003.

Economist. Economist Intelligence Unit Democracy Index 2006 http://www.economist.com/media/pdf/DEMOCRACY_TABLE_2007_v3.pdf; accessed 08/08/2007, 2006.

Farrell, J. and Shapiro, G. Standardization, Compatibility, and Innovation. *Rand Journal of Economics* 16, 70–83, 1985.

Fiorinio, D. J. Rethinking Environmental Regulation. *Harvard Environmental Law Review* 23, 441–469, 1999.

Gunningham, N. A., Kagan, R. A., and Thornton, D. *Shades of Green*. Stanford, CA: Stanford University Press, 2003.

Harbaugh, R., Maxwell, J. and Roussillon, B. The Groucho Effect of Uncertain Standards. Working paper. Indiana University, Kelly School of Business Department of Business Economics and Public Policy, 2006.

Hardin, G. The Tragedy of the Commons, *Science* 162, 1243–1248, 1968.

Haufler, V. The Kimberly Process, Club Goods, and Public Enforcement of Private Programs. In *Voluntary Programs: A Club Theory Perspective*, edited by Matthew Potoski and Aseem Prakash, MIT Press, forthcoming.

Hobbes, T. (1651) Leviathan. http://oregonstate.edu/instruct/phl302/texts/hobbes/leviathan-c.html; accessed 03/02/2007.

Hoffman, A. J. *From Heresy to Dogma*. San Francisco, CA: New Lexington Press, 1997

King, A. and Lenox, M. Industry Self-regulation without Sanctions: The Chemical Industry's Responsible Care program. *Academy of Management Journal* 43 (August), 698–716, 2000.

Kotchen, M. and Klaas van d'Veld. An Economics Perspective on Treating Voluntary Programs as Clubs. In *Voluntary Programs: A Club Theory Perspective*, edited by Matthew Potoski and Aseem Prakash, MIT Press, forthcoming.

Lenox, M and Nash, J. Industry Self-Regulation and Adverse Selection: A Comparison Across Four Trade Association Programs. *Business Strategy and the Environment* 12(6), 343–356. 2003.

March, J. and Olsen, J. *Rediscovering Institutions*. New York: The Free Press, 1989

McGuire, M. Private Good Clubs and Public Goods Club. *Swedish Journal of Economics* 74, 84–99, 1972.

North, D. C. *Institutions, Institutional Change and Economic Performance*. New York: Cambridge University Press, 1990.

North, D. C. and Weingast, B. Constitutions and Commitment: Evolution of Institutions Governing Public Choice in 17th-Century England. *Journal of Economic History* 49, 803–832, 1989.

Olson, M., Jr. *The Logic of Collective Action*. Cambridge, MA: Harvard University Press. 1965.

Ostrom, E. *Governing the Commons*. Cambridge University Press, 1990.

Ostrom E., Walker, J. and Gardner, R. *Rules, Games, and Common-Pool Resources. University of Michigan Press*. 1994.

Pigou, A. C. *The Economics of Welfare*. 4th ed. London: McMillan. 1960[1920].

Porter, M. and van der Linde, C. Toward a New Conception of the Environment-Competitiveness Relationship. *Journal of Economic Perspectives* 9, 97–118, 1999.

Potoski, M. and Prakash, A. Green Clubs and Voluntary Governance: ISO 14001 and Firms' Regulatory Compliance. *American Journal of Political Science* 49(2), 235–248. 2004.

———. Covenants with Weak Swords: ISO 14001 and Firms' Environmental Performance. *Journal of Policy Analysis and Management* 24(4), 745–769. 2005.

Prakash, A. *Greening the Firm*. Cambridge, UK: Cambridge University Press, 2000.

Prakash, A. and Potoski, M. *The Voluntary Environmentalists*. Cambridge, UK: Cambridge University Press, 2006a.

———. (2006b) Racing to the Bottom? Globalization, Environmental Governance, and ISO 14001. *American Journal of Political Science* 50(2): 347–361, 2006b.

———. Investing Up: FDI and the Cross-National Diffusion of ISO 14001. *International Studies Quarterly* 51(3), 723–744, 2007.

Rees, J. The Development of Communitarian Regulation in the Chemical Industry. *Law and Policy* 19(4), 477–528, 1997.

Rivera, J., de Leon, P. and Koerber, C. Is Greener Whiter Yet? The Sustainable Slopes Program after Five Years. *Policy Studies Journal* 34(2), 195–224, 2006.

Rivera, J. and deLeon, P. Is Greener Whiter? The Sustainable Slopes Program and the Voluntary Environmental Performance of Western Ski Areas. *Policy Studies Journal* 32(3), 417–437, 2004.

Sasser, E., Prakash A., Cashore, B., and Auld, G. Direct Targeting as NGO Political Strategy: Examining Private Authority Regimes in the Forestry Sector. *Business and Politics* 8(3), 1–32, 2006.

Schultz, M, Mouritsen, J., and Gabrielsen, G. Sticky Reputation. *Corporate Reputation Review* 4(1), 24–41, 2001.

Tiebout, C. M. A Pure Theory of Public Expenditure. *Journal of Political Economy* 64, 416–424, 1956.

Welch, E.W., Mazur, A., and Bretschneider, S. Voluntary Behavior by Electric Utilities. *Journal of Policy Analysis and Management* 19 (Summer), 407–425, 2000.

Williamson, O. E. 1985. *Economic Institutions of Capitalism*. New York: Free Press.

Winter, S.C. and May, P. J. Motivation for Compliance with Environmental Regulations. *Journal of Policy Analysis and Management* 20(4), 675–698, 2001.

Wiseman, J. The Theory of Public Utility—An Empty Box. *Oxford Economic Papers* 9, 56–74, 1957.

Weigelt, K. and Camerer, C. Reputation and Corporate Strategy: A Review of Recent Theory and Applications. *Strategic Management Journal* 9(5), 443–454, 1988.

Notes

1.   There is parallel literature that focuses on recruitment to voluntary programs: who joins and why (Arora and Cason, 1999; Delmas and Montes-Sancho, 2007). Because the attributes of the participants are likely to influence program efficacy, recruitment and efficacy issues are linked. Given endogeneity issues, scholars studying program efficacy have sought to adopt a Heckman approach wherein the recruitment issue is dealt with in the selection equation.

2.   We owe this point to Tim Büthe.

3.   We owe this point to David Baron.

4.   This could also be viewed as the "social license" to operate (Gunningham et al., 2003)

5.   As Alberini and Segerson (2002:17) note: "under a voluntary approach, a polluter will not participate unless his payoff (broadly defined) is at least as high as it would be without participation."

6.   We recognize that there is a well established literature examining how factors such enforcement frequency, sanctioning, actor preferences, sociological factors, and procedural fairness influence regulatee's propensities to obey laws (Hoffman, 1997; Winter and May, 2001). Space considerations do not allow us to elaborate on these issues.

7.   *The Economist* (2007) labels only 28 out of 167 countries as full democracies.

8.   Of the 177 countries examined in the 2007 Foreign Policy Failed State Index, 32 are listed as failed (Alert category), and another 97 in the danger of failing (Warning category).
http://www.fundforpeace.org/web/index.php?option=com_content&task=view&id=99&It emid=140; accessed 08/08/2007.

9.   It is analytically important to differentiate benefits that have characteristics of private goods (rival and excludable) from ones that have characteristics of club goods (non-rival excludable). There is a tendency to subsume clubs benefits under private benefits (see, for example, Delmas and Keller, 2005).

10.   Porter and van der Linde (1995) assume that firms systematically fail to uncover opportunities to reduce costs and well designed governmental regulations can help firms identify such opportunities. While this might have been true in the 1970s and the 1980s, we are not aware of evidence that suggests that such opportunities continue in the 21st century. There is a further danger: an excessive reliance on rosy win-win scenarios distracts the attention from the trade-offs environmental issues entail, and therefore the politics they engender. While firms should certainly be encouraged to identify inefficient pollution, public policy should not put excessive faith in such measures.

11.   Regarding the importance of the institutional context for branding benefits, our research on the cross-country ISO 14001 diffusion suggests that that ISO 14001 adoption levels in importing countries influence ISO 14001 adoption levels in exporting countries (Prakash and Potoski, 2006b). Further, the commitment to ISO 14001 in the home countries of multinational corporations influences ISO 14001 uptake in the host countries of their subsidiaries (Prakash and Potoski, 2007).

12.   In his Nobel Prize acceptance speech, Coase (1991) points to the tendency of his critics to benchmark imperfect markets against perfect governments. He calls for recognizing that all institutions fail and for undertaking comparative analysis of how various imperfect institutions fare in the context of a given objective. This important caution needs to be exercised by detractors (who tend to focus on club failures and ignore

governmental failures) and supporters (who tend to focus on government failures and overlook club failures) of voluntary clubs.

13. If stakeholders are unable to distinguish between effective voluntary clubs and greenwashes, they may treat all programs as failures, and fail to reward any firm for its program participation. Such problems could lead to a "lemons market" (Akerloff 1970) for voluntary environmental programs in which weak programs drive effective ones out of the market. What is important for clubs—and perhaps even central—is that they build and communicate a brand identity that stakeholders understand and find credible.

14. Arguably, shirking might be inadvertent. While there might be goal convergence between participants and club sponsors, the participants may not correctly understand club requirements or possess means to adhere to them. While this is theoretically possible, we have not found examples in the context of management standards where clubs requirements are seldom in the form of complex, technical terms that some participants might not comprehend. Club requirements are often quite simple and straightforward. Hence, we expect that much of the shirking is likely to be willful.

15. While it is theoretically simple to talk about club standards, some stakeholders might find it difficult to evaluate the extent to which specific standards generate positive environmental externalities. Sophisticated stakeholders, such as well funded environmental groups or government regulators, may be able to interpret a club's brand signals. Less sophisticated stakeholders such as ordinary consumers may need some assistance in translating the brand signal into useful information for guiding their purchases. They may take cues from established actors such as NGOs which are known for their technical expertise. Some may seek other types of information shortcuts, such as the attributes of the sponsor, to evaluate a club's brand signal.

16. This can also be modeled as agency conflict where club participants are agents working on behalf of club sponsors to produce positive environmental externalities.

17. See Rees (1997) work on communitarian regulations in this regard.

18. Monitoring can have four variants: first party (internal auditing), second party (conducted by firms in the same industry as in Responsible Care prior to 2002), third party (conducted by accredited auditors but paid for by the audited party), and fourth party (conducted by accredited auditors that have no financial relationship with the audited party). First- and second-party auditing are not considered credible. To keep our framework simple, we do not discuss them. Fourth-party auditing is very rare and therefore less interesting to examine from a policy perspective. By and large, third-party auditing is the gold standard in voluntary programs.

19. Kotchen and Van d'Veld (forthcoming) are notable exceptions.

20. However, there are situations where industry clubs are established not by firms but by non-governmental organizations that wish to regulate firms' environmental policies. In the forestry industry, non-governmental organizations established the Forest Stewardship Council and began lobbying forestry firms to join it. Forestry firms were not comfortable with this club simply because they did not want an adversarial actor to decide the stringency of club standards (Sasser et al., 2006). Thus, key forestry firms sought to and succeeded in establishing an industry-sponsored club, the Sustainable Forestry Initiative.

21. Environmental groups might believe that government-sponsored clubs are more credible in relation to industry-sponsored clubs. This might be because they typically have greater access to influence program design and are therefore are less prone to industry capture (Ayres & Braithwaite, 1992).

22. http://www.sfiprogram.org/erp.cfm; accessed 08/21/2007.

23. http://www.iso.org/iso/en/stdsdevelopment/whowhenhow/how.html;accessed 08/21/2007.

24. http://www.isealalliance.org/; accessed 08/21/2007.

25. In addition to industry reputation, firms have reputations and so do their products. Toyota Camry's aggregate reputation is a function of Camry's reputation, Toyota's reputation, and the Japanese automobile industry's reputation. Which reputation type will dominate in specific contexts, and why, is a question worthy of further research.

Chapter 6

The Diffusion of Voluntary International Management Standards: Responsible Care, ISO 9000 and ISO 14001 in the Chemical Industry

Magali Delmas and Ivan Montiel

Introduction

The last two decades have been marked by the development and diffusion of many industry voluntary environmental standards. Through these private or non-governmental regimes, firms commit voluntarily to improve their environmental management practices beyond compliance. These include, for example, the international environmental management standard ISO 14001, the Responsible Care standard for the chemical industry, the Sustainable Forestry Initiative (SFI) standard and the Forest Sustainable Council (FSC) standard. While these standards bear some similarities, they also differ on important characteristics related to the type of actors who make the rules, the industries targeted, the content of the standard, how commitments are verified and whether compliance mechanisms exist. When trying to understand the factors that explain the diffusion of such a diverse set of standards, one wonders whether the same set of conditions independently explains their adoption or whether their development is interdependent. In other words, does the initial adoption of some environmental standards trigger or hamper the adoption of other standards? Do standards intermingle?

Scholars analyzing the factors that explain the international diffusion of voluntary environmental standards such as ISO 14001 have emphasized the role of national institutional environments and the role of forces related to trade (Christmann & Taylor, 2001, Corbett & Kirsch, 2001, Delmas, 2005, Kollman &

145

Prakash, 2001). However, scholars have typically analyzed these standards independently through cross industry analyses and little is known about their interaction at the industry level. In this paper, we argue that environmental management standards should not be analyzed in isolation but in conjunction with other standards, because the initial adoption of some standards could explain the adoption of others.

There are two competing arguments to explain the interaction between environmental management standards. The first considers standards as exclusive of each other and competing with each other. Indeed, some scholars have explained the emergence of voluntary standards as a self-regulatory tool used by industry to hamper the creation of more stringent regulations or standards (King & Lenox, 2000, Prakash, 1999). For example, the Responsible Care program was initially set-up by the chemical industry to avoid potential regulations following the Bhopal accident (King & Lenox, 2000, Prakash, 1999). As another example, in the forestry industry the SFI standard was launched by the American Forest & Paper Association (AF&PA) within two years of the FSC standard, and was established by a diverse group of stakeholders including representatives from environmental and social groups. Since 1995, the SFI standard, which was less stringent than the FSC standard has enrolled roughly eight times as many North American acres (136 million) in its certification scheme and more total acreage worldwide than the FSC has done in 10 years (Overdevest, 2004). Some researchers have cast doubts on the effectiveness of industry codes of conducts and whether these could be used as a protection against more stringent standards (King & Lenox, 2000). Are industry standards actually effective in hampering the adoption of more stringent initiatives? Is it more difficult for more "stringent" standards to diffuse if less stringent standards are already established by the industry?

The alternative argument states that industry standards could provide information and learning opportunities for firms and could potentially pave the way for future and more stringent standards. The argument infers that with an increase in the number of adopters, uncertainties related to the risks and benefits of such voluntary practices will fade. Voluntary standards may become common practice and become the norm accepted by a broader range of firms.

Of course, the strength of each argument varies according to the specific characteristics of the standards and of their potential combination. Some standards may be similar and these similarities may make them compete with each other while other standards may complement each other. Additionally, these standards do not operate in an institutional vacuum. The characteristics of national governments and civil society should also mitigate the relationship between standards.

To understand the diffusion of international standards we need to define a comprehensive model that includes interactions between standards as well as interactions between standards and their institutional environment. In this paper we develop and test a model that explains the adoption of voluntary standards within an industry. We develop hypotheses related to interactions between standards, the role of support groups such as international NGOs and governments, and forces related to trade to explain the international diffusion of voluntary environmental standards.

Within the context of the chemical industry, we test whether the adoption of the international environmental management system ISO 14001 was favored or hampered by the adoption of other management quality, health, safety and environment standards namely Responsible Care and ISO 9000. Both ISO 9000 and ISO 14001 were designed by the International Organization for Standardization (ISO), an international non-governmental network of the national standards institutes of 156 countries. Responsible Care was developed by the chemical industry only. We also test whether the European Eco-Management & Audit Scheme (EMAS) issued by the European Commission to certify environmental management systems (EMSs) among European organizations has an impact on the adoption of ISO 14001. We test our hypotheses in 113 countries during the period from 2000 to 2003.

Our results show that voluntary management standards in the chemical industry feed on rather than compete with each other. We find that the propensity of the industry to self-organize may facilitate the adoption of ISO 14001. Furthermore, we find that the adoption of ISO 14001 may be easier for companies that have adopted the international standard ISO 9000. In addition, we find some support for the hypothesis that governmental endorsement for voluntary environmental management standards in the form of the adoption of EMAS helps the diffusion of ISO 14001. Finally, our results show that the role of civil society in raising the level of concern toward environmental issues also helps explain diffusion of an international environmental management standard such as ISO 14001. We contribute to the literature on the diffusion of policy innovations by showing the cumulative effect of management standards and the importance of national institutional environments in facilitating the diffusion of international standards. Currently, there are active discussions in policy circles regarding whether environmental standards should be designed for specific industries or for organizations across industries. We contribute to this debate by showing that both approaches are complementary rather than in competition.

In the first part of the paper, we provide a review of the literature on the diffusion of international voluntary standards and describe the main characteristics of the voluntary standards that are the focus of our analysis. We subsequently develop hypotheses on the international diffusion of ISO 14001 based on three main mechanisms, namely cultural norms, support groups and trade ties. The third section of the paper is dedicated to the description of the different variables used to measure each of the factors influencing the adoption of the standard and the methodology to test the hypotheses. The fourth section discusses the results of the statistical analysis. The last two sections of the paper discuss the policy implications of our research and a conclusion.

Literature Review

Diffusion is the process by which an innovation is communicated through certain channels over time among the members of a social system (Rogers, 1995). The literature on policy diffusion is concerned with the chronological and geographic patterns of the adoption of a policy innovation across government units (Mossberger & Wolman, 2003). This literature has identified three main driving forces by which a policy occurs: the dynamics of the international system, national factors and the characteristics of the policy instrument (Tews, Busch, & Jorgens, 2003). Voluntary codes of conduct differ from traditional governmental policies because they are initiated by private actors rather than governments. Even though private governance mechanisms differ from policy processes, they do not operate in a political vacuum. The growing literature on the diffusion of international standards indicates that a complex interplay of factors influences the international spread of voluntary standards. Scholars have shown how the pattern of interactions between businesses and government within a country influences corporate decisions to adopt international standards (Delmas, 2002, Moon & deLeon, 2005, Potoski & Prakash, 2004). The main finding is that a less adversarial government stance toward a firm enhances the adoption of ISO 14001. Countries that have a long history of cooperation and trust between government and businesses can lower the uncertainty perception about their ISO 14001 investment and are likely to promote ISO 14001 (Moon & deLeon, 2005). The second important diffusion mechanism of international voluntary standards is related to the openness of the country to trade, where firms mimic the behavior of other firms adopting voluntary standards in other countries. For example, Kollman and Prakash found that trade linkages encourage ISO 14001 adoption if countries' major export markets have adopted this voluntary regulation (Kollman & Prakash, 2001).

While these studies emphasize the role of national institutional environments and openness to trade, little research has investigated how specific characteristics of a standard may impact its diffusion and how standards interact with each other. The only exception relates to the link between ISO 9000 the quality management standard and ISO 14001 which has been identified in several articles (Christmann & Taylor; 2001; Delmas, 2006; Moon & deLeon, 2005; Prakash & Potoski, 2006). One of the reasons why little research exists on the interaction between ISO 14001 and other industry standards is that most of these studies use a cross industry approach. This approach can be explained by the fact that industry level information has been made available only recently by the International Organization for Standardization (ISO).

Responsible Care, ISO 14001, ISO 9000 and EMAS

International voluntary management standards have been identified as private governance mechanisms established, monitored and enforced by private actors to govern their own conduct (Prakash, 2000). We describe below the characteristics of the four standards examined by this study. These standards can be distinguished based on who makes the rule, the content of the rule, how the commitment is verified and whether compliance mechanisms exist. First, some of these standards are designed by industry associations while others represent multi-stakeholders initiatives involving environmental NGOs and government or industry representatives. Second, some standards are industry specific while others are applicable to a wide range of industries. Third, some include third party verification while others do not. Finally, some include performance measurements while others focus on processes. Table 6.1 compares Responsible Care, ISO 14001, ISO 9000 and EMAS based on these main characteristics.

Responsible Care

Responsible Care is an Environmental, Health and Safety (EHS) voluntary code of conduct within the chemical industry (Howard, Nash, & Ehrenfeld, 2000). It is developed, enforced and monitored by national chemical associations. The objective of the program was to regain public trust by demonstrating that chemical firms could be responsible corporate citizens who could self-regulate (King & Lenox, 2000). A related objective was to limit the significant negative externalities imposed on the whole chemical industry by accidents occurring in any firm (Prakash, 2000). The program was first developed in 1985 in Canada and in 1988 in the United States. Today 52 national chemical associations in different countries have joined the program (ICCA, 2005) (See Appendix 6.1) National chemical trade associations can mandate or advise members to adopt Responsible Care. Members conduct self-evaluations annually and rate themselves on a scale and report their evaluation to the chemical association (Prakash, 2000).

Table 6.1 Comparison of Responsible Care, ISO14001, ISO9000 and EMAS

Voluntary Program	Responsible Care	ISO 14001
Date of publication	1996	1987
Who makes the rules?	Industry	NGOs, national standard organizations and industry
What is the content of the standard?	Environmental Health & Safety management system	Environmental Management System (EMS)
How is the commitment verified/compliance mechanisms?	Trader association	Third party certification
Audience	Chemical Industry	Multi Industry

	ISO 9000	EMAS
Date of publication	1985 in Canada	1993 in Europe
Who makes the rules?	NGOs, national standard organizations and industry	European Commission
What is the content of the standard?	Quality management	EMS and environmental
How the commitment Verified/compliance Mechanisms?	Third party certification	Third party certification
Audience	Multi Industry	Multi Industry

ISO 14001

In 1996, ISO formally adopted the international environmental management standard ISO 14001, to implement and certify Environmental Management System (EMS). An EMS is one of the tools that an organization can use to implement an environmental policy. It consists of "a number of interrelated elements that function together to help a company manage, measure, and improve the environmental aspects of its operations" (Welford, 1996).

Unlike Responsible Care, ISO 14001 is designed to be adopted by any type of organization in any industrial sector. But the main difference between the Responsible Care program and ISO 14001 is that ISO 14001 can be third party certified.[1] Although organizations seeking ISO 14001 can self-declare, there are greater benefits with third party certification notably in reinforcing the credibility of certifications with customers, regulatory agencies, and the community. Because of third party certification, ISO 14001 can be more costly than Responsible Care. The costs of certification vary widely, depending on the size of the company, the nature of its operation, and the environmental system already in place. Estimates range from less than $50,000 for small firms to greater than $200,000 for larger firms (Watkins & Gutzwiller, 1999). These estimations involve the certification process only and do not take into account the cost of organizational changes that firms may have to carry out to attain the ISO 14001 standard. We therefore need to understand the circumstances under which a chemical company would be willing to incur the cost of adopting ISO 14001 in addition to Responsible Care.

ISO 9000

ISO 14001 was developed on the heels of the success of the international quality standard ISO 9000 which was initially issued in 1986. ISO 9000 is concerned with the steps taken by organizations to fulfill customers' quality requirements, applicable regulatory requirements, while aiming to enhance customer satisfaction, and achieve continual improvement of its performance in pursuit of these objectives (ISO, 2005). By December of 2003, more than half million facilities had adopted the standard. ISO 9000 and ISO 14001 bear similarities in their processes but they aim to improve different elements of an organization (quality versus the environmental impact of operations).

EMAS

In 1993, the European Commission adopted the Eco-Management and Audit Scheme (EMAS) Regulation, which established a voluntary system in which industrial sites could participate by implementing an EMS and pledge to achieve continual improvement in environmental performance (Kollman & Prakash, 2002).[2] Although voluntary, EMAS was established by the European Commission, an executive body composed of members of the European Union countries, rather than from industry or non-governmental organizations. The standard requires not only third party certification but also companies to issue a public statement with information on their environmental performance (Delmas, 2002).

These four standards represent a diverse set of standards which allows us to study the interactions between the various standards. What are the advantages of adopting only one standard as compared to adopting several standards? Would the advantages of one solution versus the other vary according to the national context? Previous analyses on the Responsible Care–ISO 14001 link based on the US context found that Responsible Care participants were less likely to get ISO 14001 certification (King, Lenox, & Terlaak, 2005). One explanation was that many chemical firms already had well functioning EMS such as Responsible Care and modifying their EMS to agree with ISO 14001 was perceived as an unnecessary cost (Prakash, 1999). These previous studies have focused exclusively on the United States and it is unclear whether the results would hold in other national contexts. More evidence exists relating to the link between ISO 9000 and ISO 14001, although some of it is mixed. Some research shows that firms that adopt ISO 9000 are more likely to adopt ISO 14001 (Darnall, 2003, Delmas, 2002, 2005; Moon & deLeon, 2005, Potoski & Prakash, 2004) while other analyses have not found a consistent positive relationship between both standards (King, Lenox, & Terlaak, 2005).

ISO 14001 is particularly suited to studying the question of the interaction between standards for several reasons. First, it was issued 11 years after Responsible Care, 10 years after the ISO 9000 standard, and a couple of years after EMAS. Furthermore, ISO 14001 exhibits a number of features desirable for econometric identification. ISO 14001 was adopted in various countries over time and a great disparity exists in terms of adoption rates between specific countries. By December 2003, a total of 66,070 firms had adopted ISO 14001 in 113 countries. In the United States, the total number of ISO 14001 certificates was 3,553; while in Europe, the number of certificates was 31,997. With reference to the chemical sector, in 2003 there were 3,761 certificates worldwide. By December 2003, Japan already had 907 chemical facilities that were ISO 14001 certified, while the United States had only 135 (ISO, 2003). See Appendix 6.2 for a depiction of the number of ISO 14001 certificates by country in the chemical industry in 2003.

Hypothesis Development

The main finding of the diffusion theory is that, for most members of a social system, the innovation-decision depends heavily on the innovation-decisions of other members of the system (Rogers, 1995). It is well established that the introduction of an innovation may affect the diffusion process of another innovation, if the two are sufficiently related by function or application (Alpert, 1994). Two opposing views are related to the role of previous innovation on the likelihood of diffusion of additional innovations. The first view relates to arguments of path dependency where firms are locked-in with existing technologies and incur high coordination costs to switch to new ones. The second view relates to learning associated with the initial innovation that helps firms adopt subsequent innovations. Therefore, in some scenarios the previous adoption of specific innovations might help the subsequent diffusion of new ones. However, the opposite reality is also possible, where the co-existence of innovations is hampered by one dominant innovation that prevents others from diffusing.

What is the case for the cumulative diffusion of international management standards? The implementation of an EMS and the subsequent ISO 14001 certification can be considered as administrative innovations, rather than a technological innovation. A technological innovation is an idea for a new product, process or service while an administrative innovation pertains to the policies of recruitment, allocation of resources, and the structuring of tasks, authority and reward (Daft, 1978). Despite these differences, studies on administrative innovations show that their diffusion process has the same structure as the diffusion of technological innovations, i.e., a logistic function resulting in a S-shaped curve (Teece, 1980, Venkatraman, Loh, & Koh, 1994). We discuss below competing hypotheses on the role of the adoption of previous management standards on the adoption of later management standards.

Norms of Exclusivity

The diffusion literature related to the impact of path dependency on the adoption of standards, highlights the difficulty that firms have in changing their technological trajectory once they have invested significantly in a standard (Bessen & Saloner, 1988, Katz & Shapiro, 1985). Firms with significant investments in alternative EMSs would find it less attractive to modify their existing EMS to fit the ISO 14001 standard (Prakash, 1999). This is particularly true if the new standard is associated with uncertainty related to its benefits and costs, something that is particularly relevant for an emerging standard such as ISO 14001. In addition, the adoption of ISO 14001 may be riskier than the adoption of Responsible Care. In the case of ISO 14001, the legal issue that can prevent some firms from considering the implementation of ISO 14001, is the potential discovery of regulatory violations that firms have not yet identified or resolved. ISO 14001 may lead to the discovery of non-compliance with applicable environmental regulations (Delmas, 2000). The identification of violations during the implementation phase or during self-audits or third party audits can lead to potential liabilities (Orts & Murray, 1997). As Responsible Care did not require environmental audits, the issue of potential liabilities did not arise. In addition, Responsible Care initially did not face the problem of path dependency since most chemical firms did not have established EMSs when Responsible Care was created (Prakash, 1999).

Norms are common practices whose value to an actor stems largely from their prevalence in a population (Elkins & Simmons, 2005). In the case of Responsible Care, firms may be subjected to norms of "exclusivity." As Potoski and Prakash (2005) have demonstrated, voluntary standards can be perceived as "clubs" where firms receive specific benefits because they belong to a specific community. Responsible Care and ISO 14001 are examples of club goods as one cannot price the discrete units of goodwill benefits generated by them. Firms will have incentives to pay membership fees only if such benefits are made excludable (Prakash, 1999). Can a firm belong to several clubs without endangering the reputation of their original club? If the norm within the industry is to participate in the "industry" standard, would memberships in multiple voluntary initiatives jeopardize the exclusivity of the industry "club" membership? In that case, norms established by the industry could potentially work against multiple memberships. As Prakash stated: "the CMA needs to protect the brand equity of Responsible Care in the light of competition from initiatives such as ISO 14001 (...). If ISO 14001 become the de facto international standard, the chemical industry will lose its distinctive advantage vis-à-vis other industries in terms of claiming long-standing commitments to safer EHS practices" (Prakash, 2000, p.202). Firms may therefore be subjected to norms of exclusivity where they are discouraged to participate in competing standards. In light of these arguments, we develop the following hypothesis related to the relationship between the adoption of Responsible Care and ISO 14001:

Hypothesis 1. The greater the diffusion of Responsible Care in a particular country, the less the number of ISO 14001 certificates in the chemical industry within that country.

Norms and Learning

The opposite argument regarding the interaction between voluntary standards relates to how norms evolve with the initial adoption of a standard. First, firms that have prior EMS implementation experience may be less likely to be skeptical about ISO 14001 certification. This is especially true because of the initial uncertainty related to the benefits of the standard. Furthermore, it might be easier to certify with ISO 14001 if a firm has already implemented the Responsible Care program. Although a few exceptions exist, in most cases the environmental management aspect of the Responsible Care program will be equivalent to the ISO 14001 requirements. Indeed, in some countries such as Lithuania, Norway or India, national chemical associations support the adoption of the ISO 14001 standard within their member companies (ICCA, 2005). Responsible Care firms will incur lower costs to access the information required to implement the ISO 14001-based EMS than firms that have not implemented any type of EMS. In addition, experts in the chemical processing industry state that by upgrading an existing Responsible Care to comply with ISO 14001, a company can add depth, rigor and credibility to its existing programs (Gilbertsen & Kowalski, 2004). We therefore predict that:

Hypothesis 2A. The greater the diffusion of Responsible Care in a particular country, the greater the number of ISO 14001 certificates in the chemical industry within that country.

The relationship between ISO 9000 and ISO 14001 is different from the one between Responsible Care and ISO 14001. ISO 9000 has become the norm for those organizations that aim to certify their quality management practices. ISO 14001 somehow complements the quality management system by establishing a similar system to manage environmental impact but addressing slightly different audiences. While ISO 9000 aims to improve quality and facilitate business objectives, ISO 14001 aims to improve environmental performance and facilitate relationships with not only market actors, but also non-market actors such as regulatory agencies and NGOs. There are clear economies of scope between both standards, and successful implementation of ISO 9000 facilitates the adoption of ISO 14001. In fact, because of the similarities between these standards and their implementation, consultants and certifiers of ISO 9000 also became consultants and certifiers of ISO 14001 (Mazurek, 2001). These consultants and certifiers could provide information about ISO 14001 certification during the process of advising their clients about ISO 9000. Therefore, in a country where a significant number of firms have adopted the ISO 9000 standard, it is likely that consultants and firms will have more knowledge about how to implement ISO 14001 than in a country where few ISO 9000 standards have been adopted. The role of these consultants and certifiers may be the key at the take-off phase of any innovation, when firms need help in understanding how to implement a management standard. Thus, we predict the following relationship between the quality standard ISO 9000 and the environmental standard ISO 14001:

Hypothesis 2B. The greater the number of ISO 9000 certificates in the chemical industry within a country, the greater the number of ISO 14001 certificates in the chemical industry within that country.

Support Groups: The Role of Government and Civil Society

Non-governmental initiatives such as international environmental standards do not operate in a cultural and institutional vacuum. Research has shown that voluntary initiatives operate under the shadow of the government and are facilitated by an active civil society (Delmas & Terlaak, 2001, Moon & deLeon, 2005). In addition to the influence that the previous adoption of management standards might have in the diffusion of ISO 14001, the position of other types of stakeholders such as the government and the civil society within each country toward international environmental issues and environmental voluntary management standards, could also shape the diffusion process.

The Role of Government

Scholars in institutional economics have analyzed how the interplay between government action and the structure of a nation's political institutions can shape the ability of a company to make private investments (Levy & Spiller, 1994). In particular, researchers note that policy uncertainty results in lower levels of investment and that even favorable government policies need to be credible if they are to facilitate investments (Henisz, 2000). The credibility and effectiveness of a government's commitment to a specific policy varies with its political and social institutions. Two examples of a government's commitment are the effectiveness of a nation's regulatory framework and the credibility of institutions that hold governments accountable for their actions (Henisz, 2000, Levy & Spiller, 1994, Lupia & McCubbins, 1998).

As firms are very dependent on the legal environment surrounding environmental protection, governmental commitment to both international policy issues and environmental protection is particularly important in explaining the diffusion of environmental management standards. As ISO 14001 is a management system that goes beyond existing command-and-control regulations, firms may view ISO 14001 as a tool to help their organizations comply with existing regulations and anticipate more stringent regulations. A government's commitment to the environment will therefore increase the perceived benefits of adopting ISO 14001. By contrast, uncertainty over the government commitment to environmental protection will result in fewer incentives for firms to invest in ISO 14001 efforts. Contexts of uncertainty regarding governmental commitment may lead to questioning the value of an unclear emerging standard than of a more mature standard that provides clearly identified benefits. We therefore hypothesize that:

Hypothesis 3A. The higher the involvement of the country's government in international relations and environmental protection policies, the greater the number of ISO 14001 certificates in the chemical industry within that country.

In addition, the attitude of governments toward environmental management standards should play a role in helping their diffusion. Governments that are sympathetic to such standards will be able to provide incentives to firms seeking their adoption. For example, in Europe the European Commission paved the way to environmental management standards by adopting EMAS. EMAS was the first international EMS standard implemented in the world. It provided Europe with some experience in EMS standardization when ISO 14001 was put into place. Furthermore, EMAS, the European standard developed by the European Commission benefited from strong support by European authorities that promoted its diffusion into European firms. They also facilitated the development of a certification system with "verifiers" and consulting companies. These factors reduced the search and information costs for European firms. The two elements, experience and regulatory promotion of the standard facilitated the development of ISO 14001 in Europe by limiting transaction costs associated with the adoption of the standard and favoring the demand for ISO 14001 from stakeholders. Although EMAS continues to differ from ISO 14001 in its depth and demands with regard to commitment, transparency and environmental performance, the structure of the environmental management system is analogous to the structure of ISO 14001. ISO 14001 could become the first step to the adoption of a more stringent EMAS standard. Therefore we hypothesize that:

Hypothesis 3B. Countries implementing EMAS will experience a higher number of ISO 140001 certificates in the chemical industry.

The Role of Civil Society
In addition to governments, other stakeholders, such as the community in the form of Non-Governmental Organizations (NGOs), may exert pressure on businesses to adopt certain practices and may assist in the diffusion of ideas among their member countries. Meyer et al. (1997) have shown that the global spread of environmental discourse and organizations was especially stimulated by non-governmental actors such as the United Nations (Meyer, Frank, Hironaka, Schofer, & Tuma, 1997). NGOs have become sophisticated communicators and are perceived as instigators of change in the global marketplace. It has been shown that under increasing pressure from environmental and labor activists, multilateral organizations, and regulatory agencies in their home countries, multinational firms are adopting international environmental standard certification such as ISO 14001 (Gereffi, Garcia-Johnson, & Sasser, 2001).

ISO 14001 may help firms to respond to NGO environmental pressures by enabling them to improve their environmental performance and communicate with NGOs. In turn, the degree of involvement of civil society in NGOs might be seen as another support group helping the diffusion process of ISO 14001. In their cross-sectional analysis of the international adoption of ISO 14001, Potoski and Prakash (2004) found that countries whose citizens join international NGOs have more ISO 14001 certifications. Implementing an ISO 14001 EMS encourages companies to write their environmental statements, have people designated to respond to NGOs demands, and organize information within the firm so that it is easily accessible, documented and organized. Moreover, by having a system in place, it may be easier to disclose information to NGOs and the community when any problems or complaints arise. We thus expect that:

Hypothesis 4. The higher the civil society activism in the form of involvement in International NGOs within a particular country, the greater the number of ISO 14001 certificates in the chemical industry within that country.

The Role of Trade Ties

Economic and social linkages between firms across countries offer channels for the transfer of management practices across borders. Multinationals are widely recognized as key agents in the diffusion of practices across national borders, through the transmission of organizational techniques to subsidiaries and to other organizations in the host country (Arias & Guillen, 1998, Christmann & Taylor, 2001). Firms that export to countries where a high number of local firms have adopted a management standard may need to adopt the same standard to export to these countries or to trade with local firms there. Guler et al. (2002) have shown such behavior, which they call "cohesion in trade," for the case of ISO 9000. Prakash and Potoski have also shown that this behavior was significant in predicting the adoption of ISO 14001 across countries (Prakash & Potoski, 2006). Besides the influence that trade ties may have on ISO 14001 adoption rates, competitive bandwagon pressures may arise from a threat of lost competitive advantage. Firms may also adopt the same practices because not doing so would place them at a disadvantage relative to the competition and erode their edge in the market place. Guler et al. (2002) identified such behavior for the case of ISO 9000. According to this argument, firms competing with countries that have a higher adoption rate of ISO 14001 should mimic their competitors' behavior and adopt ISO 14001. We therefore expect:

Hypothesis 5. The higher the trade ties with countries that have been proactive in the adoption of ISO 14001, the greater the number of ISO 14001 certificates in the chemical industry within that country.

In conclusion, we expect that normative behavior related to the adoption of the Responsible Care, ISO 9000 and EMAS will impact the ISO 14001 adoption rates within the chemical sector. In addition, two other diffusion mechanisms related to national and international support groups and to trade ties will also shape the adoption rates. Our model of diffusion of environmental management standards is depicted in Figure 6.1.

Figure 6.1 Factors Related to the International Diffusion of ISO14001 in the Chemical Industry

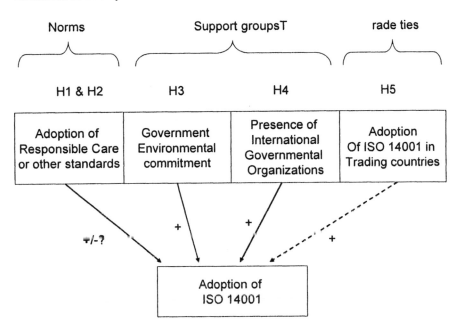

Notes: _____ denotes hypothetical relationships that are confirmed or partly confirmed by our empirical analysis

------- denotes hypothetical relationships that are not confirmed by our empirical analysis

Data and Method

We have compiled a panel dataset of the total number of ISO 14001 certified organizations within the chemical sector in 113 countries between 2000 and 2003. The dependent variable is the cumulative number of chemical facilities certified in each country for the period 2000-2003, as reported by the International Standardization Organization (ISO) in Geneva. The year 2000 was the first year that the ISO provided the number of certificates within a country by industry sector. Previously, ISO only recorded total number of ISO 14001 certificates by country. The reference month for the number of certificates was December of each year. We obtained measures for the independent variables from secondary databases. We measured all independent variables with a one-year lag.

Responsible Care. To account for the influence of the Responsible Care program on the diffusion of ISO 14001 in the chemical industry we created two variables. The first variable was created by taking the number of years that passed since a country's National Chemical Association (NCA) joined the Responsible Care program until the study year. The second set of variables differentiate between countries whose NCA requires all its members to join the Responsible Care program, countries whose NCA allows a voluntary decision to adopt Responsible Care and countries whose NCA does not participate in the program. The two binary variables included in the analysis are Required Responsible Care and Voluntary Responsible Care. Every year the International Council of Chemical Associations (ICCA) publishes a Responsible Care Status Report (ICCA, 2002). This report was used to collect some of the information to construct both variables. However, information for some of the countries was not available in the report. We contacted all 46 National Chemical Associations by e-mail and/or phone to collect the missing information.

ISO 9000 standard. We included a variable representing the number of chemical facilities with the ISO 9000 certification in the focal country, as reported by the International Standardization Organization to measure the existing experience with international process management standards.[3]

The role of the government. We use two variables to account for the role of the government in international and environmental matters and one variable representing the adoption of EMAS in Europe. First, we generated a measure that represents the involvement of a country in international environmental treaties related to the environmental impacts caused by the chemical industry. Several authors have used such variables to measure governmental commitments to environmental protection (Corbett & Kirsch, 2001, Frank, 1997). The EarthTrends Data Tables on Environmental Institutions and Governance from the World Resources Institute identify the main international environmental treaties and provide information on ratification dates (EarthTrends, 2003). This variable was calculated by taking the number of years that passed since a given nation ratified a given treaty. We focused on the three treaties related to the chemical industry: The Kyoto Protocol, the United Nations Framework Convention on Climate Change, and the Vienna Convention about Ozone. Countries that did not ratify a treaty were assigned zero. Countries with a higher score can thus be considered as first movers on the international environmental scene.

The second measure is a variable that accounts for the role of the government in international policy. We use the number of Intergovernmental Organizations (IGOs) that a country's government has joined. The Union of International Associations publishes the Yearbook of International Organizations annually (UIA, 2000-2003). They collect information about both International NGOs and Inter-Governmental Organizations (IGOs) by country. Previous researchers made use of the Yearbook to study different issues such as how social capital affects democracy (Paxton, 2002), the structure of the world culture (Boli & Thomas, 1997), the inequality of the world polity (Beckfield, 2003), the structure of the world environmental regime (Meyer, Frank, Hironaka,

Schofer, & Tuma, 1997), and the adoption of the ISO 14001 standard across all industry sectors (Potoski & Prakash, 2004).

The third variable represents the presence of the European Commission Eco-Management Audit Scheme (EMAS) in a particular country and the impact it has on the adoption rates of ISO 14001 within the chemical industry. The variable EMAS which takes the value of one for those countries where EMAS had already started the diffusion process in each particular year.

The role of civil society. To measure the degree of pressure exerted by the civil society, we introduced a variable representing the number of International NGOs in each country. This variable is also gathered from the Yearbook of International Organizations. We use the number of international NGOs in each country as a proxy for the degree of the civil society involvement in international policy issues.

Cohesion in trade within the chemical industry. To approximate cohesion in trade, we adapted the measure developed by Guler et al. (2002), which captures how strongly a country is tied to other countries through trade and through the extent to which ISO certificates have already diffused in these countries. Unlike Guler et al., we used exports instead of total trade, as we expected the imitation effect to flow through export ties. Indeed, focal countries are more likely to be affected by the practices of their customers than by the rest of the world, as they must establish legitimacy to export to customers. Formally, the cohesion in trade measure for country i at time t is:

$$\text{Cohesion in Trade}_{it} = \sum_{j} \text{ISO}_{jt-1} \times \left(\text{Exports}_{ij}/\text{Exports}_{i}\right)^2$$

where ISO_{jt-1} is the number of certificates for country j at time $t-1$, Exports_{ij} is the exports from country i to country j in 1999,[4] and Exports_{i} is country's total exports during the same period. The data on export ties between each pair of countries came from Feenstra et al., 2005.

Competitive trade within the chemical industry. We measured competition in the network of world trade within the chemical industry by an adjusted structural equivalence measure. Structural equivalence for each country i as of year t, is measured by the Pearson rank correlation coefficient between the proportion of country i's exports within the chemical industry, to all other countries (except j), and the proportion of country j's exports to all other countries (except i), weighted by the sum of ISO 14001 certificates in the chemical industry in all other countries j as of year $t-1$. It is a first-order measure because it only takes into account direct ties between pairs of countries. Formally, for each country i, the competitive trade is:

$$\text{Competitive Trade}_{it} = \sum_{j} \text{ISO Chem}_{jt-1} \times corr\left(\text{Exports}_{i}/\text{Exports}_{j}\right)$$

where ISO_{jt-1} is the number of ISO 14001 certificates in the chemical industry for country j at time $t-1$, corr (Exports_{i}, Exports_{j}) is the Pearson correlation coefficient between the percentage of country i's exports with all other countries an the percentage of country j's exports with all other countries for 1999.

Size of the national chemical industry. To control for the extent of adoption in a country at any given time, it would be ideal to compare the number of certifications within the chemical industry with the maximum number of potential certifications, e.g., the number of chemical establishments, but this information does not exist for most of the countries included in this study. We tried to solve this problem using two alternate control variables. The first alternative is to deflate certification counts using GDP and population. GDP has been used as a deflator (Corbett & Kirsch, 2001, Guler, Guillen, & Macpherson, 2002), but it does not represent the actual number of firms that could potentially be certified. The second alternative is to use the number of chemical establishments by country available at the Industrial Statistics Database created by the United Nations Industrial Development Organization (UNIDO). Although this second alternative is our ideal measure, this database only contains information for 51 out of our 113 countries. We thus used the GDP per capita measure in most of our regression models.

Foreign Direct Investment. We also control for the impact of the presence of foreign multinationals with a variable that represents the value of inward foreign direct investment (FDI) as percentage of Gross Domestic Product (GDP). This measure was obtained from the World Bank's Development Indicators Database for the years 1999–2002.

Level of ISO 14001 diffusion within the country. Finally we control for the level of ISO 14001 diffusion in each country by including the number of years since the first ISO 4001 certificate was awarded in that particular country. This variable allows us to establish control between early and late ISO 14001 adopters. Table 6.2 summarizes the descriptive statistics and correlation coefficients of all our variables.

Estimation

Our dependent variable, which represents the cumulative number of ISO 14001 certificates in the chemical industry per country, has two characteristics: it is a count variable, and it includes observations clustered at zero and observations far in the right tail of the distribution (see Appendix 6.2). Because of these characteristics, our dependent variable has a variance higher than its mean and is thus over-dispersed. Poisson regression is specifically designed for count dependent variables. Unfortunately, it assumes that the mean and variance of event counts are equal (Greene, 2003). When individual counts are more dispersed than the Poisson model, the negative binomial model can be used, because a random term reflecting unexplained between-subject differences is included in the regression model (Gardner, Mulvery, & Shaw, 1995). Therefore, we ran a negative regression model with random effects[5] using a panel dataset. The test of the inclusion of random effects is highly significant in our full model

Table 6.2 Descriptive Statistics and Correlations

	Variable	Mean	SD	1	2	3	4	5	6
1	ISO14001 in Chemical	27.29	95.23	1					
2	Required Responsible Care	0.33	0.47	0.23	1				
3	Voluntary Responsible Care	0.13	0.33	0.11	-0.27	1			
4	Years in Responsible Care	3.39	4.38	0.38	0.47	0.57	1		
5	ISO9000 in Chemical	2.80	2.30	0.43	0.43	0.41	0.72	1	
6	EMAS	0.16	0.36	0.21	0.37	0.16	0.50	0.38	1
7	Years in ISO14001	2.82	2.25	0.33	0.52	0.31	0.71	0.73	0.45
8	International NGOs	6.84	0.83	0.33	0.52	0.38	0.75	0.80	0.59
9	International Chemical Treaties	16.06	4.82	0.23	0.10	0.21	0.38	0.39	0.20
10	InterGovernmental Organizations	3.90	0.26	0.26	0.40	0.20	0.49	0.54	0.60
11	Cohesion in Trade	3.77	1.26	-0.05	-0.35	-0.13	-0.29	-0.41	-0.34
12	Competitive Trade	6.13	1.11	0.15	0.19	0.21	0.34	0.43	0.25
13	FDI	0.72	1.29	-0.12	0.09	0.19	0.21	0.06	0.23
14	GDP x capita	8.81	1.03	0.30	0.39	0.34	0.65	0.61	0.54
15	Chemical Establishments	6.12	1.66	0.33	0.33	0.24	0.48	0.59	0.21

	Variable	7	8	9	10	11	12	13	14
7	Years in ISO14001	1							
8	International NGOs	0.73	1						
9	International Chemical Treaties	0.43	0.43	1					
10	InterGovernmental Organizations	0.49	0.71	0.30	1				
11	Cohesion in Trade	-0.18	-0.48	0.05	-0.44	1			
12	Competitive Trade	0.42	0.47	0.20	0.32	-0.09	1		
13	FDI	0.04	0.19	-0.00	0.12	-0.06	0.03	1	
14	GDP x capita	0.64	0.70	0.28	0.42	-0.31	0.47	0.18	1
15	Chemical Establishments	0.41	0.59	0.54	0.48	-0.44	-0.36	-0.14	0.34

Note: coefficients| >0.12 are significant at the $p < 0.01$

(χ^2= 270.80, p=0.000), indicating that unobserved firm effects exist. The panel negative binomial model that we used is represented by the following equation:

$$\ln \lambda_{it} = \beta' X_{it} + \mu_i + \varepsilon_{it}$$

where X is a vector of characteristics of the country i at time t, μ_i is a group specific random element, similar to ε_{it} except that for each group, there is only a single draw that enters the regression identically in each period. We ran the model using the *xtnbreg* command in the Stata 7 statistical software (Stata, 2001).

Results

Table 6.3 summarizes the test results of the direct effects of the different explanatory variables on the adoption of ISO 14001 within the chemical industry using six different models. In the first three models we use GDP as the measure of industry size. In Models 4 to 6 we use the number of chemical establishments instead of GDP as a control for the size of the sector but, due to the large number of missing values, the number of observations dropped from 357 to only 104 and the number of countries from 103 to only 51.[6]

Due to collinearity issues, we use different measures of the effect of Responsible Care in separate models. In Models 1 and 4 we use the two binary variables to control for the presence of required and voluntary Responsible Care while in Models 2 and 5 we use the number of years since Responsible Care was adopted by the country's national chemical association. Last, we add two additional models, 3 and 6, in which we exclude the variable International NGOs[7] to show that even though this variable is highly correlated with some of the other independent variables, our results do not vary when it is included in the first two models.

Hypotheses 1 and 2A predict opposite effects of the experience with the National Chemical Association's Responsible Care program on the diffusion of ISO 14001 within the chemical sector. We use different measures to test for the impact of Responsible Care experience. We find that both variables, the number of years since National Chemical Association (NCA) of a particular country joined the Responsible Care (p<0.01 in Model 3 and p<0.05 in Models 2, 5 and 6), and whether Responsible Care is required to join a particular NCA are positive and significant (p<0.01 in Models 1 and 4). Our results support our hypothesis 2A, which predicts a positive relationship between the experience with Responsible Care and the likelihood of adopting ISO 14001.

Table 6.3 Negative Binomial of the Number of Chemical ISO14001 Certifications

	Model 1	Model 2	Model 3
	GDP as control for size of the industry		
Required Responsible Care	1.17**		
	(0.32)		
Voluntary Responsible Care	0.39		
	(0.37)		
Years in Responsible Care		0.08*	0.11**
		(0.04)	(0.03)
ISO9000 in Chemical	0.36**	0.31**	0.36**
	(0.07)	(0.07)	(0.06)
EMAS	-0.42	-0.37	-0.20
	(0.29)	(0.29)	(0.28)
Years in ISO14001	0.12+	0.16*	0.18**
	(0.06)	(0.06)	(0.06)
International NGOs	0.66*	0.74*	
	(0.34)	(0.32)	
International Chemical Treaties	0.00	-0.02	-0.02
	(0.03)	(0.03)	(0.02)
Intergovernmental Organizations	0.41	0.49	0.69+
	(0.40)	(0.36)	(0.36)
Cohesion in Trade	0.10	0.01	-0.08
	(0.11)	(0.10)	(0.09)
Competitive Trade	0.10	0.09	0.11+
	(0.06)	(0.06)	(0.06)
FDI	-0.10*	-0.11*	-0.10*
	(0.05)	(0.05)	(0.05)
GDP x capita	0.32+	0.23	0.35*
	(0.17)	(0.16)	(0.15)
Chemical Establishments			
Constant	-11.80**	-10.89**	-7.91**
	(2.50)	(2.53)	(2.12)
Observations	357	357	357
Number of id	113	113	113
Log Likelihood	-811.53	-819.07	-821.86

Continued on next page

Table 6.3—Continued

	Model 4	Model 5	Model 6
	Chemical Establishments as control for industry size		
Required Responsible Care	1.47**		
	(0.49)		
Voluntary Responsible Care	0.62		
	(0.58)		
Years in Responsible Care		0.12*	0.12*
		(0.05)	(0.05)
ISO9000 in Chemical	0.35**	0.28**	0.28**
	(0.09)	(0.09)	(0.09)
EMAS	0.98*	0.96*	0.95*
	(0.41)	(0.40)	(0.38)
Years in ISO14001	-0.01	-0.00	-0.00
	(0.14)	(0.12)	(0.12)
International NGOs	-0.03	-0.02	
	(0.49)	(0.49)	
International Chemical Treaties	0.08*	0.04	0.04
	(0.04)	(0.03)	(0.03)
Intergovernmental Organizations	-0.17	0.11	0.10
	(0.59)	(0.55)	(0.53)
Cohesion in Trade	0.02	-0.11	-0.11
	(0.19)	(0.18)	(0.16)
Competitive Trade	0.10	0.26	0.25
	(0.33)	(0.34)	(0.29)
FDI	-0.17+	-0.22*	-0.22*
	(0.09)	(0.09)	(0.09)
GDP x capita			
Chemical Establishments	0.21*	0.16	0.16
	(0.10)	(0.10)	(0.10)
Constant	-3.99	-4.44	-4.52
	(3.47)	(3.28)	(2.88)
Observations	104	104	104
Number of id	51	51	51
Log Likelihood	-317.21	-321.49	-321.50

Note: Standard errors in parentheses **$p<0.01$, *$p<0.05$, +$p<0.1$

Hypothesis 2B predicts a positive effect of the number of ISO 9000 certifications in the chemical industry on ISO 14001 adoption. All our models test for the impact of ISO 9000, and the variable is positive and significant ($p<0.01$), supporting our second hypothesis.

To understand the magnitude of these effects we calculate incidence-rate ratios. These ratios indicate, for example, that an additional year in the Responsible Care program increases the expected number of ISO 14001 chemical facilities in a particular country by a factor of 1.08, that is, 8% when other variables are held constant. Hence, for a country with 12 chemical facilities with ISO 14001, if they had an additional year in Responsible Care the expected number of ISO 14001 was 13. The effect that Responsible Care membership requirements have on the adoption of ISO 14001 among chemical facilities is much stronger. In those countries where the National Chemical Association asks for Responsible Care as a membership requirement, the number of ISO 14001 certified facilities increases by a factor of 3.23, or 323%. Similarly, in the case of the European EMAS in Model 4, in those countries where EMAS is present, the number of ISO 14001 certified facilities increases by a factor of 2.60, or 260%.

Hypothesis 3A predicts that the role of a particular government in international policy issues and the credibility of its governmental commitment to the environment will positively influence the adoption of ISO 14001 by chemical firms. We test these effects using two measures: a variable representing the involvement in international environmental treaties concerning the chemical sector and a variable representing the number of Intergovernmental organizations that a particular government belongs to. Our results do not show support for the role that the government might play on the decision to adopt ISO 14001 in the chemical industry. Even though we find some significant results in two models, these disappear when other independent and control variables are included. The level of governmental commitment toward the environment does not seem to impact the early diffusion of ISO 14001 in the chemical industry. One explanation for this result could be that such variables impacted the adoption of ISO 14001 indirectly by influencing the initiation of the Responsible Care program which in turned facilitated the diffusion of ISO 14001.

Hypothesis 3B predicts a positive effect of the implementation of EMAS within a country on ISO 14001 adoption. The variable EMAS, controlling for the presence of the European standard for Environmental Management System, is not significant in the first three models. However, the same variable is positive and significant ($p<0.05$) in the last three models. It may not be surprising that the effect of EMAS is not significant in the models representing all the countries of our sample since EMAS is only implemented in Europe. The last three models include a smaller subset of countries (51) in which the presence of EMAS has a positive effect on ISO 14001 adoption rates within the chemical industry.

Hypothesis 4 states that the level of community activism and involvement in international policy issues measured by the number of international NGOs will enhance the adoption of ISO 14001 in the chemical sector. The results in models 1 and 2 support our hypothesis since the variable representing the number of international NGOs is positive and significant ($p<0.05$). Therefore, the level of community activism and its involvement in international NGOs in a particular country favors the adoption of ISO 14001 within the chemical industry. The same variable is not significant when we use Chemical Establishments as the control variable for industry size.

Hypothesis 5 states that trade ties with countries that have been proactive in the adoption of ISO 14001 will impact the adoption of ISO 14001 in the focal country. Contrary to what one would expect, the cohesion in the trade variable is not shown to be significant, indicating that at the early stages of ISO 14001 adoption in the chemical sector, the trade ties between countries do not impact the diffusion rates of the standard. With regard to the competitive trade variable, the variable does not show any significant effect on adoption either, which indicates that the competitor's behavior toward ISO 14001 does not influence its diffusion in the chemical sector. These results differ from previous findings where cohesion in trade was found to explain the international diffusion of ISO 9000 and ISO 14001 (Guler, Guillen, & Macpherson, 2002). As mentioned earlier these studies were across industries and did not include specific industry effects. Industry level variation is expected due to different levels of export-dependence and pollution intensity. So it is possible that the role of bilateral trade would be a less important driver of the adoption of ISO 14001 in the chemical industry than in other industries. For example, studies have shown that the role of supplier relationships are important in the automotive industry with the US Big Three automotive manufacturers (Ford, General Motors, and Chrysler) requesting their suppliers to adopt ISO 14001 (Delmas & Montiel, 2007). Some of the results of earlier studies may be driven by the weight of industries for which trade ties play an important role in the diffusion of environmental standards.

The variable representing foreign direct investment (FDI) is negative and significant; indicating that high levels of investment are associated with low levels of adoption of the standard among chemical firms. Countries with a high level of FDI are generally countries with low level of development. It is therefore not surprising that the sign of the FDI variable is the opposite of the GDP per capita variable which exerts a significant and positive effect on the number of ISO 14001 certificates. Multinationals may therefore not bring sufficient pressure to promote the diffusion of ISO 14001 in developing countries.

Finally, the variable representing the number of years since ISO 14001 entered a country is positively significant in the first three models, indicating that countries that are the early adopters of ISO 14001 are also more likely to see high numbers of adoptions within the chemical sector. As we noted, other trend variables such as the number of years of existence of the Responsible Care program in the country also showed significant positives. This result shows an acceleration of the phenomenon of adoption over the years.

Discussion

Most authors recognize the fact that voluntary environmental standards do not operate in isolation, but within the context of larger cultures or national regulations. However, very few acknowledge that they also operate in concert with other private or semi-private environmental governance mechanisms.

We started our paper by highlighting the competing hypotheses provided by the diffusion literature concerning the impact of existing standards on the likelihood of success of a new standard. Firms could be subjected to norms of exclusivity where they are discouraged to participate in competing standards. Alternatively, firms could learn about the benefits of voluntary standards from the initial adoption of the industry standard and become more likely to adopt subsequent standards. Our findings show support for the latter explanation. We find that in the early stages of diffusion of an international environmental standard, previous adoption of other standards will shape the adoption of the latter. In particular, we find that in the case of the international environmental standard ISO 14001 in the chemical industry, the previous adoption of both the National Chemical Association's Responsible Care program, the quality standard ISO 9000 and the European EMAS standard enhanced the diffusion of ISO 14001. We find that regardless of their characteristics, all these standards enhance the diffusion of ISO 14001. We therefore conclude that environmental management standards feed on each other and that previous standards accelerate the adoption rates of subsequent ones. In the chemical context, firms that had already joined the Responsible Care program reinforce their environment, health and safety management system by also pursuing ISO 14001 certification. These results are consistent with previous findings about the impact of trade association membership in the decision to adopt new voluntary programs. For example, Rivera (2004) found that trade association membership impacted the decision to adopt the Certification for Sustainable Tourism (an environmental voluntary program for the tourism industry) among the Costa Rican hotel industry (Rivera, 2004). In our case, previous adoption of the Responsible Care program, which is promoted and managed by chemical trade associations in the different countries, impacts the decision to adopt a second voluntary program, the international voluntary standard ISO 14001.

In addition, we have argued that other institutional factors may drive the diffusion of a new industry standard within a particular sector. We predict that institutional pressure from governments and the civil society enhances the adoption of ISO 14001 within the chemical industry. We find some support to the argument that the adoption of voluntary but "governmental" environmental management system standards can help the diffusion of ISO 14001. In the early stages of ISO 14001 diffusion, we also find that other institutional pressures can drive the chemical sector to adopt the standard such as pressures from civil society in the form of Non-Governmental Organizations (NGOs). It is well known how the chemical sector has been targeted by the civil society due to its well-documented impacts on the environment (OECD, 2001). Chemical companies might adopt ISO 14001 to send a signal of good environmental behavior to NGOs who might have been skeptical about the effectiveness of the Responsible Care Program.

Our study provides a bridge between the literature on the international diffusion of non-governmental standards and the policy diffusion literature. We show the cumulative effect of management standards in specific institutional settings, notably when non-market actors such as NGOs are involved in pressurizing firms to adopt a new standard. We test a comprehensive set of factors to explain the diffusion of ISO 14001 and find that previous standards and NGOs play a major role in the diffusion of ISO 14001 in the chemical industry. While the policy diffusion literature has highlighted the importance of policy characteristics in predicting policy diffusion, the literature on the diffusion of non-governmental standards had paid less attention to the characteristics of international voluntary standards, probably because of the lack of existing data at the industry level. We show that this factor should not be forgotten as it is a major influence, at least in the chemical industry.

Unlike previous studies we do not find a significant role for government commitment in international environmental affairs or trade ties for the chemical industry adopting voluntary standards. Regarding the role of governments, our results show that more specific commitment to environmental management standard explains better the adoption of further standards rather than general commitment toward the environment. This is consistent with previous studies that showed the importance of a non-adversarial institutional environment to facilitate the adoption of ISO 14001 (Kollman & Prakash, 2001, Delmas, 2005, Moon & deLeon, 2005). In addition, it is possible that government efforts may impact indirectly on ISO 14001 through the adoption of Responsible Care. Regarding the role of trade ties, it is possible that national trade associations in the chemical industry play a more important role than forces related to bilateral trade to explain the diffusion of voluntary standards. Previous studies may not have identified industry specificities in that regard because they aggregated industry effects.

Our analysis is not without limitations. We first need to point out that our purpose is to analyze chemical companies' adoption strategy toward the new ISO 14001 standard considering that two other voluntary standards, ISO 9000 and Responsible Care were already diffused in some of the countries of analysis. Some of the institutional factors that explain the adoption of ISO 14001 might also have explained the previous adoption of the ISO 9000 and/or Responsible Care standards. However, because these previous standards were issued more than 10 years prior to ISO 14001, and because of data limitations (for example there are no data on the initial number of adoption per country for ISO 9000) it is not possible to test the factors that explain the initial adoption of these older standards. Furthermore, we want to state that additional factors such as quality customer requirements for ISO 9000 and industrial accidents and fatalities for

Responsible Care might have explained the previous adoption of these standards. However, it is not the purpose of our study to determine the factors that drove companies to adopt Responsible Care in the first place.

Further research should investigate whether adoption decisions in the future, when the standard is better established, will differ from our findings. Scholars could also investigate whether similar patterns of adoption can be identified in other industries. In addition, future analyses will need to study the current strategies undertaken by some countries to integrate some of these industry standards. For instance, in the United States, the American Chemical Council (ACC) has recently designed a combined Responsible Care-ISO 14001 certification program called RC-14001 (Chemical Week, 2002, p.51). It will be interesting to observe whether or not other industries will follow the ACC initiative and design similar programs to simplify the adoption of both standards in specific countries and whether this has an impact on adoption rates. We identified links between the Responsible Care standard and ISO 14001 in terms of how one standard can influence the diffusion of the other. However, we did not investigate how the standards influence each other in terms of their content. Both ISO 14001 and Responsible care are continuously evolving over time. Further research should analyze how standards influence the content of each other.

Policy Implications and Conclusion

Our research has important policy implications. Industry codes of conduct have been sometimes criticized as being developed by industries to protect themselves from more stringent standards (King & Lenox, 2000, Overdevest, 2004). Our research shows that this may not always be the case and that industry standards can pave the way for the next generation of standards that are more rigorous. Trade associations play an important role in fostering collective action behavior. Our results indicate that policy makers could build on the coordination abilities of trade associations to facilitate the diffusion of voluntary standards. We suggest that it is possible to envisage incremental approaches, where firms start initially with "easier" standards, learn about these and subsequently move to more stringent standards. Some researchers have argued that voluntary codes covering a wider gamut of industries may be preferable to industry level codes because generalized codes reduce stakeholders' transaction costs of monitoring as well as facilitating an inter-industry comparison (Prakash, 2000). Our research shows that "generalist" codes of conducts such as ISO 14001 should not be opposed to industry codes such as Responsible Care as both could co-exist.

Policy makers in charge of designing new voluntary standards should take into account the previous existence of other standards. Rather than designing a new standard with similar and competing characteristics than existing ones, policy makers should focus on complementary standards.

In summary, voluntary environmental standards should not be treated as alternative to one another but rather as complementary to each other. Few studies have examined how combinations of voluntary standards or combinations of voluntary standards with public ordering could be integrated into an optimal regulatory mix (Gunningham, Grabosky, & Sinclair, 1998). We need more studies that show how the design of complementary combinations of policy instruments tailored to particular environmental goals and circumstances will be more effective in improving the environment. Such studies would help to connect the emerging literature on the diffusion of environmental management standards to the literature on policy diffusion.

Bibliography

Alpert, Frank. 1994. "Innovator Buying Behavior Over Time: The Innovator Buying Cycle and the Cumulative Effects of Innovations." *Journal of Product & Brand Management* 3(2): 50–62.

Arias, Maria Eugenia an d Mauro F. Guillen. 1998. "The Transfer of Organizational Management Techniques Across Borders." In *The Diffusion and Consumption of Business Knowledge*, ed. Jose Luis Alvarez. London: Macmillan.

Beckfield, Jason. 2003. "Inequality in the World Polity: The Structure of International Organization." *American Sociological Review* 68(3): 401–24.

Bessen, James and Garth Saloner. 1988. "Compatibility Standards and the Market of Telecommunication Services." Santa Monica, CA: Rand.

Boli, John and George M. Thomas. 1997. "World Culture in the World Polity: A Century of International Non-Governmental Organization." *American Sociological Review* 62(2): 171–90.

Chemical Week. 2002. "Industry Debuts RC-14001." www.chemweek.com, (April 17, 2002).

Christmann, Petra and Glen Taylor. 2001. "Globalization and the Environment: Determinants of Firm Self-regulation in China." *Journal of International Business Studies* 32(3): 439–58.

Corbett, Charles J. and David A. Kirsch. 2001. "International Diffusion of ISO 14000 Certification." *Production & Operations Management* 10(3): 327–42.

Daft, Richard L. 1978. "A Dual-Core Model of Organizational Innovation." *Academy of Management Journal* 21(2): 193–210.

Darnall, Nicole. 2003. Why Firms Adopt ISO 14001: An Institutional and Resource-based View. In *Best Paper Proceedings: Sixty-first Meeting of the Academy of Management Conference*, ed. D. Nagao, Seattle, WA: Academy of Management, A1-A6.

Delmas, Magali. 2000. "Barriers and Incentives to the Adoption of ISO 14001 by Firms in the United States." *Duke Environmental Law & Policy Forum* 11(1): 1–38.

———. 2002. "The Diffusion of Environmental Management Standards in Europe and in the United States: An Institutional Perspective." *Policy Sciences* 35: 91–119.

———. 2005. "The Take-off Period in the Diffusion of International Standards: The Case of ISO 14001." Donald Bren School of Environmental Science & Management, University of California, Santa Barbara.

Delmas, Magali and Ann Terlaak. 2001. "A Framework for Analyzing Environmental Voluntary Agreements." *California Management Review* 43(3): 44–63.

Delmas, Magali and Ivan Montiel. 2007. "The Adoption of ISO 14001 Within the Supply Chain: When Are Costumer Pressures Effective?" Institute for Social, Behavioral, and Economic Research. ISBER, Paper 10, University of California, Santa Barbara.

EarthTrends. 2003. "Earth Trends Data Tables on Environmental Institutions and Governance: Global Governance: Participation in Major Multilateral agreements." [www.document] http://earthtrends.wri.org/ (accessed 23 January 2005).

Elkins, Zachary and Beth Simmons. 2005. "On Waves, Clusters, and Diffusion: A Conceptual Framework." *The Annals of the American Academy of Political and Social Science* 598(1): 33–51.

Feenstra, Robert C., Robert E. Lipsey, Haiyan Deng, Alyson C. Ma and Henry Mo. 2005. "World Trade Flows, 1962–2000." NBER Working Paper No. W11040, Cambridge, MA.

Frank, David J. 1997. "Science, Nature, and the Globalization of the Environment, 1870-1990." *Social Forces* 76: 409–35.

Gardner, William E., Edward Mulvery and Esther Shaw. 1995. "Regression Analyses of Counts and Rates: Poisson, Overdispersed Poisson, and Negative Binomial Models." *Psychological Bulletin* 118(3): 392–404.

Gereffi, Gary, Ronie Garcia-Johnson and Erika Sasser. 2001. "The NGO-Industrial Complex." *Foreign Policy* 125: 56–65.

Gilbertsen, Robert H. and Thomas A. Kowalski. 2004. "Responsible Care meets ISO." *Chemical Processing: The Digital Resource of Chemical Processing Magazine.*

Greene, William H. 2003. *Econometric analysis* 5th Edition. New York: MacMillan.

Guler, Isin, Mauro F Guillen and John Muir Macpherson. 2002. "Global Competition, Institutions, and the Diffusion of Organizational Practices: The International Spread of ISO 9000 Quality Certificates." *Administrative Science Quarterly* 47(2): 207–32.

Gunningham, Neil, Peter Grabosky and Darren Sinclair. 1998. *Smart Regulation: Designing Environmental Policy*. Oxford, UK: Oxford University Press.

Henisz, Witold J. 2000. "The Institutional Environment for Economic Growth." *Economics and Politics* 12(1): 1–31.

Howard, Jennifer, Jennifer Nash and John Ehrenfeld. 2000. "Standard and Smokescreen? Implementation of a Voluntary Environmental Code." *California Management Review* 42(2): 63–82.

ICCA. 2002. "ICCA Responsible Care Status Report 2002." Brussels, Belgium: International Council of Chemical Associations.

———. 2005. "Responsible Care 1985–2005." Brussels, Belgium: International Council of Chemical Associations.

ISO. 2005. "ISO 9000 and ISO 14000 in brief." Geneva, Switzerland: International Organization for Standardization.

———. 2003. "The ISO Survey of ISO 9000 and ISO 14001 Certificates." Geneva, Switzerland: International Organization for Standardization.

Katz, Michael and Carl Shapiro. 1985. "Network Externalities, Competition and Compatibility." *American Economic Review* 75(3): 424–40.

King, Andrew, Michael Lenox and Ann K. Terlaak. 2005. "The Strategic Use of Decentralized Institutions: Exploring Certification with the ISO 14001 Management Standard." *Academy of Management Journal* 48(6): 1091–106.

King, Andrew and Michael Lenox. 2000. "Industry Self-Regulation without Sanctions:

The Chemical Industry's Responsible Care Program." *Academy of Management Journal* 43(4): 698–716.

Kollman, Kelly and Aseem Prakash. 2002. "EMS-based Environmental Regimes as Club Goods: Examining Variations in Firm-level Adoption of ISO 14001 and EMAS in UK, US and Germany." *Policy Sciences* 35: 43–67.

———. 2001. "Green by Choice? Cross-national Variation in Firms' Responses to EMS-based Environmental Regimes." *World Politics* 53: 399–430.

Levy, Bran and Pablo Spiller. 1994. "The Institutional Foundations of Regulatory Commitment: A Comparative Analysis of Telecommunications Regulation." *Journal of Law Economics and Organization* 10(2): 201–46.

Lupia, Arthur and Matthew McCubbins. 1998. "Political Credibility and Economic Reform: Do Politicians Intend to Keep the Promises they Make?" Washington, DC: World Bank.

Mazurek, Janice 2001. "Third-Party Auditing of Environmental Management Systems: US Registration Practices for ISO 14001." Washington, DC: National Academy of Public Administration.

Meyer, John W., David J. Frank, Ann Hironaka, Evan Schofer and Nancy B. Tuma. 1997. "The Structuring of a World Environmental Regime: 1870–1990." *International Organization* 51(4): 623–51.

Moon, Seong-gin and Peter deLeon. 2005. "The Patterns of Institutional Interaction and ISO 14001 Adoptions." *Comparative Technology and Society* 3(1): 35–57.

Mossberger, Karen and Harold Wolman. 2003. "Policy Transfer as a Form of Prospective Policy Evaluation: Challenges and Recommendations." *Public Administration Review* 63(4): 428–40.

OECD. 2001. *OECD Environmental Outlook for the Chemicals Industry*. Paris: OECD.

Orts, Eric and Paula Murray. 1997. "Environmental Disclosure and Evidentiary Privilege." *University of Illinois Law Review* (1997): 1–69.

Overdevest, Christine. 2004. "Codes of Conduct and Standard Setting in the Forest Sector: Constructing Markets for Democracy?" *Industrial Relations/Relations Industrielles* 59(1): 172–98.

Paxton, Pamela. 2002. "Social Capital and Democracy: An Interdependent Relationship." *American Sociological Review* 67(2): 254–77.

Potoski, Matthew and Aseem Prakash. 2004. "Regulatory Convergence in Non-government Regimes? Cross-national Adoption of ISO 14001 Certifications." *The Journal of Politics* 66(3): 885–905.

———. 2005. "Green Clubs and Voluntary Governance: ISO 14001 and Firm's Regulatory Compliance." *American Journal of Political Science* 49(2): 235–248.

Prakash, Aseem. 1999. "A New-institutionalist Perspective on ISO 14000 and Responsible Care." *Business Strategy and the Environment* 8(6): 322.

———. 2000. "Responsible Care: An Assessment." *Business & Society* 39(2): 183–209.

Prakash, Aseem and Matthew Potoski. 2006. "Racing to the Bottom? Trade, Environmental Governance and ISO 14001." *American Journal of Political Science* 50(2): 350–64.

Rivera, Jorge. 2004. "Institutional Pressures and Voluntary Environmental Behavior in Developing Countries: Evidence from the Costa Rican Hotel Industry." *Social & Natural Resources* 17: 779–97.

Rogers, Everett M. 1995. *Diffusion of Innovations*. 4th Edition. New York: The Free Press.

Stata. 2001. "Stata Reference Manual Vol.4." College Station, Texas: Stata Press.

Teece, David J. 1980. "The Diffusion of an Administrative Innovation." *Management Science* 26(5): 464–70.

Tews, Kerstin, Per-Olof Busch and Helge Jorgens. 2003. "The Diffusion of New Environmental Policy Instruments." *European Journal of Political Research* 42(4): 569–600.

UIA. 2000–2003. *Yearbook of International Organizations.* Union of International Organizations: Munchen.

Venkatraman, N., Lawrence Loh and Jeongsuk Koh. 1994. "The Adoption of Corporate Governance Mechanisms: A Test of Competing Diffusion Models." *Management Science* 40(4): 496–507.

Watkins, Richard and Edwin Gutzwiller. 1999. "Buying into ISO 14001." *Occupational Health & Safety* 68(2): 52–54.

Welford, Richard. 1996. *Corporate Environmental Management: Systems and Strategies.* London: Earthscan.

Notes

1. Responsible Care has evolved over time. After the period of our study, Responsible Care programs in some countries required a third party certification. We discuss this in the concluding section.

2. EMAS became effective on April 10, 1995.

3. We need to point out that information about the number of certifications for 1999 is not available from the ISO Survey. Therefore, for our first year of analysis, year 2000, we were unable to use a one-year lag information and we decided to use the 2000 information. For the remaining years we were able to use lagged ISO 9000 adoption rates. To ensure consistency in our results, we also ran the analysis for the 3-year period (2001–2003) and found the same significant results.

4. The year 1999 is the last year for which World Trade Flows database includes data on Exports.

5. We use the random effect model because a fixed effect model would disregard all countries without any ISO 14001 certificates within the chemical sector by 2003, 26.

6. See Appendix 6.2 for a list of countries included in each model.

7. We calculate the variance inflation factor for the linear regression. The results show that the variable International NGOs is highly correlated with some of the independent variables. Hence, we exclude this variable from our analysis in Models 3 and 6 to ensure that our results are consistent.

Appendices

Appendix 6.1 Responsible Care Member Countries and Year of Adoption

Country	Adoption year	Country	Adoption year
Argentina	1992	Lithuania	2002
Australia	1989	Malaysia	1994
Austria	1992	Mexico	1991
Belgium	1991	Morocco	1998
Brazil	1992	Netherlands	1990
Bulgaria	2002	New Zealand	1991
Canada	1985	Norway	1993
Chile	1994	Peru	1996
Colombia	1994	Philippines	1996
Czech Rep.	1994	Poland	1992
Denmark	1995	Portugal	1993
Ecuador	1999	Singapore	1990
Estonia	2002	Slovak Rep.	1996
Finland	1992	Slovenia	2002
France	1990	South Africa	1994
Germany	1991	South Korea	1999
Greece	1995	Spain	1993
Hong Kong	1992	Sweden	1991
Hungary	1992	Switzerland	1992
India	1993	Taiwan	1997
Indonesia	1997	Thailand	1996
Ireland	1992	Turkey	1993
Israel	2001	United Kingdom	1989
Italy	1992	United States	1985
Japan	1990	Uruguay	1998
Latvia	2002	Venezuela	2002

Appendix 6.2 Countries Included in the Study (2003 Data)

Country	# ISO 14001 (2003)	# ISO Chemical (2003)
Albania*	0	0
Algeria	0	0
Angola	0	0
Argentina	286	5
Austria*	500	21
Azerbaijan*	5	0
Bahrain	3	0
Bangladesh	4	0
Belarus	4	0
Bolivia	7	0
Brazil*	1008	54
Bulgaria*	17	2
Cambodia	1	0
Cameroon	1	0
Canada*	1274	36
Chile	99	6
China*	5064	0
Colombia*	135	12
Cote d'Ivoire	0	0
Czech Republic*	519	32
Denmark*	486	5
Ecuador*	1	0
Egypt, Arab Rep.	195	20
El Salvador	0	0
Estonia*	74	1
Fiji	1	0
Finland*	1128	57
France*	2344	128
Gabon	0	0
Georgia*	0	0
Germany*	4144	778
Ghana	0	0
Greece	126	8
Guatemala	1	0
Honduras	6	0
Hungary*	770	37
Iceland	3	0
India*	879	97

Continued on next page

Country	# ISO 14001 (2003)	# ISO Chemical (2003)
Iran, Islamic Rep.*	88	0
Ireland	218	10
Israel*	163	29
Italy*	3066	204
Jamaica	1	0
Japan*	13416	907
Jordan*	39	13
Kazakhstan	4	0
Kenya	1	0
Korea, Rep.*	1495	166
Kuwait	0	0
Kyrgyz Rep.*	0	0
Latvia*	3	0
Lithuania*	72	1
Malaysia	370	17
Mauritius	1	0
Mexico*	406	19
Morocco	6	1
Mozambique	0	0
Nepal	1	0
Nicaragua	0	0
Niger	2	0
Nigeria	8	2
Norway*	350	6
Oman*	2	1
Pakistan	26	1
Panama*	2	0
Papua New Guinea	1	0
Peru	31	0
Philippines*	174	2
Poland*	555	8
Portugal*	248	16
Romania*	96	9
Russia*	48	6
Senegal*	0	0
Seychelles	1	0
Sierra Leone	0	0
Singapore*	523	21

Continued on next page

Appendix 6.2—Continued

Country	# ISO 14001 (2003)	# ISO Chemical (2003)
Slovak Republic	165	14
Slovenia	205	0
South Africa	378	34
Spain*	4860	216
Sri Lanka	11	0
Sudan	0	0
Sweden*	3404	29
Syrian Arab Rep.*	34	1
Tajikistan	0	0
Tanzania	0	0
Thailand*	736	75
Togo	0	0
Trinidad & Tobago	9	0
Tunisia	18	?
Turkey*	240	14
Turkmenistan	1	0
Uganda	3	0
Ukraine	7	1
United Kingdom*	5460	117
United States	3553	135
Uruguay	32	8
Uzbekistan	0	0
Venezuela*	20	0
Vietnam	56	14
Yemen, Rep.	0	0
Zambia	0	0

Note: *Countries included in Models 4 to 6 presented in Table 6.3.

Chapter 7

Is Greener Whiter Yet?
The Sustainable Slopes Program
After Five Years

Jorge E. Rivera, Peter deLeon,
and Charles Koerber

Introduction

For some time now, public policy and management scholars have been interested in identifying mechanisms that encourage environmental protection by businesses. Public policies, in terms of environmental regulations, monitoring, penalties, institutional norms, and economic incentives, have historically been identified as positively related to regulatory compliance. Recently, these factors have also been identified with an increased likelihood of participation in voluntary environmental programs (VEPs) that seek to promote proactive corporate environmental protection in more flexible and cost-efficient ways (Carmin, Darnall, and Homens 2003; Delmas and Toffel 2004; Khanna 2001; King and Lenox 2000; Rivera 2004). Indeed, much of the current federal government's environmental policies are predicated upon VEP-type programs. Yet, empirical evidence is still scant and contradictory about whether voluntary initiatives are effective alternative environmental policy instruments (Darnall 2003a; Khanna 2001; King and Lenox 2000; Potoski and Prakash 2005; Rivera and Delmas 2004; Welch, Mazur, and Bretschneider 2000).

In August 2004, the *Policy Studies Journal* published Professors Rivera and deLeon's review of the Sustainable Slopes Program (SSP), which examined the initial effectiveness of this voluntary program as articulated by the National Ski Areas Association (NSAA). Their empirical findings indicated institutional pressures often seemed to be motivating ski areas' participation in the SSP; however, "despite these institutional pressures, participant ski areas seem[ed] to be correlated with lower third-party environmental performance ratings" (Rivera and deLeon 2004, 417); that is, the SSP appeared in the beginning to be attracting the "dirtier" ski areas. They suggested that this behavior was at least partially indicating, in an Olsonian (1965) way, "free rider" behavior, or using a VEP to garner, if not necessarily deliver, environmental laurels. Much to the surprise of its authors, the article generated immediate and intense media coverage, with articles being published in multiple media outlets including *The Denver Post* (two front page Business section stories and a supportive editorial based on the research), *The Rocky Mountains News*, the *Los Angeles Times*, *The Seattle Post*, the *Boston Globe*, the *Salt Lake City Tribune*, *CBS News*, *MSNBC News*, the *Aspen Daily News*, *Vail Trail News* and, some weeks later, the *New York Times*.

Most of the stories were supportive, a few were more "balanced," others, especially those from the ski areas' and their trade association's publications, were slightly more critical, and a few were outright hostile. The crux of the criticism centered around two major points. First, that the 2001 data represented a single "snapshot" in time focused on the first year of the SSP program. Thus, even if the analysis itself were correct (a judgment to which SSP proponents do not necessarily subscribe), it reflected the initial dilemmas of any "startup program," i.e., the analysis did not accurately represent the "results" of an established program, and, besides, surely the subsequent n-year data would reflect favorably on the SSP. Second, the National Ski Area Association strongly derided the use of materials collected by the Ski Area Citizens' Coalition, claiming they were unreliable and strongly biased against ski areas' justifiable profit concern (e.g., in terms of area expansion) (Dorsey 2004; Link 2005). In short, while the article was clearly "academic," it had, in the best traditions of the literature in public affairs, touched a much broader set of interests.

This current study seeks to contribute to both the immediate discussion as to the "success" of the SSP program by specifically taking the criticisms into analytic account and, just as important, by using a more longitudinal (i.e., five-year) data set. In addition, we will begin an initial discussion on the general viability of the VEP concept, using the SSP as a representative case by evaluating the link between participation in VEPs and different areas of corporate environmental performance.

Following this introduction, we first outline the theoretic underpinnings of the analysis. The next section describes the major contextual elements of the western ski industry and the Sustainable Slopes Program. Then, we provide details about our methodological approach and articulate how we have changed the analysis to address the complaints over the initial assessment of the SSP. The following sections present the analytic findings and their discussion as well as our conclusions.

Conceptual Framework

Motivations for Participation in Voluntary Environmental Programs

The literature on voluntary environmental programs (VEPs) shows a growing consensus consistent with neo-institutional theory that gives external pressures a significant role in determining the adoption of these initiatives (Arora and Cason 1996; Darnall 2002; Delmas 2002; Khanna and Damon 1999; Potoski and Prakash 2005; Welch, Mazur, and Bretschneider 2000). Neo-institutional theory proposes that the choices of rationally-bounded managers are restricted and shaped by a taken-for-granted social and cultural environment that provides a sense of social legitimacy to organizations (Meyer and Rowan 1977; Powell and DiMaggio 1991; Scott 2001). The most important elements of this social and cultural context include institutions such as shared beliefs, norms, formal rules, symbols and ceremonial traditions that define legitimate behavior (Meyer and Rowan 1977; Powell and DiMaggio 1991).

Neo-institutional scholars (Suchman 1995) challenge the notion that businesses are exclusively profit-seeking and emphasize the importance of achieving social legitimacy for long term business survival and competitiveness. Legitimate businesses are those whose actions are seen or presumed to be "desirable, proper, or appropriate within some socially constructed system of norms, values, beliefs, and definitions" (Suchman 1995, 574). Institutions that determine social legitimacy exert coercive, normative, and mimetic pressures that have an isomorphic effect, leading businesses that operate in the same organization field to adopt similar structures and strategies (Powell and DiMaggio 1991).

Accordingly, recent empirical studies have found a statistically significant association between higher participation in VEPs and institutional pressures such as higher regulatory and monitoring requirements and greater community and environmentalist demands (Arora and Cason 1996; Darnall 2002; Delmas 2002; Khanna and Damon 1999; Potoski and Prakash 2005; Welch, Mazur, and Bretschneider 2000). Additionally, these studies indicate higher adoption of these initiatives by publicly-traded and larger firms that are more visible and thus attract stronger institutional pressures to show superior environmental management (Arora and Cason 1996; Darnall 2002; Delmas 2002; Khanna and Damon 1999; King and Lenox 2000; Rivera 2004; Winter and May 2001). In the case of the U.S. western ski industry, Rivera and deLeon's (2004) initial assessment of the SSP also found similar institutional pressures and firm characteristics significantly related to the adoption of this program.[1]

Effectiveness of Voluntary Environmental Programs

Despite the emerging consensus about the factors and firm characteristics significantly associated with participation in VEPs, research still shows contradictory
perspectives and problematic evidence regarding a fundamental question for
those interested in exploring the use of VEPs as alternative instruments of environmental policy (Andrews 1998; Carmin, Darnall, and Homens 2003; Khanna
2001; Potoski and Prakash 2005): *Are voluntary programs effective in promoting higher environmental performance among their participants?* Let us therefore elaborate on the two basic alternative perspectives regarding the environmental effectiveness of voluntary programs.

The first theme proposes that voluntary programs serve as effective policy
tools to promote enhanced environmental protection. Supporters of voluntary
initiatives hypothesize that these programs provide specific incentives in the
form of increased environmental management flexibility, technical assistance,
and enhanced "green reputation" that directly encourage participants to adopt
superior environmental protection practices (Delmas and Terlaak 2001; Khanna
2001). VEPs' flexibility and technical assistance protocols can allow firms to
adopt an expanded variety of environmental management practices and technologies that are more cost-efficient than those required by command-and-control
regulations (Delmas and Terlaak 2001; Moon 2005). The sharing of "best practices" and environmental management systems (EMS) approaches, typical of
voluntary programs, may also facilitate environmental innovation and organizational learning at different levels of the firm thus permitting a firm to adopt environmental protection practices found to be more cost efficient and effective
(King and Lenox 2000). Because of their expected superior environmental practices, VEP participants may credibly improve their "green" reputation and use it
to gain higher sales and/or price premiums from environmentally aware consumers (Reinhardt 1998). For instance, hotel facilities participants in the Costa
Rican Certification for Sustainable Tourism appear to gain statistically significant premium prices (Rivera 2002). In addition, a firm's credible "green" reputation may help participants to enhance their environmental legitimacy and thus
develop better relations with regulators and environmentalists that can preempt
more stringent oversight and stringent regulations (Darnall 2003b; Lyon and
Maxwell 2001)

Additionally, even for those VEPs that lack independent monitoring, sanctions and/or rewards, neo-institutional scholars have posited that voluntary programs may trigger a socialization process involving external peer and industry-
wide pressures that compel members to self-regulate in order to gain or maintain
a collective "green" reputation and trust from its corporate peers, regulators,
stakeholders, and, ultimately, consumers (Granovetter 1985; Hoffman 1999;
King and Lenox 2000). VEPs' institutional socialization tactics may involve
technical assistance visits and meetings, use of formal symbols—such as envi-

ronmentally friendly, i.e., "green" labels—to identify participants, periodic public reports highlighting best and worst practices participants, peer pressures, and
endorsement by important industry players and regulatory agencies, and environmental groups (DiMaggio and Powell 1983; Hoffman 1999; King and Lenox
2000). To be sure, a few studies have suggested that voluntary initiatives that
include some of these institutional socialization mechanisms, such as the U.S.
Environmental Protection Agency's (EPA) 33/50 program and ISO-14001, may
have respectively been associated with lower toxic release inventory (TRI)
emissions and environmental compliance by their participants (Dasgupta 2000;
Khanna and Damon 1999; Potoski and Prakash 2005).

On the other hand, some scholars have depicted VEPs as relatively ineffective environmental policy instruments. For years they have posited that in general, firms seldom engage in collective action efforts beyond their narrow self-
interest unless socially-constrained by strong institutional pressures in the form
of monitoring and sanctions for lack of cooperation (Hardin 1968; Olson 1965;
Ostrom 1990; Williamson 1975). *Absent these strong institutional pressures, we
propose that purely voluntary environmental programs are unlikely to promote
superior environmental performance because of their lack of coercive mechanisms to prevent opportunistic participants from free-riding on program benefits*
such as "green" reputation, technical assistance, etc. (King and Lenox 2000;
Rivera and deLeon 2004; Toffel 2005). In this case, opportunism[2] is distinguished from usual self-interest seeking as a behavior in which voluntary program participants deliberately evade and/or misrepresent performing agreed-on
environmental practices aimed at promoting higher environmental performance
(Wathne and Heide 2000; Williamson 1975, 1985).[3]

The opportunistic challenges faced by voluntary programs, with no monitoring and sanctions, arise from the non-excludable public good nature of some
of the benefits they provide to participants (Darnall 2002; King and Lenox 2000;
Potoski and Prakash 2005). For instance, once created by the program, credible
"green" reputations are enjoyed by all adopting firms including those opportunistically free-riding with low environmental performance because they are not
differentiated from truly environmentally proactive firms (Darnall 2003a; King
and Lenox 2000). To be sure, empirical evidence from recent evaluations of
VEPs has generated doubts about the environmental effectiveness of these initiatives (Carmin, Darnall, and Homens 2003; Khanna 2001; Moon 2005). These
studies suggest that voluntary initiatives such as the Chemical Industry's Responsible Care, ISO-14001, and the U.S. Department of Energy's Global Climate Challenge may attract firms with questionable environmental performance.
Once enrolled these firms do not appear to improve significantly their environmental performance (King and Lenox 2000; Toffel 2005; Welch, Mazur, and
Bretschneider 2000). In the case of the ski industry's Sustainable Slopes Program, initial evidence also suggests that its participants are more likely to have
lower environmental performance (Rivera and deLeon 2004).

Lastly, we need to appreciate that there are distinctions between different
areas of environmental performance and voluntary programs effectiveness. The

arguments about the role of institutional pressures in preventing opportunistic behavior can shed light on another important and related issue that has scarcely been addressed by scholarly research: *Which distinct areas of environmental performance are more likely to be improved by firms joining a voluntary environmental program?* Most studies examining the environmental effectiveness of voluntary environmental initiatives have used the amount of toxic releases as a proxy for environmental performance because of the general lack of data about other areas of corporate environmental performance (Khanna 2001; Toffel and Marshall 2004). Yet, of course, environmental performance is a multidimensional concept that includes not only pollution emissions but also other areas of environmental protection, such as wildlife and habitat management, resource conservation, and footprint reduction (Starik and Rands 1995). Indeed, the SSP and other voluntary initiatives include a comprehensive list of environmental practices and standards that incorporate these and other recognized dimensions of environmental protection. Thus, it can be expected that VEP participants that do not face strong institutional pressures in the form of monitoring and sanctions for non-compliance would selectively adopt different environmental management practices depending on their cost, technical difficulty, visibility for stakeholders, and benefits.

Accordingly, *we propose that participant firms would be less likely to adopt those areas of environmental protection that are more costly and have uncertain long-term benefits with little short-term payoffs for firms.* For instance, practices such as wildlife protection and "footprint" reduction, despite their significant importance for environmental protection, offer no immediate financial benefits to ski areas (Porter and van der Linde 1995; Walley and Whitehead 1994). However, resource conservation practices that seek to reduce the use of energy, water, and other materials are known to offer shorter term payoffs making them more likely to be adopted by participants (Walley and Whitehead 1994).

The Context of Western Skiing: Principal Actors and Programs

Skiing has proven to be a very popular recreational activity in the United States and particularly in the western half of the country, constituting an important part of the area's tourism and recreation economy (Hudson 2000). Despite rapid growth in the 1960s and 1970s, during the 1980s and 1990s, the ski industry experienced relatively consistent (i.e., a low-growth rate) demand in terms of the number of skier visits (Hudson 2000; NSAA 2004b).[4] More recently, even though the ski industry has faced a number of challenges (e.g. economic uncertainty in the United States and increased travel related security concerns), ski resorts nation-wide experienced an increased number of skier visits over the last four ski seasons, particularly in the Rocky Mountains and western United States (NSAA 2004a, 2005b). The 2000 through 2004 ski seasons resulted in an average of 56 million skier visits per year, compared to an average of 52 million skier visits per year between 1982 and 1999; the three best years in terms of skier visits occurred within the last four years (NSAA 2004a, 2004b). In addition snowboarding continues to grow in popularity, albeit at a modest rate. The increase in skier visits has been accompanied by a consolidation and stabilization in the number of ski resorts operating within the United States. Since 2000, there have been approximately 490 ski resorts in operation each season compared to 727 resorts in operation during the 1984-85 season (NSAA 2004c).

Given the favorable climate and terrain for skiing, resorts located in the western United States are particularly popular skiing destinations. Western ski resorts, while fewer in absolute numbers, tend to attract more skiers than resorts in other parts of the country. Skier visits to resorts in the Rocky Mountains and Pacific West accounted for 54% of all skier visits during the 2003-04 season while states in these regions contain only 34% of the ski resorts operating in the United States in 2004 (NSAA 2004b, 2004c). Resorts in the Rocky Mountain region also commanded higher average lift ticket prices ($61.08) compared to the overall average ($53.95) (NSAA 2004a). Resorts in the western United States are also more likely to operate on federal lands. Unlike resorts in the eastern United States, over 90% of resorts in the West are operated on property leased from the U.S. Forest Service (USFS) under a special permitting process (SACC 2005).

A number of special interest groups have criticized the relationship between the ski industry and the USFS for the low rents charged to ski resorts for the use of public lands. Additionally, the USFS and the NSAA have created a number of partnership arrangements under which the parties work together to promote ski sports (Briggs 2000; Clifford 2002; Wharton 1997b). In a 1997 speech to the ski industry, Mike Dombeck, the then-head of the USFS, reflected on this relationship when he stated that outdoor recreation had surpassed timber logging as the most important activity in national forests and that there were over 31 million skier visits to national forest lands in 1996 (Wharton 1997a).

Ski resorts operating on USFS-controlled land must obtain special operating permits, abide by various environmental regulations, and pay permit fees based on the fair market value of the use of the land using a formula that considers the revenue ski resorts generate from the use of USFS lands (e.g., revenue from lift tickets, ski schools, and facilities on forest lands). USFS fees range from 1.5% to 4.0% of a ski resort's adjusted gross revenue from activities on national forest land (United States Code 2003). Despite the requirement that fees be based on fair market value, a number of General Accountability Office (GAO) reports have found that the USFS has not been collecting appropriate fees from ski resorts (GAO 1996; Rogers 2002; Rogers 2003).

The USFS's increased focus on recreation has coincided with a decrease in federal appropriations for the USFS and increased pressures on the agency to generate revenues from the management of forest lands (Clifford 2002). There are also concerns that fees generated from economic activity on USFS lands are used in part to fund special accounts and trust funds which are exempt from Congress' annual appropriation process but are used to finance local community projects and partially pay for overhead expenses such as equipment purchases and/or employee salaries (Gorte 2000; Gorte and Corn 1995). Some have argued that the use of this receipt-sharing process may create perverse incentives for local USFS offices faced with reduced federal appropriations (Gorte 2000).

The Sustainable Slopes Program

Environmentalists have long been critical of the U.S. ski industry and the USFS's seemingly lax oversight of ski areas on federal lands (Briggs 2000; Clifford 2002; Glick 2001). In the late 1990s, the NSAA's decision to create the Sustainable Slopes Program (SSP) followed years of criticism by environmental groups concerned with the environmental impact resorts have on sprawl, air quality, water quality, and wildlife (Briggs 2000). The 1998 arson attack on a Vail ski lodge, purportedly the work of a radical environmental group concerned about an expansion project undertaken by Vail, received widespread media attention, seemingly united environmentalists, and subjected the ski industry to significant scrutiny (Glick 2001; Sachs 2002).

In the aftermath of the arson attack, the NSAA met and worked with various stakeholders—including ski resorts, governmental organizations, and environmental groups—to develop an environmental charter for the ski industry (NSAA 2000; Sachs 2002). Following this collaborative process, in June 2000 the NSAA launched the Sustainable Slopes Program (SSP) and issued *Sustainable Slopes: The Environmental Charter for Ski Areas* (NSAA 2000). In addition to articulating an environmental vision and mission statement for the industry, the environmental charter's goal has been to demonstrate the ski industry's "commitment to good environmental stewardship" and "provide a framework for resorts across the country to implement best practices, assess environmental performance, and set goals for improvement in the future" (NSAA 2000, 2).

A number of governmental and non-profit organizations partnered with the NSAA in the creation of the SSP including the U.S. Environmental Protection Agency, U.S. Forest Service, Colorado Department of Public Health & Environment, U.S. Department of Energy, Conservation Law Foundation, Leave No Trace, Inc., and The Mountain Institute (NSAA 2000). According to the NSAA (2005a): " The number one reason for supporting Sustainable Slopes, expressed either directly or indirectly by all Partnering Organizations, is that it leads to improved environmental performance." A few of these partnering organizations have also provided significant funding for the SSP. For example, the U.S. Forest Service contributed $30,000 to finance the creation of the SSP and later funded data collection efforts used by the NSAA in the creation of SSP annual reports (Clifford 2002; NSAA 2005a). The SSP annual reports have also been funded by the National Fish and Wildlife Foundation (NSAA 2001). However, a number of prominent environmental organizations (e.g., The Sierra Club, The Nature Conservancy) that were involved in the SSP creation program chose not become official partners in the SSP program (NSAA 2000).

The SSP charter (NSAA 2000) involves 21 general categories of environmental protection for ski area planning, operations, and outreach (see Table 7.1). Since the creation of the SSP in 2000, the NSAA has issued Sustainable Slopes annual reports highlighting environmental activities of endorsing resorts and reporting on the progress of resorts in incorporating the environmental principles into their operations. Over the years, the number of resorts endorsing the SSP has increased from 160 in 2000 (33% of U.S. ski areas) to 178 in 2005 (36% of U.S. ski areas) (NSAA 2000, 2005a). However, it is important to underscore that the number of resorts completing the SSP's annual self-assessment tool, a key part of the program, fell from a high of 90 (52%) resorts in 2002 to 54 (30%) resorts in 2005 (NSAA 2002, 2005a). The 22% decline in submission of self-assessment reports has been experienced notwithstanding the prominent role given to responding ski areas in the SSP annual reports and despite the partial funding provided by the USFS to collect these self-assessment data.

For all its efforts, the SSP has not reduced tensions between the ski industry and certain environmental groups and the media that have criticized the SSP for its lack of performance standards and independent oversight and for ignoring many important areas of environmental protection (see e.g., Hartman and Zalaznick 2003; Langeland 2002). As the U.S. EPA liaison to the SSP noted in a *Vermont Law Review* article:

> The challenge for Sustainable Slopes lies in its implementation. It is a voluntary program, so ski resorts opt-in with non-binding obligations. If resorts do not employ suggested actions or do not report annually, there are no consequences. Independent of fulfilling the twenty-one principles, resorts remain able to use the program logo for marketing and advertising (Sachs 2002).

Methodology

Statistical Analysis

Because a ski area's environmental performance is not exogenous to its decision to adopt the SSP, we employed a recursive two-stage approach proposed by Heckman (1978, 1979) that corrects for self-selection bias in the estimation of the effects of voluntary programs. The specific application of this recursive methodology to assess benefits of voluntary environmental programs is outlined by Khanna and Damon (1999, 4-5, 13) and applied by the growing number of studies that have assessed the benefits of voluntary environmental programs (Khanna and Damon 1999; Maddala 1986; Potoski and Prakash 2005; Rivera 2002; Rivera and deLeon 2004; Welch, Mazur, and Bretschneider 2000). Also, to avoid endogeneity, control variables that vary over time were lagged one year in both stages. To elaborate:

Stage One. In this step, we model ski resorts' participation in the SSP by using a probit regression specification with panel data. Subsequently, we use

Table 7.1 Basic dimensions of ski areas' environmental performance*

Basic dimension	SSP General environmental protection categories	SACC Environmental protection criteria
1. Expansion management	1. Planning, design, and construction	1. Maintaining ski terrain within the existing footprint
		2. Preserving undisturbed lands from development
		3. Preserving environmentally sensitive areas
2. Natural resources conservation	2. Water use for snowmaking	4. Promoting and implementing recycling, and water, land, and energy conservation strategies
	3. Water use for facilities	5. Conserving water and energy by avoiding new snowmaking
	4. Water use for landscaping and summer activities	
	5. Energy use for facilities	
	6. Energy use for snowmaking	
	7. Energy use for lifts	
	8. Energy use for vehicle fleets	
	9. Waste reduction	
	10. Product re-use	
	11. Recycling	
3. Pollution management	12. Water quality management	6. Minimizing traffic, emissions, and pollution.
	13. Wastewater management	7. Protecting water quality
	14. Potentially hazardous wastes	
	15. Air quality	
	16. Visual quality	
	17. Transportation	
4. Wildlife and habitat management	18. Fish and wildlife management	8. Protection of threatened or endangered species
	19. Forest and vegetative management	9. Wildlife habitat protection
	20. Wetlands and riparian areas	
	21. Education and outreach	

Source: SACC, 2005 and NSAA, 2000

*A detailed list of the underlying variables used for assessing each environmental protection criterion is available online at SACC's website (http://www.skiareacitizens.com/criteria.html).

this probit model to calculate each ski resort's probability of participation in the Sustainable Slopes Program. The control variables included in these probit models seek to account for federal and stakeholder institutional pressures known to affect participation in the SSP and other voluntary environmental programs (Khanna 2001; Rivera and de Leon 2004).

$$D_{it} = \delta_i + a_i X_{1it} + \varepsilon_{1it}; \quad (1)$$

Where:
i = ith ski area
t = observation year
D_{it} = Decision to participate in the SSP
δ_i = Regression constant term
X_{1it} = Vector of independent variables (federal government oversight, stock exchange trading, size, state location)
a_1 = Regression coefficients for vector of independent variables
ε_{1it} = Equation 1's random error term

Stage Two. In this stage of the analysis, we model the different dimensions of ski resorts' environmental performance using a random effects specification[5] estimated with a mixed generalized linear regression technique (MGLR) deemed appropriate for unbalanced panel data (Greene 2000; Little 1995).[6] The estimated probability of participation in the SPP calculated in the initial step is used here as an independent variable to assess the effect of SSP participation on environmental performance (Greene 2000; Khanna and Damon 1999; Maddala 1986). The second stage regression model also includes control variables previously found to be associated with corporate environmental performance (Darnall 2002; Delmas 2002; Khanna 2001; King and Lenox 2000; Potoski and Prakash 2005; Rivera and de Leon 2004). Our second-step model specification is represented by the following equations:

$$Y_{it} = \alpha_i + b_2 X_{2it} + c_i P_{it} + \varepsilon_{2it}; \quad (2)$$

Where:
Y_{it} = ith ski area's environmental performance at yeat t
α_i = Regression constant term
X_{2it} = Vector of independent variables (federal government oversight, stock exchange trading, size, and index of state environmentalism)
P_{it} = Probability of participation in the SSP
ε_{2it} = Equation 2's random error term

The use of Heckman's two-stage recursive methodology for estimating self-selection models has been criticized by some because the first and second stage models usually share all or almost all identifier variables (Puhani 2000). If a linear probability model is used in stage one for determining the inverse Mill's ratio (probability of participation variable introduced on the second stage), collinearity problems between this ratio and other independent variables arise in the second stage (Maddala 1986, 267-71; Olsen 1980, 1818-19). Thus, is has been suggested that application of the Heckman methodology requires the use of identifying variables associated with the dependent variable in stage one but not associated with the dependent variable in stage two.

This methodological issue was initially addressed by Olsen (1980) in an article published in *Econometrica* and more recently by other authors (Greene 2000, 926-946; Maddala 1986, 267-71). They show that the Heckman techniques that use a probit model for stage one and a linear model for the second stage do not suffer problems of identification even when a similar set of independent exogenous variables is used for both stages. This is because the probit model involves a nonlinear function of its independent variables and thus the Mill's ratio calculated from it "is a nonlinear function of the exogenous variables in the model" (Olsen 1980, 1818).

Data and Measures

Building upon Rivera and deLeon's (2004) initial cross-sectional assessment of the SSP, we collected panel data on SSP adoption, environmental performance, and independent control variables (e.g., ski resort location, ownership, size, etc.) for five years between 2001 and 2005. Information about SSP adoption was obtained from the program's official annual reports and website. Environmental performance dimensions data were obtained from the dis aggregated Ski Area Citizens' Coalition annual scorecard rankings. Data for the independent variables was gathered from individual ski areas' internet homepages, Travelocity.com, the National Ski Areas Association, the USFS, and the stock markets in New York and Toronto.

Our final sample consisted of 110 U.S. western ski areas which equates to approximately 62% of the 178 facilities operating in the western United States in 2005.[7] Included in this sample were 76 ski areas that as of the summer of 2005 had received third-party environmental performance ratings and 34 ski areas randomly drawn from the western ski resort population. The use of this sample to estimate the first and second step regression models is described below.

Probit Regression Pooled Data. Because once enrolled in the SSP ski areas are not excluded from the program, their adoption decision does not have to be made every year. Thus, as suggested by Khanna and Damon (1999), once a ski area has adopted the SPP, it is dropped from the dataset. Conversely, non-adopters could choose to participate in any following year. For instance, ski areas that joined the program in 2001 are included two times in the probit regression pooled data, once as non-members in 2000, and then as SSP members in 2001 (Khanna and Damon 1999). The resulting pooled data used for the probit analysis includes 233 observations.

Environmental Performance Dimensions Models. In the case of the second step regression models, all ski area observations for which environmental performance data were available between 2001 and 2005 were used resulting in an unbalanced panel dataset of 350 observations.

In the following paragraphs, we describe the measures of the variables included in our analysis beginning with the different dimensions of environmental performance, participation in the SSP, and then following with the independent variables.

Measure of Environmental Performance Dimensions. Following the approach used by Rivera and deLeon (2004), publicly available data obtained from the Ski Area Citizens Coalition (SACC) annual scorecard listing were used to estimate ski areas' environmental performance. SACC is a partnership of nonprofit environmental organizations located in the western United States. Since 2000, SACC has conducted assessments of the environmental performance of western ski resorts and annually publishes the results online as Environmental Scorecard Grades (http://www.skiareacitizens.com). Ski areas are assigned letter grades from A (best) to F (worst) based on their percentage compliance with multiple environmental performance criteria. The environmental criteria's underlying variables and the grading methodology are available online at SACC website (http://www.skiareacltizens.com/criteria.html). The information used to estimate scorecard grades is obtained from government documents collected through Freedom of Information Act requests.[8] Additional information is gathered from onsite visits, an annual ski area survey, individual ski resorts' websites, corporate reports, and external sources such as media articles published by trade magazines, business press, and the general media (Dorsey 2004; SACC 2005).

Since their initial publication, SACC's scorecard grades have received increasing recognition as a measure of ski areas' environmental performance not only by specialized ski publications and websites but also by mainstream media in the United States and abroad including: *The New York Times, Denver Post, Rocky Mountains News, Los Angeles Times, Seattle Post, CNN* and *ESPN*.[9] Nevertheless, it is important to underscore that the National Ski Area Association (NSAA) has vehemently criticized the use of Environmental Scorecard Grades as "an unaudited, inherently flawed, and biased measure of resort environmental performance" (Dorsey 2004). The NSAA also strongly portrays the Ski Area Citizens' Coalition as an alliance of radical environmental groups whose goal is to obstruct the expansion of the industry (Dorsey 2004; Link 2005). In particular, NSAA representatives criticize the scorecard for placing undue emphasis on penalizing ski areas involved in expansion related activities, such as real estate development, and those refusing to respond to SACC annual surveys (Baird 2004; Blevins 2004; Dorsey 2004; Janofsky 2000).

To be sure, the controversial perspectives surrounding the use of environmental performance data are not unique to SACC's scorecard grades. They are inherent in other widely used sources of environmental performance information such as, for example, self-reported TRI data gathered by the U.S. Environmental Protection Agency (King and Lenox 2000; Toffel and Marshall 2004). It is not surprising that "hard" environmental performance data are seldom available given that in the United States less than 1% of large regulated facilities received inspection of their air, water, and land pollution between 1996 and 1998 (Potoski and Prakash 2005). Thus, SACC scorecard grades and other measures of environmental performance widely used in the literature are clearly imperfect measures based on judgment and interpretation of qualitative and quantitative data that inherently involve human error and biases (Waddock 2003). In this sense, the human judgments used to develop the SACC scorecard ratings "are in many respects no different from the interpretations that underlie financial and accounting statements, which also rely on the (sometimes erroneous and sometimes felonious as witnessed in the first year of the millennium) judgments of auditors, accountants, and financial analysts to determine materiality" (Waddock 2003).

In light of the putative problems presented by the SACC scorecard, we chose to extend the approach taken in the initial evaluation of the SSP (Rivera and de Leon 2004). First, we tried to obtain alternative data that could verify or challenge the findings of the SACC environmental scorecard. An obvious alternative were the SSP members' annual self-reported environmental performance assessments collected by the NSAA, gathered in part through funding from the USFS (NSAA 2005a). On different occasions, we contacted the NSAA's Director of Public Policy seeking to gain access to these data. Unfortunately, NSAA chose to maintain the proprietary nature of these self-reported assessments and, therefore, we were denied access to these data.

The only additional publicly available indication of ski resorts' environmental performance available was the Golden Eagle Award given annually to ski resorts in recognition of their environmental excellence. This award is currently being administered by the NSAA and was previously run by Mountains Sport Media, publisher of *Ski Magazine* (NSAA 2005a). It is noteworthy that in the 2000 to 2004 period, Golden Eagle awardees also received SACC's highest environmental scorecard grades in four of five cases, suggesting a high correlation between these two independent proxies of superior environmental performance.

Second, we followed an alternative approach aimed at addressing concerns related to the SACC scorecard's "overemphasis" on penalizing expansion related activities. Instead of using SACC's overall Environmental Scorecard Grades, we used the disaggregated data to estimate percentage compliance ratios for four basic dimensions of ski areas' environmental performance: 1. expansion management; 2. natural resources conservation; 3. pollution management, and 4. wildlife and habitat management. Table 7.1 also lists the SACC scorecard criteria that we selected to be included under each dimension. It is important to note that we excluded SACC criteria that did not fit these categories or that were not used consistently over the period 2001 to 2005.[10] Finally, we also estimated *overall environmental performance* for each ski area as the non-weighted average of the four basic environmental performance dimensions' percentage compliance ratios.

Measure of Other Variables. *Adoption of the Sustainable Slopes Program* is measured using a discrete variable that takes a value of one for enrolled facilities and zero for non-participants. Low, medium, and high levels of *federal government environmental oversight* are measured respectively by identifying the type of private, mixed, and public land ownership occupied by ski area facilities. As suggested by previous authors (Briggs 2000; Clifford 2002; Rivera and deLeon 2004) facilities located on public land owned by the federal government faced significantly higher levels of environmental oversight. *Ski area size* is calculated as the total amount of skiable acres possessed by each ski area. *Ownership by a publicly-traded firm* is measured by a dummy variable equal to one for ski areas belonging to corporations traded on a stock exchange and zero otherwise. *Probability of participation in the SSP* is measured on a zero to one continuous scale and its values were estimated using the probit model calculated in the first stage of the statistical analysis (Hartman 1988; Khanna and Damon 1999). Lastly, the level of *state environmental pressures* is measured with two alternative proxies: state location or Mazur and Welch's (1999) index of state environmentalism used by other researchers (Potoski and Prakash 2005; Toffel 2005). This index is estimated using four standardized indicators: 1. state membership in the largest U.S. environmental organizations; 2. level of pro-environmental public opinion as measured by National Opinion Research Center; 3. congressional delegation's League of Conservations Voters pro-environmental ranking; and 4. state's environmental policy implementation strength ranking (Mazur and Welch 1999).

Results and Discussion

Table 7.2 shows descriptive statistics for SSP participation and performance rates for different areas of environmental protection. Descriptive statistics for the independent variables for 2005 are presented in Table 7.3. These descriptive figures suggest that, as has been the case for the overall population of U.S. ski resorts, level of SSP participation for our sample of western ski resorts has increased less than 3% over the 2001 to 2005 period (see Table 7.2). Regarding overall environmental performance, the descriptive results indicate that the proportion of ski areas (SPP members and non-members) receiving the lowest rates (F grades) has decreased from about 28% in 2001 to 12% in 2005, with the mid-rate environmental performance ranking (C grades) increasing the most from approximately 21% in 2001 to about 51% in 2005 (see Table 7.2). It is also interesting to note that in terms of individual dimensions of environmental protection, Expansion Management is the dimension where the largest proportion of sampled ski resorts (45.45%) received the highest grade (A grade).

Table 7.2 Descriptive statistics for program participation and overall environmental performance

Variable/Year	2001		2002		2003		2004		2005		Full period (2001-05)	
	N	Percent	N	Percent	N	Percent	N	Percent	N	Percent	N	Percent
Sustainable Slopes adoption												
Yes	79	71.82%	81	73.64%	82	74.55%	81	73.64%	82	74.55%	405	73.64%
No	31	28.18%	29	26.36%	28	25.45%	29	26.36%	28	25.45%	145	26.36%
Total	110		110		110		110		110		550	
Overall environmental performance (percentage score for SSP members and non-members)												
77 to 100 (A)	4	7.02%	4	5.71%	4	5.71%	4	5.26%	3	3.90%	19	5.43%
60 to <77 (B)	7	12.28%	7	10.00%	7	10.00%	13	17.11%	5	6.49%	39	11.14%
45 to <60 (C)	12	21.05%	21	30.00%	28	40.00%	33	43.42%	39	50.65%	133	38.00%
35 to <45 (D)	18	31.58%	24	34.29%	15	21.43%	16	21.05%	21	27.27%	94	26.86%
<35 (F)	16	28.07%	14	20.00%	16	22.86%	10	13.16%	9	11.69%	65	18.57%
Total	57		70		70		76		76		350	
Average performance	44.86 (16.23)		45.66 (14.52)		47.65 (15.44)		50.66 (15.44)		48.00 (12.48)		47.53 (14.82)	

Table 7.3 Descriptive statistics for the year 2005

Variable	N	Percent	Variable	N	Percent
Expansion management (percentage score)			Federal government oversight		
77 to 100 (A)	35	45.45%	Lower	19	17.27%
60 to <77 (B)	12	15.58%	Medium	15	13.64%
45 to <60 (C)	11	14.29%	Higher	76	69.09%
35 to <45 (D)	7	9.09%	Total	110	
≤35 (F)	12	15.58%			
Total	77				
Mean score		67.30 (26.31)			
Natural resource conservation			Ownership by a publicly traded firm		
77 to 100 (A)	3	3.95%	Yes	10	9.09%
60 to <77 (B)	3	3.95%	No	100	90.91%
45 to <60 (C)	6	7.89%	Total	110	
35 to <45 (D)	11	14.47%			
≤35 (F)	53	69.74%			
Total	76				
Mean score		31.37 (18.04)			
Pollution management			Size (thousand acres)		
77 to 100 (A)	0	0.00%	0 - 1	57	51.82%
60 to <77 (B)	12	15.58%	1> - 2	28	25.45%
45 to <60 (C)	54	70.13%	2> - 3	17	15.45%
35 to <45 (D)	0	0.00%	3> - 4	6	5.45%
≤35 (F)	11	14.29%	4> - 5	2	1.82%
Total	77		Total	110	
Mean score		50.54 (11.19)	Mean score		1.3 (1.04) [a]
Wildlife and habitat management			State location		
77 to 100 (A)	0	0.00%	Alaska	2	1.82%
60 to <77 (B)	0	0.00%	Arizona	2	1.82%
45 to <60 (C)	36	46.75%	California	20	18.18%
35 to <45 (D)	6	7.79%	Colorado	25	22.73%
≤35 (F)	35	45.45%	Idaho	8	7.27%
Total	77		Montana	8	7.27%
Mean score		32.17 (19.97)	New Mexico	8	7.27%
			Nevada	4	3.64%
			Oregon	8	7.27%
			Utah	13	11.82%
			Washington	9	8.18%
			Wyoming	3	2.73%
			Total	110	

[a]Standard deviations are in parentheses.

Indeed, no ski resorts received an A grade for pollution management and wild-life protection and only 3.95% scored an "A" for natural resource conservation (see Table 7.3).

Adoption of the Sustainable Slopes Program

Findings for two probit regression specifications that model ski areas' participation decisions are presented in Table 7.4. Each model uses a different proxy for state environmental pressures: Model 1 relies on state location whereas Model 2 uses Mazur and Welch's index of state environmentalism (1999). Given that the two models are statistically significant ($P<0.01$) and offer similar results, we only discuss the results of Model 2.[11,12] In accordance with previous research on voluntary environmental programs, the probit findings indicate that ski areas are significantly more likely to participate in the SSP when facing higher levels of federal government oversight ($p<0.05$) (Darnall 2003a; Henriques and Sadorsky 1996; Khanna and Damon 1999; Rivera 2004). Also, consistent with previous studies of VEP participation, the results suggest that larger ski area size ($P<0.01$), and greater levels of state environmental pressures ($p<0.05$) are significantly correlated with adoption of the SSP (Darnall 2002; Khanna 2001; King and Lenox 2000; Toffel 2005).[13] The effect of ownership by a publicly traded firm is less conclusive as only Model 2 suggests a positive relationship with SSP participation at 90% confidence. Given that participation in the SSP has changed little over the 2001-2005 period, it is not surprising that our findings are congruent with Rivera and deLeon's (2004) assessment of the first year participation in the Sustainable Slope Program.

Overall, this evidence is consistent with neo-institutional theory concepts suggesting that coercive pressures in the form of regulatory demands, arising at either the federal or state level, are a key incentive for promoting corporate "green" signaling in the form of adoption of self-regulatory initiatives, such as the Sustainable Slope Program (Darnall 2003a; Delmas and Terlaak 2001). Similarly, larger ski areas and those traded in the stock market are more visible to a wider array of stakeholders (i.e., the media, environmentalists, consumers, the industry association) that exert stronger normative institutional pressures on these facilities to show greater proactive environmental behavior (Darnall 2003a; King and Lenox 2000). Thus, we suggest that independent of their actual environmental practices, these resorts use SSP adoption as a relatively low-cost and conspicuous "green legitimacy" building mechanism that may help to preempt additional environmental regulatory demands (Darnall 2003b; Lyon and Maxwell 2001). Larger or publicly traded facilities may also find the adoption of SSP practices easier because they tend to have more resources and greater access to innovative environmental management technologies as compared to smaller or privately owned ski areas (Hoffman 1999; King and Lenox 2000).

Table 7.4 Results from probit regression models[1]
(Dependent variable: Participation in the Sustainable Slopes Program)

	Model 1	Model 2
Constant	-1.68 (0.42)[a] ***	-2.50 (0.36)***
Federal government environmental oversight		
High (Public land)	1.29 (0.32)***	1.17 (0.28)***
Medium (Public-private land)	1.81 (0.42)***	1.69 (0.34)***
Ownership by publicly trade firm	0.99 (0.84)	1.45 (0.78)*
Size (thousand of acres units)	0.73 (0.17)***	0.66 (0.14)***
State environmental pressures		
Index of state environmentalism		1.21 (0.51)**
State location		
Alaska	-1.13 (0.70)	
Arizona	-0.12 (0.72)	
California	0.51 (0.34)	
Idaho	-1.34 (0.46)***	
Montana	-0.59 (0.47)	
New Mexico	-1.03 (0.43)**	
Nevada	-0.81 (0.44)*	
Oregon	0.72 (0.55)	
Utah	-0.24 (0.41)	
Washington	-0.32 (0.42)	
Wyoming	-1.19 (0.61)**	
N	233	233
-2 Log L	216.45	236.57
χ^2 for covariates	91.46***	71.34***
Percent correctly classified	83.8	80.2

[1]Model 1 is used to predict ski areas' probability of participation given that it has a higher percentage of correctly classified adoption decisions.
[a] Standard errors are in parentheses.   Prob: = *prob<0.10; ** prob<0.05; *** prob < 0.01

Environmental Effectiveness of the SSP

More important than identifying factors associated with participation is determining whether adoption of voluntary programs, such as the SSP, actually promotes higher environmental performance by participants (Andrews 1998; Potoski and Prakash 2005). Seeking to address this question, we estimated five different regression models that analyze the outcome of the SSP in different areas of environmental protection: Overall environmental management, expansion management, natural resource conservation, pollution management, and wildlife and habitat management (see Table 7.5) For all models, the chi-square statistic indicates a significant fit for the independent variables included in the models (P<0.01) (alternative model specifications are displayed on endnote 14).[14]

Model 3 on Table 7.5 presents the results for overall environmental performance. We find that the coefficient on probability of participation is not statistically significant, even at 90% confidence. This finding indicates that ski areas' adoption of the SSP is not significantly correlated with higher overall environmental performance for the 2001-2005 period. Similarly, the results suggest that during this period, enrollment in the SSP does not have a statistically significant correlation with higher performance in the following individual dimensions of environmental protection: expansion management (See Model 4), pollution management (Model 6), and wildlife and habitat management (Model 7). In these three cases, the coefficients on the probability of participation variable are statistically insignificant (P<0.1). Compared to non-adopting ski resorts, SSP participants only appear to show a statistically significant correlation with higher Natural Resource Conservation performance rates (P<0.05; see Model 5).

These results indicate lack of statistical evidence to conclude that between 2001 and 2005, ski areas adopting the SSP displayed superior performance levels than non-participants for most areas of environmental protection. SSP adoption only seems to be associated with higher performance in natural resources conservation practices. These non-significant findings are consistent with the neo-institutional theory arguments positing that purely voluntary initiatives are bound to suffer free-riding behavior because of their lack of robust coercive and normative mechanisms that can differentiate between proactive and opportunistic participants (Hardin 1968; King and Lenox 2000; Olson 1965; Ostrom 1990; Williamson 1975).

As highlighted by Rivera and de Leon (2004) in their initial selection effect assessment of the SSP: a significant number of poor environmental performing facilities appear to self-select into the program because the program's charter did not established performance-based standards, did not require independent third-party monitoring of its members' environmental practices, and lacked sanctions or rewards for respectively poor or superior environmental performance (Dorsey 2004; Rivera and deLeon 2004; Sachs 2002). Our five-year treatment effect evaluation contributes to the initial SSP assessment by showing

Table 7.5 MGL regression results
(Dependent variable: environmental performance)

	Overall environmental performance (Model 3)	Expansion management (Model 4)	Natural resources conservation (Model 5)	Pollution management (Model 6)	Wildlife and habitat Management (Model 7)
Constant	55.96 (5.29)[1] ***	85.12 (8.81)***	31.87 (7.94)***	57.53 (5.38)***	62.16 (7.56)***
Federal government oversight					
High (Public land)	-7.00 (3.86)*	-4.68 (5.94)	-13.32 (6.21)**	-0.52 (4.23)	-10.38 (6.38)
Medium (Public-private land)	-10.81 (4.61)**	-8.54 (7.01)	-18.97 (7.53)**	1.20 (5.13)	-17.45 (7.92)**
Ownership by publicly traded firm	-2.06 (4.18)	-15.97 (6.65)**	-2.28 (5.51)	-2.15 (4.42)	-3.81 (6.40)
Probability of participation	8.75 (8.32)	-11.90 (14.00)	32.70 (12.43)**	12.59 (8.41)	-4.27 (11.85)
Size (thousands of acres units)	-4.47 (2.1)**	-7.0 (3.5)**	-7.0 (3.1)**	2.0 (2.1)	-0.45 (2.9)
State environmental pressures	-0.19 (7.57)	9.60 (12.61)	16.66 (11.31)	-14.71 (7.65)*	-7.76 (10.65)
N	348	348	348	348	348
-2 Log L	-590.6	-321.1	-223.7	-481.9	-117.9
χ^2 for covariates	272.27***	330.34***	191.37***	175.92***	88.79***

[1] Standard errors are in parentheses.
Prob: = *prob<0.10; ** prob<0.05; *** prob < 0.01.

lack of statistical evidence suggesting that once enrolled and over time, enough participants improve their practices in agreed-upon SSP dimensions of environmental protection such as expansion management, pollution management, and wildlife and habitat management. Facing the SSP's weak institutional mechanisms for preventing opportunistic behavior, it appears that once enrolled, program participants may predominantly adopt those environmental management practices that are highly visible, such as recycling, or those that offer immediate short-term benefits with relatively small investments such as energy and water conservation (Porter and van der Linde 1995; Walley and Whitehead 1994).

To be sure, our findings suggest that compared to non-adopting ski areas, the only dimension of environmental protection for which SSP members seem to show a statistically significant improvement is natural resources conservation. This dimension includes recycling, energy, and water conservation practices (see Table 7.1) that profit-driven firms are more likely to adopt without an institutional socialization process spurred by strong coercive and normative pressures (Delmas 2002; Hoffman 1999; King and Lenox 2000; Scott 2001). On the other hand, the other three major dimensions of environmental protection involve practices that may not have evident short-term financial benefits, or as in the case of relatively more profitable pollution prevention measures, require larger financial investments that run against ski areas' capital budget constraints (Walley and Whitehead 1994).

Regarding the control variables included in the environmental performance specifications, we found that ski areas' location on federal land or mixed land appears to have a statistically significant correlation with lower overall environmental performance (Model 3) and natural resource conservation performance (Model 5). In addition, location in mixed land also shows a significant correlation with lower wildlife and habitat management performance (Model 6). The coefficient on ownership by a publicly-traded firm (Model 4) also indicates a statistically significant association with lower performance for expansion management. Finally, larger ski areas appear to have a statistically significant correlation with lower overall environmental performance ($P<0.05$). Similarly, larger ski areas are significantly related to lower performance rates for expansion management (Model 4) and natural resource conservation (Model 5).

These findings for ski areas located on federal or mixed land were unexpected (Henriques and Sadorsky 1996; Khanna 2001). After all, ski areas occupying federal land administered by the USFS are periodically subjected to greater coercive institutional pressures in the form of enhanced government oversight through a Special Use Permit process. These Special Use Permits call for ski areas' operations and development plans to be consistent with USFS resource management plans and fee structures (Briggs 2000; Clifford 2002; Rivera and deLeon 2004). Holding Special Use Permits also involves obtaining approval of Environmental Impact Statements for any new development.

Yet, the lower performance of ski areas occupying national forest lands may reflect weak institutional pressures that result from at least three contradictory mandates and conflict of interest conditions experienced by the USFS. For instance, as suggested by Rivera and deLeon (2004), the USFS has opposing mandates that require it to regulate ski areas' environmental impacts and concurrently promote ski industry growth. Second, promoting increasing economic activities on national forest land directly increases the hundreds of millions of dollars annually allocated to the off-budget trust funds sometimes used by the USFS to partially finance overhead expenses such as employee salaries (Dombeck 2000; Gorte and Corn 1995).[15] Third, the USFS is required by law to share 25% of its gross commercial revenue from national forests with local counties for roads and school financing (Gorte 2000; Rey 2005).[16] Accordingly, local western congressional representatives and county officials with national forest lands in their districts tend to actively advocate for increasing economic activities in national forests against the demands from environmentalists for reduced economic activity (Dombeck 2000; Gorte 2000; Rey 2005). In addition, it can also be argued that the lack of exclusive private property rights intrinsic to ski areas located on federal land preempts any incentives that ski firms may have to engage in environmental protection practices that involve uncertain long-term benefits (Hardin 1968; Olson 1965; Ostrom 1990).[17]

Despite the higher visibility of ski areas owned by publicly traded corporations, the lack of evidence linking them to higher scores for overall environmental performance, natural resources conservation, pollution management, and wildlife habitat management was not surprising. The same can be said of their significant association with lower expansion management performance. Wall Street does not exert normative environmental pressures on firms and instead focuses on demanding consistent double digit increases in financial performance which, in the case of ski resorts, is accomplished by focusing on aggressive real estate development and expansion activities that inherently have a negative impact on the environmental footprint of ski resorts (Hudson 2000; Palmeri 2003). The emphasis on quarterly profits also reduces the appeal of investments in other areas of environmental protection that involve uncertain long-term payoffs (Walley and Whitehead 1994). We suggest that a similar underlying logic applies to the overall lower environmental performance shown by larger ski areas that are known for their aggressive focus on real estate development around skiable terrain (Palmeri 2003).

Conclusions

This study contributes to answering a basic issue regarding the use of VEPs as alternative environmental protection policy tools: *Are voluntary programs effective in promoting higher environmental performance by participant firm facilities?* We also contribute to the literature by highlighting the importance of analyzing an additional issue related to the environmental policy effectiveness of voluntary environmental initiatives: *Which distinct areas of environmental per-*

formance are more likely to be improved by firms joining a voluntary environmental program? We addressed these two questions by assessing the implementation in the western United States of the Sustainable Slopes Program (SSP), a voluntary initiative established by the National Ski Areas Association.

Consistent with neo-institutional theory, our findings indicate that participation in the SSP is related to coerceive and normative pressures in the form of enhanced federal oversight and higher state environmental demands exerted by state agencies, local environmental groups, and public opinion (Darnall 2003a; Khanna 2001; King and Lenox 2000; Rivera 2004). Additionally, our five-year study found no statistical evidence to conclude that compared to non-participants SSP ski areas have higher overall environmental performance or higher scores in the following individual dimensions of environmental protection: expansion management, pollution management, and wildlife and habitat management. SSP participants only appear to show a statistically significant correlation with higher natural resource conservation performance rates.

These findings are also consistent with the neo-institutional perspective argument that purely voluntary initiatives that lack specific performance-based standards, third-party oversight, rewards for exceptional behavior, and/or sanctions for poor performance are bound to suffer free-riding behavior because of their lack of robust institutional mechanisms that can differentiate between proactive and opportunistic participants (Hardin 1968; Olson 1965; Ostrom 1990; King and Lenox 2000; Rivera and deLeon 2004; Scott 2001; Williamson 1975).

Facing SSP's weak institutional mechanisms for preventing opportunistic behavior, it appears that once enrolled, ski areas may predominantly adopt natural resources conservation practices that are known to be easier and more visible for their customers (such as recycling) or those that offer immediate short-term benefits with relatively small investment such as energy and water conservation (Porter and van der Linde 1995; Walley and Whitehead 1994). Unfortunately, without an effective institutional socialization process spurred by strong coercive and normative pressures, we found no evidence of similar adoption of practices affecting other major dimensions of environmental protection such as expansion management and wildlife habitat management. These other dimensions may not have evident short-term financial benefits or customer visibility, or as in the case of relatively more profitable pollution prevention measures require larger financial investments that run against firms' capital budget constraints (Delmas 2002; Hoffman 1999; King and Lenox 2000; Scott 2001; Walley and Whitehead 1994).

For policy makers, the findings of this study suggest reservations about a priori assuming that purely voluntary programs can be effective in promoting comprehensive superior environmental protection. Of course, given the limited nature of this particular inquiry, we cannot judge VEPs in general. However, we do present the distinct possibility that purely voluntary environmental initiatives are much more problematic than their proponents would generalize. Most importantly, this research suggests caution for federal agencies about officially endorsing industry sponsored voluntary environmental initiatives—such as the ski industry's SSP—that lack independent monitoring, performance standards, and any type of sanctions/rewards for poor/ superior environmental performance. Finally, it is important to stress an important limitation of our study. Although the Ski Areas Citizens' Coalition's Environmental Scorecard is the best available measure of ski areas' environmental performance, its validity has been strongly challenged by the National Ski Areas Association. We repeatedly requested access to alternative environmental performance data collected by the SSP but NSAA officials denied us access to the data. In future studies in this area we hope researchers may be able to access these proprietary environmental performance data collected by the SSP or are able to use other alternative environmental performance measures.

Fall 2008 Postscript

Perhaps partially in response to the large amount of news media stories critical of the Sustainable Slopes Program (SSP), in 2006 the National Ski Areas Association (NSAA) expressed its intention to update it. As part of this revision, the NSAA acknowledged: "The need to shift from facilitating group reporting and blanket accountability to supporting the individual [ski] resorts in their efforts to improve their environmental performance" (NSAA, 2006: page 4-1).

NSAA considered these changes necessary as it came to view the SSP as a "maturing voluntary program" that has to emphasize "ever higher levels of performance while continuing to encourage broad participation and efforts across the industry" (NSAA, 2006: page 4-1). This new perspective resulted in a new emphasis on encouraging individual ski resorts to produce annual environmental reports. In 2006, the SSP official Annual Reports stopped claiming that the number one reason for partnering organizations (e.g. U.S. Environmental Protection Agency and U.S. Forest Service) to support the program was that "it leads to improved environmental performance." Also, for the first time in 2007, NSAA sought to improve the credibility and openness of the SSP by encouraging its participants to obtain third-party certification with nationally recognized certification organizations (NSAA, 2007: 1–4). Additionally, the SSP launched a US$10,000 fund to support the adoption of the program's principles among its participant resorts (NSAA, 2008: 4-1). As scholars that have studied the SSP since 2001, we view these intended changes with interest and hope that they may indeed result in more environmental accountability and transparency among ski resorts participating in this voluntary initiative.

However, it is very important to verify these announced changes against actual implementation. As we discussed in the article, adoption of third-party oversight, performance-based standards, and sanction/rewards are necessary conditions for voluntary programs to be effective at promoting enhanced environmental performance by their participations. The SSP's new support for cred-

ible third-party oversight, that can help reduce free-riding behavior by participant ski resorts, has resulted in a small number of ski resorts receiving different
types of independent environmental certifications. As of October 2008, two ski
resorts—Aspen-Snowmass (CO) and Jackson Hole (WY)—have received comprehensive certification of their environmental management practices by ISO
14001. Also, with the help of the NSAA we were also able to identify a few
other examples of ski resorts gaining independent certification of some of their
environmental management practices. They include: 1. Mammoth (CA) and
Grand Targhee (WY) obtaining Climate Registry Certification for their reduction of greenhouse gases; 2. Vail (CO), Crystal Mountain (MI), Northstar-at-
Tahoe (CA), and Mammoth (CA) receiving Leadership in Energy and Environmental Design (LEED) Certification for some of their new buildings; and 3. Six
additional ski resorts—Snowmass (CO), Wolf Creek (UT), Tamarack (ID),
Ragged Mountain (NH), Angel Fire (NM), and Stowe Mountain (VT)—earning
different kinds of Audubon Certification for specific environmental protection
projects and practices.

The actions taken by this select group of ski resorts is no doubt encouraging
and provides a more credible indication of their actual adoption of proactive
beyond compliance environmental protection practices. Yet, we believe that it
remains to be seen whether other non third-party certified SSP participant resorts have actually improved their performance in the different areas of environmental protection assessed in this article for the 2001–2005 period.

Bibliography

Andrews, R. 1998. "Environmental Regulation and Business Self-Regulation." *Policy Sciences* 31: 177–197.

Arora, S. and T. Cason. 1996. "Why do Firms Volunteer to Exceed Environmental Regulations? Understanding Participation in EPA's 33/50 program." *Land Economics* 72: 413–32.

Baird, J. 2004. "Utah ski areas rated low on environment." *The Salt Lake Tribune*, September 12, page B1.

Blevins, J. 2004. "It's Not Easy Being Green: Ski Areas Dispute Analysis of Their Environmental Records." *Denver Post,* August 30.

Briggs, J. 2000. "Ski Resorts and National Forests: Rethinking Forest Service Management Practices for Recreational Use." *Boston College Environmental Affairs Law Review* 28: 79–118.

Carmin, J., N. Darnall, and J. Homens. 2003. "Stakeholder Involvement in the Design of
U.S. Voluntary Environmental Initiatives: Does Sponsorship Matter?" *Policy Studies Journal* 31 (4): 527–543.

Clifford, H. 2002. *Downhill Slide: Why the Corporate Ski Industry is Bad for Skiing, Ski
Towns, and the Environment.* San Francisco: Sierra Club Books.

Darnall, N. 2002. "Why Firms Signal 'Green': Environmental Management System Certification in the United States." Ph.D. Dissertation: University of North Carolina-
Chapel Hill.

————. 2003a. "Why Firms Certify to ISO 14001: An Institutional and Resource-Based View." *Academy of Management Conference's Best Paper Proceedings*, Seattle, Washington. The Academy of Management. Pages B1–B6.

————. 2003b. "Motivations for Participating in a Voluntary Environmental Initiative: The Multi-state Working Group and EPA's EMS Pilot Program." In S. Sharma and M. Starik eds. *Research in Corporate Sustainability: The Evolving Theory and Practice of Organizations in the Natural Environment.* Boston: Edward Elgar Publishing. Pages 123–154.

Dasgupta, N. 2000. "Environmental Enforcement and Small Industries in India: Reworking the Problem in the Poverty Context." *World Development* 28 (5): 945–967.

Delmas, M. 2002. "The Diffusion of Environmental Management Standards in Europe and in the United States: An Institutional Perspective." *Policy Sciences* 35 (1): 91–119.

Delmas, M., and A. Terlaak. 2001. "A Framework for Analyzing Environmental Voluntary Agreements." *California Management Review* 43 (3): 44–63.

Delmas, M. A., and M. W. Toffel. 2004. "Stakeholders and Environmental Management Practices: An Institutional Framework." *Business Strategy & the Environment* 13 (4).

DiMaggio, P., and W. Powell. 1983. "The Iron Cage Revisited: Institutional Isomorphism and Collective Rationality in Organizational Fields." *American Sociological Review* 48:147–160.

Dombeck, M. 2000. *Letter of Resignation as Chief of the US Forest Service.* Washington, D.C.: United States Forest Service.

Dorsey, J. 2004. "Debunking the SACC Scorecard." *NSAA Journal* (October/November): 11–13.

GAO. 1996. *U.S. Forest Service. Fees for Recreation Special-Use Permits Do Not Reflect Fair Value.* December.

Glick, D. 2001. *Powder Burn.* New York: Public Affairs.

Gorte, R. 2000. RS20178: *Forest Service Receipt-Sharing Payments: Proposal for Change.* Washington, D.C.: Report to Congress by the Congressional Research Service.

Gorte, R. and L. Corn. 1995. *The Forest Service Budget: Trust Funds and Special Accounts.* Washington, D.C.: Congressional Research Service Report to Congress, 96-604 ENR.

Greene, W. H. 2000. *Econometric Analysis.* 4th ed. Upper Saddle River, New Jersey: Prentice-Hall, Inc.

Granovetter, M. 1985. "Economic Action and Social Structure: The Problem of Embeddedness." *American Journal of Sociology* 91: 481–510.

Hardin, G. 1968. "The Tragedy of the Commons." *Science* 162:1243–1248.

Hartman, R. S. 1988. "Self-Selection Bias in the Evaluation of Voluntary Energy Conservation Programs." *Review of Economics and Statistics* 70: 448–458.

Hartman, B., and M. Zalaznick. 2003. "Impeccable Peaks or Sloppy Slopes?" *Vail Daily* February 23. At http://www.eaglevalleyalliance.org/sloppy_slopes.htm. Accessed on May 18, 2005

Heckman, J. 1978. "Dummy Endogenous Variables in a Simultaneous Equation System." *Econometrica* 46 (6): 931–959.

————. 1979. "Sample Selection Bias as a Specification Error." *Econometrica* 47 (1): 153-161.

Henriques, I., and P. Sadorsky. 1996. "The determinants of an environmental responsive firm: An empirical approach." *Journal of Environmental Economics and Management* 30: 381-395.

Hoffman, A. 1999. "Institutional Evolution and Change: Environmentalism and the U.S. Chemical Industry." *Academy of Management Journal* 42: 351–371.

Hsiao, C. 1986. *Analysis of Panel Data.* New York: Cambridge University Press.

Hudson, S. 2000. *Snow Business: A Study of the International Ski Industry.* New York: Cassell.

Janofsky, M. 2000. "Environmental Groups' Ratings Rile Ski Industry." *New York Times,* December 3.

Khanna, M. 2001. "Non-Mandatory Approaches to Environmental Protection." *Journal of Economic Surveys* 15 (3): 291–324.

Khanna, M., and L. Damon. 1999. "EPA's Voluntary 33/50 Program: Impact on Toxic Releases and Economic Performance of Firms." *Journal of Environmental Economics and Management* 37: 1–25.

King, A., and M. Lenox. 2000. "Industry Self-Regulation Without Sanctions: The Chemical Industry Responsible Care Program." *Academy of Management Journal* 43: 698–716.

Langeland, T. 2002. "Green Room or Greenwash?" *Colorado Springs Independent.* February 14–20. <http://www.csindy.com/csindy/2002-02-14/news3.html>. Accessed May 18, 2005.

Link, G. 2005. National Ski Areas Association's Director of Public Policy. Interview by authors. Lakewood, Colorado. March 29, 2005.

Little, R. 1995. "Modeling the Drop-Out Mechanism in Repeated-Measures Studies." *Journal of the American Statistical Association* 90: 1112–1121.

Lyon, T. P., and J. Maxwell. 2001. "Voluntary Approaches to Environmental Regulation: An Overview." In M. Franzini and A. Nicita eds. *Economic Institutions and Environmental Policy.* Aldershot, UK: Ashgate Publishing Ltd. Pages 75–120.

Maddala, G. S. 1986. *Limited-Dependent and Qualitative Variables in Econometrics.* New York: Cambridge University Press.

Mazur, A., and E. Welch. 1999. "The Geography of American Environmentalism." *Environmental Science & Policy* 2: 389–396.

Meyer, J., and B. Rowan. 1977. "Institutional Organizations: Formal Structure as Myth and Ceremony." *American Journal of Sociology* 80:340–363.

Moon, S. G. 2005. "Contexts, Timing, and Corporate Voluntary Environmental Behavior: A New Look at Voluntary Participation in the Environmental Protection Agency's Green Lights Program." Ph.D. Dissertation, University of Colorado, Denver

National Ski Areas Association (NSAA). 2000. *Sustainable Slopes: The Environmental Charter for Ski Areas.* Denver: National Ski Areas Association.

———. 2001. *Sustainable Slopes Annual Report 2001.* Denver: National Ski Areas Association.

———. 2002. *Sustainable Slopes Annual Report 2002.* Denver: National Ski Areas Association.

———. 2004a. *Kottke National End of Season Survey 2003–4 Preliminary Report.* Denver: National Ski Areas Association.

———. 2004b. *Estimated U.S. Ski Industry Skier Visits by Region.* http://www.nsaa.org/nsaa/press/2004/skiervisits.pdf. Accessed on May 18, 2005.

———. 2004c. *494 U.S. Ski Resorts in Operation During 2003–2004 Season.* http://www.nsaa.org/nsaa/press/2004/03-04-sa-number-history.pdf. Accessed on May 18, 2005.

————. 2005a. *Sustainable Slopes Annual Report 2005*. Denver: National Ski Areas Association.

————. 2005b. *Preliminary Report Indicates 2004/05 Season as Fourth Best on Record.* http://www.nsaa.org/nsaa/press/2005/nc-05-prelim-kottke.asp. Accessed on May 20, 2005.

Olsen, R. 1980. "A Least Squares Correction for Selectivity Bias." *Econometrica* 48 (7): 1815–1820.

Olson, M. 1965. *The Logic of Collective Action: Public Goods and the Theory of Groups.* Cambridge, MA: Harvard University Press.

Ostrom, E. 1990. *Governing the Commons: The Evolution of Institutions for Collective Action.* New York: Cambridge University Press.

Palmeri, C. 2003. "An Uphill Battle on the Slippery Slopes: Can Cheap Tickets and Snowboard 'Terrain' Save the Ski Resorts?" *Business Week,* Issue 3815: 44. January 13, 2003.

Porter, M. and C. van der Linde. 1995. "Green and Competitive." *Harvard Business Review*, September-October: 149–163.

Potoski, M., and A. Prakash. 2005. "Green Clubs and Voluntary Governance: ISO 14001 and Firms' Regulatory Compliance." *American Journal of Political Science* 49 (2): 235–248.

Powell, W. and P. DiMaggio. Eds. 1991. *The New Institutionalism in Organizational Analysis.* Chicago: University of Chicago Press.

Puhani, P. 2000. "The Heckman Correction for Sample Selection and its Critique." *Journal of Economic Surveys* 14 (1): 53–68.

Reinhardt, F. L. 1998. "Environmental Product Differentiation: Implications for Corporate Strategy." *California Management Review* 40 (4): 43–73.

Rey, 2005. Congressional Testimony before the Subcommittee on Public Lands and Forests by Mark Rey, Under Secretary of Natural Resources and Environment, USDA. Washington DC, February 8. http://www.fs.fed.us/congress/109/senate/oversight/rey/020805.html. Accessed April 4, 2006.

Rivera, J. 2002. "Assessing a Voluntary Environmental Initiative in the Developing World: The Costa Rican Certification for Sustainable Tourism." *Policy Sciences* 35: 333-360.

Rivera, J. 2004. "Institutional Pressures and Voluntary Environmental Behavior in Developing Countries: Evidence from Costa Rica." *Society and Natural Resources* 17: 779–797.

Rivera, J. and P. deLeon. 2004. "Is Greener Whiter? The Sustainable Slopes Program and the Voluntary Environmental Performance of Western Ski Areas." *Policy Studies Journal* 32 (3): 417–437.

Rivera, J., and M. Delmas. 2004. "Business and Environmental Policy: An Introduction." *Human Ecology Review* 11 (3): 230–234.

Rogers, P. 2002. "Cold Cash: Ski Resorts Profit on Cheap U.S. Land." *San Jose Mercury News,* April 7.

————. 2003. "Forest Service to Review Rents Paid by Ski Resorts." *Knight Ridder Tribune Business News,* January 10.

Rubin, D. 1976. "Inference and Missing Data." *Biometrika* 63: 581–592.

Sachs, R. F. 2002. "National Perspective on Mountain Resorts and Ecology." *Vermont Law Review* 26 (3): 515.

Scott, R. W. 2001. *Institutions and Organizations*. 2nd ed. Thousand Oaks, CA: Sage Publications.

Ski Area Citizen's Coalition (SACC). 2005. *"How are ski areas graded?"* http://www.skiareacitizens.com/criteria.html. Accessed on May 15, 2005.

Starik, M., and G. P. Rands. 1995. "Weaving an Integrated Web: Multilevel and Multi-system Perspectives of Ecologically Sustainable Organizations." *Academy of Management Review* 20 (4): 908–935.

Suchman, M. 1995. "Managing Legitimacy: Strategic and Institutional Approaches." *Academy of Management Review* 20 (3): 571–610.

Toffel, M. 2005. "Voluntary Environmental Management Initiatives: Smoke Signals or Smoke Screens?" Ph.D. Dissertation: University of California, Berkeley.

Toffel, M., and J. Marshall. 2004. "Improving Environmental Performance Assessment: A Comparative Analysis of Weighing Methods Used to Evaluate Chemical Release Inventories." *Journal of Industrial Ecology* 8 (1–2): 143–172.

United States Code, 2003. Section 497c. http://frwebgate.access.gpo.gov/cgi-bin/getdoc.cgi?dbname=browse_usc&docid=Cite:+16USC497c. Accessed on May 15, 2005.

Walley, N., and B. Whitehead. 1994. "It is Not Easy Being Green." *Harvard Business Review* May–June: 46–52.

Wathne, K., and J. Heide. 2000. "Opportunism in Interfirm Relationships: Forms, Outcomes, and Solutions." *Journal of Marketing* 64: 36–51.

Waddock, S. 2003. "Myths and Realities of Social Investing." *Organization & Environment* 16 (3): 369–380.

Welch, E., A. Mazur, and S. Bretschneider. 2000. "Voluntary Behavior by Electric Utilities: Levels of Adoption and Contribution of the Climate Challenge Program to the Reduction of Carbon Dioxide." *Journal of Policy Analysis and Management* 19 (3): 407–425.

Wharton, T. 1997a. "Recreation Bumps Logging as Top use of America's Forests." *The Salt Lake Tribune* December 4.

———. 1997b. "Forests' Overseer Promotes Public Lands Partnerships." *The Salt Lake Tribune* December 6.

Williamson, O. 1975. *Markets and Hierarchies: Analysis and Antitrust Implications.* New York: The Free Press.

———. 1985. *The Economic Institutions of Capitalism.* New York: The Free Press.

Winter, S. C., and P. J. May. 2001. "Motivation for Compliance with Environmental Regulations." *Journal of Policy Analysis and Management* 20 (4): 675.

Notes

1. Rivera and deLeon's (2004) manuscript provides a detailed outline of a neo-institutional theory model of participation in voluntary programs that interested readers should examine. Khanna and Damon (1999) also develop an alternative model of voluntary participation in the initiatives.

2. Williamson (1975, 6) originally defined opportunism as "self-interest seeking with guile." He later characterized guile as "lying, stealing, cheating, and calculated efforts to mislead, distort, disguise, obfuscate, or otherwise confuse" (Williamson 1985, 47).

3. Free riding is understood as avoiding cooperating in the provision of a collectively produced good while expecting to derive individual benefit from it (Delmas and Keller 2005; Olson 1965, 1990).

4. The term skier visit refers to one skier or snowboarder visiting a resort for any portion of one day (NSAA 2005b).

5. A fixed-effects model is inappropriate due to the time-invariant nature of some of the independent variables (Hsiao 1986). A Housman test is normally used to select between fixed and random effects models for specification without time-invariant independent variables (Greene 2000).

6. The MGLR technique is better suited to handle unbalanced panel data than the traditional generalized least squares techniques (Little 1995; Rubin 1976). This mixed linear regression methodology employs a maximum likelihood estimation approach and allows the unknown random error vector to exhibit both correlation and heterogeneous variances (Little 1995).

7. We classified western ski areas as those located in the Rocky Mountains and Pacific West regions of the U.S.

8. These government document--available online at SACC's website--include among others: USFS environmental impact statements, master development plans, expansion proposals, and forest management plan revisions; and also formal biological opinions prepared by the U.S. Fish and Wildlife Service (SACC 2005).

9. A quick Google search of the term "ski area environmental scorecard grades" generates links to over 200 stories and articles on the score card rankings and more than 500 hits.

10. Criteria left out involve for instance: a) Opposing/supporting environmentally sound policy positions and b) those that in the early 2000s penalized ski areas for not responding to SACC's annual survey.

11. Model 1 yields a slightly higher percentage of correctly classified participation decisions and it is used to estimate the values of ski area's probability of participation in the SSP -- one of the independent variables included in the second stage of the regression analysis. Calculating the probability of participation with Model 1 also reduces the chance of overidentification as this model does not includes all the same independent variables used in the second stage of the analysis (see note 6).

12. To assess heteroskedasticity problems in the probit models, we used the David and Mackinnon test: It did not indicate problems ($P<0.05$).

13. State location, the alternative measure of state environmental pressures used in Model 1, similarly suggest that domicile in states with lower environmental pressures, such as Idaho ($P<0.01$), New Mexico ($P<0.05$), Nevada ($P<0.01$), and Wyoming ($P<0.05$), is significantly related to lower participation in the SSP.

14. We thank one of the anonymous reviewers for requesting that we explore alternative model specifications that may have revealed the presence of identification problems in the second stage of analysis (see description of these possible problems on the Methodology section of this article). To do so, we re-calculated all the second stage MGL regression models excluding the following independent variables: 1) ski area size and 2) ownership by publicly traded firm. These two variables showed the highest collinearity with the probability of participation variable (inverse Mill's ratio) calculated in stage one and thus could have led to identification problems. See table below for findings of alternative model specifications:

Table 7.6 New MGL regression results:[a]
Excluding size and ownership by publicly traded firm as control variables
(Dependent variable: environmental performance dimensions)

	Overall environmental performance (Model 3)	Expansion management (Model 4)	Natural resources conservation (Model 5)	Pollution management (Model 6)	Wildlife and habitat management (Model 7)
Constant	0.53 (0.051)[b]	0.89 (0.074)	0.091 (0.10)	0.56 (0.05)	0.62 (0.069)
Probability of participation	-0.053 (0.056)	-0.039 (0.083)***	0.29 (0.10)**	0.050 (0.053)	-0.082 (0.073)
N	348	348	348	348	348
-2 Log L	-609.8	-459.4	-74.8	-504.7	-140.2
χ^2	282.89***	362***	182.62***	174.31***	87.86***

[a]: Additional independent variables included in the models (Federal government oversight and state environmental pressures) not shown.
[b]: Standard errors are in parentheses.
Prob: ▨ *prob<0.10; ** prob<0.05; *** prob < 0.01.

With the exception of the Expansion Management regression (Model 4), all other models produced similar results for the probability of participation variable (our key independent variable of interest in the analysis). In the case of the Expansion Management regression the new coefficient for the probability of participation variable shows a negative and significant association with the dependent variable (expansion management percentage score). This specific new finding actually suggests that in expansion related practices, SSP participants have lower performance than non-participants.

15. Forest Service trust fund allocations are independent of the U.S. Congress' annual appropriation process (Gorte and Corn 1995; Dombeck 2000).

16. Since 1908, the 25 Percent Fund Act (16 U.S.C. sec. 500) has required these payments in lieu of property taxes Rey, 2005).

17. We thank Nicole Darnall for pointing out this alternative explanation.

Chapter 8

Assessing the Performance of Voluntary Environmental Programs: Does Certification Matter?

Nicole Darnall and Stephen Sides

Introduction

Over the past 20 years, considerable efforts have been expended by governments, industry and third-party organizations to develop and promote organizational participation in voluntary environmental programs (VEPs). In general, VEPs set forth a specific rationale to identify and guide the pursuit of improved environmental performance, in turn offering participants benefits for doing so.

Scholarly research has sought to explore the rationale for participation in VEPs and for undertaking certain activities that go beyond environmental compliance requirements.[3, 5, 31] Other studies have begun to recognize that VEP design characteristics may influence their proper functioning.[47, 51, 15] These evaluations have found that certain VEP design deficiencies, specifically the absence of third-party oversight of performance monitoring, invite "free-ridership" on the part of some participants, and "shirking" of underlying program commitments. VEPs lacking sufficient oversight therefore have been questioned for their intent and their benefits bestowed on participants.

Related to the environmental performance of VEPs, previous scholarship has suggested that VEPs—even those without third-party monitoring—are a means for improving participants' environmental performance.[32] However, in other instances, scholarship has demonstrated that participation in VEPs lacking oversight does not improve environmental performance.[34, 51, 52] Numerous questions therefore remain first about the overall utility of VEPs in that, as yet, we know little about whether these programs collectively are meeting their environmental goals. Second, questions remain about whether or not third-party monitoring of participants' adherence to program goals improves VEP efficacy.

To address these research needs, this study integrates the results of previous VEP research using meta-analytic techniques to develop a broader quantitative perspective of VEP performance. This analysis offers two contributions to organizational research on voluntary environmental governance. First, previous VEP scholarship has been equivocal in establishing a link between VEP participation and subsequent environmental improvements. One reason is that prior research has focused generally on evaluating the efficacy of individual programs and so a broader view of the efficacy of VEP participation is not understood. This study builds on previous VEP research findings to establish a much needed overall assessment of their efficacy. In so doing, this research evaluates the entire body of peer-reviewed VEP literature and provides critical insights regarding the relationship between participation and improved environmental performance.

The second contribution of our analysis is that it distinguishes among the two most common subcategories of programs—those requiring self-monitoring as opposed to third-party certification. In making this distinction, we examine the proposition that ISO 14001, which requires certification and independent third-party monitoring, improves participants' environmental performance to a greater degree than programs requiring self-monitoring alone. It offers evidence that *overall* VEP participants' environmental performance is worse than non-participants, especially for programs that require participants to self-monitor their adherence to program goals. Further, participants in ISO 14001 *as a group* exhibit inconclusive environmental performance improvements.

Understanding Voluntary Environmental Programs

VEPs have been characterized under the broader rubric of voluntary environmental action, comprising several distinct categories of activity including negotiated agreements, unilateral projects, and sector and cross-sector alliances.[53] More formally, VEPs are defined as programs, codes, agreements, and commitments that encourage organizations to voluntarily reduce their environmental impacts beyond the requirements established by the environmental regulatory system.[9] VEPs emerged in the late 1980s in response to criticisms about the overly prescriptive and often inefficient nature of the traditional command-and-control approach to environmental regulation.[18] While there was widespread recognition of the problems with traditional regulation, there lacked consensus on how to achieve reform, particularly in the face of prevailing beliefs that restructuring would spur political and social confrontation.[18] VEPs emerged as an alternative means for improving environmental conditions outside the regulatory development process.[9] Not only did these programs address a number of environmental concerns being raised by citizens and interest groups, they also avoided the complex and costly conflicts that often are associated with regulatory reform.[4]

Over 200 VEPs exist in the United States at the regional and national level,[9, 17] and even more programs operate within states and localities. The Environmental Protection Agency (EPA) is the largest sponsor of US-based VEPs. By the end of the 1990s, some 13,000 companies were participating in EPA sponsored VEPs.[40] These programs account for 1.6%[41] of EPA's $4.3 billion dollar operating budget, or approximately $69 million.[57] This cost has raised concerns from VEP critics who take issue with the fact that EPA has struggled to satisfy its Congressional mandate of ensuring environmental compliance within the regulated community. Agency officials and scholars alike argue that achieving regulatory compliance has lagged in large part because of limited Congressional funding for regulatory inspections and audits[18] and other budgetary reductions at a time when the agency's mandated responsibilities are increasing.[45] Given these circumstances, some suggest that government funding for VEPs should be reallocated towards helping ensure compliance with existing laws rather than managing non-regulatory programs, especially since empirical studies of VEP performance lack consistency.

In some instances researchers have offered evidence that participation in government-sponsored VEPs improves environmental performance[32] while other studies show that government sponsored VEPs[21] and VEPs that involved significant government involvement in their development[50, 51] do not. Studies which fail to show support for the idea that government developed VEPs improve environmental performance attribute their findings to weak VEP design. VEPs having weak program structures are characterized by their inability to ensure that participants implement program goals, to require regular monitoring, or to mandate periodic reporting requirements.[15] In instances where participant reporting is required, program managers rarely verify whether the reporting is accurate.

One reason why VEPs are developed with weak design structures is that program managers are balancing the need for rigor with the goal of providing a flexible means for participants to move beyond the parameters established by the traditional regulatory system. A tension therefore emerges between program managers' desires to encourage more widespread VEP participation and the need to ensure that program goals are met.[17] However, government agencies defend their VEPs. For instance, EPA claims that the general public has saved nearly $6 billion, conserved 603 million gallons of water, saved nearly 770 trillion British thermal units (BTUs) of energy and cut more than 438,000 tons of emissions.[58]

Government VEPs are not the only programs under scrutiny in that concerns also have been raised about the utility of industry sponsored VEPs.

These programs generally focus on encouraging participation by firms within a specific industrial sector. The emergence of sector-specific industry VEPs was prompted by public concerns regarding the environmental performance of firms and by appeals to promote consistent environmental management among industry association members.[22, 26] Criticisms about these VEPs have been lodged by NGOs and research scholars alike[6, 34] who have suggested that, like government-developed VEPs, VEPs designed entirely by industry associations lack appropriate implementation, monitoring, and reporting protocols that would lead to improved environmental performance outcomes.

One way to remedy VEP design weaknesses is to develop programs that require external third-party oversight and certification. Although less prevalent than other types of VEPs, certified VEPs have significant popularity because of their external monitoring and reporting features. ISO 14001 is the most widely recognized third-party certified VEP. By April 2005, more than 88,800 facilities worldwide had certified to ISO 14001, of which, 4,671 facilities were US based.[43] ISO 14001 requires participants to implement an environmental management system (EMS). EMSs consist of a collection of internal policies, assessments, plans and implementation actions,[10] affecting the entire organizational unit and its relationships with the natural environment. Once certified, the ISO 14001 label indicates that the company has implemented a management system that documents the firm's pollution aspects and impacts and identifies a pollution prevention process[5] which is continually improved over time.[16]

VEPs have several commonalities. First, they all require participant firms to establish environmental targets and statements of environmental goals.[15] They also have comparable administrative requirements in the form of written agreements, letters of intent, or memoranda of understanding committing the participant to achieving program goals.[15] However, these programs differ in one significant way. Government- and industry-sponsored VEPs generally are "self-monitoring" programs in that conformance with program goals is assured by VEP participants self-reporting their adherence to program requirements.[15] By contrast, ISO 14001 requires external certification by an independent third-party which confers additional external legitimacy[5] about participants' environmental commitments. Further, the certification process is more likely to formalize managerial commitment towards achieving environmental performance goals.[54]

VEPs and Their Relationship with Environmental Performance

In spite of the equivocal findings in previous research, there are several reasons why we would expect all types of VEPs to improve participants' environmental performance. First, VEPs establish environmental performance goals which may help focus participants' environmental management activities, enhance internal oversight of environmental improvement,[33] and rally around a common cause. Second, most VEPs offer participants technical assistance, such as pollution prevention training, that can help firms meet program goals. Other ways in which VEPs can offer assistance is in the form of direct grants to hire environmental consultants. More prevalent in government sponsored VEPs, direct grants subsidize VEP implementation increasing participants' access to external expertise that can fortify their environmental management capabilities.[16] Subsidized technical assistance of all sorts therefore can encourage greater environmental performance gains.

Outside of creating environmental goals and providing technical assistance, VEPs generally establish peer networks among member firms. These networks allow for the exchange of information on best management practices. Information exchange also helps facilitate VEP implementation and may further assist participants in gaining knowledge that helps strengthen their environmental management capabilities. Further, VEP participation can encourage greater collaboration within the firm. That is, by participating in a VEP, firms may improve their internal networks by collaborating across multiple operational areas, which creates broader organizational support for achieving VEP goals.[46] All these functional attributes of VEPs work collectively to encourage participants to improve their environmental performance.

Hypothesis 1: Organizations participating in VEPs have improved environmental performance.

VEP Oversight and Environmental Performance

Numerous VEP design features may affect participants' environmental performance, including program sponsorship. For instance, government-sponsored programs are designed with a greater diversity of stakeholder involvement which avoids agency favoritism for one interest group or position.[9] At the same time, industry sponsored programs are argued to lack rigorous implementation, monitoring, and reporting regimes and lead to lower environmental standards.[34, 6] Despite these propositions, industry, government, and nonprofit VEP sponsors develop programs with similar administrative, environmental, and conformance requirements.[15] As a result, other VEP design features, such as program oversight, may go further in explaining variations in environmental performance across different types of programs.

In general, there are three distinct "levels" of program oversight—internal assessments, self-reports to program sponsors, and external monitoring by an independent third-party auditor.[15] Most program sponsors require participants to either self-report their environmental performance to program sponsors or rely on audits by independent third-parties. For this reason, and because programs requiring internal assessments generally do not involve public disclosure of environmental information, previous empirical research typically has focused on the latter two types of VEPs to evaluate program efficacy.

In comparing VEPs that require self-reporting and external certification, we anticipate that certification programs may increase participants' environmental performance to a greater degree. This belief is based in large part on institutional arguments that external verification changes the dynamics of a collective action and causes individuals to more seriously consider their group obligations.[42] In the case of VEPs, external certification may motivate participants to respond more earnestly to program requirements[48] since participants undergo third-party evaluation that assesses their conformance to program standards. In the process, participants may be more likely to formalize managerial commitment towards achieving more ambitious environmental goals,[54] and institutionalize existing pollution prevention programs by getting more value from what has already been developed.[14] Further, independent review offers a greater degree of accountability and reduces opportunities for participants to behave opportunistically (King & Lenox, 2000; Davies et al., 1996). Additionally, companies that fail certification or have their certification revoked may face reputational penalties in the eyes of external stakeholders.

By contrast, VEPs that rely on self-reports of participants' environmental performance rarely undergo additional verification even by program sponsors.[15] As such, these programs create opportunities for participants to report that they are achieving program goals when in fact they are not. In such instances, participants have an incentive to free-ride and inaccurately "signal" that they are managing their environmental impacts to a greater extent than non-participants.[20, 15] In so doing, participants may receive program benefits without changing their environmental behavior or meeting program goals. Because of the greater opportunities for free-riding, we hypothesize that participants in self-monitored programs will improve their environmental performance to a lesser degree than participants in VEPs requiring external certification.

Hypothesis 2: Participation in certified VEPs is associated with greater improvements in environmental performance than participation in self-monitored VEPs.

Methods

To evaluate our hypotheses, we relied on meta-analytic techniques that considered the aggregate relationship between VEP participation and environmental performance. This approach was used to integrate the entire body of VEP literature to offer more generalized insights regarding the relationship between VEPs, their monitoring regimes, and environmental performance.

Inclusion Criteria

The first step in preparing for the meta-analysis was to determine the population of studies relevant for inclusion. For the purposes of this study, we relied on Carmin, Darnall & Mil-Homen's[9] definition of a VEP: any program, code, agreement or commitment that encouraged business organizations to voluntarily reduce their environmental impacts beyond that required by the environmental regulatory system. The population of VEP studies was limited to programs that operate or operated in the United States (to control for the regulatory environment) and those that measured participants' environmental performance by way of pollution reductions. We defined environmental performance as an objective quantitative change in pollution or conditions contributing to the same (i.e. recycling, pollution prevention and time out of compliance). This definition focused the population of studies on those that demonstrated changes in actual or relative facility emissions, discharges and releases or off-site transfer of wastes, numbers of compliance citations, etc. Our definition excluded studies that did not consider pollution changes and eliminated studies that employed categorical or descriptive measures of environmental performance.

The population was further limited to studies evaluating regional or national programs and VEPs that were designed to have business organizations as their participants as opposed to government organizations, communities, or individuals. Suitable VEP studies were required to be published in a peer-reviewed journal. As such, they would have undergone extensive scrutiny by the scientific community.

Finally, there is an inevitable selection bias associated with VEP participation in that participation is voluntary. In the presence of selection bias, estimating the relationship between VEP participation and environmental performance would lead to an error term that is correlated with the participation decision. Since the error term captures the effects of all omitted and imperfectly measured variables, any regressors that are correlated with the unmeasured or mis-measured factors will end up proxying for them. A two-stage estimation approach corrects for self-selection bias.[24] Applied to the VEP setting, the factors that determine VEP participation (first stage) are estimated simultaneously with the factors that determine its environmental performance (second stage). To account for selection bias in the meta-analysis, the population of eligible studies was restricted to scholarship that utilized these two-stage estimation procedures.

Data

Studies that met our inclusion criteria were identified by conducting an exhaustive literature search using ABI/Inform (ProQuest). ABI/Inform provides access to the full text of over 1,800 US and international business, environmental, economic and policy related journals. Searches were conducted in May 2006 and covered the years 1982 to 2006. Cross-citations also were explored from previous VEP studies.[2, 15, 20, 31, 35, 46, 47, 50]

Some 60 studies evaluating aspects of VEPs were identified and evaluated for salient characteristics that would support their inclusion in the meta-analysis. Of these, 11 assessed the environmental performance of VEPs and controlled for selection bias. After further consideration, two of these studies were omitted. In one instance,[2] the paper evaluated adopters of an environmental management system without distinguishing whether adoption was part of a formal VEP (see Table 8.1). The second study by Rivera & deLeon[51] was excluded because an updated paper by Rivera, deLeon & Koerber[52] was published in 2006 with more comprehensive data. The updated study is included in the meta-analysis.

Table 8.1 VEP studies excluded[1] from the meta-analysis

Reference	VEP Evaluated	Dependent Variable	Empirical Approach and Exclusion Rationale
Anton, Deltas & Khanna (2004)	Evaluates firms' EMS for evidence of increased comprehensiveness, TRI data, as well as separate assessment of regulatory and market pressures	TRI emissions, releases and off-site transfers as well as hazardous air pollutant releases	Standard Poisson and negative binomial models assesses development of an EMS without regard to whether it was part of a VEP.
Rivera & deLeon (2004)	Evaluates participants in the National Ski Areas Association's *Sustainable Slopes* program	Environmental "scorecard" based on quantitative measures	Two-stage probit model estimating factors predicting both participation and environmental performance; excluded because an updated study was published in 2006 with more comprehensive data. The updated study is included in the meta-analysis.

Ultimately, 9 studies met our selection criteria and were included in the analysis. This number is significant considering that a meta-analysis can be performed on as few as two qualifying studies since statistical power is limited only by the data utilized in the original studies.[36] Since the total number of observations evaluated in the original studies is in excess of 30,000 firms, the

---

[1] This table lists studies that used some form of environmental performance measure and controlled for selection bias. Other VEP studies (not listed) were excluded because they did not evaluate environmental performance, and instead focused on participation attributes or economic factors.

Table 8.2 Summary of VEPs included in the analysis

Name of Program	Brief Description
33/50 Program	• Sponsored by EPA • Program that sought to engage participants in verifiable pollution prevention activities • One of the earliest government sponsored programs, attracted a large number of participants from US industry • Goals were to reduce certain emissions, discharges and waste streams by 33 percent by 1992 and then 50 percent by 1995 • Participants self-reported their progress towards established goals
Climate Challenge Program	• Sponsored by the US Department of Energy • Addresses an unregulated emission (carbon dioxide) • Participants encouraged to develop flexible approaches to achieve self-established goals • Formalized by written agreement
ISO 14001	• Sponsored by the International Organization for Standardization, a nonprofit organization, using input from numerous advisory groups and constituencies • Establishes an effective and verifiable environmental management system • Participation requires certification to the standard by an approved registrar • Administration of ISO 14001 is managed by registrars in each country • Participation expanded as a result of supply chain mandates
Responsible Care	• Sponsored initially by the Canadian Chemical Producers Association and later adopted by the US Chemical Manufacturers Association (now known as the American Chemistry Council) • Required for all industry association members • Established codes for addressing critical health, safety and environmental management responsibilities • Participants self-reported their progress towards established goals • Only recently has the program required third-party performance audits
Sustainable Slopes Program	• Sponsored by the National Ski Areas Association • Involves 21 specific environmental "charters" for participating ski areas • Annual self-assessment required • Independent assessment of environmental performance used in analysis

meta-analysis had sufficient statistical power to arrive at a meaningful conclusion about the overall efficacy of VEPs that were included in this study.

The 9 studies evaluated 11 different environmental performance measures across 5 VEPs. Four VEPs required self-reports of environmental performance (33/50, Climate Challenge, Responsible Care®, and Sustainable Slopes) and one required certification (ISO 14001). Table 8.2 describes each of these programs in greater detail. Table 8.3 offers a descriptive summary of the studies included in the meta-analysis.

Table 8.4 summarizes the data included in the meta-analysis calculations. It identifies the VEP type (self-monitoring or certified), the environmental performance measure used, as well as the effect size and weight for each environmental performance measure.

Empirics

There are three advantages to utilizing a meta-analytic approach. First, meta-analysis is less concerned with the underlying study statistics—whether they are significant or not—and more concerned with the relative "size" of the observed effects. Second, meta-analysis corrects for sampling errors associated with studies of differing sizes.[25] For instance, VEP studies with fewer observations are susceptible to sampling errors that in turn weaken the inferences that can be derived from that study. Meta-analysis corrects for these concerns by weighting the "effects" observed in individual studies according to the sample size, reducing the weight of small sample studies and, in turn, reducing sampling error in the comparison.[28] Third, meta-analysis allows for the quantitative comparison of multiple studies that evaluate related dependent variables.[36] These comparisons can be made regardless of whether the relationships in the original study are statistically significant.[30]

It is important to note that meta-analysis does not require that dependent variables be identical. Typically there is variability among dependent variables because candidate studies inevitably have different measures of that variable.[30, 36, 25, 23] Further, variability is anticipated among study features (including research models and data sources) and their attributes, and there is increasing acceptability to include more divergent study characteristics.[30, 36, 25, 23] For this reason, published meta-analytic research commonly utilizes broad measures of their dependent and independent variables.[44, 8, 49] Related to the VEP setting, variability also exists in the population of studies evaluating environmental performance. Types of environmental performance measures that have been used include reductions in toxic releases[32, 34, 33, 46] and carbon dioxide emissions,[61] time out of compliance with air pollution regulations,[47] and environmental scorecards that evaluate participant recycling and pollution prevention.[52]

Table 8.3 VEP studies included in the meta-analysis

Reference	VEP Evaluated	Dependent Variable	Empirical Approach
Khanna & Damon (1999)	Study of chemical industry participants in EPA's *33/50 Program* using TRI data	33/50 releases, Superfund site involvement	Two-stage least squares "participation" model, with predicted probability of participation and defined measure of environmental performance.
Gamper-Rabindran (2006)	Evaluates EPA's *33/50 Program* participants with respect to environmental performance	Percent reduction in 33/50 Program releases	Program participation integrated as a binary endogenous variable and compared to pre-33/50, 33/50, and post-33/50 program year releases. Two-stage model applied.
King & Lenox (2000)	Evaluates *Responsible Care* with respect to environmental performance and (estimated) facility production	Relative emissions and sector emissions using weighted TRI data	Covariance matrix and fixed-effect model relate VEP participation to environmental performance measures, while controlling for endogeneity through two-stage modeling.
King, Lenox & Terlaak (2005)	Study of participants in *ISO 14001* utilizing Toxic Release Inventory data	Calculated index of environmental performance focused on waste management	Discrete time, random-effect probit regression analysis two-stage) focusing on cross sectional data to evaluate defined environmental performance measures.
Potoski & Prakash (2005a)	Analysis of US facilities participating in *ISO 14001*	Logged and absolute index-weighted emissions	Treatment effects model and probit model, with endogeneity adjustments, focus on monitoring and enforcement measures
Potoski & Prakash (2005b)	Analysis of US facilities participating in *ISO 14001*	Time out of compliance with air pollution regulations	Two-stage OLS model of monitoring and enforcement measures affecting environmental performance .
Rivera, de Leon & Koerber (2006)	Follow-up study of western ski resorts in the *Sustainable Slopes* program	Environmental "scorecard" based on quantitative measures	Recursive two-stage probit model using environmental performance as a predictor of participation.
Vidovic & Khanna (2007)	Evaluates EPA's *33/50 Program* participants with respect to environmental performance	Percent reduction in 33/50 Program releases	A two-step procedure involving a probit model predicting participation, followed by an analysis of participants' TRI releases.
Welch, Mazur & Bretschneider (2000)	Evaluates data from largest electric utilities participating in EPA's *Climate Challenge Program*	Predicted and actual emissions for carbon dioxide and other priority air pollutants	Logit regression analysis with elements to address endogeneity. Beta coefficients provided on program participants representing high percentage of annual carbon dioxide emissions from electric utilities

Table 8.4 Description of included studies and meta-analytic calculations

Author (Year)	VEP Name	Program Type	Environmental Performance Measure	Extracted Statistical Data†		Meta-analysis Calculations	
				Difference Covariate Means	Regression Coefficient/ Result	Calculated Effect Size (ES)	Calculated Weight [1/(se)²]
Gamper-Rabindran (2006)	33/50	Self-monitored	33/50 releases—indexed to industry-type		0.54	0.54	22.72
Khanna & Damon (1999)	33/50	Self-monitored	33/50 releases—indexed to probability of participation	-2.40		- 0.477	28.57
King & Lenox (2000)	Responsible Care	Self-monitored	(1) Relative emissions (2) Sector emissions Mean of (1) & (2)		0.08 0.27 0.175	-- -- 0.36	-- -- 117.6
Rivera, de Leon & Keorber (2006)	Sustainable Slopes	Self-monitored	Quantitative environmental "scorecard"	0.43		0.20	122
Vidovic & Khanna (2007)	33/50	Self-monitored	33/50 releases indexed to participation		0.109	0.88	59
Welch, Mazur & Bretschneider (2000)	Climate Challenge	Self-monitored	Carbon dioxide reduction		0.09††	0.09	42
King, Lenox & Terlaak (2005)	ISO 14001	Certified	(1) Index of Observed Waste Generation (Environmental Performance) (2) Waste transfer off-site Mean of (1) & (2)		-0.02 0.03 0.005	-- -- 0.02	-- -- 435
Potoski & Prakash (2005a)	ISO 14001	Certified	Logged Emissions Reduction— CERCLA-TRI Weighting		-0.0134	-0.03	109
Potoski & Prakash (2005b)	ISO 14001	Certified	Time out of compliance with air pollution regulations		-0.0768	-0.16	142

† Unless otherwise noted, a negative sign denotes that the study found evidence that VEP participation was associated with reductions in pollution and a positive sign denotes that the study showed VEP participation was associated with increases in pollution.

†† Study found no statistically significant relationship between VEP participation and pollution reductions.

With respect to accounting for how VEP participation was measured, all of the studies included in the analysis make use of either a dummy variable accounting for participation or utilize regression to establish a predicted probability of participation, which is then compared against actual participation to validate the empirical model. As such, actual comparisons of the two groups—participants and non-participants—was possible.

While some studies included in the meta-analysis allowed for direct comparison of the covariate mean environmental performance of VEP participants and non-participants, others required that the effect size be estimated. To arrive at these estimations we utilized regression coefficients (r) from previous studies to calculate an observed mean standardized effect level. This effect level characterizes the critical differences in environmental performance (a continuous variable) between VEP participants and non-participants (a dichotomous variable). It is calculated using the point-serial formula[36]:

$$ES = \delta = \frac{2r}{\sqrt{1 - r^2}}$$

To correct for sampling and measurement error, studies were assigned a weight (ω) based on the inverse square of the standard error of the effect size.[36] This weight was calculated as a function of the number of VEP participants and non-participants in the study, and integrating a random effects constant (v) that accounts for variability across the observed effects:

$$\omega = \frac{1}{(se)^2 + v}, \text{ where } se = \sqrt{\frac{n_1 + n_2}{n_1 n_2} + \frac{ES}{2(n_1 + n_2)}}$$

For some study correlation coefficients, the standard errors often are not provided, or have a problematic determination, particularly where the r distribution is skewed and the population sample size is large.[13] Given that the standard error is necessary in determining the sample weight, we used Lipsey & Wilson's (2001)[36] procedure for calculating the Fisher Zr transformed correlation coefficient as an estimate of the effect size:

$$ES_{Zr} = 0.5 \ln [1+r/1-r]$$

Using the Fisher Zr transformed correlation coefficients, the standard error calculation is as follows:

$$se = \sqrt{\frac{1}{n - 3}}$$

Two of the studies included in our analysis used more than one environmental performance measure to assess the efficacy of a single VEP (i.e., King, Lenox & Terlaak, 2005; King & Lenox, 2000).[34, 33] These studies had the potential to influence the meta-analysis results to a greater degree (Glass, McGraw & Smith, 1981).[23] To avoid bias related to the inclusion of more than one environmental performance measure per study, we took an *average* of the environmental performance measures and used this value in the meta-analysis. Doing so kept with conventions aimed at avoiding duplicate (covariate) contributions.[23] The average weighted effect size across all studies in the meta-analysis was then calculated as follows (Lipsey & Wilson, 2001):[36]

$$\overline{ES} = \frac{\sum (\omega \times ES)}{\sum \omega}$$

To assess whether or not the studies included in the analysis were estimating the same population mean, we performed a homogeneity test. This test assesses the variability in the data, and defines the underlying model that can be used in calculating the effect size used for comparison purposes.[36] Homogeneity tests rely on a Q statistic, which is distributed Chi-square. A positive homogeneity test would indicate similarity across the studies' measures and requires meta-analytic estimation by way of a fixed effects model. Otherwise, a random effects model should be used.

While our hypotheses differ from those in a typical empirical evaluation in that they are tested using results from previous studies, meta-analysis derives additional quantitative insights on the comparisons established in these original studies—and can support new findings. To evaluate Hypothesis 1, all studies were assessed without regard to their underlying monitoring regime. The results of our homogeneity test (Q=69.0) indicated that a random effects model should be applied to evaluate the variability between overall VEP participation and environmental performance (see Table 8.5). To evaluate Hypothesis 2, the studies were divided into two distinct subsets—self-monitored programs and certified programs. Self-monitoring programs were defined as VEPs requiring participants to self-report their fulfillment of program expectations, whereas certified VEPs were defined as VEPs requiring independent verification that participants were fulfilling program requirements. Six studies evaluated self-monitoring programs (33/50, Climate Challenge, Responsible Care, and Sustainable Slopes). Based on the results of our homogeneity test (Q=51.0), a random effects model was used to compare these programs. Three studies were recognized as evaluating certified VEPs and in each instance those studies evaluated ISO 14001 participation (see NOTE below). Consistent with the fact that the three studies evaluated the same VEP, the results of our homogeneity test (Q=5.2, p<0.01) indicated that the data were homogeneous and that a fixed effects model should be applied to compare these programs.

While several of the studies evaluated the same VEP, each represents an independent assessment (sampling) of participants' environmental performance in addition to a unique dependent variable measure conforming to our definition.

There are advantages to this approach in that having multiple studies of the same population and different measures of the dependent variable [11,12] allows for the correction for sampling error and improves the reliability of the relationship being explored. [60]

Results

Table 8.5 describes the results of our meta-analysis models. It shows that across all programs, non-participants demonstrated a 7.7% stronger environmental performance than participants. Further, the results of our confidence interval (95%) suggested that non-participants' environmental performance improved between 1.8% and 13.6% more than VEP participants. These findings did not support of Hypothesis 1, which states that organizations participating in VEPs will have improved environmental performance.

NOTE: ISO 14000 series consists of 23 standards constituting the ISO 14000 "family." One such standard is ISO 14001. This standard which *requires* certification, whereas the others do not. In some instances a firm may claim it conforms to ISO 14001, but does not obtain certification. However, our analysis does not include studies that consider whether or not individual participants claim to be certified. Rather, it includes studies that examine actual certification.

Table 8.5 Summary of aggregate findings—
Relating VEP participation to environmental performance

VEP Studies Included	Number of Environmental Performance Measures	Meta-analysis Model	Meta-analysis Outcome †	Standard Error	Z-Score	C.I. (95%)	Test of Heterogen-eity††
All (9)	11	Random Effects	0.077	0.030	2.6	0.018 to 0.136	Q=69.0
Self-monitored (6)	7	Random Effects	0.240	0.034	6.8	0.173 to 0.307	Q=51.0
Certified (3)	4	Fixed Effects	-0.025	0.038	0.7	-0.1 to 0.05	Q= 5.2*

† Meta-analysis outcome is an aggregate finding that combines the effects found in previous studies. A negative value indicates that VEP participation was associated with reductions in environmental impacts as compared to non-participants whereas a positive value indicates that VEP participation was associated with increases in environmental impacts.

†† A significant Q statistic indicates that data are homogeneous in nature and should be evaluated using a fixed effects model. An insignificant Q statistic indicates that data are heterogeneous and should be evaluated using a random effects model.

* Statistically significant at $p<0.01$.

When considering environmental performance in self-monitored programs, there was strong evidence that suggested participants failed to improve their environmental performance over non-participants. More specifically, non-participants demonstrated a 24% greater improvement in environmental performance than participants in self-monitored programs. Further, a confidence interval (95%) of these findings indicated that the mean level of environmental performance improvement for non-participants was between 17% and 30% greater than participants in self-monitoring VEPs.

In evaluating the environmental performance of participants in ISO 14001, the results showed that participation was associated with a 2.5% improvement in environmental performance over non-participants. However, the related confidence interval (95%) indicated that the mean level of environmental performance improvements was between a 10% improvement and a 5% decrease in performance. As such, while overall performance may improve, because the confidence interval spans zero, there was inconclusive evidence regarding whether or not ISO 14001 certification leads to improved environmental performance. Combined, these findings offer some support Hypothesis 2, which states that participation in certified VEPs is associated with greater improvements in environmental performance than participation in self-monitored VEPs. However, they offer little evidence that participants in ISO 14001 had stronger environmental performance improvements than non-participants.

To consider the importance of VEP monitoring further, we assessed the variance explained in participants' environmental performance due to VEPs being either self-monitored or certified (ISO 14001). The Q statistics for the two groups were compared by way of a random effects analog to the one-way Analysis of Variance (ANOVA).[36] This procedure offers equivalent results to estimating a regression model with a single dummy variable (self-monitored VEP participant or ISO 14001 certified participant). In so doing, the procedure compares estimates the "within" study variation and the "between" study variation to arrive at an overall conclusion as to whether the self-monitored and certified VEPs demonstrate equivalent environmental performance improvements. The results of the ANOVA analog show that the Q "between study" group data (Q=12.8, $p<.01$) account for a significant amount of the variability in our data, which affirms that our groupings are statistically valid (see Table 8.6). Differences in VEP monitoring regimes therefore explain significant variation in participants' environmental performance changes.

Table 8.6 ANOVA analog comparison of VEP groupings

	Heterogeneity Measure—Q-statistic				
	All VEPs (Q_{TOT})	Self Monitored VEPs (Q_{SELF})	Certified VEPs (Q_{CERT})	Within Study Groups ($Q_W = Q_{CERT} + Q_{SELF}$)	Between Study Groups ($Q_B = Q_{TOT} - Q_W$)
Number of Studies	9	6	3	--	--
Degrees of Freedom	8	5	2	7 (9 studies – 2 groups)	1 (2 groups-1)
Calculated Q—see Table 8.5	69.0	51.0	5.2	--	--
Calculated Q— ANOVA analog[†]	--	--	--	56.2	12.8*

† The ANOVA analog tests for whether or not groupings (related to self-monitored and certification programs) account for significant variability in observed environmental performance improvements.
* Statistically significant at $p<0.01$, indicating that the monitoring grouping explains significant variability in environmental performance.

Discussion and Conclusions

Scholars and practitioners have presented numerous concerns about the overall utility of VEPs, especially since we know little about whether these programs collectively are meeting their environmental goals. This research helps address these issues by aggregating the results found in previous studies to arrive at an overall conclusion about the efficacy of VEPs. Our findings indicate that there is little evidence that *overall* VEP participation is associated with improved environmental performance. Rather, non-participants improve the environment 7.7% more than VEP participants. These unexpected findings are explained in part by differences in VEP design in that significant variations exist among the two most common subcategories of programs—those requiring self-monitoring as opposed to third-party certification.

In comparing these two VEP monitoring regimes, this study shows that *on average* non-participants demonstrate a 24% stronger environmental performance improvement than participants in self-monitored VEPs. By contrast, participants in ISO 14001, which requires external certification by an independent third-party auditor, *on average* shows modest environmental performance improvements (2.5%) over non-participants. However, because the mean level of environmental improvements for ISO 14001 participants ranges between 10% and -5%, we are not confident that ISO 14001 certification leads to real environmental improvements.

Participants in self-monitored VEPs self-evaluate their adherence toprogram requirements and submit reports to program managers of their progress. However, conformance is rarely verified, and if it is, there exists no mechanism to expel participants that fail to meet the VEP's environmental goals (Darnall & Carmin, 2005).[15] Situations such as these invite widespread free-ridership and shirking of VEP goals (King & Lenox, 2000; Rivera, 2002).[34, 50] Participants therefore derive program benefits (such as increased recognition for a proactive environmental strategy) without conforming to VEP requirements (Darnall & Carmin, 2005).[15]

While ISO 14001 requires certification by an independent third-party auditor, which reduces some opportunities for free-riding, it fails to incorporate two important VEP design features that would help ensure that participants improve their environmental performance. First, ISO 14001 does not require that third-party audits be publicly disclosed. Such disclosure may succeed in improving participants' environmental performance because they are held accountable to a greater degree.[46] The second design weakness of ISO 14001 is that it does not have a strong sanctioning mechanism. Indeed, firms that are granted ISO 14001 certification rarely are decertified if they fail to maintain conformance with the standard.[7] Moreover, in the unlikely event that a firm is decertified, ISO does not publish summary statistics for these companies. This design policy differs from positions taken by other certified VEPs. For instance, 16 participants of the Sustainable Forestry Initiatives' (SFI) original 45 members were expelled from the program for failure to uphold the standard.[1] SFI publicly disclosed conformance information on its website to maintain external credibility for its VEP and enhance the legitimacy of participants that successfully maintain their certification (see NOTE below).

To address the problem of free-riding, participants in both self-monitored and certified VEPs need to be separated in some way such that companies which

---

NOTE: SFI was developed as an industry-initiated third-party certification VEP. Industry representatives worked in concert with representatives from the environmental, professional, conservation, academic and public sectors to design this program. On January 1, 2007, the program became fully independent and it is governed by Sustainable Forestry Initiative, Inc. (SFI, Inc.).

fulfill program requirements are differentiated from participants that fail to do so. Imposing greater monitoring and expelling free-riders is one way to create this separation, in that firms intending to free-ride would be discouraged from participating in a VEP or removed for their nonconformance.[15] By preventing shirking—in both sponsor-monitored and certified VEPs—VEPs would encourage a virtuous cycle of reputational improvements for VEPs and their participants. That is, participants would be more likely to contribute to the maintaining the VEP's reputation because they believe other members will do so as well.[47, 55]

However, weak VEP goals may explain why program participants do not demonstrate greater environmental improvements than nonparticipants. Goal setting theory suggests that goals serve an energizing function[37] for organizations. Specific and challenging goals result in a higher performance than moderate or easy attainable goals.[38] The highest level of effort generally occurs when a task is moderately difficult and the lowest levels occur when the task is either very easy or very hard. Relating these issues to VEPs, in fact participants may be adhering to program goals. However, if programs are designed with goals that are weaker than the internal environmental performance targets established by nonparticipating firms, participants will be less likely to outperform nonparticipants.

We originally hypothesized that participation in ISO 14001 would lead to greater environmental performance changes than participation in self-monitored programs. While our findings support this proposition, it is only because self-monitored programs appear to perform so poorly. Indeed, both types of programs fail to offer compelling evidence that their participants improve the environment to a greater degree than non-participants. Combined, our findings point to the hazards of developing VEPs with weak design structures. While it is important to recognize that program managers are balancing the need for ensuring program efficacy with the goal of providing participants flexibility, flexibility in program design (as currently implemented) can compromise the ability of these programs to improve participants' environmental performance.

Our findings have important implications for policy makers who promote VEPs in that the programs evaluated in this study do not demonstrate any real environmental performance improvements. However, it is important to ask "what is the role of these programs?" If VEPs are designed for the single purpose of encouraging participants to improve the environment to a greater degree than non-participants then these programs may have little tangible merit. These conclusions are consistent with recent evaluations criticizing government-sponsored VEPs for their inability to determine success, failure, and ideal models for future program development.[58] In the absence of developing stronger design features, VEP critics may be justified in their concerns about the overall utility of these programs.

However, VEPs may also serve a more nuanced (but equally important) role. Even if a firm's participation represents a purely symbolic act, many VEP participants implemented performance-improving environmental practices prior to the existence of the VEP. Strong empirical evidence of this relationship has been found for ISO 14001 adopters[33] as well as companies that participated in EPA's 33/50 program.[32] That is, many firms use VEP participation as a vehicle for communicating their previous environmental improvements in an effort to gain external social and economic rewards.[33] In instances such as these, there is a "decoupling" between substantive environmental improvements related to the symbolic act of VEP participation.[33] Coupling of symbol and substance then occurs after the VEP is developed in that the program serves as a vehicle for firms to credibly communicate their prior activities.[33] In the absence of the VEP, there would be no way for companies to communicate their previous environmental improvements and obtain value from them. However, prior environmental improvements may also increase the marginal cost for VEP participants to achieve greater pollution reductions since their low-hanging fruit has been picked. By contrast, to the extent that nonparticipating firms are engaging in pollution reductions for the first time, they can more readily make small changes in their operating procedures that lead to greater environmental gains. These distinctions may partially explain why VEP participants do not demonstrate greater environmental improvements.

It is also important to recognize that VEPs rely on flexible approaches to encourage environmental improvement. In some instances, this flexibility may help participants foster collaborative relationships between government and the regulated community that promotes shared learning and capacity development.[15] In other instances, VEPs have influenced corporate attitudes regarding the environment and management practices. While these activities may have little impact on VEP efficacy, they can create a foundation for long-term environmental stewardship.[15, 41]

Related to the regulatory realm, there may be additional merit for promoting VEPs outside of demonstrating efficacy. For instance, VEPs can investigate and promote innovative environmental policy ideas[19] when political resistance prevents the adoption of more powerful mandatory plans.[39] Such ideas can be tested and evaluated before they are implemented across the regulated community.[15] As such, in asking the question "what is the role of these programs?" the answer may be much broader than was originally conceived by their program designers.

In arriving at our conclusions, this research imposed numerous inclusion and exclusion criteria before deeming a study suitable for comparison in this analysis. Despite our detailed approach, there are reasons to interpret our findings cautiously. The limited number of existing VEP studies prevented us from utilizing a multiple regression analysis. Rather, this study evaluated the relationship between VEP monitoring regimes and participants' environmental performance by way of a random effects analog to the one-way ANOVA. The ANOVA analog offers useful insights about the relationship between VEP participation, program monitoring, and participants' environmental performance

(D. Wilson, personal communication, September 17, 2007). While our findings draw on more than 30,000 observations of VEP participant and non-participant behavior, and include VEPs that had reporting, monitoring, administrative, and conformance requirements which are typical of many VEPs, we believe care should be exercised in extrapolating our findings to predict the environmental performance outcomes of other VEPs, especially those with more (or less) robust accountability requirements. Moreover, this study did not account for the important, but difficult to quantify intangible effects of VEP participation, such as changes in attitudes or management practices. While these issues may have a trivial influence on VEP efficacy, they can lead to behavioral changes that benefit the natural environment in the future.[15, 41]

As the variety and number of VEPs grows, and as markets and other stakeholders increasingly rely on these programs to gauge firms' environmental performance, it is essential to understand more about their purpose and efficacy. Additionally, as more resources are dedicated to VEP development and implementation, it will be increasingly important to understand which design characteristics lead to greater environmental improvements. Future research should evaluate this latter issue in particular. For instance, some VEPs (e.g., Responsible Care®) were designed as self-monitored VEPs (see NOTE below), but recently added third-party auditing requirements. By studying programs such as these we might be able to better understand the impact that monitoring regimes have on participant shirking and the extent to which third-party monitoring helps achieve program goals within the same VEP. Such an evaluation also would offer stronger empirical evidence regarding the merit of external auditing. Additionally, future studies would benefit by comparing the efficacy of ISO 14001 with other certified VEPs (like SFI) that couple certification with public disclosure requirements in addition to sanctions that expel nonconforming participants. Doing so would offer important evidence about the incremental environmental performance gains offered by various VEP design features.

In sum, the research presented in this paper builds on the inconsistent findings of previous research to establish a much needed overall assessment of VEP efficacy. It offers two contributions to organizational research on voluntary environmental governance, in addition to areas for future study. First, it provides a broader view of the efficacy of VEPs as alternative environmental governance tools and presents critical insights regarding the relationship between participation and improved environmental performance. Second, this research distinguishes among the two most common subcategories of programs—those requiring self-monitoring as opposed to third-party certification. It offers

NOTE. King & Lenox (2000)[34] evaluated the efficacy of Responsible Care. Their study was completed during the time in which the program required self-monitoring only.

evidence that *overall* VEP participants' environmental performance is worse than non-participants, especially for programs that require participants to self-monitor their adherence to program goals. Further, participants in ISO 14001 *as a group* exhibit inconclusive environmental performance improvements. Finally, this research demonstrates the need for future research to consider the varying purposes of VEPs and how specific design features can increase their value as tools for environmental governance.

Notes

1. American Forest and Paper Association. (2001). *The SFI Program: A Bold Approach to Sustainable Forest Management*, www.afandpa.org/forestry/sfi_frame, last accessed December 2001.

2. Anton, Wilma Rose Q., George Deltas, and Madhu Khanna (2004). "Incentives for environmental self-regulation and implications for environmental performance," *Journal of Environmental Economics and Management* 48(1): 632–654.

3. Arora, Seema and Timothy N. Cason (1996). "Why do firms volunteer to exceed environmental regulations? Understanding participation in EPA's 33/50 program," *Land Economics* 72: 413–432.

4. Baggott, Robert (1986). "By voluntary agreement: The politics of instrument selection," *Public Administration* 64(1): 51–67.

5. Bansal, Pratima and Trevor Hunter. (2003). "Strategic explanations for the early adoption of ISO 14001," *Journal of Business Ethics* 46(3): 289–299.

6. Barber. Jeffrey. (1998). "Responsible action or public relations? NGO perspectives on voluntary initiatives," *Industry and Environment*, 21(1–2): 19–22.

7. Barrow, Christopher J. (2005). *Environmental Management and Development*. London: Taylor & Francis. Inc.

8. Boyle, Kevin J., Gregory L. Poe and John C. Bergstrom (1994). "What do we know about groundwater values? Preliminary implications from a meta analysis of contingent valuation studies," *American Journal of Agricultural Economics* 76 (December). 1055–1061.

9. Carmin JoAnn, Nicole Darnall and Joao Mil-Homens (2003). "Stakeholder involvement in the design of U.S. voluntary environmental programs: Does sponsorship matter?" *Policy Studies Journal* 31: 527–543.

10. Coglianese Cary and Jennifer Nash (eds.) (2001). *Regulating from the Inside: Can Environmental Management Systems Achieve Policy Goals?* Washington, DC: Resources for the Future.

11. Cook, Thomas D. and Donald T. Campbell (1979). *Quasi Experimentation: Design and Analysis Issues for Field Settings*. Boston: Houghton-Mifflin.

12. Cooper, Harris M. (1989). *Integrating Research: A Guide for Literature Reviews* (2nd edition). Newberry Park, CA: Sage Publications.

13. Cooper, Harris M. & Larry V. Hedges (1994). *The Handbook of Research Synthesis*. Newberry Park., CA: Sage Publications.

14. Darnall, Nicole. (2006). "Why firms mandate ISO 14001 certification," *Business & Society* 45(3): 354–381.

15. Darnall, Nicole and JoAnn Carmin (2005). "Cleaner and greener? The signaling accuracy of U.S. voluntary environmental programs," *Policy Sciences* 38: 71–90.

16. Darnall, Nicole and Daniel Edwards Jr. (2006). "Predicting the cost of environmental management system adoption: the role of capabilities, resources and ownership structure," *Strategic Management Journal* 27(2): 301–320.

17.   Darnall, Nicole, JoAnn Carmin, Nicole Kreiser and Joao. Mil-Homens (2003). *The Design & Rigor of U.S. Voluntary Environmental Programs: Results from the VEP Survey,* Department of Political Science & Public Administration, North Carolina State University and Department of Urban Studies and Planning, Massachusetts Institute of Technology.

18.   Davies, Terry, Janice Mazurek, Kieran McKarthy and Nicole Darnall (1996). *Industry Incentives for Environmental Improvement: Evaluation of U.S. Federal Initiatives.* Washington, DC: Resources for the Future, Center for Risk Management.

19.   Delmas, Magali A. and Ann K. Terlaak. (2001). "A framework for analyzing environmental voluntary agreements," *California Management Review* 43: 44–62.

20.   Delmas, Magali and Arturo Keller (2005). "Free riding in voluntary environmental programs: The case of the U.S. EPA WasteWise program," *Policy Sciences* 38(2-3): 91–106.

21.   *Gamper-Rabindran, Shanti. (2006). "Did the EPA's voluntary industrial toxics program reduce emissions? A GIS analysis of distributional impacts and by-media analysis of substitution," *Journal of Environmental Economics and Management* 52: 391–410.

22.   Garcia-Johnson, Ronnie. (2000). *Exporting Environmentalism: U.S. Multinational Chemical Corporations in Brazil and Mexico.* Cambridge, MA: MIT Press.

23.   Glass, Gene V., Barry McGaw and Mary Lee Smith (1981). *Meta-Analysis in Social Research.* Beverly Hills (CA): Sage Publications.

24.   Greene, William H. (2003). *Econometric Analysis.* 5th Edition. Upper Saddle, NJ: Prentice-Hall.

25.   Hedges, Larry and Ingram Olkin (1985). *Statistical Methods for Meta-Analysis.* San Diego, CA: Academic Press, Ltd.

26.   Hoffman, Andrew. (1997). *From Heresy to Dogma: An Institutional History of Corporate Environmentalism.* San Francisco: New Lexington Press.

27.   House, Robert J. and Phillip M Podsakoff. 1994. "Leadership effectiveness: Past perspectives and future directions for research." In J. Greenberg (Ed.), *Organizational Behavior: The State of the Science* (pp. 45–82). Hillsdale, NJ: Lawrence Erlbaum Associates.

28.   Hunt, Morton M. (1997). *How Science Takes Stock: the Story of Meta-Analysis.* New York: Russell Sage Foundation.

29.   Hunter, John E. (1997). "Needed: A ban on the significance test," *Psychological Science* 8: 3–7.

30.   Hunter, John E. and Frank L. Schmidt (2004). *Methods of Meta-Analysis: Correcting Error and Bias in Research Findings.* Thousand Oaks, CA: Sage Publications.

31.   Khanna, Madhu and Wilma Rose Q. Anton (2002). "Corporate environmental management: Regulatory and market-based incentives," *Land Economics* 78: 539–558.

32.   *Khanna, Madhu and Lisa Damon (1999). "EPA's voluntary 33/50 program: Impact on toxic releases and economic performance of firms," *Journal of Environmental Economics and Management* 37(1): 1–17.

33. *King, Andrew A., Michael J. Lenox and Ann Terlaak (2005). "The Strategic use of decentralized institutions; Exploring Certification with the ISO 14001 management standard," *Academy of Management Journal* 48(6): 1091–1106.

34. *King, Andrew A. and Michael J. Lenox (2000). "Industry self-regulation without sanctions: The chemical industry's Responsible Care program." *Academy of Management Journal* 43(4): 698-716.

35. Lenox, Michael and Jennifer Nash (2003). "Industry self-regulation and adverse selection: a comparison across four trade association programs," *Business Strategy and the Environment* 12(6):343–360.

36. Lipsey, Mark W. and David B. Wilson (2001). *Practical Meta-Analysis.* Thousand Oaks, CA: Sage Publications, Inc.

37. Locke, Edwin A. and Garry P. Latham. 2002. "Building a practically useful theory of goal setting and task motivation" *American Psychologist* 57: 705–15.

38. ———. 1990. *A Theory of Goal Setting and Task Performance.* Englewood Cliffs, NJ: Prentice Hall.

39. Lyon, Thomas P. (2003). *Voluntary versus Mandatory Approaches to Climate Change Mitigation.* Washington, DC: Resources for the Future, Issue Brief 03-01.

40. Mazurek, Janice (2002). "Government sponsored voluntary programs for firms: An initial survey," in T. Dietz & P.C. Stern, eds. *New Tools for Environmental Protection: Education, Information and Voluntary Measures,* Washington, DC: National Academy Press, pp. 219–234.

41. Morgenstern, Richard and William A. Pizer (2007). *Reality Check: The Nature and Performance of Voluntary Environmental Programs in the United States, Europe, and Japan.* Washington, DC: Resources for the Future.

42. Olson, Mancur. (1965). *The Logic of Collective Action.* Cambridge, MA: Harvard University Press.

43. Peglau, Reinhard (2005). *ISO 14001 Certification of the World.* Berlin: Federal Environmental Agency.

44. Orlitzky, Marc and John D. Benjamin (2001). "Corporate social performance and firm risk: A meta-analytic review," *Business and Society* 40(4): 369–396.

45. Portney, Paul R. and Richard N. Stavins. (eds.) (2000). *Public Policies for Environmental Protection.* Washington, DC: Resources for the Future.

46. *Potoski, Matthew and Aseem Prakash (2005a). "Covenants with weak swords: ISO 14001 and facilities' environmental performance," *Journal of Policy Analysis and Management* 24(4): 745.

47. *——— (2005b). 'Green clubs and voluntary governance: ISO 14001 and Firms' Regulatory Compliance,' *American Journal of Political Science* 49(2): 235.

48. Prakash, Aseem. (2000). *Greening the Firm.* Cambridge, UK: Cambridge University Press, p.286.

49. Ringquist, Evan. (2005). "Assessing evidence of environmental inequities: A Meta-Analysis,' *Journal of Policy Analysis and Management* 24(2): 223–247.

50. Rivera, Jorge. (2002). "Assessing a voluntary environmental initiative in the developing world: The Costa Rican certification of sustainable tourism," *Policy Sciences* 35: 333–360.

51. Rivera, Jorge and Peter deLeon (2004). "Is greener whiter? Voluntary environmental performance of western ski areas," *Policy Studies Journal* 32(3):417–438.

52. Rivera, Jorge, Peter deLeon and Charles Koerber (2006). "Is greener whiter yet? The Sustainable Slopes Program after five years," *Policy Studies Journal* 34(2): 195–224.

53. Rondinelli, Dennis A. and Ted London (2003). "How corporations and environmental groups cooperate: Assessing cross sector alliances and collaborations," *Academy of Management Executive* 17(1): 62–76.

54. Rondinelli, Dennis A. and Gyula Vastag (2000). "Panacea, common sense, or just a label? The value of ISO 14001 environmental management systems," *European Management Journal* 18: 499–510.

55. Scholz, John T. and Mark Lubell. 1998. "Adaptive political attitudes: Duty, trust and fear as monitors of tax policy." *American Journal of Political Science* 42: 398–417.

56. US Environmental Protection Agency (2004). US Environmental Protection Agency, Performance Track Program, http://www.epa.gov/performancetrack/program/index.htm.

57. US Environmental Protection Agency (2007). *FY2008 EPA Budget in a Brief.* Washington, DC: USEPA, Office of the Chief Financial Officer, EPA-205-S-07-001.

58. US Office of Inspector General (2007). *Voluntary Programs Could Benefit from Internal Policy Controls and Systematic Management Approach.* Washington, DC: USOIG, Report No. 2007-P-00041, September 25.

59. *Vidovic, Martina and Neha Khanna (2007). "Can voluntary pollution prevention programs fulfill their promises? Further evidence from the EPA's 33/50 Program," *Journal of Environmental Economics and Management* 53:180–195.

60. Webb, Eugene J., Donald Campbell, Richard Schwartz, Lee Sechrest and Janet Groves (1981). *Nonreactive Measures in the Social Sciences.* Boston: Houghton-Mifflin.

61. *Welch, Eric, Allan Mazur and Stuart Bretschneider (2000). "Voluntary behavior by electric utilities: Levels of adoption and contribution of the Climate Challenge Program to reduction of carbon dioxide," *Journal of Policy Analysis and Management* 19(3): 407.

Denotes study included in meta-analysis.

Chapter 9

Can Voluntary Environmental Regulation Work in Developing Countries: Lessons from Case Studies

Allen Blackman

Introduction

The conventional approach to industrial pollution control is to establish laws requiring firms to cut emissions. Voluntary regulation, by contrast, provides incentives—but not mandates—for pollution control. The four main types of voluntary regulation are: environmental agreements negotiated between regulators and industry; public programs (administered by regulators or third parties) that individual firms are invited to join; public disclosure initiatives that collect and disseminate information on participants' environmental performance; and unilateral commitments made by firms (Khanna 2001).[1] In industrialized countries, such regulation has become quite popular (OECD 1999, 2003). Less well known is that environmental authorities in developing countries, particularly those in Latin America, also have embraced this approach and are rapidly putting initiatives in place. For example, over the past decade, regulatory authorities in Colombia, Chile, and Mexico have negotiated dozens of high-profile voluntary "clean production agreements" with dirty industrial sectors (Jiménez 2007; Hanks 2002). Other types of voluntary regulation, including state-run voluntary audit, labeling, and public disclosure programs, are also increasingly common (Rivera 2002; Blackman et al. 2007; García, Sterner and Afsah 2007).

Although voluntary environmental initiatives in industrialized countries share many features with those in developing countries, their objectives are gen-

239

erally different. Policymakers in industrialized countries typically use voluntary regulation to encourage firms to overcomply with mandatory regulations; those in developing countries generally use it to help remedy rampant noncompliance with mandatory regulation. For example, an explicit goal of national clean production initiatives in both Chile and Colombia has been to foster compliance with mandatory regulation (Jiménez 2007; Blackman et al. 2006). Given that voluntary regulation in developing countries is usually a frontline compliance strategy rather than an effort to move beyond compliance, the stakes for its success are high.

But is voluntary regulation likely to have significant environmental benefits in developing countries? Two opposing views are emerging in the nascent literature on the topic. Some argue that voluntary regulation holds considerable promise for developing countries (Hanks 2002; World Bank 1999). As is well known, policymakers in these countries face an array of barriers to enforcing mandatory regulation, including weak institutions, incomplete legal foundations, and limited political will (Russell and Vaughn 2003; Eskeland and Jimenez 1992). According to its proponents, voluntary regulation sidesteps these constraints because, by definition, it does not depend directly on mandatory regulation to motivate polluters to improve their environmental performance. Rather, it relies on at least two other types of incentives. First, by raising the profile of firms' environmental performance, voluntary regulation can boost pressures placed upon polluters by consumers, capital markets, nongovernmental organizations, and community groups. For example, a firm participating in a negotiated voluntary agreement could, in principle, receive positive publicity that increases its sales, enhances its access to financial capital, and deflects criticism from environmental advocates. Second, voluntary initiatives often subsidize investments in pollution abatement. These subsidies can be pecuniary—for example, grants or loans for pollution control equipment—but more often they are informational—for example, seminars, brochures, and one-on-one interactions that provide technical assistance in pollution abatement. Such nonpecuniary subsidies are reputed to be a leading "soft" benefit of voluntary regulation.

Notwithstanding those arguments, there are at least four reasons to doubt that voluntary regulation can be effective in developing countries.

(i) Weak regulatory pressure. Case studies suggests that a "background threat" of mandatory regulation is often a critical motivation for firms to participate in and comply with voluntary regulatory initiatives (Khanna 2001; Lyon and Maxwell 2002). This finding implies that voluntary regulatory instruments are unlikely to perform well in countries where mandatory regulation is weak.

(ii) Weak nonregulatory pressure. Many of the nonregulatory factors that reputedly motivate firms to participate in and comply with voluntary regulation—including pressure from consumers, capital markets, nongovernmental organizations, and community groups—are relatively anemic in developing countries.

Niche markets for "green" products are smaller than in industrialized countries; capital markets, including stock markets, are thinner; and environmental nongovernmental organizations and advocacy groups are relatively weak and scarce (Fry 1988; Wehrmeyer and Mulugetta 1999).

(iii) Regulatory capture. Regulatory processes and programs in developing countries are often heavily influenced by industrial interests, a phenomenon often referred to as regulatory capture (Russell and Vaughn 2003). This is likely to be a particular problem with initiatives that are the outcome of a negotiation between regulators and industry, such as clean production agreements. Where regulatory capture is a problem, polluters will be able to block monitoring and enforcement mechanisms, third-party participation, individual penalties for noncompliance, quantified baselines and targets, and other measures that are widely seen as prerequisites for effective voluntary initiatives (OECD 1999). A closely related concern is that in developing countries, voluntary regulation can be used to preempt or delay effective mandatory regulation by creating an environmental "Potemkin Village"—a false impression that regulators and polluters are making progress on environmental problems. If this is the case, one cannot argue that, whatever its weaknesses, voluntary regulation can only improve environmental quality. Rather, voluntary regulation can have real environmental costs, which must be weighed against any possible benefits.

(iv) Preponderance of small-scale firms. Small-scale and informal (unlicensed and unregistered) firms are more prevalent in developing countries than in industrialized countries (Blackman 2006). Using voluntary regulation to control pollution from such firms is problematic. They may be less susceptible to many of the regulatory and nonregulatory pressures that create incentives for compliance with voluntary initiatives, including those generated by green consumers and capital markets. Also, they may be more likely to free-ride on the activities of larger participants in voluntary initiatives.

How have these arguments for and against the use of voluntary regulation in developing countries played out in practice? The literature on the topic is quite thin, and to my knowledge, a broad assessment has yet to appear. Among the studies that have been published, all but two focus on evaluating a single initiative, and none have compared and contrasted different types of initiatives to shed light on the advantages and disadvantages of each.[2] Related research on industrialized countries may not generalize to developing countries, where voluntary regulation is often used for different purposes and where the institutional and socioeconomic context is dissimilar.

To help fill this gap, this paper presents case studies of three voluntary initiatives: a series of negotiated agreements in Mexico, a public program in Mexico, and a public disclosure scheme in India. Two criteria were used to select the three case studies. First, we chose case studies of three types of voluntary regulation to facilitate comparison. The disadvantage of this cross-cutting focus is, of course, a more limited understanding of each type of initiative. Second, we chose case studies that could be extracted from recently completed or ongoing research (Blackman and Sisto 2006; Blackman et al. 2007; Powers et al. 2007). The additional contributions of the present paper are to compare and contrast the three initiatives focusing on broad themes (including the four "concerns" discussed above) rather than methodological details, to place them in context via a review of the literature, and to distill policy and research prescriptions.

Because three case studies constitute a small nonrandom sample of voluntary initiatives, we need to be cautious in drawing conclusions. That said, our analysis suggests that although voluntary environmental regulation in developing countries is a risky endeavor, initiatives that are carefully designed and deployed can be effective. The risks can be minimized by emphasizing the dissemination of information about pollution and pollution abatement options and by avoiding voluntary tools in certain situations—those where regulatory and non-regulatory pressures for improved environmental performance are weak and where polluters can dictate the terms of the initiative.

The remainder of the paper proceeds as follows. The second section presents a review of existing case studies of voluntary regulation in developing countries. The third section presents a case study of negotiated voluntary agreements between regulatory authorities and leather tanneries in Guanajuato, Mexico. The fourth section offers a case study of Mexico's Clean Industry Program, a national voluntary audit program. The fifth section presents a case study of India's Green Ratings Project, a public disclosure program. The sixth section compares and contrasts the three initiatives, and the last section presents policy prescriptions and suggestions for future research.

Literature

Although the growing popularity of voluntary regulation worldwide has spurred a boom in research on the topic (for reviews, see Harrison 1999; Khanna 2001; Lyon and Maxwell 2002; and Morgenstern and Pizer 2007), only a few studies have focused on developing countries. This section reviews this thread of the literature. We restrict attention to the three types of voluntary regulation represented by our case studies—negotiated agreements, public programs, and public disclosure—paying particular attention to the four concerns discussed in the introduction.[3]

Negotiated Agreements

Case studies of voluntary environmental agreements negotiated between regulators and industry highlight the importance of both regulatory pressure and regulatory capture in explaining success and failure: they suggest that such agreements are more effective when accompanied by a credible threat of mandatory regulation, and less effective when polluters are able to block design elements aimed at holding them to environmental performance targets. Jiménez (2007) analyzes Chile's extensive experience with sector-wide negotiated voluntary agreements, the result of a 2001 national policy aimed at improving compliance with mandatory regulation. The negotiated agreements complemented a reasonably effective mandatory regulatory system and included specific environmental performance targets, clear deadlines, third-party monitoring, sanctions for noncompliance, and pollution abatement subsidies. Jiménez uses rigorous policy evaluation ("matching") techniques along with detailed plant-level survey data to compare the environmental performance of plants that participated in voluntary agreements with similar plants that did not participate. He concludes that the voluntary agreements did in fact spur environmental performance.

Esterling Lara's (2003) evaluation of negotiated agreements in Colombia is far less positive. These agreements grew out of an effort to improve compliance with 1993 laws that completely overhauled the nation's environmental regulatory system. Virtually all the agreements lacked specific targets, deadlines, third-party monitoring, sanctions, and subsidies. The specific targets that industry committed to in the agreements were overwhelmingly procedural—for example, holding meetings, forming committees, and generating reports. Even so, Esterling Lara found that in a sample of 13 voluntary agreements, on average industry kept only about a third of these low-level commitments.

Both Dvorák, Lisa, and Sauer (2002) and Freitas and Gereluk (2002) present case studies of voluntary agreements intended to preempt more stringent mandatory regulations. Dvorák, Lisa, and Sauer analyze a 1995 agreement between the Ministry of the Environment and a national trade association of washing powder producers in the Czech Republic that was used by the trade association to head off mandatory rules on phosphate content. The targets set under the agreement were relatively lax, and the authors conclude that as a result, the agreements probably had few environmental benefits. Freitas and Gereluk evaluate a 1995 Brazilian agreement negotiated among the national government, representatives of industry, and labor unions to limit workplace exposure to benzene, a carcinogen. The agreement revamped an unrealistic 1994 regulation that mandated zero exposure: it set less stringent industry-specific standards, established rules for handling and storing benzene, and set up monitoring procedures. According to Freitas and Gereluk, notwithstanding some shortcomings, investment in benzene abatement, benzene exposure, and the incidence of benzene-related occupational illness have all declined significantly since the agreement was signed.

Public Programs

The handful of studies of developing country voluntary public programs—that is, programs administered by regulators or third parties that require participating firms to meet environmental performance or procedural standards—suggest that they can have environmental benefits, and that external pressures applied by regulators and other stakeholders motivate firms to participate. Rivera (2002, 2004) analyzes the Costa Rican Certification for Sustainable Tourism program, a voluntary initiative that aims to reduce the adverse environmental impacts of hotels. Using detailed data on more than 150 hotels, Rivera finds that government monitoring, trade association membership, and an orientation toward green consumers drive participation. Furthermore, he finds that only those participating hotels that overcomplied with program standards were rewarded with higher room prices and more customers, a result that suggests that nonparticipants are not able to free-ride on the investments of participants.

Blackman and Bannister (1998) evaluate an early-1990s voluntary program aimed at persuading managers of more than 300 small-scale brick kilns in Ciudad Juárez, Chihuahua (Mexico) to substitute clean-burning propane for dirty traditional fuels, including used tires and scrap wood. Roughly half the kilns in the city joined the program, even though switching to propane dramatically increased production costs. Blackman and Bannister attribute the program's success partly to stepped-up pressures applied by regulators, trade associations, and community organizations, and to subsidies paid to propane adopters.

Several papers examine International Standards Organization (ISO) 14001 certification, a voluntary program that requires participating plants to identify their negative environmental impacts, establish goals for reducing them, and design an environmental management plan to meet these goals. Using survey data from more than 200 Mexican manufacturing plants, Dasgupta, Hettige and Wheeler (2000) find that plants that are frequently inspected by regulators, are publicly owned, and have more educated employees are more likely to obtain ISO 14001 certification. They also find that certified plants are more likely to comply with mandatory regulation. Christmann and Taylor (2001) use similar methods to examine ISO 14001 certification in a sample of more than 100 Chinese firms. They find that firms that are owned by or sell to multinationals and those that export to developed countries are more likely to be certified. Finally, Roht-Arriaza (1997) examines the potential for ISO 14001 certification to generate significant improvements in environmental performance in the 18 countries that belong to the Asia-Pacific Economic Corporation. She concludes that in isolation, this voluntary program is unlikely to lead to such improvements because it requires firms only to adopt management procedures, not to meet performance standards, and has weak information, reporting, and accreditation requirements.

Public Disclosure

Only a few published studies examine developing country voluntary programs that collect, verify, and disseminate information on firms' environmental performance. All present positive evaluations. García, Sterner, and Afsah (2007) and Blackman, Afsah, and Ratunanda (2004) analyze Indonesia's widely acclaimed Program for Pollution Control, Evaluation, and Rating (PROPER), a quasi-voluntary initiative (at first, participation was mandatory) that assigns plants easy-to-understand color-coded rankings and disseminates these rakings to create incentives for compliance through "honor and shame." García, Sterner, and Afsah use econometric techniques to demonstrate that the program led to significant reductions in polluting emissions. Blackman, Afsah, and Ratunanda present plant-level survey results that suggest the program spurred pollution reductions mainly by providing the managers with new information about their plants' emissions and abatement opportunities. Finally, Wang et al. (2004) describe pilot public disclosure programs in two Chinese cities: Zhenjiang, Jiangsu, and Hohot, Inner Mongolia. These "GreenWatch" programs also assign participating facilities simple color coded rankings. The authors find that the two pilot programs have had significant positive impacts and recommend expanding them to other Chinese cities.

Negotiated Agreements in Mexico[4]

This section presents a case study of four negotiated voluntary agreements used to control pollution generated by hundreds of tanneries in León, Guanajuato (Mexico). As we shall see, the agreements amounted to an almost entirely unsuccessful effort to circumvent legal, institutional, and other barriers to enforcing mandatory regulation.

Background

León, Mexico's leather goods capital, is a sprawling industrial city of some one million inhabitants in the north-central state of Guanajuato. Approximately 1,200 tanneries are scattered throughout the city. For the most part, they supply small local shoemaking and leather wear factories. The vast majority of the tanneries employ fewer than 15 workers, and about a third are informal. They generate organic liquid wastes, inorganic liquid wastes (notably sulfur and chromium), and solid wastes (mainly sludge infused with toxic chemicals). Since 2000, the organic liquid wastes have been treated by a municipal wastewater treatment plant, but the solid wastes and inorganic liquid wastes remain uncontrolled and are a leading contributor to the severe degradation of the Lerma-Chapala watershed, one of Mexico's largest. The number, small size, dispersion, informality, and local economic importance of León's tanneries make them an exceptionally challenging target for environmental regulatory authorities.

The Impetus for Voluntary Regulation

Although pollution from tanneries in León has been a serious problem for decades, significant pressure for remedial action did not develop until the mid-1980s, following the launch of a campaign to improve surface water quality in the Lerma-Chapala watershed. Despite this pressure, in the 1980s and 1990s, local regulators faced severe constraints that more or less ruled out relying principally on a conventional mandatory approach and made negotiated voluntary agreements a logical choice. Specifically, regulators lacked the legal, institutional, physical, and civic infrastructure needed to use mandatory tools. The requisite legal infrastructure included clear regulations governing both the discharge of liquid wastes into municipal sewers and the classification, handling, and storage of hazardous wastes. The former were not promulgated until 1998. Although hazardous waste regulations were promulgated in 1993, written materials clarifying how they applied to tanneries were not available until 1997.[5] The institutional infrastructure needed to regulate tanneries included capable state and municipal regulatory authorities. Yet Guanajuato's environmental regulatory agency was not established until the mid-1990s, León's sewer authority was not founded until 1985, and a municipal environmental authority was not established until the next decade. The physical infrastructure needed to control tannery pollution included facilities to treat inorganic liquid wastes, organic liquid wastes, and hazardous solid wastes. Of these three types of infrastructure, to date, only one—a facility to treat organic wastes—has been built, and it did not begin operating until 2000. Finally, the civic infrastructure needed to control tannery pollution included public support for regulating tanneries in León. There is virtually no evidence that citizens of León—either individually as voters and consumers or collectively via nongovernmental and community organizations—have ever placed significant political pressure on tanners to improve pollution control. One reason is that, as the leading employer in the city, the leather goods industry enjoys considerable political and popular support.

The Four Agreements

Starting in 1987, Mexican regulatory authorities negotiated a series of four voluntary environmental agreements with leather tanners in León. The agreements had several common characteristics. Each was signed by tannery trade associations and by federal and local regulators, and each was administered by local regulators. Each committed the tanners to completing specified pollution control measures within two to four years, and each committed regulators to making investments needed to fill gaps in regulatory infrastructure and to providing tanners with pecuniary and nonpecuniary pollution abatement subsidies. Unfortunately, the outcome of each negotiated agreement was also the same. Tanners—and to a lesser extent regulators—abrogated virtually all of their commitments.

Signed in July 1987, the first agreement committed the tanners to undertaking low-cost pollution prevention and control measures—namely, to installing sedimentation tanks and recycling tanning baths—within two years. For their part, regulators agreed to promulgate standards needed to control discharges into the local sewer system. Of these provisions, only one was carried out: most tanners installed sedimentation tanks, which were urgently needed to prevent the city's sewers from clogging.

In light of the failure of the first voluntary agreement, regulators negotiated a second agreement in October 1991. It focused on a new pollution control strategy: building a series of common effluent treatment plants to control inorganic liquid wastes. Tanners committed to relocating to a series of industrial parks where the plants would be built. The city of León agreed to pass new zoning legislation that would facilitate relocation, register all tanneries, and build municipal solid and organic liquid waste treatment facilities. The agreement did not specify who would pay for relocating the tanneries and building the effluent treatment plants. The second tannery agreement spurred only one real accomplishment—city authorities set aside a plot of unimproved land for the creation of a large tanning industrial park. By 1993, efforts to control tannery pollution had once again come to a standstill.

After an international incident involving the death of thousands of migratory birds wintering at a reservoir polluted by tannery wastes in the winter of 1994–1995, pressure for tannery pollution control was revived, and a third voluntary agreement was signed in June 1995. It more or less repeated the provisions of the first two agreements. In addition, federal, state and municipal authorities agreed to finance an education and research center to build public support and a scientific foundation for tannery pollution control. Again, none of these commitments were kept.

The fourth voluntary agreement was signed in March 1997. It included a new twist on the usual strategy for controlling tannery liquid wastes: the city would build a series of common effluent treatment plants as well as segregated sewer systems to transport wastes to these plants and would charge tanners fees to pay for this infrastructure. Individual tanners instead of trade association representatives were required to sign the agreements. The signatories of the fourth voluntary agreement ignored virtually all its terms with two exceptions: city authorities built a municipal plant to treat organic (but not industrial) liquid wastes and dug an unimproved pit for the disposal of tannery sludge. Stakeholders in León have not negotiated a fifth agreement, and the environmental problems generated by tanneries persist.

A Public Program in Mexico[6]

This section presents a case study of the Clean Industry Program (also known as the National Environmental Auditing Program), Mexico's flagship national voluntary environmental program. The case study suggests that, unlike some voluntary public programs in industrialized countries, the Clean Industry Program does not chiefly attract already-clean plants seeking positive publicity. Rather, it attracts a significant number of relatively dirty plants and, therefore, likely has a positive impact on environmental quality.

Background

Established in 1992 as a branch of the national environmental ministry, the Federal Environmental Attorney General's Office (PROFEPA) is charged with monitoring and enforcing environmental regulations in areas where the federal government has jurisdiction, including particularly dirty industrial sectors (e.g., petroleum), certain pollutants (e.g., air emissions), and certain geographic regions (e.g., the U.S.-Mexico border). This broad mandate is exceptionally challenging given PROFEPA's limited human and financial resources (Brizzi and Ahmed 2001).

To help overcome these challenges, in its first year of operations, PROFEPA created the Clean Industry Program. It was designed to leverage PROFEPA's limited resources by shifting some of the burden for monitoring onto the private sector. It operates as follows. Plants volunteering to join the program pay for an environmental audit by an accredited third-party, private sector inspector. The audit determines what pollution control and prevention procedures the plant has in place and what additional procedures are required to comply with all existing environmental regulations. Following the audit, the plant agrees in writing to correct all violations or deficiencies by a specified date. PROFEPA, in exchange, agrees not to penalize the plant for the identified violations until that date has passed. If the plant abides by this agreement, it is awarded a Clean Industry certificate that exempts it from regulatory inspections for two years. Akin to a seal of good housekeeping, this certificate is sometimes used in marketing campaigns.

Hence, the Clean Industry Program provides a basket of incentives for participation and compliance that includes both "carrots" and "sticks." The main carrots are an enforcement amnesty and the Clean Industry certificate, which can be used as a marketing tool. The main stick is the threat of enforcement of mandatory environmental regulations for plants not in the program. The Clean Industry Program is now quite popular. The number of participating plants grew from 77 in 1992 to roughly 3,500 in 2005.

Do Only Clean Plants Join?

A pervasive concern about voluntary public programs, in both industrialized and developing countries, is that they may not actually generate significant environmental benefits. Some research suggests that such programs mostly attracts plants that are already relatively clean because clean plants pay a minimal cost to meet the programs' environmental performance targets but can reap significant benefits. Therefore, it is said, the programs do not improve environmental quality and primarily serves as public relations vehicles—for both industry and regulators (Vidovic and Khanna 2007; Morgenstern and Pizer 2007).

Unfortunately, the credible plant-level data on the environmental performance of Mexican firms needed to test this hypothesis simply do not exist. Therefore, we use a proxy: records of PROFEPA fines. To determine whether relatively clean plants are joining the Clean Industry Program, we examine the relationship between PROFEPA fines and participation in the Clean Industry Program.

We construct a plant-level data set by merging registries of manufacturing plants compiled by the Mexican Ministry of Economics and PROFEPA. The result is a sample of 61,821 plants of which 541 participated in the Clean Industry Program and 61,280 did not. Variables include the dates and amounts of fines from 1987 through 2004 as well as the plants' geographic location, sector, scope of market, gross sales, equity, and whether it exports, imports, and is a government supplier.

Simple summary statistics indicate a strong correlation between PROFEPA fines and participation in the Clean Industry Program (Table 9.1). Plants that participated in the program were fined far more often and far more heavily than nonparticipants: 20 percent of participants were fined versus only three percent of nonparticipants, and the average fine was 89,923 pesos for participants versus 36,530 pesos for nonparticipants.

Table 9.1 Mexican Environmental Attorney General's Office (PROFEPA) fines, 1987–2004

Sample → ↓	Clean Industry participants+ participants	non- Clean Industry participants	Clean Industry nonparticipants
All plants	(n = 61,821)	(n = 541)	(n = 61,280)
Fined	3.17%	20.15%	3.02%
Plants that were fined	(n = 1,611)	(n = 98)	(n = 1,513)
Total fines (n)	2,658	155	2,503
Average fines/plant (n)	1.50	1.43	1.50
Average fine (pesos)	39,847.34	89,923.43	36,530.21

Although suggestive, this simple correlation does not prove causation. It may just reflect differences in underlying characteristics of plants. For example, it could be that large plants are more likely to be fined by PROFEPA and are also more likely to participate in the Clean Industry Program. The correlation also does not indicate whether the timing of PROFEPA fines and of participation suggests causation: it tell us nothing about the interval between the two events or even which comes first.

To control for plant characteristics and timing, we employ an econometric (duration) model, described in detail in Blackman et al. (2007). The results are summarized in Figure 9.1, a graph of the relationship between (i) the hazard ratio—the effect of a PROFEPA fine on the probability of joining the Clean Industry Program—and (ii) the number of years that have elapsed since the most recent fine. (More precisely, the hazard ratio is the ratio of the conditional probability of joining the program given a fine to the conditional probability of joining absent a fine.) The figure also includes 95 percent confidence intervals. The hazard ratio is positive and significantly different than unity (i.e., no effect on the probability of joining the program) for t between one and three. The appropriate interpretation is that a PROFEPA fine raised the probability that a plant would join the Clean Industry Program for three years following the fine. Figure 9.1 shows that, on average, the likelihood of joining the Clean Industry Program more than doubles for three years after a fine.

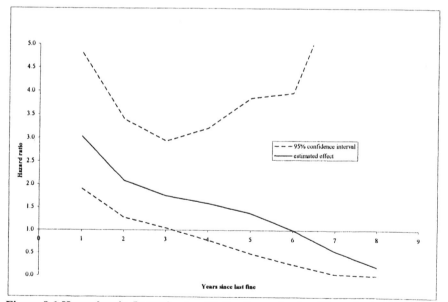

Figure 9.1 Hazard ratio (hazard rate with fine/hazard rate without fine) as function of time since last fine for plants participating in Clean Industry Program (Mexico).

This graph provides compelling evidence of a causal relationship between PROFEPA fines and participation in the Clean Industry Program. In particular, the temporal pattern of the effect—the fact that the closer one is in time to a fine, the greater the probability of participation—suggests that regulatory activity causes participation.

Impacts on Environmental Quality

Our results suggest that the Clean Industry Program is not simply a public relations scheme that primarily attracts already-clean firms. Rather, its participants include a significant number of dirty firms under pressure from regulatory authorities.

Official records indicate that the vast majority of firms that joined the Clean Industry Program signed agreements with PROFEPA to eliminate deficiencies identified in their audits, complied with these agreements, and were ultimately awarded Clean Industry certificates. However, our analysis cannot say whether the Clean Industry Program actually motivated these improvements in environmental performance. It could be that the plants that joined the program would have taken the same or similar actions even if they had not joined (presumably because they were being fined by PROFEPA and wished to avoid further sanctions). Hence, our results can be interpreted as a preliminary indication—but by no means proof—that the Clean Industry Program has generated significant environmental benefits.

Public Disclosure in India[7]

This section presents a case study of the Green Rating Project (GRP), a public disclosure pollution control program in India. The case study suggests the program has had a significant environmental benefit by spurring abatement at particularly dirty industrial facilities.

Background

India's phenomenal economic growth during the past 15 years, averaging more than 6 percent per year, has had severe environmental consequences that, in turn, have sparked public demand for environmental protection. In the mid-1990s, the Centre for Science and Environment (CSE), arguably India's best-known and most influential environmental nongovernmental organization, began work on the Green Ratings Project (GRP), a public disclosure pollution control program. GRP background materials state that the program was inspired by the Council of Economic Priorities, a now-defunct U.S. nongovernmental organization that provided investors with annual ratings of the environmental performance of U.S. companies, and that the GRP was urgently needed to shore up India's weak environmental regulatory institutions.

To date, the GRP has rated the environmental performance of large plants in four pollution-intensive industrial sectors: pulp and paper, chlor-alkali, cement, and automobiles. Plants are assigned a numerical score ranging from 0 to 100 and are awarded symbolic "leaves" depending on their score: five leaves for scores of 75 and above, four for 50–74, three for 35–49, two for 25–34, one for 15–24, and none for 14 and below. The GRP scores are based on an evaluation of the plant's life-cycle environmental impacts, from the sourcing and processing of raw materials to the manufacture, use, and disposal of products. The exceptionally detailed data needed to conduct this cradle-to-grave analysis are collected from questionnaires administered to participating plants, along with secondary data provided by local environmental regulatory institutions and other sources. To give plants an added incentive to respond to questionnaires, CSE assigns those that fail to do so a score of zero and a rating of no leaves. According to CSE, self-reported data are carefully checked by the organization's inspectors and compared with the secondary data. Both the questionnaires used to collect the data and the methodology used to analyze it have been designed by a panel of leading technical experts in each rated sector. In addition, to ensure objectivity and transparency, the entire GRP program is supervised by a panel comprising high-level representatives of industry, government, the judiciary, academia, and nongovernmental organizations.

In addition to informing the public about plants' environmental performance, the GRP also informs plants about their pollution and pollution abatement options. CSE uses the primary and secondary data it collects to construct a detailed environmental profile of each plant that is sent to the facility for review before being released to the public. CSE also publishes specific recommendations for improving environmental performance in each sector.

Impact on the Pulp and Paper Sector

Has the GRP actually motivated participating plants to improve their environmental performance? Answering this question requires data on the environmental impacts of participating plants for several years before and several years after a rating. Such data are available for only one sector—pulp and paper, the first sector rated by GRP (in 1999) and the only sector to have been rated a second time (in 2004). CSE based these two ratings on annual survey data on India's largest pulp and paper plants for the years 1996 through 2003. All plants with a production capacity exceeding 100 tons per day in 1998 were included in the first rating. The resulting sample comprises 28 plants that collectively were responsible for 59 percent of national pulp and paper production. Of these 28 plants, 22 were rated a second time in 2004.[8] The 1996–2003 panel data make it possible to assess the impact of the 1999 GRP rating on the environmental performance of these 22 plants.

Table 9.2 provides a preliminary indication of the impact of the GRP on 21 of these 22 plants.[9] The table shows that environmental performance of the 21 plants was generally poor in both 1999 and 2004. In both ratings, no plants received more than three leaves. The table does not provide a clear indication that the GRP spurred significant improvements in environmental performance: only a few plants moved from lower to higher rankings between 1999 and 2004, and several moved in the opposite direction. However, after 1999, CSE changed the GRP rating criteria to make them significantly more stringent. Therefore, the 1999 and 2004 ratings are not comparable, and it is necessary to examine the data that underpin the ratings to determine how environmental performance actually changed over time.

Table 9.2 Green Ratings Project (India) pulp and paper plant ratings, 1999 and 2004

2nd rating (2004)	1st rating (1999)			
	1 leaf	2 leaves	3 leaves	*Total plants*
1 leaf	5	2	0	7
2 leaves	2	8	1	11
3 leaves	0	2	1	3
Total plants	7	12	2	21

Emissions data suggest that environmental performance of particularly dirty plants—those that received one leaf in the 1999 rating—did in fact improve significantly during 1999, the year of the first GRP rating. Figures 9.2–9.4 present average annual emissions data for the 21 sample plants for the years 1996–2003. They show that emissions of the three most common measures of water pollution—biochemical oxygen demand (BOD), chemical oxygen demand (COD), and total suspended solids (TSS)—from plants that received a one-leaf rating declined dramatically in 1999.

Although these figures demonstrate that poorly performing plants' emissions declined after the 1999, they are not definitive proof that the GRP ratings drove these reductions. The changes may have been due to contemporaneous industry-wide market and regulatory pressures. Powers et al. (2007) uses econometric techniques to control for such factors. Specifically, they control for community pressure as measured by the socioeconomic characteristics of the communities surrounding participating plants, market pressure as measured by product mixes and prices of inputs and outputs, and exogenous technological change as measured by the industry-wide trend in pollution levels prior to 1999. The results strongly suggest that the GRP drove emissions reductions for plants that received a one-leaf rating in 1999. These findings comport with previous analyses of public disclosure programs in developing countries that show that disclosure has the greatest impact on poorly performing plants (García, Sterner, and Afsah 2007; Blackman, Afsah, and Ratunanda 2004). Intuition suggests that such plants would be more responsive to public disclosure because their marginal costs of controlling emissions are relatively low (since they have not yet taken advantage of inexpensive abatement opportunities) and because the marginal benefits are relatively high (since poorly performing plants are probably under the most pressure from regulators and communities).

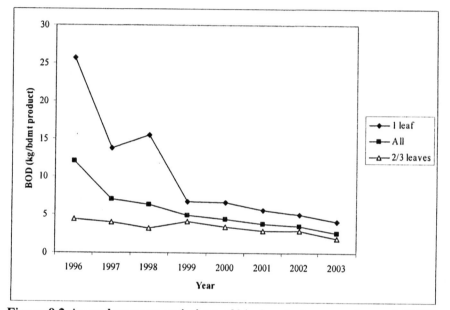

Figure 9.2 Annual average emissions of biochemical oxygen demand (BOD) from 21 pulp and paper plants participating in Green Ratings Project (India), by performance rating (leaves).

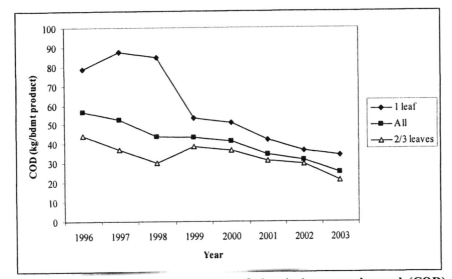

Figure 9.3 Annual average emissions of chemical oxygen demand (COD) from 21 pulp and paper plants participating in Green Ratings Project (India), by performance rating (leaves).

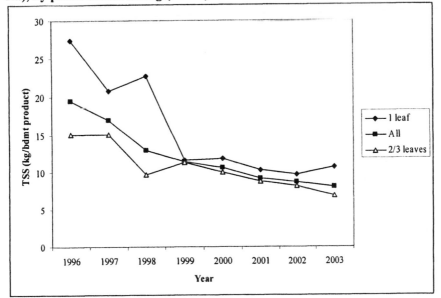

Figure 9.4 Annual average emissions of total suspended solids (TSS) from 21 pulp and paper plants participating in Green Ratings Project (India), by performance rating (leaves).

Discussion

We have presented three case studies intended to shed light on the prospects for voluntary regulation in developing countries. The case study of negotiated voluntary agreements in León, Guanajuato, paints a decidedly pessimistic picture of these prospects, while the case studies of the Clean Industry Program in Mexico and the Green Ratings Project in India provide grounds for optimism. Why were the Mexican negotiated agreements less successful? We will argue that various characteristics of the negotiated agreements made them particularly susceptible to the dangers of using voluntary regulation in developing countries—namely, weak regulatory pressures for improved environmental performance, weak nonregulatory pressures, and regulatory capture. In addition, these agreements were not effective in leveraging preexisting pressures by publicizing noncompliance.

Weak Regulatory Pressure

As discussed above, research on voluntary regulation in developing countries suggests that a background threat of mandatory regulation is an important driver of participation in and compliance with voluntary regulation. This research implies that voluntary regulation is unlikely to work in situations where such threats are not credible. The León case study bears out this prediction. Regulatory authorities in León were not able to threaten mandatory regulation because the legal, institutional, civic, and physical infrastructure they needed for enforcement was woefully incomplete. By the time the biggest gaps had been filled in the late 1990s, tanners had already abrogated three voluntary agreements without being punished and had little reason to believe that continued noncompliance would be sanctioned.

The institutions that administer the Clean Industry Program and the Green Ratings Project, on the other hand, carry a much bigger enforcement stick. PROFEPA, which runs the Clean Industry Program, is a national regulatory institution and likely has more capacity—including trained staff, funding, and political will—than do local regulators in the state of Guanajuato. PROFEPA regularly levies hefty fines for noncompliance, whereas local environmental regulatory authorities have sanctioned tanneries only infrequently. Although the Green Ratings Project is not a regulatory institution, the program likely brings to bear considerable regulatory pressure. It exposes and then vigorously publicizes noncompliance of the leading polluters. The effect is to both inform national and local environmental regulatory institutions about noncompliance and generate public pressure for these institutions to take quick action to remedy the problem. Thus, one could argue that the Clean Industry Program and the Green Ratings Project have been more successful than negotiated agreements in León because the organizations that run these programs use voluntary regulation to leverage a credible enforcement threat, whereas the regulatory authorities in León tried to use it to compensate for the lack of such a threat.

Weak Nonregulatory Pressure

A second concern about using voluntary regulation in developing countries is that nonregulatory pressures are unlikely to take up the slack for weak mandatory regulation. In León, this appears to have been the case. Nonregulatory actors such as community groups and consumers never created significant incentives for tanners to improve their environmental performance. By contrast, these actors almost certainly generated such incentives in the Clean Industry Program and the Green Ratings Project. Both programs disseminate information about environmental performance at the national level, where pressures from external stakeholders are presumably stronger than at the local level. The Green Ratings Project was designed expressly for this purpose. Although the Clean Industry Program was not, it has a similar effect: plants that graduate from the program receive national publicity.

Regulatory Capture

A third concern about using voluntary regulation in developing countries is that it will be captured by private sector lobby groups and may even lower environmental quality by preempting or forestalling mandatory regulation. The characteristics of the four voluntary agreements in León suggest that they were, in fact, captured by the tannery lobby. The agreements were mostly toothless, lacking quantified baselines and targets, transparency, monitoring and enforcement mechanisms, and individual penalties for noncompliance. Moreover, since the four agreements coincided with a prolonged period of negligible environmental progress, it is not unreasonable to suggest that they actually fostered this inactivity by creating the appearance—albeit less and less credible—of forward motion. In short, one could argue that the agreements did more harm than good. The evidence for regulatory capture is much less compelling in the case of the Clean Industry Program and especially the Green Ratings Project. The Clean Industry Program is administered by a national-level institution that likely has more power relative to polluters than the local regulators who administered the León voluntary agreements, and the Green Ratings Project is administered by a nongovernmental organization.

Preponderance of Small-Scale Firms

A fourth concern about using voluntary regulation in developing countries is that industrial sectors are often dominated by small firms that may be less susceptible to pressures applied by regulators, consumers, communities, and capital markets. This concern appears to have been well founded in the case of the León voluntary agreements. The leather tanning sector in León is dominated by small firms that have been particularly difficult for regulators to identify, monitor, and sanction; these firms rely principally on retained earnings instead of banks and stock markets for financing; they have received almost unwavering support from the local community; and they sell the lion's share of their product to small-scale local shoemakers, who have minimal incentives to vet the environmental performance of their suppliers. By contrast, both the Clean Industry Program and the Green Ratings Project focus on large-scale plants. Such plants are easier for regulators to monitor and sanction; need banks and capital markets for financing; sell their products in national and international markets (where consumers presumably care more about environmental quality); and are more likely to be targeted by environmental nongovernmental organizations and community groups.

Information Dissemination

A final reason that the tannery voluntary agreements were less successful than the Clean Industry Program and the Green Ratings Project relates not to the potential dangers of using voluntary regulation in developing countries but to one of the reputed benefits—disseminating information to firms about their emissions and the various options for abating it. In general, the provision of such information is likely to fill a gap in developing countries. Firms in industrialized countries typically pay consultants to perform environmental audits, a practice that implies it is costly to collect environmental performance data. In countries like Mexico and India, where formal regulatory pressure is less stringent and factories have little incentive to pay these costs, one would expect polluters to be ill informed about their emissions and the options for reducing them. Only the third tannery voluntary agreement contained explicit provisions for fostering such informational mechanisms, and these provisions, like most others in the agreements, were more or less ignored. By contrast, both the Clean Industry Program and the Green Ratings Project emphasize disseminating information to participating firms. The Clean Industry Program has done this via a third-party environmental audit, and the Green Ratings program has done it via environmental profiles and sector-wide recommendations for pollution control and prevention.

Conclusion

Before considering the policy implications of our case studies, a caveat is in order: our sample of three voluntary initiatives is obviously small and nonrandom and tells us little about how frequently similar programs and outcomes are observed in practice. Therefore, care must be taken in trying to distill policy lessons. Notwithstanding this limitation, the three case studies do provide some insights into the prospects for voluntary regulation in developing countries. The broad, if somewhat obvious, inference is that using voluntary regulation in developing countries is clearly risky—but not doomed to failure. The likelihood of success depends on the design and deployment of the initiatives. The case studies enable us to make four recommendations in this regard.

First, voluntary regulation is unlikely to be successful in situations where both regulatory and nonregulatory pressures for improved environmental performance are lacking. Our case studies and those reviewed suggest that polluters do not make good on voluntary commitments for purely altruistic reasons. Rather, they do so to avoid present or future expected costs generated by regulators, product markets, capital markets, employees, and communities, or to reap rewards for compliance offered by these stakeholders. When these costs and rewards are minimal, compliance will be low. For example, for the leather tanneries in León, sanctions for abrogating negotiated agreements applied by regulators and others were minimal, and the outcome was predictable. It is important to point out, however, that well-designed voluntary initiatives can enhance regulatory and nonregulatory pressures for improved environmental performance. For example, the Clean Industry Program does this by improving PROFEPA's information about polluters via an environmental audit, and by enhancing their reputations with "green" consumers. The Green Ratings Project has similar benefits. Hence, while some preexisting pressures for improved environmental performance are a necessary condition for successful voluntary regulation, the hope is that voluntary regulation will leverage these pressures.

Second, voluntary initiatives are unlikely to be successful when they do not incorporate design features now widely viewed as prerequisites for success: quantified baselines and targets, transparency, monitoring and enforcement mechanisms, and individual penalties for noncompliance. The tannery negotiated agreements lacked all of these mechanisms, but the Clean Industry Program and the Green Ratings Project featured all of them. Ultimately, an absence of these design elements may signal regulatory capture. It is probably no accident that among the three types of voluntary initiatives represented by our case studies— negotiated agreements, public programs, and public disclosure—these design characteristics were missing in negotiated agreements. As the name implies, such agreements are the result of a direct negotiation between regulators and industry, a process that naturally leads to situations where the private sector has considerable influence over the content of the agreement.

Third, national programs are more likely to be effective than local ones because they tap into a broader and deeper set of nonregulatory pressures, target large-scale firms that are relatively easy to monitor, and are run by national-level environmental authorities that usually wield a more credible threat of enforcement than local regulators. The one local initiative in our set of three case studies—negotiated agreements in León—was also the least successful. The exception to this rule, however, would be cases where regulatory and nonregulatory pressures for improved environmental performance are weak at the national level but strong in certain localities, such as capital cities or border cities (e.g., Blackman and Bannister 1998).

Fourth, the case studies indicate that disseminating information about pollution and abatement options to participating firms and the public at large can boost the effectiveness of voluntary initiatives. The two initiatives reviewed in this paper that emphasized information dissemination were more successful than the one that did not. One constraint is that in developing countries, collecting reliable plant-level environmental performance information is costly. However, the public sector need not bear all of these costs. For example, in the Clean Industry Program, these costs are shifted onto polluters, who must pay for third-party audits, and in the Green Ratings Project, they are split between participating plants and a nongovernmental organization.

Finally, our case studies and review of the literature suggest that further research on voluntary regulation in developing countries is needed. As discussed earlier, research on the topic is rare, and comparative studies are even rarer. Research in several specific areas would be particularly helpful. First, more comparative studies are needed to shed light on the advantages and disadvantages of different types of voluntary regulation and to test the preliminary hypotheses presented in this section.

Second, we need to better understand whether voluntary regulation actually has measurable environmental benefits in developing countries. A major challenge in conducting such research is acquiring reliable plant-level panel data on environmental performance—information that is hard to come by in most developing countries (because it does not exist or is tightly held) and that often must be collected via a survey. An advantage of studying public disclosure pollution control programs is that they typically generate the data needed for such evaluations. Another major challenge in evaluating the environmental benefits of voluntary regulation is determining what plants' environmental performance would have been had they not participated in the voluntary initiative—the counterfactual or baseline problem alluded to in our discussion of the Clean Industry Program and Green Ratings Project. A common tactic in quantitative research is to compare the environmental performance of a matched sample of participating and nonparticipating plants (Jiménez 2007) or to control for factors other than participation that may explain changes in environmental performance among participants (Powers et al. 2007).

Third, further research is needed to identify the factors that drive the improved environmental performance of participants in voluntary initiatives. A variety of methods can be used to address this question, including regression analysis (Jiménez 2007; Blackman and Bannister 1998), survey research (Blackman et al. 2004), and choice experiments (Wernstedt et al. 2006). Finally, given that voluntary regulation in developing countries is typically used to achieve compliance with mandatory regulations rather than to move beyond them, further research is needed on the relationship between voluntary and mandatory regulation and on how this relationship creates special challenges and opportunities for regulators.

Bibliography

Blackman, Allen. (ed.). *Small Firms and the Environment in Developing Countries: Collective Impacts, Collective Action.* Washington, DC: Resources for the Future Press, 2006.

Blackman Allen, and Geoffrey J. Bannister. "Community Pressure and Clean Technology in the Informal Sector: An Econometric Analysis of the Adoption of Propane by Traditional Mexican Brickmakers." *Journal of Environmental Economics and Management* 35, no. 1 (1998): 1–21.

Blackman, Allen, and Nicholas Sisto. "Voluntary Environmental Regulation in Developing Countries: A Mexican Case Study." *Natural Resources Journal* 46, no. 4 (2006): 1005–42.

Blackman, Allen, Shakeb Afsah, and Damayanti Ratunanda. "How Does Public Disclosure Work? Evidence from Indonesia's PROPER Program." *Human Ecology Review* 11, no. 3 (2004): 235–46.

Blackman, Allen, Sandra Hoffman, Richard Morgenstern, and Elizabeth Topping. "Assessment of Colombia's National Environmental System (SINA)." Report. Washington, DC: Resources for the Future (2006).

Blackman, Allen, Bidisha Lahiri, William Pizer, Marisol Rivera, and Carlos Muñoz. "Voluntary Environmental Regulation in Developing Countries: Mexico's Clean Industry Program." Discussion Paper 07-36. Washington, DC: Resources for the Future (2007).

Brizzi, Adolfo, and Kulsum Ahmed. "A Sustainable Future." Pp. 117–132 in *Mexico: A Comprehensive Development Agenda for the New Era,* edited by Marcelo Guigale, Olivier Lafourcade, and Vinh H. Nguyen. Washington, DC: World Bank, 2001.

Christmann, Petra, and Glen Taylor. "Globalization and the Environment: Determinants of Firm Self Regulation in China." *Journal of International Business Studies* 32, no. 3 (2001): 459–58.

Dasgupta, Susmita, Hemamala Hettige, and David Wheeler. "What Improves Environmental Performance? Evidence from Mexican Industry." *Journal of Environmental Economics and Management* 39 (2000): 39–66.

Dvořák, Antonin, Ales Lisa, and Petr Sauer. "Negotiated Voluntary Environmental Agreements: Cases in the Czech Republic." Pp. 206–218 in *Voluntary Environmental Agreements: Process, Practice and Future Use,* edited by Patrick ten Brink. Sheffield, UK: Greenleaf Publishing, 2002.

Eskeland, Gunnar, and Emmanuel Jimenez. "Policy Instruments for Pollution Control in Developing Countries." *World Bank Research Observer* 7, no. 2 (1992): 145–69.

Esterling Lara, Angel. "Evaluación y Perspectivas de los Convenios de Concertación para una Producción Más Limpia En Colombia. Aplicación de un Modelo de Evaluacion Estrategica a los Convenios de Concertacion." Final Report to Colombian Ministry of Environment, Housing and Territorial Development. Bogotá (2003).

Freitas, Nilton, and Winston Gereluk. "A National Tripartite Agreement on Benzene in Brazil." Pp. 176–190 in *Voluntary Environmental Agreements: Process, Practice and Future Use,* edited by Patrick ten Brink. Sheffield, UK: Greenleaf Publishing, 2002.

Fry, Maxwell. *Money, Interest, and Banking in Economic Development.* Baltimore: Johns Hopkins University Press, 1988.

García, Jorge, Thomas Sterner, and Shakeb Afsah. "Public Disclosure of Industrial Pollution: The PROPER Approach for Indonesia?" *Environment and Development Economics* 12, no. 6 (2007): 739–756.

Hanks, Jonathon. "A Role for Negotiated Environmental Agreements in Developing Countries." Pp. 159–176 in *Voluntary Environmental Agreements: Process, Practice, and Future Use,* edited by Patrick ten Brink. Belgium: Institute for European Environmental Policy, 2002.

Harrison, Kathryn. "Talking with the Donkey: Cooperative Approaches to Environmental Protection." *Journal of Industrial Ecology* 2, no. 3 (1999): 51–72.

Haslam, Paul Alexander. "The Corporate Social Responsibility System in Latin America and the Caribbean." FOCAL Policy Paper FPP-04-1. Canadian Foundation for the Americas (2004).

Higley, Charles, Frank Convery, and François Lévêque. "Voluntary Approaches: An Introduction." Paper presented at CAVA International Policy Workshop on the Use of Voluntary Approaches, Brussels, Belgium, February 1, 2001.

Jiménez, Orlando. "Voluntary Agreements in Environmental Policy: An Empirical Evaluation for the Chilean Case." *Journal of Cleaner Production* 15 (2007): 620–37.

Khanna, Madhu. "Economic Analysis of Non-Mandatory Approaches to Environmental Protection." *Journal of Economic Surveys* 15, no 3 (2001): 291–324.

Lyon, Thomas, and John Maxwell. "Voluntary Approaches to Environmental Regulation: A Survey." In *Economic Institutions and Environmental Policy,* edited by M. Frazini and A. Nicita. Aldershot and Hampshire: Ashgate Publishing, 2002.

Morgenstern, Richard, and William Pizer (eds.). *Reality Check: The Nature and Performance of Voluntary Environmental Programs in the United States, Europe, and Japan.* Washington, DC: Resources for the Future Press, 2007.

Organization for Economic Co-operation and Development (OECD). *Voluntary Approaches for Environmental Policy: An Assessment.* Paris: OECD Environment Directorate, 1999.

———. *Voluntary Approaches for Environmental Policy: Effectiveness, Efficiency and Usage in Policy Mixes.* Paris: OECD Environment Directorate, 2003.

Powers, Nicholas, Allen Blackman, Thomas Lyon, and Urvashi Narain. "Does Public Disclosure Reduce Pollution? Evidence from India's Pulp and Paper Industry." Working Paper. Washington, DC: Resources for the Future (2007).

Rivera, Jorge. "Assessing a Voluntary Environmental Initiative in the Developing World: The Costa Rican Certification for Sustainable Tourism." *Policy Sciences* 35 (2002): 333–60.

———. "Institutional Pressures and Voluntary Environmental Behavior in Developing Countries: Evidence from Costa Rica." *Society and Natural Resources* 17 (2004): 779–97.

Roht-Arriaza, Naomi. "Environmental Management Systems and Environmental Protection: Can ISO14001 Be Useful within the Context of APEC?" *Journal of Environment and Development* 6, no. 2 (1997): 292–316.

Russell, Clifford, and William Vaughan. "The Choice of Pollution Control Policy Instruments in Developing Countries: Arguments, Evidence and Suggestions." Pp. 331–373 in *International Yearbook of Environmental and Resource Economics*, vol. VII, edited by Henk Folmer and Tom Tietenberg. Cheltenham, UK: Edward Elgar, 2003.

Utting, Peter. *The Greening of Business in Developing Countries: Rhetoric, Reality and Prospects.* London: United Nations Research Institute for Social Change and Zed Books, 2002.

Vidovic, Martina, and Neha Khanna. "Can Voluntary Pollution Control Programs Fulfill Their Promises? Further Evidence from EPA's 33/50 Program." *Journal of Environmental Economics and Management* 53 (2007): 180–95.

Wang, Hua, Jun Bi, David Wheeler, Jinnan Wang, Dong Cao, Genfa Lu, and Yuan Wang. "Environmental Performance Rating and Disclosure: China's GreenWatch Program." *Journal of Environmental Management* 71, no. 2 (2004): 123–33.

Wehrmeyer, Walter, and Yacob Mulugetta (eds.) *Growing Pains: Environmental Management in Developing Countries.* Sheffield, UK: Greenleaf Publishing, 1999.

Wernstedt, Kris, Peter Meyer, Anna Alberini, and Lauren Heberle. "Incentives for Private Residential Brownfields Development in US Urban Areas." *Journal of Environmental Planning and Management* 49, no. 1 (2006): 101–19.

World Bank. *Greening Industry: New Rules for Communities, Markets, and Governments.* New York: Oxford University Press, 1999.

Notes

* I'm grateful to Peter deLeon, Jorge Rivera, three anonymous reviewers, and seminar participants at Catholic University of Chile, Johns Hopkins University School for Advanced International Studies, and Monterrey Institute of Technology for helpful comments and suggestions. Thanks are also due to Bidisha Lahiri, Tom Lyon, Carlos Muñoz, Urvashi Narain, Billy Pizer, Nick Powers, Marisol Rivera, and Nick Sisto for collaborating on the three case studies summarized in this paper.

1. Taxonomies of voluntary regulation differ but typically include these four categories. See also Lyon and Maxwell (2002), Higley, Convery, and Lévêque (2001), and OECD (1999, 2003).

2. Hanks (2002) and Utting (2002) compare cases studies of voluntary regulation in developing countries. Both are limited to one type of voluntary regulation: the former examines negotiated agreements, and the latter mainly examines unilateral commitments.

3. See Utting (2002) and Haslam (2004) for reviews and case studies of the fourth main type of voluntary regulation (unilateral commitments) in developing countries.

4. This section is drawn from Blackman and Sisto (2006).

5. Prior to the 1988 passage of the General Law of Ecological Balance and Protection of the Environment (LGEEPA), Mexico's second comprehensive federal environmental law, regulations governing both liquid and hazardous wastes were confused, incomplete, and at least in the state of Guanajuato, roundly ignored. LGEEPA assigned local governments the responsibility of regulating liquid discharges into municipal sewer systems, the main repository for tannery liquid effluents in León. However, it was not until 1998 that

León finally promulgated regulatory standards for such discharges. LGEEPA charged the federal government with regulating hazardous wastes, but the federal government did not issue implementing regulations regarding hazardous wastes until 1993 and did not clarify how these regulations applied to tanneries until four years later.

6. This section is based on Blackman et al. (2007).

7. This section is drawn from Powers et al. (2007).

8. Of the six plants that were rated in the first period but not the second, five were permanently closed and one was temporarily closed after the first rating.

9. One plant, BILT Graphics, answered CSE questionnaires and was assigned an environmental performance score but not a "leaves rating" because it was not in operation for the entire sample period. Of the six plants that were included in the first rating but not the second, one received two leaves and five received one leaf. Six plants were rated in the second phase, but not in the first. Of these plants, three received three leaves, one received two leaves, one received one leaf, and one received zero leaves.

Chapter 10

Voluntary Environmental Programs: A Canadian Perspective

Irene Henriques and Perry Sadorsky

Canadian environmental policy has traditionally emphasized command and control environmental regulations. Although not as stringent as U.S. policy, which prescribes mandatory quantity limits on emissions of pollutants or the use of specific abatement technology, Canadian command and control policy has primarily been enabling rather than mandatory with an emphasis on achieving targets or goals via cooperation and negotiation between specific polluters and government (Valiante, 2002). While these regulations have protected the environment, the command-and-control regulatory approach has some limitations; including expensive and protracted development and enforcement processes; jurisdictional constraints on subject matter, approach and scope; vulnerability to inconsistent enforcement due to staff and resource cutbacks; and a tendency toward inflexibility and over-formality (Webb, 2004). Together these limitations tend to promote end-of-pipe pollution controls rather than pollution prevention while imposing steep costs on both firms and regulators (Coglianese & Nash, 2001).

A growing belief in the need to provide flexibility to firms and lower the cost of environmental protection has led many governments, industry groups and individual companies to consider using voluntary environmental programs (VEPs) that encourage voluntary actions to pollution and prevention (Morgenstern and Pizer, 2007; Paton, 2000). VEPs, therefore, come in many forms and structures. We define VEPs as commitments not required by legislation or regulations;[1] are agreed to by one or more individuals or organizations; are intended to influence or control behavior; and are applied in a consistent manner or set to reach a consistent outcome (Webb, 2004). A loose taxonomy for classifying VEPs has evolved. According to Morgenstern and Pizer (2007), VEPs can be classified as public voluntary programs, negotiated agreements between business and government, or unilateral agreements by industrial firms. Public VEPs involve environmental agencies inviting firms to voluntarily meet specified standards or adopt clean technologies (Khanna, 2001). Participants in these programs sign nonbinding letters of intent and progress in the program is monitored by self reporting. Governmental bodies develop the programs and firms are invited to participate. Specific terms of the program are, in general, not negotiated. Examples of public VEPs in the United States include the 33/50 Program, Green Lights and the Climate Wise Program. In depth cases studies of the 33/50 Program and the Climate Wise Program are found in Morgenstern and Pizer (2007). Examples of Canadian public voluntary program include the Voluntary Challenge and Registry (VCR) Program and the Accelerated Reduction and Elimination of Toxics Initiative (ARET).

Negotiated VEPs involve the government environmental agencies negotiating with a firm or trade association on abatement targets, timelines and plans (Khanna, 2001; Morgenstern & Pizer, 2007). Such negotiations usually provide regulatory relief in exchange for pollution reductions in excess of status quo standards (Khanna, 2001). These agreements are used in Canada, the EU, Japan and the United States, are usually legally non-binding and their implementation varies across countries. Examples of negotiated VEPs include the United States EPA's Common Sense Initiative and Project XL, Denmark's program on industrial energy efficiency, the United Kingdom's Voluntary Climate Agreements, and Japan's Keidanren Voluntary Action Plan on the Environment (Morgenstern & Pizer, 2007). Examples of negotiated national voluntary agreements in Canada include industry specific Environmental Performance Agreements, Canadian Pesticide Container Management Program, the Recycling Program for Rechargeable Batteries, and the Refrigerant Management Canada Program.[2] Although there do exist regional public and negotiated VEPs in Canada, our focus in this paper will be on more widely applicable national programs.

Unilateral agreements, on the other hand, occur without direct government involvement and include unilateral corporate programs aimed at environmental stewardship. The interest in promoting voluntary environmental action and pollution prevention has been accompanied by a growing number of business-initiated unilateral actions to change corporate culture and management practices via the introduction of environmental management systems (EMS), industry level codes of environmental management such as the Responsible Care program developed by the Canadian Chemical Producers' Association and international EMS certification programs such as the International Standards Organization's (ISO) ISO 14001. EMSs represent an organizational change within corporations and an effort for self-regulation by defining a set of formal environmental policies, goals, strategies and administrative procedures for improving environmental performance (Coglianese & Nash, 2001).

This paper discusses the theoretical motivations for firms to adopt VEPs in general and examines Canada's experience with these three types of VEPs—

public, negotiated and unilateral agreements—to assess whether the motivating factors are present. We then argue that the institutional, political and regulatory framework governing environmental policy in Canada does not provide the conditions necessary to effectively promote superior corporate environmental protection across jurisdictions. Despite the lack of government directed voluntary environmental programs, there has been considerable interest by both the private sector and civil society who have taken the lead by developing unilateral agreements. Using existing literature and our current research, we examine the factors that motivate firms in Canada to participate in unilateral agreements and the characteristics of firms with the higher environmental performance.

Motivations for Adopting VEPs

Why would a firm participate in a voluntary environmental program? The traditional economics literature assumes that profit-maximizing firms take prices and regulations as given and therefore have no incentive to control pollution in the absence of environmental regulations or go beyond compliance with existing regulations (Cropper & Oates, 1992). The current management and economic literature, however, does not support this assertion nor does it support the assumption that profit-maximizing firms necessarily take regulations as given (Morgenstern & Pizer, 2007). In fact, the environmental management literature suggests that participation in VEPs provides a variety of potential benefits to firms such as relief from existing environmental regulation (like a burdensome tax), the pre-emption of regulatory threats or the influencing of future regulations (Khanna & Anton, 2001; Henriques & Sadorsky, 1996; Lyon & Maxwell, 2002; Alberini & Segerson, 2002); cost efficiency (Hart & Ahuja, 1996); improved stakeholder relations (Arora & Cason, 1999; Henriques & Sadorsky, 1996, 1999); and the possibility of receiving technical assistance in kind or via some kind of incentive mechanism. Hence, organizations are motivated to increase their internal efficiency and external legitimacy, which can lead to competitive advantage and shareholder value creation (Hart, 1995; Hart & Milstein, 2003).

Firms may participate in VEPs in order to gain relief from existing environmental regulation or the pre-emption of regulatory threats or the influencing of future regulations. Lyon and Maxwell (2002, 2004) provide a survey of the economic models used to analyze how firms can optimize their corporate regulatory strategy via the pre-emption of tougher regulations and the weakening of future regulations. Under certain conditions, these models explain the adoption of a VEP as an attempt to avoid the traditional regulatory/legislative process. Moreover, the models all highlight the cost savings that arise from VEPs via reduced transaction costs and/or compliance costs. The caveat in all these models, of course, is that the regulators and/or politicians are motivated to maximize social welfare. In addition, participation in VEPs may also build important intangible benefits such as goodwill and trust between the organization and the government which may, in turn, reduce monitoring costs.

Firms may participate in VEPs in order to increase cost efficiency and reduce risk through pollution prevention. Better utilization of inputs results in less waste and emissions from the production of goods and services and this, in turn, leads to lower costs for inputs and waste disposal (Hart, 1995; Hart & Milstein, 2003). While businesses can practice pollution prevention and eco-efficiency through better management of their resources and capabilities (Hart, 1995), VEPs can provide an additional stimulus to reduce emissions and waste by encouraging the sharing and adoption of best practices between divisions within the same firm as well as between firms within the same industry (especially through benchmarking and trade associations). Environmental management systems (EMSs) like ISO 14001, for example, which is built on similar principles as those used in total quality management systems, provide a systematic process for waste generation and risk reduction (Darnall, 2002) and effective management of an organization's environmental performance can lead to tangible and intangible benefits over both the short and long term (Darnall & Edwards, 2006).

Dow Chemical's Waste Reduction Always Pays (WRAP) and Chevron's Save Money and Reduce Toxics (SMART) are two examples of unilateral programs aimed at reducing waste and emissions through eco-efficiency. 3M's Pollution Prevention Pays (3P) program is one of the most widely cited examples of a program that cut costs and simultaneously improved environmental performance. The 3M's 3P program was initiated in 1975 and for the first time gave ordinary workers the opportunity to identify opportunities for waste reduction. Between 1975 and 1990, 3M cut total emission by 50% (530,000 tons). Over this same period of time, the company claims to have saved $500 million by cutting the costs of raw materials, compliance, disposal, and liability (Hart & Milstein, 2003). More generally, empirical research by Christmann (2000) clearly demonstrates that with the right set of skills and capabilities (like employee involvement and continuous improvement) pollution prevention and waste minimization strategies do lower costs and increase profits. Consequently, pollution prevention is one of the most direct ways for a company to increase shareholder value.

Firms may participate in VEPs in order to foster better relationships with stakeholders. In fact, stakeholder engagement is one of the best ways for organizations to build intangible assets which can lead to competitive advantage. Stakeholders are defined as "any group or individual who can affect or is affected by the achievement of the organization's objectives" (Freeman, 1984: 46). The literature on how stakeholders influence organizational strategy argues that firms will pay attention to primary (Clarkson, 1995), salient (Mitchell, Agle & Wood, 1997) or influential (Frooman, 1999) stakeholders. The power these stakeholders exert over a firm is dependent on whether these stakeholders have control of critical resources the firm requires for effective continued operation (Henriques & Sharma, 2005). Important primary stakeholders in the environmental arena include consumers, who are looking for "greener" alternatives; regulators who control a firm's license to operate; employees who are looking for a better working environment; and shareholders/owners who are concerned about future liabilities associated with environmental risks.

Current research in stakeholder theory suggests that secondary stakeholders also need to be engaged. Secondary stakeholders are not directly involved in the organization's economic transactions per se, and tend not to have control over critical organizational resources (Mitchell, Agle & Wood, 1997; Sharma & Henriques, 2005), but have the capacity to mobilize public opinion in favor of, or in opposition to, the organization (Freeman, 1984). Secondary stakeholders' ability to mobilize public opinion has increased significantly with the advent of the internet as well as their ability to influence primary stakeholders such as consumers and government (Henriques & Sharma, 2005). Secondary stakeholders include environmental groups, community groups, the media, labor unions and industry associations (Hoffman, 2001). Consequently, stakeholders, both primary and secondary, have the potential to signal their environmental preferences to firms and if addressed (via, perhaps a VEP) may lead to improved environmental and economic performance via reduced emissions and increased benefits (tangible and intangible) respectively. Hence, engaging primary and secondary stakeholders is particularly useful to firms in establishing intangible values like goodwill, legitimacy, reputation, and trust which enable an organization to differentiate itself from its competitors and build competitive advantage. For example, in a recent publication by the World Bank's International Finance Corporation (IFC, 2007), numerous case studies are used to illustrate the benefits associated with stakeholder engagement. According to the IFC, "the risks associated with poor stakeholder relations—and opportunities provided by constructive ones—are now better understood by the private sector and financial investors alike. Companies that have grasped the importance of actively developing and sustaining relationships with affected communities and other stakeholders throughout the life of their project, and not simply during the initial feasibility and assessment phase, are reaping the benefits of improved risk management and better outcomes on the ground" (IFC, 2007: 1).

Firms may participate in VEPs for the opportunity to receive technical assistance in kind or via some kind of incentive mechanism. Some firms may feel that environmental issues are a serious concern that they should address, but may lack resources (e.g., labour, capital, materials, managerial skills, finances) and/or capabilities (defined as the capacity for a set of resources to perform a task or activity in an orderly manner (Hitt, Ireland, Hoskisson, Rowe, & Sheppard, 2006)) to best achieve pollution reductions. VEPs may provide government or industry sponsored technical assistance programs in the form of low cost loans to install new pollution abatement equipment or technical knowledge in the form of environmental consulting. Building an environmental management system, for example, requires an investment in time and money (e.g., human capital, physical capital). Participation in a VEP may provide a firm with a low cost way of building its resources and capabilities.

Whilst most of the discussion on participation in VEPs focuses on what motivates firms to participate, it is also interesting to offer some suggestions as to why public authorities would find it advantageous to participate in VEPs beyond the usual cost reduction motive. Volu ntary environmental programs provide opportunities for governmental agencies to gain experience with new problems and new industries (Morgenstern & Pizer, 2007). VEPs provide an opportunity for government agencies to experiment with achieving environmental improvements more quickly and more flexibly with lower administration costs than would be incurred under a command and control approach. VEPs can also foster a better relationship between business and government and more clearly provide opportunities for mutual responsibility in dealing with environmental concerns.

VEPs in Canada

While the preceding section provided the theoretical motivations for firms to adopt VEPs the reality is that there are very few ongoing national public or negotiated VEPs in Canada. More specifically, Canada's only two widely known public VEPs have expired (ARET and VCR). In fact, the public and negotiated VEPs that have been initiated, have, for the most part, been negotiated VEPs. The reasons why Canada has so few national government-initiated VEPs may be due to a combination of various institutional, regulatory and political factors. These factors are discussed below.

Institutional and Regulatory Factors

Canada is a federal state in which each of the ten provinces and three territories has considerable jurisdictional power. As the Canadian Constitution does not clearly spell out distinct jurisdictional responsibilities for each government, their responsibilities can overlap, causing the potential for uncertainty as to which level of government has the authority to regulate for specific environmental problems and objectives. As a result, the division of powers regarding environmental policy between the various levels of government flows to a great extent from jurisdiction over natural resources (Vourc'h, 2001). In general, natural resources are largely within the provincial or territorial arena giving provinces/territories the authority to legislate with respect to both publicly and privately owned resources within their respective regions. The federal government, however, has responsibility over some resources transcending provincial boundaries such as fish, as well as through its power over agriculture and navigation.

The role of provincial governments and territories

Most environmental regulation occurs at the provincial level. Provincial powers to regulate the environment come from section 92 of the Constitution Act (1967) (Boardman, 1992; Field & Olewiler, 2002). Powers include authority to legislate with respect to the management of public lands and resources, non-renewable natural resources, forestry, electricity generation, municipal institutions, property and civil rights and matters of a local or private nature. The limits to provincial authority are 1) only matters within a province or territory can be regulated; 2) the Crown and its agents may not be subject to legislation of another level of government; and 3) provinces are limited to direct taxation only (Valiante, 2002). The limit to direct taxation was used in a challenge to the Nova Scotia waste regulations that imposed a deposit on beverage containers. Certain stakeholders challenged the Nova Scotia's Deposit Refund System because it employed a half back system whereby only half the deposit was refunded and the other half was paid into a fund to support recycling and environmental awareness (C.M. Consulting, 2006). The challengers claimed that such a system was an indirect tax and inadmissible. The courts deemed the deposit valid because it was a charge that was part of a regulatory scheme, not a tax (Valiante, 2002). This taxation limit and the court challenge suggest that provinces must be careful in designing regulatory schemes which provide economic incentives or deterrents so that such incentives or deterrents are part of regulatory scheme and not an indirect way of collecting general revenue.

The emerging role of First Nations

Another very important player in the Canadian environmental public policy debate is First Nations. First Nations have gradually gained recognition of their constitutionally protected rights and have negotiated self-government and land claim agreements. As a result of the special status of First Nations' constitutionally protected rights (e.g., fish, game and timber), the involvement of First Nations in decisions that affect these rights will be judged by a much higher standard than any other type of stakeholder consultation. Moreover, according to Valiante (2002), First Nations have finalized 14 comprehensive land claims and self-government agreements, with numerous others, primarily in northern Canada and British Columbia, at different stages of negotiations. These agreements are seen as "modern treaties" and therefore have constitutional status.

The Canadian Environmental Protection Act 1999 (CEPA, 1999) places aboriginal participation on par with federal ministers and the provinces within the National Advisory Committee by enabling delegation of administration of the Act to a government or "an aboriginal people," and by requiring application of traditional aboriginal knowledge to the identification and resolution of environmental problems.

Consequently, for many resource and environmental areas and issues, responsibility is shared between federal and provincial (or territorial) governments in consultation, with affected aboriginal groups. The implication, of course, is that the two levels of government have to cooperate to act effectively. The shared nature of environmental jurisdiction has led all parties involved to use a stakeholder approach when dealing with environmental issues (Vourc'h, 2001). Various ministerial councils, such as the Canadian Council of Ministers of the Environment, have been established which use this approach (CEC, 2004). Although, the amount of public scrutiny of government decision making and setting environmental policy has been minimal until the 1990s, today the stakeholder approach implies a broader consultation with the private sector, individuals, environmental and other interest groups who may be affected. Although this negotiation approach is laudable in that a broader group is consulted, Copeland (1998) suggests that Canada's environmental policy has suffered from a lack of an integrated vision for sustainable development and from a lack of commitment to environmental goals. Consultation without vision or commitment to environmental goals may in fact lead to inferior outcomes. It is at this stage where political factors play an important role.

Political Factors

VanNijnatten (1999) provides an excellent comparison of American and Canadian approaches to environmental policy and citizen participation from the early 1970s to the late 1990s and finds political culture to be a significant difference affecting their approaches. Whereas the U.S. political culture tends toward individualism and active participation,[3] Canadian political culture tends towards passivism and elitism.[4] More specifically, VanNijnatten (1999) argues that the U.S. institutional framework is characterized by multiple power centers making it more difficult to change existing environmental policy while the Canadian institutional framework is characterized by a concentration of power at the federal or provincial levels making it easier for changes to be undertaken if other issues such as budget concerns or a lack of political will take precedence.

Between the mid-1980s to the early 1990s Canada opened up its environmental policymaking procedures and began to use multi-stakeholder consultations (MSCs). MSCs bring together multiple stakeholders, representing different interests, with the purpose of gaining a consensus on how to balance economic and environmental concerns. Participants of MSCs include multiple levels of government, different administrative agencies, and industry representatives. MSCs were widely used in formulation of Canadian environmental policy both at the federal and provincial levels. Some examples include the formation of the 1988 Canadian Environmental Protection Act (CEPA), the 1989–1990 Federal Pesticide Registration Review, the 1992 federal pulp and paper regulations, and the 1992 formation of the National Pollutant Release Inventory which was modeled on the U.S. EPA's Toxic Release Inventory (VanNijnatten, 1999). In March 2000, the Canadian government enacted the *New Canadian Environmental Protection Act, 1999* (CEPA 1999) which is an Act that gives the federal government new powers to require pollution planning for substances declared toxic (CEC, 2004).

The Canadian Environmental Protection Act (CEPA 1999) operates under the sensitive arena of shared federal and provincial jurisdiction. One of the primary purposes of CEPA is the regulation of toxic substances.[5] CEPA 1999 contains expanded goals and objectives of the federal government including pollution prevention, virtual elimination of persistent and bio-accumulative toxic substances, an eco-system approach, the precautionary principle, cooperation with other governments and biodiversity (Valiante, 2002). It also introduces a new regulatory option, namely, the use of economic instruments and market-based approaches such as deposits, refunds and tradable permits. The statute, however, does not provide any guidance as to when such economic instruments would be appropriate for the control of toxic substances or what administrative controls would be necessary to ensure consistency and accountability. These are to be worked out in guidelines and regulations to be developed in the near future.

The lack of market based instruments in Canada was also noted in a recent OECD environmental performance report for Canada which stated: " Market based instruments are insufficiently used to foster integration of environmental concerns into sectoral policies; too much emphasis is given to soft instruments like voluntary guidelines or partnerships" (OECD, 2004: p. 97). The few incentive based instruments that do exist include a small number of tradable permit systems (HCFCs, methyl bromide, NO_x and VOC emissions—limited to power plants and large industry—and transferable fishing quotas), regional deposit-refund systems, and various transportation and transportation related taxes. The limited scope of these incentives, as well as, the inability of government to integrate such incentives with voluntary environmental programs, has tended to reduce the effectiveness of such programs insofar as voluntary participation and costs are concerned.

From the early 1990s onwards, Canadian citizen participation and environmental regulation were scaled back (VanNijnatten, 1999, Paehlke, 2000). According to Paehlke (2000), this decline was due to two important events: budget cuts and right-wing provincial governments. The federal government reduced environmental spending by 32% over the period 1995 to 1998 (Paehlke, 2000). The provinces of Alberta and Ontario quickly followed the federal government's lead in reducing their budget deficits. As a result, provincial funding for the environment was drastically cut. Most of the cutbacks to environmental budgets at both the federal and provincial levels were in the areas of monitoring, enforcement, and funding. Cuts to environmental budgets need not necessarily imply an overall reduction in environmental protection provided an alternative means, say in the form of voluntary environmental programs can be found.

Public Voluntary Programs

Two of the more well know Canadian public voluntary environmental programs include the Accelerated Reduction and Elimination of Toxics Initiative (ARET) program of 1995–2000, and the Canadian Voluntary Challenge and Registry (VCR) Program. The ARET program was a pollution prevention and abatement initiative that involved stakeholders from industry, health, professional organizations, environmental groups, organized labor, and federal and provincial governments across Canada. The long term goal of ARET was 1) the virtual elimination of releases of 30 persistent, bioaccumulative and toxic substances and 2) the reduction of another 87 toxic substances to levels insufficient to cause harm. The short term (year 2000) goal of ARET was 1) to reduce persistent, bioaccumulative and toxic substance emissions by 90% and 2) to reduce all other toxic substance emission by 50%. For its time, ARET was leading edge and represented the first large scale organized voluntary environmental program in Canada (Environment Canada Review Branch, 2000). By the year 2000, ARET had attracted participation from 8 major industry sectors, 171 companies and government organizations, and 318 individual facilities. Over the course of the program, more than 70,000 tonnes of ARET substances were prevented from being released into the environment (The Green Line Environment Canada's World Wide Web site, 2003). In their final report on the ARET program, however, Environment Canada's Review Branch (2000) concluded that ARET participation was **not** one of the main factors in motivating industry to reduce releases of toxic substances. In fact, according to the report half of the reductions reported in 1997 were achieved before ARET began, a small proportion of ARET participants were responsible for the vast majority of emissions reductions, participants did not report all of their releases of ARET substances to the ARET Secretariat, and Environment Canada does not have in place an integrated information system to identify the best opportunities for using voluntary methods or participating in voluntary initiatives like ARET. The Review Branch also questioned whether the $2 million dollars spent on the development and start up of ARET was the most efficient use of federal funds especially in light of the fact that ARET participation was not one of the main factors behind the reduction in the releases of toxic substances. The Review Branch concluded that existing environmental regulations, equipment upgrades, and "beyond business as usual" decision making (unilateral voluntary environmental programs established by some companies well in advance of the ARET program) were more important factors than ARET in the reduction in toxic releases.

Antweiler and Harrison (2006) in their evaluation of the ARET Challenge have also disputed whether the reported environmental benefits were in fact attributable to the program in question. Using treatment effect regressions to determine the true impact of ARET on emissions (i.e., controlling for self-selection bias), they find that 1) releases of the ARET substances were not "virtually eliminated" as stated in the challenge; 2) there is a significant disparity between voluntary ARET reporting prior to 2001 and mandatory National Pollutant Release Inventory (NPRI) reports thereafter suggesting that there may have been some significant under-reporting of releases of these substances by ARET members; and 3) there were reductions in at most 5 out of the 17 reported ARET substances covered under NPRI. The difficulty in evaluating any voluntary program is twofold. First, is the lack of data on participating firms' performance, and if data are available, they may not have been subject to independent verification (Antweiler & Harrison, 2006). Second, is the fact that a negotiated process may provide certain flexibilities to the firms involved which make it difficult to attribute any gains in performance to the program itself. In the case of ARET, for example, participants were allowed to choose their own "base year" benchmark with up to 6 years before the 1994 launch of the program (Antweiler & Harrison, 2006).

Takahashi, Nakamura, van Kooten & Vertinsky (2001) examined firm participation in, and the impact of, the Canadian Voluntary Challenge and Registry (VCR) Program. The VCR Program was initiated in 1995 as a joint federal and provincial program to encourage industrial firms to reduce their greenhouse gas emissions. The VCR Program became a privatized incorporated, nonprofit government and industry organization in 1997 with the majority of its funding, from 1997 onwards, coming from the private sector. Participation in the VCR program and commitment to the VCR program was used as a proxy for a firm's commitment to carbon emissions reductions. Participation in the VCR Program required 1) knowledge of the existence of the VCR Program, 2) submission of a letter of intent, and 3) submission of an action plan. Using survey data collected from Canadian firms in the manufacturing, resource extraction, and transportation industries, Takahashi et al. (2001) empirically model a firm's familiarity with the VCR program, a firm's participation in the VCR Program, whether a firm had submitted a VCR action plan, and a firm's range of emission reduction goals. Probit models were estimated with variables accounting for firm size, regional and industry sector dummy variables, and a range of pressure sources stemming from environmental groups, media, industry trade associations, government, shareholders, customers, and employees.

The empirical results were mixed with no explanatory variable having a statistically significant impact across each of the four models. The empirical results suggest that participation in the VCR Program did not have an impact on a firm's range of emission reduction goals. It therefore appears that firms participated in the VCR Program for political reasons rather than for environmental concerns.

Brouhle and Raimirez (2007) find that participation in the VCR program increased between 1995 and 1999, remained relatively constant between 2000 and 2003 and dropped significantly in 2004. The levels of engagement with the VCR program are higher in provinces that have large petroleum (Alberta) or manufacturing (Ontario) industries also have higher levels. The levels of engagement with the VCR program are higher in industries like petroleum and electric utilities.

On January 1, 2005, the Canadian Standards Association acquired the VCR Program as it was removed from the Federal Climate Change Plan. Looking back at the approximate ten-year history of the VCR is enlightening. The program was a voluntary and exploratory program that did succeed in generating industry awareness and responsiveness to reduce greenhouse gas emissions. As the program proceeded, however, it became apparent that small voluntary reductions in greenhouse gas emissions by industry would do little to meet Canada's emission targets agreed to under the Kyoto Accord. The inability to curb free-riding by participants and the lack of specific emission reduction targets remained a problem. Consequently, industry and government both realized that further cuts to greenhouse gas emissions would likely need to come through stringent regulation (Lucas & Potes, 2006).

Negotiated Voluntary Environmental Programs

Against this backdrop of reduced government spending on the environment, jurisdictional issues, lack of market based instruments to complement public VEPs and the overlapping of administrative boundaries, negotiated voluntary pollution prevention initiatives (VPPIs) were developed because they were viewed by the Canadian government as being less "costly" than having to commit to environmental standards which require expertise in the area of economic/market-based policy analysis and the consensus of all provinces, territories and affected aboriginal groups (Harrison, 1995; Copeland, 1998).

In 1997, the New Directions Group, a working group composed of representatives from industry, government and non-governmental organizations, wrote a paper entitled *Criteria and Principles for the Use of Voluntary or Non-regulatory Initiatives to Achieve Environmental Policy Objectives* (Environment Canada, 2006). The four principles underlying an environmental performance agreement include effectiveness, credibility, transparency and accountability, and efficiency. The design criteria include senior level commitment from participants, clear environmental objectives and measurable results, clearly defined roles and responsibilities, consultation with affected and interested stakeholders, public reporting, verification of results, incentives and consequences, and continuous improvement. The main advantage of environmental performance agreements is the flexibility they provide to customize environmental goals. Environmental performance agreements encourage industry to strive to develop environmental protection initiatives beyond what is possible through regulation. An agreement can be used as a complement, a precursor, or an alternative to a non-voluntary instrument, such as a regulation. To date, five environmental performance agreements have expired and five are in operation (http://www.ec.gc.ca/epa-epe/en/agr.cfm). While information on the environmental performance agreements and their implementation is provided on Environment Canada's web site (http://www.ec.gc.ca/epa-epe/en/agr.cfm) concerns still remain over the transparency of the negotiation process and the role that stakeholders play in assessing the performance of these agreements. Inadequate data make it very difficult to assess the outcome of these negotiated agreements.

Canada has also entered into negotiated voluntary environmental programs to achieve beyond compliance reductions in the releases of toxic substances with specific industry sectors (such as vehicle manufactures, auto parts manufacturers, chemical producers, metal finishers, dry cleaners, and the printing and graphics industry) through Memoranda of Understanding (MOU). More specifically, a memorandum of understanding is a commonly used agreement between governments and the private sector to achieve a particular goal such as the reduction of emissions. This allows governments to achieve pollution targets without passing specific regulations. For example, a MOU was signed between Ford, General Motors and Daimler-Chrysler which commits these companies to reduce and/or eliminate the use, generation and release of 65 substances (De Gonzaque, 2001). By 2000, this MOU has resulted in the reduction or elimination of 9400 tonnes of targeted substances and over 300,000 tonnes of wastes and other substances (De Gonzaque, 2001). On the other hand, if there is a memorandum of understanding, a company cannot be prosecuted for failure to comply if it has notified the government that it needs more time, for example, to install pollution abatement equipment or if adverse economic conditions prevent compliance. This may enable some companies to delay compliance (Field & Olewiler, 2002). Moreover, most MOUs are closed industry-government collaborations with little or no input from other stakeholders which may reduce the credibility of such agreements. The Achilles heel of any voluntary program is the absence of credible verification by third parties (Van Nijnatten, 1998).

Although environmental performance agreements may have been successful in reducing specific toxic emissions of those firms involved, the number of these agreements has been very small (five concluded, five in progress). Why has there been so few participants? Firms that have the necessary resources and capabilities to reduce toxic emissions on their own may feel that they have little to gain by participating in an environmental performance agreement but may choose to participate if they believe that the benefits derived from increased goodwill with Canadian regulatory stakeholders exceed the costs of the extra oversight (Potoski & Prakash, 2004). Firms that do not have the necessary resources and capabilities to reduce toxic emissions on their own, on the other hand, may find a negotiated VEP's extra oversight less attractive (i.e., too costly) than trying to acquire the necessary resources and capabilities on their own or with the help of their industry association. The small number of firms participating in these negotiated VEPs suggests that the benefits derived from increased goodwill do not appear to exceed the costs of the extra oversight. Given that the use of economic instruments and market-based approaches such as deposits, refunds and tradable permits have not yet been extensively developed in Canada, the ability to incorporate such instruments into VEPs so as to increase the incentive for voluntary participation and reduce the costs to firms of entering these agreements do not exist.

In summary, the reasons why there may be so few national public and negotiated VEPs and little private sector participation include 1) jurisdictional sensitivities (and negotiation costs) which limit the subject matter, approach and scope of governmental VEPs; 2) Canadian political culture which is characterized by a concentration of power making it easier for governments to remove funding for environmental matters when other issues take precedence making private sector participants wary of any such program; 3) the government's inability to integrate economic instruments and market-based approaches into the their VEPs so as to increase private-sector participation; and 4) lack of negative incentives to stop firms from using a governmental VEP for political gain rather than addressing environmental concerns. Together these reasons may explain why all parties to a government initiated VEP may be reluctant to get involved.

Unilateral Agreements

While there appears to be little support for public and negotiated voluntary environmental programs in Canada, the same cannot be said for unilateral voluntary environmental programs. Canadian leadership in unilateral agreements includes industry initiated VEPs. The Responsible Care Program, for example, was developed by the Canadian Chemical Producers' Association (CPPA) and introduced in the mid-1980s. Responsible Care is an elaborate environmental management system that includes a statement of moral obligations regarding the responsible management of chemicals and chemical products. Interestingly, unlike in the United States, the CPPA represented (and continues to represent) almost all chemical manufacturers in Canada. The program's main objectives were to improve the industry's environmental performance, to improve its relationship with governments and to foster increased public trust both of which were poor following the Union Carbide Bhopal industrial disaster of December 3, 1984 (Moffet et al., 2004).

Moffet and his colleagues (2004) provide an analysis of the development of the Responsible Care Program in Canada from the perspectives of government, industry and other stakeholders. In their analysis of the development of the Responsible Care Program in Canada, they draw six valuable lessons regarding the design and process that can be transferable to other VEPs whether they are public, negotiated or unilateral agreements. The lessons include 1) the importance of sustained, senior level leadership; 2) the requirement for strong internal and external accountability mechanisms; 3) the need for participants to share both information and technological and management know-how; 4) the need to commit sufficient resources; 5) the need to bring in stakeholders' input into all phases of the program (initial design, implementation and verification); and 6) the need to set strong penalties to dissuade companies from free-riding on the benefits of being in the program while not undertaking their obligations as members of the program (Moffet et al., 2004).

The Responsible Care Program is now recognized as probably the leading sectoral VEP in the world with chemical industries in over 45 countries having adopted the program. Although the environmental performance (as measured by toxic releases) of the chemical industry in the United States improved after the inception of the Responsible Care Program, absolute improvement amongst members of the program was no faster than earlier members and slower than among non-members (King & Lenox, 2000). Unfortunately, since almost all chemical manufacturers in Canada participate in the Responsible Care Program (hence no control group), all we can state by examining the aggregate data is that there has been an improvement in environmental performance since the inception of the Responsible Care Program in Canada. Furthermore, this program is being used as a model for other industry sectors such as the electricity and pulp and paper sectors.

Henriques and Sadorsky (1996, 1999) provide one of the first and most comprehensive studies of voluntary environmental initiatives undertaken by firms in Canada. Henriques and Sadorsky (1996) develop a framework to empirically test the determinants of an environmentally responsive firm. An environmentally responsive firm is defined as a firm having formulated a plan for dealing with environmental issues. Explanatory variables were included in the analysis to proxy for pressures from customers, suppliers, shareholders, government regulation, cost of environmental controls, employees, environmental organizations, achievement of efficiency gains, neighborhood and community groups, other lobby groups, and the importance of environmental issues over the next five years. This study combined original 1992 survey data with firm specific data to create a unique cross section data base consisting of 400 firms operating in six industries across Canada. Many of the estimated coefficients on the explanatory variables were statistically significant. In particular, the empirical results found that a firm's formulation of an environmental plan is positively influenced by customer pressure, shareholder pressure, government and regulatory pressure, neighborhood and community group pressure, and the importance of environmental issues over the next five years. The formulation of an environmental plan is negatively influenced by other lobby group pressures. The results provide useful insight into how firms react to environmental issues. The results also provide policy makers with a list of determinants which can be used either as an alternative or complement to environmental regulation. The results are particularly useful in demonstrating that while environmental regulation is an important driver behind environmental responsiveness at the firm level, other variables like customer pressure, shareholder pressure, and neighborhood and community group pressure play significant roles in determining whether a firm implements voluntary environmental initiatives.

Henriques and Sadorsky (1999) set out to determine whether environmentally committed firms differed from less environmentally committed firms in their perceptions of the relative importance of different stakeholders in influencing their natural environmental practices. Environmental commitment can be measured in terms of environmental practices. Examples of environmental practices include 1) a firm has an environmental plan, 2) has a formal document describing the environmental plan, 3) has presented the plan to shareholders, 4) has presented the plan to employees, 5) has an environmental EHS unit, 6) has a board or management committee committed to dealing with environmental issues. Using cluster analysis, firms were classified into four environmental profiles: reactive, defensive, accommodative, and proactive. Empirical analysis found that firms with more proactive environmental profiles do indeed differ from less environmentally committed firms in their perceptions of the relative importance of different stakeholders. One of the major findings of Henriques and Sadorsky (1999) is that a manager's perception of a stakeholder is critical to the manager's view of the stakeholders' importance. Consequently, company's that view environmental issues as important should hire managers who share the same perspective. Another major finding of Henriques and Sadorsky (1999) is that environmentally proactive firms view regulatory, community, and organizational stakeholders as important (but not media) whereas reactive firms only view the media as important. Proactive firms are also more willing to spend the necessary time and money to effectively manage environmental issues.

Whilst much of the published research for Canada has focused on the determinants of VEPs at the firm level, little research has focused on the determinants of VEPs at the facility level, particularly in the context of an international comparison. Henriques and Sadorsky (2007a) investigate the determinants of VEPs at the facility level and provide empirical results on what determines a facility's decision as to 1) whether or not it should introduce an environmental management system, 2) whether or not to engage someone to be responsible for environmental matters, 3) whether or not it should introduce a certified environmental management system (ISO 14001 or EMAS), and 4) the comprehensiveness of a facility's EMS as proxied by the total number of specific environmental management practices implemented. These four models of VEPs are tested using manufacturing facility level data from a 2003 international survey conducted by the Organization for Economic Co-operation and Development (OECD). Data were collected from facilities operating in Canada, France, Germany, Hungary, Japan, Norway, and the United States. Empirical results show that export orientation, the influence of corporate head office, the adoption of a quality management system, the perception that the use of natural resources has a significant negative impact, and the impact of voluntary agreements each has a positive and statistically significant impact on a facility's level of commitment to the natural environment in each of the four models. Government sponsored technical assistance programs have a negative and statistically significant impact on each of the four levels of commitment to the natural environment which suggests that the greater the importance of technical assistance programs, the less likely facilities will implement their own voluntary environmental initiatives. Environmental groups were found to have no significant impact on any of the models suggesting that facilities' relationship with environmental groups is not very collaborative. Canadian facilities were not statistically different from U.S. facilities in the equations that determine a facility's choice as to whether or not to introduce an environmental management system, or whether or not a facility should introduce a certified environmental management system (ISO 14001 or EMAS). Compared to U.S. facilities, Canadian facilities were less likely to have someone responsible for environmental matters. Compared to U.S. facilities, Canadian facilities were less likely to have more comprehensive EMSs.

The Henriques and Sadorsky (2007a) study suggests two very interesting policy implications. First, the impact of inspection frequency and the influence of public authorities vary with the number of environmental practices undertaken by a facility. For facilities with few environmental practices, inspection frequency has a significant impact on the determinants of environmental practices while the influence of public authorities has no significant impact. For facilities with a larger number of environmental practices, the influence of public authorities has a negative and significant impact on the determinants of environmental practices while inspection frequency continues to have a positive impact on the determinants of environmental practices. These results suggest that it is not the regulations themselves that motivate the adoption of voluntary environmental initiatives but rather the enforcement of the regulations that has the expected impact.

A second interesting policy implication is the finding that government sponsored technical assistance programs reduces the likelihood of a facility's adoption of voluntary environmental practices. It appears that that technical assistance programs are viewed as a substitute for environmental initiatives rather than a complement and policy makers need to be aware of this.

In summary, what motivates Canadian firms to participate in unilateral agreements? A reading of the published research on Canada suggests that the main motivators to participate in any unilateral VEP are 1) to forestall or influence future regulatory developments and 2) to maintain or regain public trust by improving the environmental performance of the industry (industry-wide VEP) or firm (single firm initiative) and by improving stakeholder relations (e.g., customers, community and shareholders). Finally, top management support, accountability mechanisms, and the commitment of sufficient resources to the voluntary initiatives are critical success factors.

Performance of Unilateral Agreements

Performance of unilateral agreements can be assessed in several ways. The first, and most obvious, is to assess whether there has been a decrease in environmental emissions. In this case, the focus is on the level of emissions rather than the manner in which the emissions were reduced. The second method looks at the way in which emissions were reduced. The question here is whether the VEP has incited an organization to reduce its emissions via cleaner technology processes as opposed to end-of-pipe solutions. The benefit of this approach is that it attempts to assess whether a VEP can be used to induce long term benefits and efficiencies for all stakeholders. The third, and sometimes more difficult performance measure insofar as its link to environmental activities, is business performance. Previous studies that evaluate the broader link between an organization's environmental strategies and its business performance offer mixed results, with some studies demonstrating that an organization's proactive environmental activities leads to improved business performance (e.g., Russo & Fouts, 1997; Hart & Ahuja, 1996; Rivera 2002; Stanwick & Stanwick, 2001), and others illustrating either insignificant (Levy, 1995; Fogler & Nutt, 1975; Rockness et al., 1986) or varied findings (e.g., Khanna & Damon, 1999). As such, the argument of whether or not proactive environmental activities lead to improved business performance is far from resolved. Even less is known about how EMSs, in particular, fit into this debate. Below are two studies using Canadian data that have employed the last two measures of performance, namely the way in which emissions are being reduced and business performance.

Henriques and Sadorsky (2007b) use a dual core model of organizational innovation to determine the factors that affect a facility's decision to undertake cleaner technological innovations. Using Canadian level manufacturing data from the OECD data set mentioned above, they find that having an EMS reduces the likelihood that a Canadian facility will implement environmental technologies that change the production process. In comparison, having a TQM increases the likelihood that a facility will implement clean technologies. Administrative pressures arising from corporate headquarters and shareholders have no impact on technological innovations. External stakeholders (like regulators, community groups, environmental groups, and trade associations), employees, customers, and suppliers each increase the likelihood that facilities will use cleaner technologies. One of the policy implications from this paper is that promoting TQM is a better alternative than promoting EMS if policy makers want to implement cleaner technologies at the facility level. If policy makers, on the other hand, wish to help facilities develop the administrative systems necessary to monitor and control their environmental impacts, then promoting an EMS is a better choice.

Darnall, Henriques and Sadorsky (2008) look explicitly at whether EMSs, which are adopted at the facility level, affect facility level business performance. Using the OECD database, this study evaluates whether EMSs can create business value across multiple international settings (Canada, United States, Germany and Hungary). This study shows that facilities are driven to adopt more comprehensive EMSs in response to institutional pressures for greater external legitimacy, and desire to build upon existing complementary resources and capabilities. However, facilities that rely on their resources and capabilities such as export orientation, quality management, R&D and employee commitment in developing their EMS are more likely to improve their overall business performance relative to those facilities that are only driven by their desire to meet regulations. For policymakers, this suggests that VEPs (public, negotiated or unilateral agreements) that allow an organization to build-up their complementary resources and capabilities will be the programs that are likely to get more firms to participate via the contagion effect as more and more firms in the "VEP club" demonstrate positive business performance. The empirical results also show that manufacturing facilities located in the United States are more likely to implement a more comprehensive EMS than those located in Canada, Germany or Hungary. Facilities located in Canada, Germany and Hungary, *ceteris paribus*, have greater business performance than those located in the United States.

Canadian research examining the link between VEPs and environmental performance is now being conducted. Here efforts are being undertaken by the authors to link the Canadian OECD data with the Canadian National Pollution Release Inventory to address not only whether emissions have been reduced but also whether the toxicity levels of these emissions have followed suit.

Policy and Research Implications

Public VEPs are primarily an American phenomenon. Lyon & Maxwell (2004) suggest that this may be due to the U.S. separation of power between the executive branch and the legislative branch. The authors argue that public VEPs may arise when the legislative branch wants to pursue stronger environmental policies but cannot get its proposals through Congress or the executive branch, finds public VEPs a convenient way to reduce legislative pressure for environmental action. In Canada, however, a parliamentary system exists in which a single party controls both the executive and legislative functions. It should therefore be easier for the Canadian executive to issue credible legislative threats reducing the need for public VEPs. This may also help to explain why one of the more well known national public VEPs in Canada, the Voluntary Challenge and Registry Program, was dismantled as participants realized that the small voluntary greenhouse gas reductions would be insufficient to preempt more stringent regulation. In the case of the ARET program, representatives of environmental, labor and other public interest groups walked out of the multistakeholder process over the uncertainties of the overall goal of ARET (e.g., reduction vs elimination; voluntary vs regulatory) (VanNijnatten, 1998). Lack of data collection, analysis, reporting procedures and an integrated information system were also weaknesses surrounding ARET. Any future public VEPs in Canada must address these weaknesses.

Negotiated VEPs, on the other hand, are rarely used in the United States due to stakeholders challenging the U.S. EPA's statutory authority to achieve regulatory reform while exempting companies from complying with current statutes and regulations (Mazurek, 1998). In Canada, the shared nature of environmental jurisdiction has led all parties involved to use a stakeholder approach when dealing with environmental issues (Vourc'h, 2001). The stakeholder approach is the fundamental driver of *Policy Framework for Environmental Performance Agreements* (Environment Canada, 2001). According to this document, the four principles underlying negotiated VEPs include effectiveness (environmental performance agreements must achieve measurable results), credibility (the public must have confidence in the approach and in the parties' capacity to deliver on commitments), transparency and accountability (all parties to an environmental performance agreement must be publicly accountable), and efficiency (environmental performance agreements should be no more expensive to the parties than alternatives for equivalent environmental results). Successful multistakeholder consultation, however, is not possible without government providing all participants involved a policy framework within which consultation occurs (VanNijnatten, 1998). Although the Canadian government has the framework with which to make negotiated VEPs both credible and effective, the government's lack of commitment to an environmental vision and goals has been a perpetual problem which, along with the inability or unwillingness of government to use market based incentives as a way to increase private sector participation, reduce the interest in negotiated VEPs for all involved (Harrison, 1995; Copeland, 1998). Moreover, the memorandums of understanding (MOUs) between governments and industrial interests have proceeded with little or no outside input (VanNijnatten, 1998) which appears to contradict the four principles underlying negotiated VEPs set out by Environment Canada (Environment Canada, 2006) and the recommendations by the International Finance Corporation (IFC, 2007) that stakeholders remain actively engaged throughout the life of a project/program (VEP).

The Canadian government may also lack the necessary resources and capabilities to effectively design, promote and manage public and negotiated VEPs. Unlike government environmental offices in other OECD countries which actively recruit, hire, and promote individuals who have backgrounds (university degrees) in economics, natural resources, and policy, government policy offices in Canada are often staffed with scientists with little or no training in policy formation and implementation (Adamowicz, 2007). The lack of economic analysis in environmental policy making combined with poor or inadequate data collection may help to explain some of the difficulties in designing and implementing successful public and negotiated VEPs in Canada. These difficulties can be overcome but it requires the Canadian government to hire people trained in environmental economics and policy making and to more actively monitor, evaluate and verify the data that are being collected from environmental programs.

Unilateral agreements, on the other hand, are proliferating. Many companies have set up their own multistakeholder consultative process (e.g., Suncor, Hydro Quebec, Alcan). Our research suggests that firms in Canada are making significant commitments to environmental actions and that stakeholders such as employees/managers, consumers, community groups as well as governments are important instigators of these actions. Hence the theoretical arguments on the motivations for adopting VEPs such as gaining relief from existing environmental regulation, preempting regulatory threats or influence future regulation, increasing cost efficiency via pollution prevention, fostering better relations with stakeholders so as to build intangible values such as goodwill, legitimacy, reputation, and acquiring technical assistance are all supported.

The ability to assess these individual or industry programs, however, is difficult due to the lack of publicly available data. It is therefore necessary for researchers to undertake survey research, to collect the necessary data on the environmental activities undertaken by a facility or firm as well as information on the stakeholders that have influenced their decision making process; and a search of publicly available environmental performance data (which is only available at the facility level) such as toxic releases and worker safety information. The environmental performance of Canadian VEPs still needs to be ascertained. The authors' current research aims to address this lacuna by merging the Canadian OECD data with the Canadian National Pollution Release Inventory.

Conclusions

The theoretical literature on the motivations for adopting VEPs suggests that voluntary approaches may be more efficient by reducing the transactions and enforcement costs associated with designing and implementing mandatory regulations because VEPs replace uniform, inflexible standards by flexible, tailored agreements or by voluntary "over-compliance" efforts (Khanna, 2001). The ability of government to provide a credible threat of mandatory regulations and market incentives to increase participation would make VEPs both more efficient and effective. This, however, requires governments to have a vision and set of environmental goals which they can present to all stakeholders. In the case of Canada, the multistakeholder process could guide the government in determining the "how to" of the vision which may include negotiated VEPs. Unfortunately, for a variety of reasons discussed earlier, this has not occurred. Given the interest by civil society in environmental issues, however, this may change.

Unilateral agreements in Canada, on the other hand, are increasing. The concern for the environment by civil society eventually affects the many stakeholders a firm deals with directly or indirectly including shareholders, employees, governments, consumers, communities, aboriginal groups, environmental groups and suppliers, each of which can affect the organization's operations. The economic implications of managing an organization's environmental performance whether tangible (decreased regulatory costs, cost efficiencies, technical assistance, reduced liability) or intangible (goodwill, trust, legitimacy, increased brand image) can be significant both in the short and long term.

Voluntary agreements may have significant potential to reduce environmental impacts directly as well as change organizational culture and capabilities towards a more environmentally proactive stance. In the case of Canada, the effectiveness, efficiency and credibility of these agreements, however, need to be evaluated and monitored. Hopefully, as the credibility and performance of these VEPs increase, more creative VEPs will be designed to deal with the yet uncontrolled forms of pollution such as nonpoint sources.

Bibliography

Adamowicz, Wiktor. "Reflections on Environmental Policy in Canada." *Canadian Journal of Agricultural Economics* 55 (March, 2007): 1–13.

Alberini, Anna, and Kathleen Segerson. "Assessing Voluntary Programs to Improve Environmental Quality." *Environmental and Resource Economics* 22, no. 1–2 (June, 2002): 157–184.

Antweiler, Werner, and Kathryn Harrison. "The ARET Challenge: Evaluating a Negotiated Voluntary Challenge Program." Working paper, Department of Political Science, University of British Columbia, 2006.

Arora, Seema, and Timothy N. Cason. "Do Community Characteristics Influence Environmental Outcomes?: Evidence from the Toxic Release Inventory." *Southern Economic Journal* 65, no. 4 (April, 1999): 691–716.

Boardman, Robert. *Canadian Environmental Policy: Ecosystems, Politics, and Process.* Oxford University Press, Toronto, 1992.

Brouhle, Keith, and Donna Ramirez Harrington. "Firm Strategy and the Canadian Voluntary Climate Change and Registry (VCR)." *Business Strategy & the Environment* (2007) in press.

Christmann, Petra. "Effects of "Best Practices" of Environmental Management on Cost Advantage: The Role of Complementary Assets." *Academy of Management Journal* 43 no. 4 (August, 2000): 663–680.

Clarkson, Max B.E. "A Stakeholder Framework for Analyzing and Evaluating Corporate Social Performance." *Academy of Management Review* 20 no. 1 (January, 1995): 92–117.

C.M. Consulting, *Who Pays What?: An Analysis of Beverage Container Recovery and Costs in Canada.* 2006. http://www.env.gov.bc.ca/epd/epdpa/ips/resources/pdf/who_pays_what.pdf). Accessed September 19, 2007.

Coglianese, Gary, and Jennifer Nash. *Regulating From the Inside: Can Environmental Management Systems Achieve Policy Goals?* Washington DC: Resources for the Future, 2001.

Commission for Environmental Cooperation (CEC) of North America. *Moving Forward with Pollution Prevention in North America: A Progress Update.* Montreal, Canada, 2004.

Copeland, Brian. "Economics and the Environment: The Recent Canadian Experience and Prospects for the Future." *Industry Canada Research Publication* #8, Ottawa, 1998.

Cropper, Maureen L., and Wallace E. Oates. "Environmental Economics: A Survey." *Journal of Economic Literature*, no. 2 (June, 1992): 675–740.

Darnall, Nicole. *Why Firms Signal Green: Environmental Management System Certification in the United States.* unpublished Ph.D. Dissertation, University of North Carolina, Chapel Hill, 2002.

Darnall, Nicole, and Daniel Edwards Jr. "Predicting the Cost of Environmental Management System Adoption: The Role of Capabilities, Resources and Ownership Structure." *Strategic Management Journal* 27, no. 4 (April, 2006): 301–320.

Darnall, Nicole, Irene Henriques, and Perry Sadorsky. "Do Environmental Management Systems Improve Business Performance in an International Setting?" *Journal of International Management* 14, no. 4 (December, 2008) in press.

De Gonzaque, John. "Implementing Pollution Prevention in Canada." paper delivered at the *International Conference on Cleaner Production*, Beijing, China, September 2001. http://www.chinacp.com/eng/cpconfer/iccp01/iccp06.html. Accessed September 19, 2007.

Environment Canada. *Policy Framework for Environmental Performance Agreements.* 2001. http://www.ec.gc.ca/epa-epe/pol/en/index.cfm. Accessed September 19, 2007.

Environment Canada. *Environmental Performance Agreements.* Status Report, 2006. http://www.ec.gc.ca/epa-epe/en/stRpt.cfm. Accessed September 19, 2007.

Environment Canada Review Branch. *Evaluation of the Accelerated Reduction and Elimination of Toxics Initiative (ARET).* Final Report April 2000.

Field, Barry, and Nancy Olewiler. *Environmental Economics: Second Canadian Edition.* McGraw Hill Ryerson: Toronto, 2002.

Fogler, H. Russell, and Fred Nutt. "A Note on Social Responsibility and Stock Evaluation." *Academy of Management Journal* 18, no. 1 (March, 1975): 155–160.

Freeman, R. Edward. *Strategic Management: A Stakeholder Approach.* Pitman/Ballinger (Harper Collins): Boston, USA, 1984.

Frooman, Jeff. "Stakeholder Influencing Strategies." *Academy of Management Review* 24, no. 2 (April, 1999): 191–205.

Government of Canada. *Pollution Prevention—A Federal Strategy for Action.* 1995.

Harrison, Kathryn. "Is Cooperation the Answer?: Canadian Environmental Enforcement in Comparative Context." *Journal of Policy Analysis and Management* 14 (1995): 221–245.

Hart, Stuart L. "A Natural Resource-Based View of the Firm." *Academy of Management Review* 20, no. 4 (October, 1995): 986–1014.

Hart, Stuart L., and Gautam Ahuja. "Does It Pay to Be Green? An Empirical Examination of the Relationship between Emission Reduction and Firm Performance." *Business Strategy & the Environment* 5, no. 1 (March, 1996): 30–37.

Hart, Stuart L., and Mark B. Milstein. "Creating Sustainable Value." *Academy of Management Executive* 17, no. 2 (May, 2003): 56–69.

Henriques, Irene, and Perry Sadorsky. "The Determinants of an Environmentally Responsive Firm: An Empirical Approach." *Journal of Environmental Economics and Management* 30, no. 3 (May, 1996): 381–395.

———. "The Relationship Between Environmental Commitment and Managerial Perceptions of Stakeholder Importance." *Academy of Management Journal* 42, no. 1 (February, 1999): 87–99.

———. "Environmental Management Systems and Practices: An International Perspective." In: Johnstone N. (Ed.) *Environmental Policy and Corporate Behaviour*. Edward Elgar Publishing, in association with Organisation for Economic Co-Operation and Development, Northampton, MA. (2007a): 34–87.

———. "Environmental Technical and Administrative Innovations in the Canadian Manufacturing Industry." *Business Strategy & the Environment* 16, no. 2 (February, 2007b) 119–132.

Henriques, Irene, and Sanjay Sharma. "Pathways of Stakeholder Influence in the Canadian Forestry Industry." *Business Strategy & the Environment* 14, no. 6 (November/December, 2005): 384–398.

Hitt, Michael A., R. Duane Ireland, Robert E. Hoskisson, W. Glen Rowe, and Jerry Paul Sheppard. *Strategic Management: Competitiveness and Globalization—Concepts*. Second Canadian Edition, Thomson Nelson Canada, 2006.

Hoberg, George. "Governing the Environment: Comparing Canada and the United States." In K. Banting, G. Hobert and R. Simeon (Eds.), *Degrees of Freedom: Canada and the United States in a Changing World*. Montreal and Kingston: McGill-Queens University Press, 1997.

Hoffman, Andrew. *Competitive Environmental Strategy: A Guide to the Changing Business Landscape*. Washington, DC: Island Press, 2001.

Howlett, Michael. "Policy Instruments and Implementation Styles: The Evolution of Instrument Choice in Canadian Environmental Policy." In VanNijnatten D. L. and R. Boardman (eds.), *Canadian Environmental Policy: Context and Cases*. Oxford: Oxford University Press, 2002.

IFC. *Stakeholder Engagement: A Good Practice Handbook for Companies Doing Business in Emerging Markets*. International Finance Corporation, World Bank: Washington, DC, 2007.

Khanna, Madhu. "Non-Mandatory Approaches to Environmental Protection." *Journal of Economic Surveys* 15, no. 3 (July, 2001): 291–324.

Khanna, Madhu, and Lisa A. Damon. "EPA's Voluntary 33/50 Program: Impact on Toxic Releases and Economic Performance of Firms." *Journal of Environmental Economics and Management* 37, no. 3 (January, 1999): 1–25.

King, Andrew, and Michael J. Lenox. "Industry Self-Regulation Without Sanctions: The Chemical Industry's Responsible Care Program." *Academy of Management Journal* 43, no. 4 (August, 2000): 698–716.

Levy, David L. "The Environmental Practices and Performance of Transnational Corporations." *Transnational Corporations* 4 (1995): 44–67.

Lucas, Alistar R, and Veronica Potes. "Voluntary Greenhouse Gas Emission Reductions: The Rise and Fall of VCR Inc." Paper No. 2, ISEEE, University of Calgary, 2006.

———. *Corporate Environmentalism and Public Policy*. Cambridge: Cambridge University Press, 2004.

Lyon, Thomas P., and John Maxwell. "Voluntary Approaches to Environmental Regulation: A Survey." In M. Franzini and A. Nicita (eds.), *Economic Institutions and Environmental Policy*. Aldershop and Hampshire: Ashgate Publishing, 2002.

Mazurek, Janice. The Use of Voluntary Agreements in the United States: An Initial Survey. ENV/EPOC/GEEI(98)27/Final, Paris, France: OECD, 1998.

Mitchell, Ronald K., Bradley R. Agle, and Donna J. Wood. "Toward a Theory of Stakeholder Identification and Salience: Defining the Principle of Who and What Really Counts." *Academy of Management Review* 22, no. 4 (October, 1997): 853–886.

Moffet, John, Francois Bregha, and Jane F. Middelkoop. "Responsible Care: A Case Study of a Voluntary Environmental Initiative." in K. Webb (ed.) *Voluntary Codes: Private Governance, The Public Interest and Innovation.* Ottawa: Carleton Research Unit for Innovation, Science and Environment, 2004: 177–207.

Morgenstern, Richard D., and William A. Pizer. *Reality Check: The Nature and Performance of Voluntary Environmental Programs in the United States, Europe, and Japan.* Resources for the Future, Washington, D.C. USA, 2007.

OECD. *Environmental Performance Reviews: Canada.* OECD: Paris, 2004.

Paehlke, Robert. "Environmentalism in One Country: Canadian Environmental Policy in an Era of Globalization." *Policy Studies Journal* 28 no. 1 (Spring, 2000): 160–175.

Paton, Bruce. "Voluntary Environmental Initiatives and Sustainable Industry." *Business Strategy & the Environment* 9, no. 5 (September/ October, 2000): 328–338.

Potoski, Matthew, and Aseem Prakash. "The Regulation Dilemma." *Public Administration Review* 64, no. 2 (2004): 137–148.

Rivera, Jorge. "Assessing a Voluntary Environmental Initiative in the Developing World: The Costa Rican Certification for Sustainable Tourism." *Policy Sciences* 35 (March/April, 2002): 333–360.

Rockness, Joanne, Paul Schlachter, and Howard O. Rockness. "Hazardous Waste Disposal, Corporate Disclosure, and Financial Performance in the Chemical Industry." in: Neimark, M. (Ed.) *Advances in Public Interest Accounting* 1: JAI Press, Greenwich, 1986: 167–191.

Russo, Michael V., and Paul A. Fouts. "A Resource-Based Perspective on Corporate Environmental Performance and Profitability." *Academy of Management Journal* 40, no. 3 (June, 1997): 534–559.

Sharma, Sanjay, and Irene Henriques. "Stakeholder Influences on Sustainability Practices in the Canadian Forest Products Industry." *Strategic Management Journal* 26, no. 2 (February, 2005): 159–180.

Stanwick, Peter A., and Sarah D. Stanwick. "CEO Compensation: Does it Pay to Be Green?" *Business Strategy & the Environment* 10, no. 3 (May/June, 2001): 176–182.

Takahashi, Takaya., Masao Nakamura, G. Cornelis van Kooten, and Iian Vertinsky. "Rising to the Kyoto Challenge: Is the Response of Canadian Industry Adequate?" Journal of Environment Managemen Vol. 63, No. 2 (October 2001): 149-161.

The Green Line. Environment Canada's World Wide Web site, (2003). http://www.ec.gc.ca/nopp/aret/en/index.cfm. Accessed September 19, 2007.

Valiante, Marcia. "Legal Foundations of Canadian Environmental Policy." In VanNijnatten D. L. and R. Boardman (eds.), *Canadian Environmental Policy: Context and Cases.* Oxford: Oxford University Press, 2002.

VanNijnatten, Debra L. "The Day the NGOs Walked Out." *Alternatives Journal* 24, no. 2 (1998): 10–15.

———. "Participation and Environmental Policy in Canada and the United States: Trends Over Time." *Policy Studies Journal* 27, no. 2 (Summer, 1999): 267-287.

Vourc'h, Ann. "Encouraging Environmentally Sustainable Growth in Canada." Economics Department Working Papers No. 290, OECD (2001).

Webb, Kernaghan. *Voluntary Codes: Private Governance, the Public Interest and Inno-vation*. Ottawa: Carleton Research Unit for Innovation, Science and Environment, 2004.

Notes

1. Note that while a VEP is not required by legislation or regulations, this does not suggest that there are no legal aspects associated with its implementation or that the VEP may have been implemented as a result of regulations.

2. For more details on these and other voluntary programs see the OECD Environment Directorate at http://www2.oecd.org/ecoinst/queries/index.htm

3. According to VanNijnatten (1999), these attributes are expressed in the horizontal and vertical fragmentation of the American institutional framework where the separation of powers system provides for coequal executive and legislative branches that are designed specifically to check one another. Together with extensive public access to information, substantial interest group activism and the ability of interest groups to take legal action, Hoberg (1997) has characterized the American political process as one of "pluralist legalism."

4. According to VanNijnatten (1999), these attributes are expressed in elitist origins with the fusion of the executive and legislative branches, the dominance of the lower house, strong political parties and the hierarchical structure of ministerial responsibility in the administrative branch. Together this places a high degree of concentration of policy-making capacity in the political executive. Hence, the Canadian political process is less pluralist, less open, less adversarial and more informal than the U.S. process (VanNijnatten, 1999).

5. For a complete discussion see Valiante (2002).

Chapter 11

Concluding Opinion:
Voluntary Environmental Programs:
Are Carrots Without Sticks Enough
for Effective Environmental
Protection Policy?

Jorge E. Rivera and Peter deLeon

During the last few decades, Voluntary Environmental Programs (VEPs) and the protection they implied became one of the most used public policy alternatives to promote environmental protection in the United States, and, to some degree, in other nations as well. In general terms, VEPs are self-regulatory agreements with firms and industries that commit themselves to improve their environmental protection practices. Not surprisingly, they come in many forms and structures, from strictly voluntary initiatives with no required standards, no reporting, and no evaluative oversight to third-party certification programs with specific performance-based requirements, rigorous assessments, and differential rewards or sanctions. Voluntary environmental programs also vary in terms of their industry and country focus and their unilateral or joint sponsorship by government agencies, industry, and environmental groups.

This volume has highlighted several types and models for VEPs. To briefly summarize, they can include: (1) initiatives established and encouraged by regulators, such as the U.S. Environmental Protection Agency (EPA), including the Performance Track Program; (2) collaborative, negotiated agreements between firms, regulators, environmentalists, and other stakeholders (e.g., the U.S. Department of Agriculture's Organic Certification program); and (3) unilateral programs promoted by industry and/or environmental non-profit organizations and the cooperation of government agencies, such as the U.S.

National Ski Areas Association's Sustainable Slopes Program and the Forest Stewardship Council Certification.

As was noted earlier, the number of VEPs in the US alone now numbers in the hundreds, clearly a trend whose time has come. Yet, despite their widespread popularity and increased use, VEPs are highly controversial, mostly because of the many challenges they face to actually promote enhanced environmental performance by their participants, but at least partly for the regulatory position they tacitly (sometimes, manifestly) espouse. Arguably, those problems are endemic to regulations in general, but certainly to VEPs in specific.

The classified ad below, recently profiled in a *New York Times* story illustrates a few of most important challenges confronted by those seeking to promote the use of VEPs as effective win-win environmental policy alternatives to traditional command-and-control regulations. First and most important, VEPs surely imply and perhaps present the image (or reality) of opportunistic "green washing" behavior by program participants. Second, it is necessary, albeit problematic, to document the distinguishing characteristics of the few credible programs among the hundreds of VEPs established in the United States alone. The *Times* article reads as follows:

chicago craigslist > city of chicago > real estate—by broker

$279000 1BD & 2BD Condos in Eco-Friendly, LEED Certified Building! (River North) (map)

Reply to: see below
Date: 2009-02-18, 4:15PM CST

With only six units per floor on each of its 10 residential stories, 9 West Erie has a friendly and intimate atmosphere. An eco-friendly building pursuing LEED certification, it will implement earth-friendly design and construction, recycled materials, as well as energy efficient appliances and building systems. Pre-construction pricing is still available. To view a full listing with pictures and a virtual tour, click here.[1]

This ad reflects one of the difficulties with a VEP, or in this case "when is a VEP not a VEP" and what that distinction suggests. That is, a careful reading of this listing by someone with expertise in voluntary environmental certification may help most readers of Craigslist realize that a "building *pursuing* LEED certification" (emphasis added) is not quite the same as a "LEED *certified* building."[2] Any building, even the most energy inefficient, can *pursue* LEED certification. However, LEED certification can only be received by buildings that demonstrate superior environmental and energy management practices.

Furthermore, LEED certification can only be granted to *finished* buildings and these Chicago condos have not been built yet. To be sure, many (including Craig!) might have not noticed the possibly "misleading" nature of the Craigslist headline and just relied on the commonly held reputation of LEED as a highly credible indicator of a successful VEP. Rather, the issue should be: what is the purpose of a LEED construction? Only then can we consider whether a "successful" LEED equals a "successful" VEP.

Regarding the second challenge, even environmental policy experts have a very difficult time identifying the small number of credible VEPs among the hundreds of self-regulation initiatives established in the United States by government agencies, industry, and nonprofit organizations. Part of this problem, of course, is that the definition of a VEP has been seen to vary as a function of the context in which it is situated; not surprisingly, then, the calibration of what constitutes "success" varies just as widely, if not more so.

To illustrate this second point, let us return to the Craigslist advertisement above and think about the following questions: how many workaday consumers know what LEED is, let alone how it is measured and/or reported? Or do you agree that it constitutes the "preeminent" voluntary environmental certification in the U.S. building industry? Leaving aside the probability of the average consumer knowing the answers, these questions could easily stump the VEP expert. A third question, then, is why are the results of a VEP so open to mistaken judgments?

Our colleague Allen Blackman, from Resources for the Future, also pointed out another key challenge faced by VEPs established under the premise that credible "green" signals are highly valued in the market place: When reading the advertisement, Blackman has observed that perhaps most consumers would not consider "green" (i.e., environmentally oriented) attributes as necessary conditions for purchasing a home and would be just as happy to be able to afford a brand new condominium in a comfortable part of Chicago. We saw an analogous situation when we reviewed U.S. ski areas: repeatedly we were told that the American skiers—nominally serious environmentalists—were more concerned with the location of a resort rather than paying more for a "green" lift ticket. Granted, the "green" certification awarded by the rare credible VEPs is valued by other stakeholders such as government agencies, environmentalists, the media, and large corporations under the scrutiny of watchdog groups. Yet, this challenge remains to the consumer at large in the United States (and we suspect beyond American borders as well). Most people when surveyed say that they care about protecting the environment but, as workaday consumers, most are not yet willing to pay or able to afford certified environmentally friendly products, a condition that renders the recognition and acknowledgment of the "successful" VEP as problematic, at best.

The authors in this volume are fully aware of the critical nature of some these observations and, while not necessarily completely agreeing with them, realize that they are not made lightly. In one specific case, for more than a decade now, Rivera's academic research and scholarly publications have been focused on the study of voluntary environmental programs both in the United States and developing countries, at first arguing for the establishment of VEPs in lieu of the suspect command and control regulations, and, more recently, in evaluating such programs. And as our colleagues have noted, VEPs offered great promise for an environmental researcher seeking to emphasize an innovative environmental policy tool that could potentially be able to: (1) reduce implementation and monitoring costs for governments; (2) create greater flexibility, reduce compliance costs, and preempt new regulations and stricter oversight for business; and (3) simultaneously achieve superior corporate environmental performance. Alas, empirical data are stubborn things. Overall, the growing body of credible evidence on VEPs suggests strong caution about the early enthusiasm for these initiatives as alternatives to traditional command-and-control regulations. In brief, this evidence suggests an emerging consensus on the following points:

First, stringent environmental regulations or a credible threat of their adoption are necessary conditions for VEPs to attract a large number of business participation. We are reluctant to admit that the attractiveness of the VEPs is predicated on the growing likelihood that a more invasive set of government-mandated regulations are imminent but perhaps the threat is useful in this case; that is, "mandated" might be necessary to secure the "voluntary." Second, except for a few remarkable exceptions, most environmental self-regulation initiatives currently established in the United States are *strictly voluntary* and thus lack critical necessary conditions to reduce "free-riding" behavior by participant businesses. The most important of these conditions are:

1. Specific performance-based standards of environmental protection adopted by participant companies;
2. Periodic independent third-party audits that verify the adoption of these standards; and
3. Rewards and sanctions that publicly recognize the different levels of audited performance obtained by VEP participants.

Third and most importantly, *strictly voluntary environmental programs* not only tend to attract the firms characterized as high polluting firms as participants (again, possibly as a ploy to avoid more restrictive governmental intervention) but once enrolled these business show *lower* rates of environmental performance improvement than those firms who chose not to participate.

In other words, and most worrisome, VEPs originally conceived and trumpeted as "win-win" policy alternatives are actually—*in the strictly voluntary form typical of the United States.*—seen to be serving the interest of dirty businesses to the exclusion of environmental protection interests.

Finally, this emerging consensus after more than a decade of empirical social science research on VEPs suggests two basic policy implications:

1. Federal and state government agencies should stop creating and/or endorsing strictly voluntary programs that do not include the specific institutional conditions for preventing the free-riding behavior highlighted above. This includes the necessity of third-party evaluation and the publication of those assessments.

2. Voluntary environmental programs need to award differential certification levels, necessarily including no certification, based on independently audited environmental performance of their participants. Avoiding the granting of blanket green certifications or recognitions to business participants regardless of true performance is vital to increase the environmental protection effectiveness of VEPs and to appeal to the small, but growing, number of environmentally aware consumers.

In sum, third-party, performance-based VEPs can be effective at helping advance environmental protection interest when used as one of many *complements* to mandatory environmental regulations. Yet, even when appropriately designed—unfortunately a rare case during the last decade in the United States—VEPs are only a first step if used as an *alternative* to mandatory regulations.

NOTES

1. L. Vestel, (2009). "Taking liberties with LEED". *New York Times,* February 19, 2009. Accessed online on February 19, 2009.
http://greeninc.blogs.nytimes.com/2009/02/19/taking-liberties-with-leed/?hp

2. LEED is the acronym identifying the Leadership in Energy and Environmental Design program, as sponsored by the U.S. Green Building Council.

Index

About the Contributors

Allen Blackman is an Economist and Senior Fellow at Resources for the Future, *a nonprofit environmental policy research institute in Washington, DC. His* work focuses on environmental issues in developing countries, specifically the use of "alternative" policy tools such as voluntary regulation, public disclosure, economic incentives, and payments for environmental services. His research has been published in a variety of books and journals including the *Policy Studies Journal,* the *American Journal of Agricultural Economics* and the *Journal of Environmental Economics and Management.*

Nicole Darnall is an Associate Professor of Corporate Sustainability and Public Policy at George Mason University. She also is a collaborative visiting fellow of the Economic and Social Research Council and the Social Science Research Council, and an Erasmus Mundus International Scholar. She investigates the reasons why companies adopt sustainability strategies, whether companies that adopt these strategies improve the environment, and whether companies that improve the natural environmental also derive business value.

Peter deLeon has written on issues regarding the stages of the policy process, with special emphasis on the role of democracy in the policy process. He has also written in the subject areas of national security, comparative science and technology policy, political corruption, and environmental regulation. He has presented his work widely, most recently at Tampere University, Finland. He is presently the director of the Ph.D. program at the School of Public Affairs at the University of Colorado Denver.

Magali Delmas is an Associate Professor of Management at the University of California Los Angeles and the director of the UCLA Center for Corporate Environmental Performance. Standing at the crossroads of policy and management, Magali Delmas' research focuses on the various interactions between environmental policy and business strategy at the national and international level. She seeks to understand how environmental policies influences firms' strategies and performance and in turn how firms help shape environmental policy. Magali Delmas' current work includes the analysis of the effectiveness of firms' voluntary actions to mitigate climate change. She is also engaged in refining current methodologies to measure and communicate firm's and products' environmental performance. Previous to embarking on an academic career, she worked at the European Commission as the economic advisor of the Director for Industry.

David Ervin is a Professor of Environmental Management, Professor of Economics and a Fellow in the Center for Sustainable Processes and Practices at Portland State University. He teaches courses in the economics of sustainability, business environmental management and global environmental issues. Prior appointments include professor and Head of Agricultural and Resource Economics at Oregon State University, professor of Agricultural Economics at the University of Missouri-Columbia, Chief of Resource Policy Branch in the U.S. Department of Agriculture's Economic Research Service, and Director of Policy Studies for the Henry A. Wallace Institute for Alternative Agriculture. He holds BS and MS degrees from The Ohio State University and a Ph.D. from Oregon State University. His current research areas include business environmental management, university-industry research relationships, and the economics of green technology.

Irene Henriques is an Associate Professor at the Schulich School of Business, York University. Her research interests span both economics and management and include the economics of R&D, industrial organization and environmental management and sustainability. She has published numerous articles in leading journals including the *Academy of Management Journal*, the *American Economic Review*, the *Journal of Environmental Economics and Management* and the *Strategic Management Journal*. She has the honor and pleasure of being the 2009 Chair of the Organizations and the Natural Environment (ONE) Division of the Academy of Management. She has also been affiliated with the OECD and the Joint Public Advisory Committee (JPAC) for the Commission for Environmental Cooperation (CEC) of North America.

Cody Jones PhD is an Adjunct Professor of Renewable Energy Engineering at Oregon Institute of Technology, and a former instructor of environmental science and sustainability at Portland State University. Research interests: the influence of regulation and managers' attitudes toward environmental protection on voluntary environmental management efforts in for-profit organizations.

Madhu Khanna is a Professor in the Department of Agricultural and Consumer Economics, University of Illinois at Urbana-Champaign. She received her PhD from the University of California at Berkeley. Her research focuses on environmental policy analysis and technology adoption. She examines the effectiveness and targeting of alternative marked-based instruments and voluntary approaches for inducing the adoption of environmentally friendly technologies. She is a member of the Environmental Economics Advisory Committee of the

Science Advisory Board of the U.S. EPA. She has served on the Board of Directors of the Association of Environmental and Resource Economists. She holds editorial positions at several environmental and agricultural economics journals. She is a University of Illinois Scholar and a Leopold Leadership Fellow.

Dinah A. Koehler is a Senior Research Associate at the Conference Board's Center for Corporate Citizenship and Sustainability. When this article was written she managed the environmental decision-making and behavior research track in the Economics and Decision-Sciences research program at the National Center for Environmental Research, EPA Office of Research & Development. Her expertise is in risk assessment, evaluation of corporate environmental behavior and performance, and risk perception. She holds a Science Doctorate from Harvard School of Public Health and a Masters from the Fletcher School at Tufts University.

Charles P. Koerber is a doctoral candidate in the Department of Strategic Management and Public Policy at The George Washington University (Washington, DC). He is also currently a Visiting Instructor in the Kogod School of Business at American University. His research interests include financial, ethical, environmental, and social reporting; voluntary environmental programs; and corporate responsibility. Email: ckoerber@gwu.edu.

Patricia Koss is an Associate Professor of Economics at Portland State University. Her teaching and research has focused on environmental and energy economics, as well as industrial organization and regulation.

Thomas P. Lyon is the Director of the Erb Institute for Global Sustainable Enterprise at the University of Michigan. He holds the Dow Chair of Sustainable Science, Technology and Commerce, with appointments in both the Ross School of Business and the School of Natural Resources and Environment. Professor Lyon is a leader in using economic analysis to understand corporate environmental strategy and how it is shaped by emerging government regulations, nongovernmental organizations, and consumer demands. His book, *Corporate Environmentalism and Public Policy*, published by Cambridge University Press, is the first rigorous economic analysis of this increasingly important topic. Professor Lyon earned his bachelor's degree at Princeton University and his doctorate at Stanford University. His current research focuses on corporate environmental information disclosure, greenwash, the causes and consequences of renewable energy policy, and voluntary programs for environmental improvement.

Laurie Manderino is a PhD candidate in Public Affairs at the University of Colorado Denver. She has worked as an environmental policy and finance consultant in the US and Europe and spent five years managing local development projects in Africa. She co-authored several papers on environmental policy development in Eastern Europe during the period of transition to market economies. She is currently conducting research on voluntary environmental programs as part of an inter-disciplinary PhD program on *Sustainable Urban Infrastructure* funded by the National Science Foundation.

John W. Maxwell is the W. George Pinnell Professor of Business, Economics and Public Policy at the Indiana University Kelley School of Business. He is a Fellow of The Royal Society for the Encouragement of the Arts, Manufactures and Commerce (FRSA), Adjunct Research Professor at the Ivey School of Business and a Fellow of the China Center for Insurance and Social Security Research, Peking University. He has published numerous articles and edited volumes on the political economy of regulation, voluntary environmental agreements, non-market strategy and conflict and cooperation over scarce resources. Maxwell's *Corporate Environmentalism and Public Policy* was published by Cambridge University Press in 2004. Prior taking up the Pinnell Professorship, Maxwell was Professor and Academic Director of the Lawrence National Center for Policy and Management at the Richard Ivey School of Business at the University of Western Ontario. Professor Maxwell has been a visiting scholar at the Department of Economics, University College London, and the School of Economics as well as the Guanghua School of Management, both at Peking University. Professor Maxwell has taught courses on the Global Environment of Business, Managerial Economics, Sustainable Enterprise, and Corporate Non-Market Strategy to undergraduate, MBA and PhD students.

Ivan Montiel is an Assistant Professor of Management at California State University, Los Angeles. His research interests include how organizations can design socially responsible and sustainable strategies while remaining competitive, business ethics, and management in Latin American countries. He has a doctorate in Environmental Science & Management from the Donald Bren School of Environmental Science and Management at University of California, Santa Barbara. Prior to joining CSULA he taught at The University of Texas, Pan American. His research has been published in *Journal of Economics & Management Strategy, Journal of Business Ethics, Policy Studies Journal, Business & Society* and *Organization & Environment*.

Matthew Potoski is an Associate Professor in the Political Science Department at Iowa State University. He serves as Co-editor of *Journal of Policy Analysis and Management* and has received the Iowa State University LAS Award for Early Achievement in Research and LAS Award for Mid Career Achievement in

Research. He has published over 30 journal articles on a variety of public management and policy issues, such as public sector contracting and service delivery, environmental policy, and voluntary regulations. He is co-author of *The Voluntary Environmentalists* (Cambridge, 2006) and the co-editor of *Voluntary Programs, A Club Theory Approach* (MIT 2009).

Aseem Prakash is a Professor of Political Science at University of Washington-Seattle. He serves as the General Editor of Cambridge University Press Series on Business and Public Policy. He is the author of *Greening the Firm: The Politics of Corporate Environmentalism* (Cambridge University Press, 2000), the co-author of *The Voluntary Environmentalists: Green Clubs, ISO 14001, and Voluntary Environmental Regulations* (Cambridge University Press, 2006), and the co-editor of *Nonprofit Accountability Clubs: Voluntary Regulation of Nonprofit and Nongovernmental Organizations* (Cambridge University Press, 2010), *Voluntary Programs: A Club Theory Perspective* (The MIT Press, 2009), *Globalization and Governance* (Routledge, 1999), *Coping with Globalization* (Routledge, 2000), *Responding to Globalization* (Routledge, 2000).

Jorge E. Rivera is an Associate Professor of Strategic Management and Public Policy at The George Washington University. Currently, he is also a Visiting Associate Research Fellow at CATIE in Costa Rica. His research focuses on the relationship between public policy and business strategies. He has published many journal articles and his work received Best Paper Awards from the Academy of Management's Organizations and Natural Environment Division in 2001 and the Policy Sciences Society in 2003. He is also the author of two forthcoming books: *Business and Public Policy* by Cambridge University Press and *Voluntary Environmental Programs: A Policy Perspective* by Lexington Press. In 2008, he was appointed as an Associate Editor of the journals: *Policy Sciences* and *Business & Society*.

Perry Sadorsky is an Associate Professor in the Schulich School of Business at York University in Toronto. His current research interests include energy and the natural environment, financial markets and the economy, corporate commitment to the natural environment, and the relationship between business performance, innovation and sustainability. He has published extensively in these areas. He has been involved in several international organizations and international working groups. He is currently Treasurer of the Organizations and the Natural Environment Division of the Academy of Management.

Stephen Sides is a doctoral student in the Department of Environmental Science and Policy at George Mason University. His research interests include organizational behavior under voluntary environmental programs (VEPs), with special emphasis on participation strategies and measures of environmental performance that can inform policymakers on the efficacy of VEPs as an instrument of constructive change.